AlphaGo Simplified

May 11, 1997, was a watershed moment in the history of artificial intelligence (AI): the IBM supercomputer chess engine, Deep Blue, beat the world Chess champion, Garry Kasparov. It was the first time a machine had triumphed over a human player in a Chess tournament. Fast forward 19 years to May 9, 2016, DeepMind's AlphaGo beat the world Go champion Lee Sedol. AI again stole the spotlight and generated a media frenzy. This time, a new type of AI algorithm, namely machine learning (ML) was the driving force behind the game strategies.

What exactly is ML? How is it related to AI? Why is deep learning (DL) so popular these days? This book explains how traditional rule-based AI and ML work and how they can be implemented in everyday games such as Last Coin Standing, Tic Tac Toe, or Connect Four. Game rules in these three games are easy to implement. As a result, readers will learn rule-based AI, deep reinforcement learning, and more importantly, how to combine the two to create powerful game strategies (the whole is indeed greater than the sum of its parts) without getting bogged down in complicated game rules.

Implementing rule-based AI and ML in these straightforward games is quick and not computationally intensive. Consequently, game strategies can be trained in mere minutes or hours without requiring GPU training or supercomputing facilities, showcasing AI's ability to achieve superhuman performance in these games. More importantly, readers will gain a thorough understanding of the principles behind rule-based AI, such as the MiniMax algorithm, alpha-beta pruning, and Monte Carlo Tree Search (MCTS), and how to integrate them with cutting-edge ML techniques like convolutional neural networks and deep reinforcement learning to apply them in their own business fields and tackle real-world challenges.

Written with clarity from the ground up, this book appeals to both general readers and industry professionals who seek to learn about rule-based AI and deep reinforcement learning, as well as students and educators in computer science and programming courses.

Mark H. Liu is an Associate Professor of Finance, the (Founding) Director of the MS Finance Program at the University of Kentucky. He obtained his Ph.D. in finance from Boston College in 2004 and his M.A. in economics from Western University in Canada in 1998. Dr. Liu has more than 20 years of coding experience and is the author of two books: Make Python Talk (No Starch Press, 2021) and Machine Learning, Animated (CRC Press, 2023).

AlphaGo Simplified
Rule-Based AI and Deep Learning in Everyday Games

Mark Liu

CRC Press
Taylor & Francis Group
Boca Raton   London   New York

CRC Press is an imprint of the
Taylor & Francis Group, an **informa** business

A CHAPMAN & HALL BOOK

Cover design images: Simply Amazing/Shutterstock and maxuser/Shutterstock

First edition published 2025
by CRC Press
2385 NW Executive Center Drive, Suite 320, Boca Raton FL 33431

and by CRC Press
4 Park Square, Milton Park, Abingdon, Oxon, OX14 4RN

CRC Press is an imprint of Taylor & Francis Group, LLC

ISBN: 978-1-032-72221-4 (hbk)
ISBN: 978-1-032-72212-2 (pbk)
ISBN: 978-1-032-72220-7 (ebk)

DOI: 10.1201/9781032722207

Typeset in Latin Modern font
by KnowledgeWorks Global Ltd.

Publisher's note: This book has been prepared from camera-ready copy provided by the authors.

To Ivey and Andrew.

Contents

Section III Reinforcement Learning

List of Figures

Preface

> "The whole is greater than the sum of its parts."
> – *Aristotle*

MAY 11, 1997, was a watershed moment in the history of artificial intelligence (AI): the IBM supercomputer Chess engine, Deep Blue, beat the world Chess champion, Garry Kasparov. It was the first time a machine had triumphed over a human player in a Chess tournament. The news garnered much media attention. But here's the twist: Deep Blue was no machine learning (ML) marvel; it was powered by traditional rule-based AI, a far cry from the modern AI we know today.

Fast forward 19 years to the electrifying showdown of 2016, where Google DeepMind's AlphaGo took on Go champion Lee Sedol. Once again, AI seized the spotlight, creating a frenzy in the media. But this time, it was a new kind of AI, driven by the incredible force of ML, particularly deep reinforcement learning, that captured the world's imagination. The strategies it employed were a game-changer, quite literally. But that's not all! The real secret to AlphaGo's success is the fact that it merged deep reinforcement learning with rule-based AI such as Monte Carlo Tree Search (MCTS) to supercharge the game strategies (the whole is indeed greater than the sum of its parts in this case).

Now, you may be wondering: What is ML, and how does it relate to AI? Why is deep learning all the rage in today's tech-driven world? This book has the answers. In these pages, you'll unravel the inner workings of traditional rule-based AI and modern ML. I'll show you how to apply these concepts to three simple yet captivating games: Last Coin Standing, Tic Tac Toe, and Connect Four. You'll dive into the exciting world of artificial intelligence through the thrilling stories of Deep Blue and AlphaGo, two groundbreaking moments that rewrote the history of AI.

For readers who are unfamiliar with these games, Last Coin Standing (the coin game from now on) is a game in which two players take turns removing one or two coins at a time from a pile of 21 coins. The player who takes the last coin is the winner. In Tic Tac Toe, two players take turns marking a cell with an X or O in a three-by-three grid. The first player to connect three Xs or Os in a row horizontally, vertically, or diagonally wins. Connect Four pits two players against each other in a quest to form a direct line of four game pieces of the same color.

Why these three games, you ask? Well, they're simple to grasp and perfect for exploring the world of rule-based AI, deep reinforcement learning (e.g., policy gradients or the actor-critic method), and other AI techniques. There is no need for you to get bogged down in complex game rules. In contrast, games like Chess and Go require a deep well of domain knowledge to devise effective strategies. Deep Blue's algorithm, for instance, uses thousands of rules to evaluate board positions in Chess. The game of Go involves complicated rules like "no self-capturing," "komi" (compensation for the first mover's advantage), and the tricky concept of "ko" (avoiding creating a previous board position). What's more, applying rule-based AI and deep learning to these three games is fast and easy and doesn't require costly computational resources. As you'll discover in this book, you can train intelligent game strategies on a regular computer in minutes or hours. As a result, the trained AI provides perfect solutions for the first two games, while Connect Four gets super-human performance. In contrast, Chess and Go require supercomputing facilities. Deep Blue blitzed through hundreds of millions of board positions each second, and AlphaGo gobbled up the processing power of 1920 CPUs and 280 GPUs. The average reader doesn't have access to such supercomputing might, which is why we choose everyday simple games to make AI learning accessible to everyone with a regular computer.

By immersing yourself in these three captivating games, you'll grasp the essence of rule-based AI, from the MiniMax algorithm to alpha-beta pruning and the exhilarating Monte Carlo Tree Search. Afterward, we'll venture into the realm of ML, specifically deep reinforcement learning – the secret sauce behind AlphaGo's victory. DeepMind's brilliant minds used the policy-gradient method and crafted two deep neural networks to train game strategies. You'll learn how to combine modern ML techniques with rule-based AI to achieve superhuman performance, just like the DeepMind team did in the epic AlphaGo showdown. Get ready for an AI journey that's not just educational but downright thrilling!

This book is divided into four parts. Part I provides an introduction to the three games and outlines how to develop strategies using rule-based AI techniques like MiniMax and MCTS. Part II delves into deep learning and its application to the three games. Part III explores the fundamentals of reinforcement learning and demonstrates how to enhance game strategies through self-play deep reinforcement learning. Finally, in Part IV, we integrate rule-based AI with deep reinforcement learning to construct AlphaGo (and its successor, AlphaGo Zero) algorithms for the three games.

Here's an overview of the book:

Part I: Rule-Based AI

Chapter 1: Rule-Based AI in the Coin Game

In this chapter, we introduce the first of the three games featured in this book: the coin game. You'll be guided through the rules of the game and learn how to create a rule-based AI that can achieve a 100% win rate against any opponent when playing in the second position.

Chapter 2: Look-Ahead Search in Tic Tac Toe

You'll delve into the rules of the second game: Tic Tac Toe. You'll learn how to develop strategies that enable the AI to plan up to three moves ahead. To think one step ahead, the AI evaluates all possible next moves to see if any of them immediately result in a win. If so, the AI takes that move. Thinking two steps ahead involves the AI trying to block the opponent from winning in their next turn. By thinking three steps ahead, the AI chooses the path that is most likely to lead to victory after three moves. In many cases, thinking three steps ahead ensures that the AI can secure a win within three moves.

Chapter 3: Planning Three Steps Ahead in Connect Four

In this chapter, you'll learn how to play Connect Four in the local game environment and develop rule-based AI strategies for the game. These AI players will think up to three moves ahead. When the AI looks one step ahead, it evaluates all possible next moves and chooses one that could lead to an immediate win. However, thinking two steps ahead in Connect Four introduces more complexity. The AI must determine whether its next move will block the opponent's win or inadvertently help them win. Our strategy for this scenario is twofold: if the AI's move blocks the opponent, it proceeds with that move; otherwise, it avoids a move that helps the opponent win in two moves. When thinking three steps ahead, the AI follows the path that is most likely to lead to victory after three moves.

Chapter 4: Recursion and MiniMax Tree Search

Up to this point, you have been hardcoding look-ahead search techniques to devise game strategies. However, extending this approach beyond three steps becomes increasingly cumbersome and prone to errors. To address this, you'll learn a more efficient method for conducting look-ahead searches: the MiniMax tree search. You'll learn how to implement the MiniMax tree search in the coin game by employing recursion, which involves calling a function within itself. This recursive approach enables the MiniMax agent to search ahead until the end of the game. As a result, the MiniMax agent is able to solve the coin game.

Chapter 5: Depth Pruning in MiniMax

You'll begin by developing a MiniMax agent for Tic Tac Toe using recursion. The MiniMax tree search method explores all potential future paths and solves the game. However, in more complex games like Connect Four, Chess, or Go, the MiniMax algorithm is unable to exhaustively explore all possible future paths in a reasonable time. To overcome this limitation, the algorithm employs a technique called depth pruning. This approach involves searching a specific number of moves ahead and then stopping the search. You'll learn how to create a MiniMax agent with depth pruning and apply it to Connect Four.

Chapter 6: Alpha-Beta Pruning

Alpha-beta pruning enhances the look-ahead search algorithm by allowing it to bypass branches that cannot impact the final outcome of the game. This optimization significantly reduces the time it takes for the MiniMax agent to decide on a move, enabling it to explore more steps ahead and develop smarter moves within a given time frame. To apply alpha-beta pruning in a game, the agent keeps track of two values: alpha and beta, which represent the best possible outcomes for the two players, respectively. Whenever $alpha > -beta$, or equivalently $beta > -alpha$, the agent stops searching a branch. You'll implement alpha-beta pruning in both Tic Tac Toe and Connect Four. By incorporating this technique, the time required for the MiniMax agent to decide on a move is reduced by up to 97%, making the algorithm much more efficient.

Chapter 7: Position Evaluation in MiniMax

Depth pruning enables a MiniMax agent to develop intelligent (though not perfect) strategies quickly in complex games. In earlier chapters, when the depth of a tree search reaches zero and the game is not yet over, the algorithm assumes a tied game. However, in many real-world games, we often have a good estimate of the outcome based on heuristics, even when the game is not over. In this chapter, you'll learn the concept of the position evaluation function and apply it to the Connect Four game. When the depth reaches zero in a tree search and the game is not over, you'll use an evaluation function to assess the value of the game state. This evaluation function provides a more accurate assessment of the game state, enabling the MiniMax agent to make more intelligent moves.

Chapter 8: Monte Carlo Tree Search

MiniMax tree search, augmented by powerful position evaluation functions, helped Deep Blue beat the world Chess champion Garry Kasparov in 1997. While in games such as Chess, position evaluation functions are relatively accurate, in other games such as Go, evaluating positions is more challenging. In such scenarios, researchers usually use Monte Carlo Tree Search (MCTS). The idea behind MCTS is to roll out random games starting from the current game state and see what the average game outcome is. After rolling out, say 1000, games from this point, if Player 1 wins 99 percent of the time, the current game state must favor Player 1 over Player 2. To select the best next move, the MCTS algorithm uses the Upper Confidence Bounds for Trees (UCT) method. This chapter breaks down the process into four steps: selection, expansion, simulation, and backpropagation. Readers learn to implement a generic MCTS algorithm that can be applied to the three games in this book: the coin game, Tic Tac Toe, and Connect Four.

Part II: Deep Learning

Chapter 9: Deep Learning in the Coin Game

In this chapter, you'll learn what deep learning is and how it's related to ML and AI. Deep learning is a type of ML method that's based on artificial neural networks. A neural network is a computational model inspired by the structure of neural networks in the human brain. It's designed to recognize patterns in data, and it contains layers of interconnected nodes, or neurons. You'll learn to use deep neural networks to design game strategies for the coin game in this chapter. In particular, you'll build and train two networks, a fast policy network and a strong policy network, to be used in the AlphaGo algorithm later in the book.

Chapter 10: Policy Networks in Tic Tac Toe

In this chapter, you'll train a fast policy network and a strong policy network in Tic Tac Toe. The two networks contain convolutional layers, which treat game boards as multi-dimensional objects and extract spatial features from them. Convolutional layers greatly improve the predictive power of neural networks and this, in turn, leads to more intelligent game strategies. To generate expert moves in Tic Tac Toe, you'll use the MiniMax algorithm with alpha-beta pruning from Chapter 6. You'll use game board positions as inputs and expert moves as targets to train the two policy neural networks. The two trained policy networks will be used in the AlphaGo algorithm later in this book.

Chapter 11: A Policy Network in Connect Four

In this chapter, you'll train a policy network in Connect Four so that it can be used in the AlphaGo algorithm later in the book. To generate expert moves, you'll first design an agent who chooses moves by using the MCTS algorithm half of the time and a MiniMax algorithm with alpha-beta pruning the other 50% of the time. You let the above agent play against itself for 10,000 games. In each game, the winner's moves are considered expert moves while the loser's moves are discarded. You'll then create a deep neural network and use the self-play game experience data to train it to predict expert moves.

Part III: Reinforcement Learning

Chapter 12: Tabular Q-Learning in the Coin Game

You'll learn the basics of reinforcement learning in this chapter. You'll use tabular Q-learning to solve the coin game. Along the way, you'll learn the concepts of dynamic programming and the Bellman equation. You'll also learn how to train and use Q-tables in tabular Q-learning.

Chapter 13: Self-Play Deep Reinforcement Learning

You'll learn to use self-play deep reinforcement learning to further train the strong policy network for the coin game. You'll learn what a policy is and how to implement the policy gradient method to train the agent in deep reinforcement learning. A policy is a decision rule that tells the agent what actions to take in a given game state. In the policy gradients method, the agent engages in numerous game sessions to learn the optimal policy. The agent bases its actions on the model's predictions, observes the resulting rewards, and adjusts the model parameters to align predicted action probabilities with desired probabilities. You'll also use the game experience data from self-plays to train a value network that predicts game outcomes based on current game states.

Chapter 14: Vectorization to Speed Up Deep Reinforcement Learning

You'll apply self-play deep reinforcement learning to Tic Tac Toe in this chapter. You'll learn to manage several challenges in the process. Firstly, unlike the coin game, where illegal moves are non-existent as players simply choose to remove one or two coins per turn, Tic Tac Toe has a decreasing number of legal moves as the game advances. You'll learn to assign negative rewards to illegal moves so the trained agent chooses only legal moves. Secondly, the computational demands of training for Tic Tac Toe are significantly higher than for the coin game. You'll learn to use vectorization to speed up the training process. Finally, this chapter will guide you through the process of encoding the game board in a player-independent manner so that the current player's game pieces are represented as 1 and the opponent's as -1. This allows the use of the same neural network for training both players. With the above challenges properly handled, you'll implement the policy gradient method in Tic Tac Toe to train a policy network. You'll also train a value network based on the game experience data.

Chapter 15: A Value Network in Connect Four

You'll apply the policy gradient method to Connect Four in this chapter. You'll learn to handle illegal moves by assigning a reward of -1 every time the agent makes an illegal move. You'll also use vectorization to speed up training. Self-play deep reinforcement learning is used to further train a policy network in Connect Four based on the policy network from Chapter 11. Readers also use the game experience data from self-play to train a value network: the network will predict the game outcome based on the board position.

Part IV: AlphaGo Algorithms

Chapter 16: Implementing AlphaGo in the Coin Game

In this chapter, you'll implement the AlphaGo algorithm in the coin game. MCTS constitutes the backbone of AlphaGo's decision-making process: it is used to find the most promising moves by building a search tree. You'll learn to use three deep neural networks you developed in earlier chapters. The strengthened policy network (from Chapter 13) selects child nodes so that the most valuable child nodes are selected to roll out games. The fast policy network developed in Chapter 9 helps in narrowing down the selection of moves to consider in game rollouts. The value network from Chapter 13 evaluates board positions and predicts the winner of the game from that position so that the agent doesn't have to play out the entire game in rollouts. When moving second, the AlphaGo agent beats the ruled-based AI player in 100% of games.

Chapter 17: AlphaGo in Tic Tac Toe and Connect Four

In this chapter, you'll create an AlphaGo agent featuring two main enhancements. Firstly, it will be versatile and capable of handling two games, Tic Tac Toe and

Connect Four. Secondly, the agent's game simulation strategy includes a choice between random moves and those suggested by a fast policy network. MCTS remains the core of the agent's decision process, involving selection, expansion, simulation, and backpropagation. Three deep neural networks, introduced in previous chapters, will enhance the tree search. You'll evaluate the AlphaGo algorithm's effectiveness in Tic Tac Toe. Against the perfect rule-based AI from Chapter 6, the AlphaGo agent consistently draws, indicating its ability to solve the game.

Chapter 18: Hyperparameter Tuning in AlphaGo

Unlike agents in the coin game or Tic Tac Toe, the AlphaGo agent in Connect Four does not fully solve the game. This chapter, therefore, focuses on identifying the optimal combination of hyperparameters in AlphaGo that yields the most effective game strategy. Grid search is a common approach for hyperparameter tuning. This process involves experimenting with different permutations of hyperparameters in the model to determine empirically which combination offers the best performance. You'll learn to fine-tune four key hyperparameters for the AlphaGo agent in Connect Four in this chapter. The optimized AlphaGo agent can defeat an AI that plans four steps ahead.

Chapter 19: The Actor-Critic Method and AlphaZero

In 2017, the DeepMind team introduced an advanced version of AlphaGo, named AlphaGo Zero (which we'll refer to as AlphaZero in this book because we apply the algorithm to various games beyond Go). AlphaZero's training relied exclusively on deep reinforcement learning, without any human-derived strategies or domain-specific knowledge, except for the basic rules of the game. It learned through self-play from scratch. AlphaZero utilizes a single neural network with two outputs: a policy network for predicting the next move and a value network for forecasting game outcomes. In this chapter, you'll learn this advanced deep reinforcement learning strategy known as the actor-critic method, applying it specifically to the coin game. You'll then integrate both the policy and value networks from the actor-critic method with MCTS for making decisions in actual games, mirroring the approach used in the AlphaGo algorithm in Chapter 16. The AlphaZero agent developed in this chapter, if playing as Player 2, can beat the AlphaGo agent developed earlier in Chapter 16.

Chapter 20: Iterative Self-Play and AlphaZero in Tic Tac Toe

You'll learn to construct an AlphaZero agent for both Tic Tac Toe and Connect Four in this chapter. You'll then implement the AlphaZero algorithm in Tic Tac Toe by integrating a policy gradient network with MCTS. To train the model, you'll start a policy gradient network from scratch and initialize it with random weights. During training, the policy gradient agent competes against a more advanced version of itself: the AlphaZero agent. As training progresses, both agents gradually improve their performance. This dynamic scenario presents a unique challenge, as the agent effectively faces a moving target. To address this challenge, an iterative self-play approach is used. Initially, you'll keep the weights of the policy gradient network, as utilized by the AlphaZero agent, constant, while updating the weights within the policy gradient network itself. After an iteration of training, the weights in the policy gradient network used by the AlphaZero agent will be updated. This process is repeated in successive iterations until the AlphaZero agent perfects its gameplay.

Chapter 21: AlphaZero in Unsolved Games

In the previous two chapters, you have used rule-based AI to periodically evaluate the AlphaZero agent to gauge its performance and decide when to stop training. Even though rule-based AI was not used in the training process directly, it was used for testing purposes to monitor the agent's performance. In unsolved games, no game-solving algorithm can be used as the benchmark. How should we test the performance of AlphaZero and decide when to stop training in such cases? In this chapter, you'll treat Connect Four as an unsolved game. To test the performance of AlphaZero and decide when to stop training, an earlier version of AlphaZero is used as the benchmark. When AlphaZero outperforms an earlier version of itself by a certain margin, a training iteration is complete. You'll then update the parameters in the older version of AlphaZero and restart the training process. You'll train the AlphaZero model for several iterations so that the AlphaZero agent becomes increasingly stronger. The trained AlphaZero agent consistently outperforms its predecessor, AlphaGo, in Connect Four!

All Python programs, along with answers to some end-of-the-chapter questions, are provided in the GitHub repository https://github.com/markhliu/AlphaGoSimplified.

Acknowledgments

This is my second collaboration with CRC Press, and the experience has been nothing short of wonderful. I extend my heartfelt thanks to Randi Slack and Solomon Pace-McCarrick for their invaluable assistance during the editorial process. I also like to thank the production team of Gabrielle Perez and Nancy Rebecca for helping me cross the finish line.

To you, the reader, I am deeply grateful for the opportunity to share my thoughts and ideas. Your engagement with my work has provided me with a precious platform to express myself and be heard. Writing this book has been a transformative journey of discovery and learning. Organizing my thoughts on the subject has not only brought clarity but has also expanded my understanding in unexpected ways. I am thankful for the personal growth this process has enabled.

Lastly, I want to express my profound appreciation to my wife, Ivey Zhang, and my son, Andrew Liu, for their unwavering support throughout this journey.

I

Rule-Based AI

## CHAPTER 1

Rule-Based AI in the Coin Game

"Can you learn stuff you haven't been programmed with so you can be, you know, more human?"

– John Connor, in Terminator 2: Judgement Day

IN THE 1991 Hollywood movie *Terminator 2: Judgement Day*, John Connor asked the Terminator, "Can you learn stuff you haven't been programmed with so you can be, you know, more human?" The simple question highlights two drastically different paradigms in artificial intelligence (AI): rule-based AI (stuff that machines have been programmed with, in John Connor's words) and machine learning (ML) – the powerhouse behind modern AI. With rule-based AI, we humans hard-code various rules onto a machine and tell the machine what to do in each situation according to the rules. ML is a new paradigm that is very different from the traditional rule-based AI. Instead of programming rules onto a computer and telling it what to do, humans feed the computer many examples and let the computer figure out what the rules are. The machine can then decide what to do in situations it has never encountered before based on the learned rules. While rule-based AI is powerful when rules are clear and relatively easy to code onto a computer, ML is especially useful in situations where coding in rules is either too difficult or downright impossible.

In this book, you'll learn both rule-based AI and ML by implementing them in three simple everyday games: the coin game, Tic Tac Toe, and Connect Four. More importantly, you'll also learn how to combine rule-based AI and ML (as AlphaGo did) to create intelligent game strategies that are far more powerful than strategies based on either AI paradigm alone. This chapter introduces you to the first of the three games: *Last Coin Standing* (also known as the coin game). You'll learn to create a game strategy based on traditional rule-based AI. The AI agent solves the game and wins 100% of the time when it moves second against any opponent.

DOI: 10.1201/9781032722207-1

The purpose of this chapter is threefold. First, it provides a local game environment for the coin game and creates a perfect solution to the game based on rule-based AI. Second, later in this book, we'll develop strategies for the coin game based on other algorithms such as MiniMax, Monte Carlo Tree Search, deep neural networks, and deep reinforcement learning. We'll use the rule-based AI developed in this chapter to test the effectiveness of various game strategies in later chapters. Third, later in this book, when we train deep learning or deep reinforcement learning game strategies (such as the policy-gradient method), we need to generate game experience data to train these models. The stronger the players in simulated gameplays, the better the trained game strategies. We'll use rule-based AI developed in this chapter to simulate intelligent gameplay. As a result, the trained agents in deep learning and deep reinforcement learning are also strong (they'll also make perfect moves and solve the game).

Nonetheless, the main takeaway from this chapter is that rule-based AI can be very effective in many situations. In fact, rule-based AI (including the look-ahead search method that we'll discuss later in this book) led to the victory of Deep Blue against the world Chess champion Garry Kasparov in 1997.

Before you get started, you'll first install Python on your computer and create a virtual environment for projects in this book.

What You'll Learn in This Chapter

- Setting up a Python virtual environment for this book
- Learning the rules of the coin game
- Playing the coin game using the local game environment
- Creating a rule-based AI agent in the coin game

1.1   SET UP A PYTHON VIRTUAL ENVIRONMENT

In this section, you'll first install Anaconda on your computer so that you can run Python programs in this book. You'll then set up a virtual environment so you'll have correct versions of various Python libraries for projects in this book. You'll use Jupyter Notebook as your integrated development environment (IDE). At the end of this section, you'll set up a file system for projects associated with the book.

1.1.1   Install Anaconda

To install Anaconda, go to the following website https://www.anaconda.com/download/success and scroll down to the bottom of the page. Then, download the latest version of Python 3 for your operating system (Windows, Mac, or Linux). If you are using a Mac, select the appropriate graphical installer depending on whether your machine has an Intel Processor or the Apple M1 chip. If you are using Linux, select the appropriate package depending on your system.

If you are using Windows or Mac, install Anaconda by clicking on the graphical installer you just downloaded. Follow the on-screen instructions to finish the installation. If you are using Linux, run the *.sh* file you just downloaded and make sure you activate the installation after that. Chapter 1 of my book *Machine Learning, Animated* [6] provides detailed instructions on how to install Anaconda on your machine.

1.1.2   Create a Virtual Environment

It's highly recommended that you create a separate virtual environment for this book. Let's name the virtual environment for this book *ags*, short for AlphaGo Simplified. Enter the following command in the Anaconda prompt (Windows) or a terminal (Mac or Linux):

```
conda create -n ags
```

Press the ENTER key on your keyboard and follow the on-screen instructions all the way through to finish the creation of the new virtual environment.

Now, we need to set up Jupyter Notebook in the newly created virtual environment on your computer. First, activate the virtual environment by running the following line of code in the Anaconda prompt (Windows) or a terminal (Mac or Linux):

```
conda activate ags
```

To install Jupyter Notebook in the virtual environment, run the following command:

```
conda install notebook
```

To launch Jupyter Notebook, execute the following command with the virtual environment activated:

```
jupyter notebook
```

1.1.3   The File System for This Book

You should first create a folder /ags/ on your computer's Desktop, which will contain all files for this book. All local modules are placed in a subfolder /utils/ within the /ags/ folder. We'll then create a subfolder /files/ within the /ags/ folder for various files (such as images and trained models) in the book.

To create the aforementioned file system, first download the file *tmp.ipynb* from the book's GitHub repository https://github.com/markhliu/AlphaGoSimplified and place it in the folder /Desktop/ags/ you just created on your computer. Open the Jupyter Notebook app on your computer in the *ags* virtual environment by following instructions in the previous subsection. After that, navigate to the folder /Desktop/ags/ and open the file *tmp.ipynb*. In a new cell in the file, run the following lines of code:

```
[1]:  import os

      os.makedirs("utils", exist_ok=True)
      with open("utils/__init__.py", "w") as f:
          f.write("")
      os.makedirs("files", exist_ok=True)
```

In the above cell, we first create a subfolder /utils/ in the folder /Desktop/ags/ on your computer. We then generate an empty file ___init___.py inside the folder /Desktop/ags/utils/ so that Python treats it as a local package. The last line of code creates the folder /Desktop/ags/files/ on your computer.

Ways to Learn Python Basics

This book assumes you have a working knowledge of the Python programming language. If not, there are various free online resources you can tap into. W3Schools provides a great free online Python tutorial: go to https://www.w3schools.com/python/ and follow the examples and exercises in the tutorial. They also provide a "Try it Yourself" editor and online compiler for you to run Python code without installing Python on your computer. Alternatively, you can pick up a Python basics book and go over it. Professor Charles Severance has a free online book, *Python for Everyone* [9]: https://www.py4e.com/.

1.2 THE COIN GAME

The coin game is a simple two-player zero-sum game. It's also known as the Last Coin Standing game. This section discusses the game rules and the solution to the coin game.

1.2.1 Rules of the Coin Game

In the coin game, there are 21 coins in a pile. Two players take turns removing coins from the pile. Each player can take either one or two coins from the pile in each turn. Players are not allowed to skip a turn or take more than two coins at a time. The player who takes the last coin in the pile wins the game.

There are different versions of the game. In some versions, the player who takes the last coin loses. In other versions, a player can take either one, two, or three coins in each turn. No matter which version we use, the central message of this chapter remains the same: rule-based AI can work very effectively in many situations.

1.2.2   Implement Rules in the Coin Game

The main goal of the book is to learn rule-based AI and ML and apply them to various real-world situations. As such, we'll abstract away from the implementation of the game rules in the three games used in this book (the coin game, Tic Tac Toe, and Connect Four). Instead, we'll modularize the three games and place the implementations in the local modules. This way, you can focus on designing game strategies with various AI algorithms without getting distracted by game rules.

Nonetheless, we'll quickly implement the coin game in the following program since it's relatively easy to do so. After that, you can play against a random player manually by entering your moves using the keyboard.

Open a new cell in the Jupyter Notebook and enter the following code in it. Here you are playing against a computer player who makes random moves. Use your keyboard to enter numbers 1 or 2 to play a game.

```
[2]:  from random import choice

coins = 21
while True:
    # Player 1 moves first, randomly
    move1 = choice([1,2])
    coins=coins-move1
    print(f'player 1 chooses {move1}; {coins} remaining')
    # Check if the game has ended
    if coins<=0:
        print('game over; player 1 won')
        break
    # Player 2 moves after that
    while True:
        move2 = input('what\'s your choice?\n')
        try:
            if int(move2)==1 or int(move2)==2:
                break
            else:
                print("please enter either 1 or 2")
        except:
            print("please enter a number in the form of 1 or 2")
    coins = coins - int(move2)
    print(f"you have chosen {move2};  {coins} remaining")
    # Check if the game has ended
    if coins<=0:
        print('game over; player 2 won')
        break
```

```
player 1 chooses 1; 20 remaining
what's your choice?
2
you have chosen 2;  18 remaining
player 1 chooses 1; 17 remaining
what's your choice?
2
you have chosen 2;  15 remaining
player 1 chooses 2; 13 remaining
what's your choice?
2
you have chosen 2;  11 remaining
player 1 chooses 2; 9 remaining
what's your choice?
2
you have chosen 2;  7 remaining
player 1 chooses 2; 5 remaining
what's your choice?
2
you have chosen 2;  3 remaining
player 1 chooses 1; 2 remaining
what's your choice?
2
you have chosen 2;  0 remaining
game over; player 2 won
```

The computer moves first and removes either one or two coins (with a 50% chance for each) from the pile. When it's your turn, you can enter either 1 or 2 as your move. If you enter anything other than 1 or 2, the program will remind you to enter a valid move and let you re-try. After each move, the program checks if the game is over. If not, it goes to the next player.

I entered number 2 in every move to speed up the game. The results show that I have won.

Run the above cell a few times to play against the computer and see if you can figure out a winning strategy. Note that the computer player's moves are different each time you play because the moves are randomly chosen.

1.2.3 A Winning Strategy

You may have figured out a winning strategy. The second player will always win if he/she follows this rule: make sure the number of coins in the pile is a multiple of three. The pile starts with 21 coins, so it's already a multiple of three. Therefore, if Player 1 takes one coin, Player 2 should take two coins; if Player 1 takes two coins, Player 2 should take one coin. With this rule, Player 2 will leave 18, 15, 12, 9, 6, and eventually 3 coins in the pile. Once there are three coins in the pile when it's Player

1's turn to play, Player 2 will win the game for sure: if Player 1 takes one coin, Player 2 takes the last two coins and wins; if Player 1 takes two coins, Player 2 takes the remaining one coin in the pile and wins.

Play the game again using the above winning strategy.

Next, we'll create a game environment for the coin game. We'll also add a graphical game window using the Python *turtle* library.

1.3 THE COIN GAME ENVIRONMENT

We'll create game environments for the three games used in this book by following the customs in OpenAI Gym. The attributes and methods in various games are identical (or close to identical) to each other. This way, you'll focus on learning rule-based AI and ML without getting distracted by the details of game rules.

In this chapter, we'll create a coin game environment, using the *turtle* library to draw graphical game windows.

1.3.1 Methods and Attributes of the Coin Game

Go to the book's GitHub repository https://github.com/markhliu/AlphaGoSimplified and download the three files *coin_env.py*, *coin_simple_env.py*, and *cash.png* and place them in the folder /Desktop/ags/utils/ on your computer. We'll use the file *coin_env.py* to represent the coin game environment. Open the file and take a look. Unless you want to learn how to create your game environments, you don't need to understand the code in the file. The file *cash.png* generates an image of a coin in the game window. The file *coin_simple_env.py* is the same as the file *coin_env.py* except that it doesn't provide a graphical game window. We'll use the file *coin_simple_env.py* later in the book when training deep learning and deep reinforcement learning game strategies (removing the game windows speeds up the training process).

Specifically, our self-made coin game environment has the following attributes:

- agent: there are two agents in the coin game environment, Players 1 and 2.
- action_space: an attribute that provides the space for all actions that can be taken by an agent. The action space is a set with two values: 1 and 2.
- observation_space: an attribute that provides the list of all possible states in the environment. We'll use an integer number between 0 and 21 to represent the number of coins left in the pile.
- state: an attribute indicating which state an agent is currently in. The state is the number of coins left in the pile, which can take an integer number between 0 and 21.
- action: an attribute indicating the action taken by an agent. The action is either 1 (removing one coin from the pile) or 2 (removing two coins from the pile).

- reward: an attribute indicating the reward to the agents because of the actions taken by them. The reward is 0 in each step unless a player has won the game, in which case the reward is 1 to the winner and −1 to the loser. There is no draw in the coin game.
- done: an attribute indicating whether the game has ended. This happens when there is no coin left in the pile.
- info: an attribute that provides information about the game. We'll set it as an empty string. We add this attribute so we have all the attributes in a typical OpenAI Gym game environment.

Our self-made coin game environment has a few methods as well:

- reset() is a method to set the game environment to the initial (that is, the starting) state. Player 1 has the turn and there are 21 coins in the pile in the initial state.
- render() is a method showing the current state of the environment graphically.
- step() is a method to make a move in the game environment and return the new state, the reward, the *done* variable, and the *info* variable based on the action taken by an agent.
- sample() is a method to randomly choose an action from the action space.
- close() is a method to close the game environment, including stopping displaying the game window.

The above methods are the same as those in a typical OpenAI Gym game environment.

1.3.2 Interact with the Coin Game Environment

Next, you'll learn to play the coin game by using the self-made game environment. First, we'll initiate the game environment and show the game window, like so:

```
[3]: from utils.coin_env import coin_game

env = coin_game()
env.reset()
env.render()
```

You should see a separate game window as shown in Figure 1.1.

If you want to close the game window, use the *close()* method, like so:

```
[4]: env.close()
```

Next, we'll check the attributes of the game environment such as the observation space and action space:

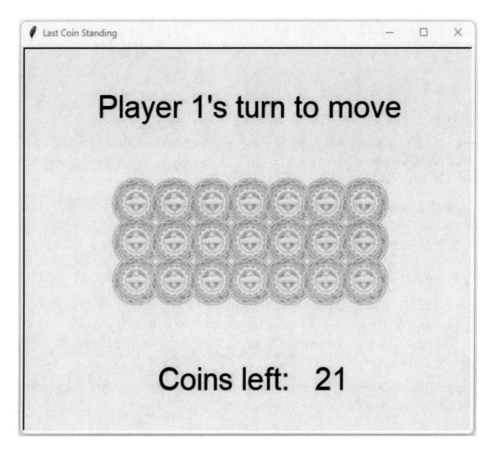

Figure 1.1　The starting game window in the coin game

```
[5]:  env=coin_game()
      # check the action space
      number_actions=env.action_space.n
      print("the number of possible actions is",number_actions)
      # sample the action space ten times
      print("the following are ten sample actions")
      for i in range(10):
          print(env.sample())
      # check the shape of the observation space
      print("the shape of the observation space is",\
            env.observation_space.shape)
```

```
the number of possible actions is 2
the following are ten sample actions
2
1
2
1
1
```

```
1
2
1
1
1
```

the shape of the observation space is (1,)

The results above show that there are two possible actions that can be taken by an agent. The meanings of the actions in this game are: 1, removing one coin from the pile and 2, removing two coins from the pile.

The *sample()* method returns an action from the action space randomly: the above results show ten different actions. The state space is a scalar: a number indicating how many coins are left in the pile.

1.3.3   Play a Complete Coin Game

Next, we'll play games in the custom-made environment. Let's first play a game by randomly selecting an action from the action space in each step for both players. After that, you'll play a game manually against a computer player who makes random moves.

The next code cell shows a complete game, in which both players randomly choose an action from the action space in each step:

```
[6]:  import time
      import random

      env = coin_game()
      env.reset()
      env.render()
      print(f"the current state is state={env.state}")
      while True:
          action = env.sample()
          time.sleep(1)
          print(f"Player {env.turn} has chosen {action}")
          state, reward, done, info = env.step(action)
          env.render()
          print(f"the current state is state={env.state}")
          if done:
              if reward==1:
                  print("Player 1 has won!")
              else:
                  print("Player 2 has won!")
              break
      env.close()
```

```
the current state is state=21
Player 1 has chosen 2
the current state is state=19
Player 2 has chosen 1
the current state is state=18
Player 1 has chosen 2
the current state is state=16
Player 2 has chosen 1
the current state is state=15
Player 1 has chosen 2
the current state is state=13
Player 2 has chosen 2
the current state is state=11
Player 1 has chosen 2
the current state is state=9
Player 2 has chosen 2
the current state is state=7
Player 1 has chosen 1
the current state is state=6
Player 2 has chosen 2
the current state is state=4
Player 1 has chosen 2
the current state is state=2
Player 2 has chosen 1
the current state is state=1
Player 1 has chosen 2
the current state is state=0
Player 1 has won!
```

The output above shows that player 1 has won. Run the above code cell several times. You'll notice that the output is different each time you run it because both players choose random moves.

1.3.4   Play the Coin Game Manually

Next, you'll learn how to manually interact with the coin game environment. You'll use your keyboard to enter either 1 or 2 in each step of the game. The program is similar to the one we created at the beginning of this chapter when we didn't use the game environment.

The following lines of code show you how:

```
[7]:   # Initiate the game environment
       env=coin_game()
       env.reset()
       env.render()
```

```
print(f"the current state is state={env.state}")
# Play a full game manually
while True:
    action = env.sample()
    time.sleep(1)
    print(f"Player {env.turn} has chosen {action}")
    state, reward, done, info = env.step(action)
    env.render()
    print(f"the current state is state={env.state}")
    if done:
        print("Player 1 has won!")
        break
    # Player 2 moves after that
    while True:
        move2 = input('what\'s your choice?\n')
        try:
            if int(move2)==1 or int(move2)==2:
                break
            else:
                print("please enter either 1 or 2")
        except:
            print("please enter a number in the form of 1 or 2")
    action = move2
    print(f"Player {env.turn} has chosen {action}")
    state, reward, done, info = env.step(action)
    env.render()
    print(f"the current state is state={env.state}")
    if done:
        print("Player 2 has won!")
        break
env.close()
```

```
the current state is state=21
Player 1 has chosen 2
the current state is state=19
what's your choice?
1
Player 2 has chosen 1
the current state is state=18
Player 1 has chosen 2
the current state is state=16
what's your choice?
1
Player 2 has chosen 1
the current state is state=15
```

```
Player 1 has chosen 2
the current state is state=13
what's your choice?
1
Player 2 has chosen 1
the current state is state=12
Player 1 has chosen 1
the current state is state=11
what's your choice?
2
Player 2 has chosen 2
the current state is state=9
Player 1 has chosen 2
the current state is state=7
what's your choice?
1
Player 2 has chosen 1
the current state is state=6
Player 1 has chosen 1
the current state is state=5
what's your choice?
2
Player 2 has chosen 2
the current state is state=3
Player 1 has chosen 2
the current state is state=1
what's your choice?
1
Player 2 has chosen 1
the current state is state=0
Player 2 has won!
```

Here I am playing second, with the winning strategy: in each step, if Player 1 chooses 1, I choose 2; if Player 1 chooses 2, I choose 1. As a result, I have won the game.

1.4   BUILD A RULE-BASED AI FOR THE COIN GAME

In this section, you'll learn to create a rule-based AI with the winning strategy. After that, you'll use the strategy to play games and test its effectiveness.

Later in this book, you'll design various types of game strategies such as MiniMax, Monte Carlo Tree Search, Deep Reinforcement Learning, and so on. We'll often test the efficacy of these strategies. Therefore, in this chapter, you'll get used to writing programs to test AI game strategies. You'll also use different players to play against each other: such as the random player versus AI, AI versus AI, and so on.

1.4.1   An AI Player in the Coin Game

Since we'll use the AI game strategy many times later in this book, we'll create an AI agent in a local module. This way, we'll simply import the function associated with the AI game strategy from the local module every time we need to use it.

Download the file *ch01util.py* from the book's GitHub repository and place it in the folder /Desktop/ags/utils/ on your computer. Open the file and take a look. In it, we have defined the following function:

```
[8]:  def rule_based_AI(env):
          if env.state%3 != 0:
              move = env.state%3
          else:
              move = env.sample()
          return move
```

The *rule_based_AI()* function takes the game environment as the input. The AI player will choose a move based on the game state (that is, how many coins are left in the pile). If the game state is a multiple of three, the AI player randomly chooses 1 or 2. Otherwise, the AI player chooses the remainder of the game state divided by 3: doing this ensures that the number of coins left in the pile is a multiple of three.

In the local module *ch01util*, we'll also create a random player who randomly selects a valid move:

```
[9]:  def random_player(env):
          move = env.sample()
          return move
```

Even though we use the game environment as an input, the move made by the random player is independent of the state. It returns either 1 or 2 randomly.

In the local module *ch01util*, we create a function that simulates a complete coin game. We can choose the two players as the two arguments for the function, like so:

```
[10]:  # Define the one_coin_game() function
       def one_coin_game(player1, player2):
           env = coin_game()
           env.reset()
           while True:
               action = player1(env)
               new_state, reward, done, info = env.step(action)
               if done:
                   break
               action = player2(env)
               new_state, reward, done, info = env.step(action)
               if done:
```

```
            break
    return reward
```

The function *one_coin_game()* simulates one full game: it takes two function names as the two arguments. For example, if we use *rule_based_AI* and *random_player* as the two arguments in the function, Player 1 will make moves based on the function *rule_based_AI()* while Player 2 will make moves based on the function *random_player()*. There is a difference between *rule_based_AI()* and *rule_based_AI*: while the former (with parentheses) indicates the calling of the function, the latter (without parentheses) is the name of the function.

Function Name versus Calling A Function

Pay attention to the difference between a function name (without parentheses) and the calling of a function (with parentheses). For example, *rule_based_AI* is just a function name while *rule_based_AI()* calls the function and executes all command lines in it. What a difference the parentheses make in this case!

We don't use the *render()* method in the *one_coin_game()* function to speed up game simulation. As a result, you won't see the game windows. The function returns the reward of the game. We can infer the outcome from the reward: if the reward is 1, Player 1 has won; if the reward is −1, Player 2 has won the game.

1.4.2   Test the Efficacy of the AI Game Strategy

Next, we'll test how often the AI player wins when it plays against a random player. We also look at the game outcomes when two AI players play against each other.

First, we simulate 1000 games when the AI player moves first and plays against a random player.

```
[11]: from utils.ch01util import (rule_based_AI,
          random_player, one_coin_game)

# Simulate 1000 games and record all outcomes
results=[]
for _ in range(1000):
    result=one_coin_game(rule_based_AI, random_player)
    results.append(result)
# Print out the game outcomes
wins=results.count(1)
print(f"The AI player has won {wins} games")
losses=results.count(-1)
print(f"The AI player has lost {losses} games")
```

```
The AI player has won 990 games
The AI player has lost 10 games
```

The AI player has won 990 games out of 1000. It lost the rest 10 games. Considering that if both players make perfect moves, the first player loses 100% of the time, the AI player has done a great job: winning 99% of the time when playing first.

Note that when you run the above code cell, you are likely to get a different outcome, but the AI player should win about 99% of the time.

Next, we test how often the AI player wins if it plays second. We simulate 1000 games when the AI player moves second and plays against a random player. Specifically, when calling the *one_coin_game()* function, we put the function name *random_player* as the first argument and function name *rule_based_AI* as the second argument.

[12]:
```python
# Simulate 1000 games and record all outcomes
results=[]
for x in range(1000):
    # important: put AI player second here
    result=one_coin_game(random_player, rule_based_AI)
    results.append(result)
# Game results: AI wins when outcome is -1
wins=results.count(-1)
print(f"The AI player has won {wins} games")
losses=results.count(1)
print(f"The AI player has lost {losses} games")
```

```
The AI player has won 1000 games
The AI player has lost 0 games
```

Since the AI player now plays second, a game outcome of −1 means that the AI player wins. The above results show that AI has won all 1000 games. Run the above cell multiple times and you will get the same outcome each time because the AI player has a perfect winning strategy.

Next, we test and see what happens if two AI players play against each other.

We simulate 1000 games when both players use the rule-based AI game strategy we developed earlier.

Specifically, when calling the *one_coin_game()* function, we put the function name *rule_based_AI* as both the first and the second argument.

[13]:
```python
# Simulate 1000 games and record all outcomes
results=[]
for x in range(1000):
    # important: put AI player second here
    result=one_coin_game(rule_based_AI, rule_based_AI)
```

```
    results.append(result)
# Print out the game results
wins1=results.count(1)
print(f"The first AI player has won {wins1} games")
wins2=results.count(-1)
print(f"The second AI player has won {wins2} games")
```

```
The first AI player has won 0 games
The second AI player has won 1000 games
```

The above results show that the second AI player has won all 1000 games. Run the above cell again and you will get the same outcome because when both players play perfectly, the second player always wins.

In this chapter, you learned the rules of the first of the three games that we use in this book: Last Coin Standing (or the coin game). You also learned how to play the coin game by using the game environment in the local module. You designed a rule-based AI game strategy that wins the game 100% of the time when playing second. You'll use the game environment to design other game strategies in later chapters.

1.5 GLOSSARY

- **Action:** A decision made by a player in a game environment.
- **Action Space:** The collection of all actions that can be taken by agents.
- **Agent:** The player of the game. All three games in this book have two players in it.
- **Game Environment:** A specialized development environment for computer games, in which agents interact with the environment and each other by taking different actions.
- **Observation Space:** The collection of all possible game states in a game environment.
- **Rule-Based AI:** A branch of artificial intelligence (AI) in which humans hard code various rules onto computers and tell them what to do in each situation.
- **Reward:** The payoff to the agents in the game based on actions taken by agents and the game outcome.
- **State:** The current situation of the game.
- **The Coin Game:** Also known as Last Coin Standing. A game in which two players take turns removing coins from a pile of 21 coins. A player must remove either one or two coins from the pile in each turn. The player who removes the last coin wins.

1.6 EXERCISES

1.1 Install Anaconda on your computer and create a virtual environment named *ags*.

1.2 Install Jupyter Notebook in the newly created virtual environment *ags*.

1.3 Run the first code cell in Section 1.1.3 to create folders /Desktop/ags/utils/ and /Desktop/ags/files/ and the file ___init___.py on your computer.

1.4 Rerun the first cell in Section 1.2.2 and enter number 5 in a step and see what happens.

1.5 Rerun the first cell in Section 1.3.2 and make sure you see the game window.

1.6 Rerun the first cell in Section 1.3.4 and use the winning strategy we discussed in the chapter to win the game.

1.7 Use the function *one_coin_game()* to simulate 1000 games and use the function name *random_player* as both the first and the second arguments. Print out the game outcomes and see how many times the first player has won and how many times the second player has won.

## CHAPTER 2

Look-Ahead Search in Tic Tac Toe

"Saying Deep Blue doesn't really think about chess is like saying an airplane doesn't really fly because it doesn't flap its wings."

– *Drew McDermott*

IN THIS CHAPTER, you'll learn to play the Tic Tac Toe game in a local game environment. You'll hard code in various rules to make the AI player think up to three steps ahead. You'll then deploy the strategies against a random player and each other and see how effective they are. Coding in rule-based AI in Tic Tac Toe in this chapter serves at least four purposes. First, you'll learn how to build an AI agent that can think up to three steps ahead and generalize the logic to other games or real-world situations. Second, it introduces you to the game environment of Tic Tac Toe, as we'll use this game to study other AI algorithms later in this book, such as MiniMax, Monte Carlo Tree Search, policy gradient, and so on. Third, in deep reinforcement learning, an agent learns from playing against intelligent opponents, and we'll use the AI players created in this chapter as opponents when we design deep reinforcement learning game strategies. Fourth, later in this book, we'll use rule-based AI to test how effective a certain game strategy is; that is, we'll use rule-based AI as our benchmark when testing the effectiveness of various game strategies.

To build an AI player who can think one step ahead, we iterate through all possible next moves and check if any one of them leads to winning the game right away. If yes, the AI player will take the move. Thinking two steps ahead means that the AI player tries to prevent the opponent from winning the next turn. The program iterates through all combinations of the next two moves and checks if there is a combination that leads to a win for the opponent. If yes, the AI player blocks the opponent's move. By thinking three steps ahead, the AI player follows the path that most likely leads to a victory after three moves. In many scenarios, thinking three steps ahead can guarantee a win for the AI player in three steps.

What You'll Learn in This Chapter

- Learning the rules of Tic Tac Toe
- Playing Tic Tac Toe in the local game environment
- Creating AI agents that can think one, two, or three steps ahead
- Testing the effectiveness of AI agents in Tic Tac Toe

2.1   THE TIC TAC TOE GAME ENVIRONMENT

In Tic Tac Toe, two players take turns marking a cell with an X or O in a three-by-three grid. The first player to connect three Xs or Os in a row horizontally, vertically, or diagonally wins.

In this section, you'll familiarize yourself with the local custom-made Tic Tac Toe game environment. The game environment also creates game windows using the *turtle* library so you can visualize a graphical representation of the game. As we did in Chapter 1 for the coin game, we'll also discuss various attributes and methods of the Tic Tac Toe game environment.

2.1.1   Methods and Attributes in Tic Tac Toe

Your main goal is to learn rule-based AI and ML and apply them to various real-world situations. We therefore abstract away from the implementation of game rules. Instead, we'll place the implementation of game rules in a local module *ttt_env*. This way, you can focus on designing game strategies with AI without being distracted by the details of game rules.

First, download the file *ttt_env.py* from the book's GitHub repository https://github.com/markhliu/AlphaGoSimplified and place it in the folder /Desktop/ags/utils/ on your computer. If you are interested in creating your own game environment, open the file and take a look at how various attributes and methods are coded in the file. Otherwise, all you need to know is the attributes and methods of the game environment, which are similar to those in a typical OpenAI Gym game environment. The game environment is similar to the one in Chapter 12 of my book *Machine Learning, Animated* [6].

Our custom-made Tic Tac Toe game environment has the following attributes:

- action_space: the collection of all actions that can be taken by the agent. The action space has nine values, from 1 to 9. We use 1 to 9 instead of 0 to 8 to avoid confusion since we don't use zero-indexing in everyday life.

- observation_space: an attribute that provides the list of all possible states in the environment. We use a NumPy array with nine values to represent the nine cells on a game board.
- state: an attribute indicating which state the agent is currently in. Each of the nine cells can take a value of −1 (occupied by Player O), 0 (empty), or 1 (occupied by Player X).
- action: an attribute indicating the action taken by the agent. The action is an integer between 1 and 9.
- reward: an attribute indicating the reward to agents because of the game outcome. The reward is 0 in each step unless a player has won the game, in which case the winner has a reward of 1 and the loser a reward of −1.
- done: an attribute indicating whether the game has ended. The variable takes value *True* when one player wins or if the game is tied.
- info: an attribute that provides information about the game. We'll set it as an empty string. We add this attribute so we have all the attributes in a typical OpenAI Gym game environment.

Our Tic Tac Toe game environment has a few methods as well:

- reset() is a method to set the game environment to the initial (that is, the starting) state. All cells on the board will be empty.
- render() is a method showing the current state of the environment graphically.
- step() is a method that returns the new state, the reward, the *done* variable, and the variable *info* based on actions taken by the two agents.
- sample() is a method to randomly choose a legal action from the action space.
- close() is a method to end the game environment.

The above methods are the same as those in Chapter 1 as well as those in a typical OpenAI Gym game environment.

2.1.2 Familiarize Yourself with the Tic Tac Toe Game Environment

We'll check the attributes and methods of the self-made game environment and make sure they work the same way as those in a typical OpenAI Gym game environment.

First, we'll initiate the game environment and show the game board as follows:

```
[1]: from utils.ttt_env import ttt

env = ttt()
env.reset()
env.render()
```

We import the *ttt* class from the local *ttt_env* module and set it as our game environment. Since we called the *render()* method in the above code cell, you should see a separate turtle window, with a game board as shown in Figure 2.1.

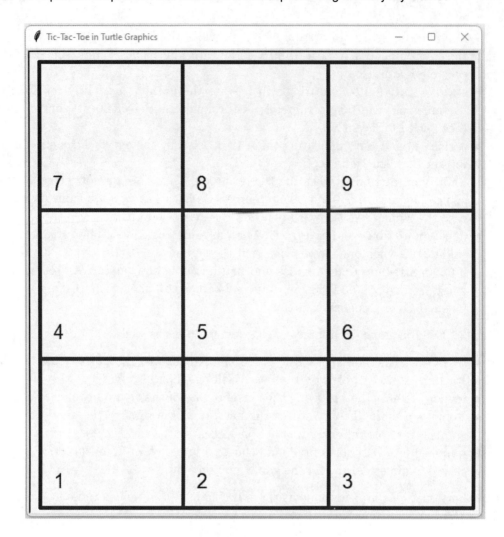

Figure 2.1 The starting game window in Tic Tac Toe

The nine cells on the game board are marked 1 through 9. After each move, the corresponding cell will be marked with an X or an O.

If you want to close the game board window, use the *close()* method, like so:

```
[2]:   env.close()
```

The next code cell checks the attributes of the Tic Tac Toe game environment:

```
[3]:   env=ttt()
       # check the action space
       number_actions=env.action_space.n
       print("the number of possible actions is", number_actions)
       # sample the action space ten times
       print("the following are ten sample actions")
```

```
for i in range(10):
    print(env.sample())
# check the shape of the observation space
print("the shape of the observation space is",\
      env.observation_space.shape)
```

```
the number of possible actions is 9
the following are ten sample actions
2
7
9
9
6
8
4
2
5
9
the shape of the observation space is (9,)
```

The meanings of the actions in this game are as follows: 1 means placing a game piece in cell 1,..., and 9 means placing a game piece in cell 9.

The state space is a vector with nine values, corresponding to the nine cells on the game board. Each cell can have a value of −1 (occupied by Player O), 0 (empty), or 1 (occupied by Player X).

2.1.3 Play Games in the Tic Tac Toe Environment

Next, we'll play Tic Tac Toe games in the custom-made environment. You'll learn to play a full game, either by letting both players select random moves or by entering moves through your keyboard.

Here we'll play a full game, by randomly choosing a valid action in each step:

```
[4]: import time

     # Initiate the game environment
     env=ttt()
     state=env.reset()
     env.render()
     # Play a full game
     while True:
         print(f"the current state is \n{state.reshape(3,3)[::-1]}")
         action = env.sample()
         time.sleep(1)
         print(f"Player X has chosen action={action}")
```

```
    state, reward, done, info = env.step(action)
    env.render()
    if done:
        print(f"game state is \n{state.reshape(3,3)[::-1]}")
        if reward==1:
            print("Player X has won!")
        else:
            print("It's a tie!")
        break
    print(f"the current state is \n{state.reshape(3,3)[::-1]}")
    action = env.sample()
    time.sleep(1)
    print(f"Player O has chosen action={action}")
    state, reward, done, info = env.step(action)
    env.render()
    if done:
        print(f"game state is \n{state.reshape(3,3)[::-1]}")
        print("Player O has won!")
        break
env.close()
```

```
the current state is
[[0 0 0]
 [0 0 0]
 [0 0 0]]
Player X has chosen action=2
the current state is
[[0 0 0]
 [0 0 0]
 [0 1 0]]
Player O has chosen action=1
the current state is
[[ 0  0  0]
 [ 0  0  0]
 [-1  1  0]]
Player X has chosen action=9
the current state is
[[ 0  0  1]
 [ 0  0  0]
 [-1  1  0]]
Player O has chosen action=4
the current state is
[[ 0  0  1]
 [-1  0  0]
 [-1  1  0]]
```

```
Player X has chosen action=8
the current state is
[[ 0  1  1]
 [-1  0  0]
 [-1  1  0]]
Player O has chosen action=7
game state is
[[-1  1  1]
 [-1  0  0]
 [-1  1  0]]
Player O has won!
```

In each step, we select an action by calling the *sample()* method in the game environment, which returns a random valid move. When printing out the game state, we use [:: −1] to switch the top and bottom rows in the NumPy array so that cells 1, 2, and 3 are in the bottom row while cells 7, 8, and 9 are in the top row. We do this to match the cell numbers in the printout with those marked on the game board in the *turtle* game windows.

The above output shows Player O has won. However, the outcome is likely different when you run the above code cell because the actions are randomly chosen.

Next, you'll manually play the Tic Tac Toe game by entering moves with your keyboard. You'll enter a number between 1 and 9 in each turn. The following lines of code show you how:

[5]:
```python
state=env.reset()
env.render()
print("enter a number between 1 and 9 as your move:")
# Play a full game manually
while True:
    print(f"game state is \n{state.reshape(3,3)[::-1]}")
    m=int(input(f"Player {env.turn}, what's your move?\n"))
    print(f"Player {env.turn} has chosen action={m}")
    state, reward, done, info = env.step(m)
    env.render()
    if done:
        print(f"game state is \n{state.reshape(3,3)[::-1]}")
        if reward!=0:
            print(f"Player {env.turn} has won!")
        else:
            print("It's a tie!")
        break
env.close()
```

```
enter a number between 1 and 9 as your move:
game state is
[[0 0 0]
 [0 0 0]
 [0 0 0]]
Player X, what's your move?
5
Player X has chosen action=5
game state is
[[0 0 0]
 [0 1 0]
 [0 0 0]]
Player O, what's your move?
1
Player O has chosen action=1
game state is
[[ 0  0  0]
 [ 0  1  0]
 [-1  0  0]]
...
Player X, what's your move?
9
Player X has chosen action=9
game state is
[[-1 -1  1]
 [ 1  1 -1]
 [-1  1  1]]
It's a tie!
```

In each turn, you enter a number between 1 and 9 on your keyboard as the move for
Player X or Player O until the game ends. In the above output, I entered moves 5,
1, 3, 7, 4, 6, 2, 8, and 9 (and in that order). The game is tied.

2.2   THINK ONE STEP AHEAD IN TIC TAC TOE

To think one step ahead in Tic Tac Toe, the AI player will iterate through all possible
next moves and check if any one of them leads to a win right away. If yes, the AI
player will take the move. Otherwise, the AI player randomly selects a move.

We'll first code in such an AI player. We'll then test the efficacy of the game strategy
by letting it play against random moves and see how often the AI player wins.

2.2.1   Create an AI Player Who Thinks One Step Ahead in Tic Tac Toe

Since we'll use the same AI game strategies in later chapters, we define a function
ttt_think1() in the local module *ch02util*. This way, we can import the AI agent

from the local module later without redefining it. Download the file *ch02util.py* from the book's GitHub repository and place it in the folder /Desktop/ags/utils/ on your computer. Open the file and familiarize yourself with the functions in it.

The function *ttt_think1()* checks if there is a move that wins the game for the AI player right away. If yes, it returns the move. Otherwise, the function returns a random move. The function *ttt_think1()* is defined as follows:

```
[6]: from copy import deepcopy


def ttt_think1(env):
    # iterate through all possible next moves
    for m in env.validinputs:
        # make a hypothetical move
        env_copy=deepcopy(env)
        state,reward,done,_=env_copy.step(m)
        # if reward is 1 or -1, current player wins
        if done and abs(reward)==1:
            # take the winning move
            return m
    # otherwise, randomly select a move
    return env.sample()
```

The function takes the current game environment as the input. We have made the function player-independent in the sense that the game strategy applies to both Player X and Player O.

We'll also define two other agents in the local module to test the look-one-step-ahead agent in Tic Tac Toe. The first one is a random player who selects a move randomly amongst all valid actions. The function, *ttt_random()*, is defined as follows in the local module *ch02util*:

```
[7]: def ttt_random(env):
    move = env.sample()
    return move
```

The second agent takes the move entered manually through the computer keyboard. The function, *ttt_manual()*, is defined as follows in the local module *ch02util*:

```
[8]: def ttt_manual(env):
    print(f"game state is \n{env.state.reshape(3,3)[::-1]}")
    while True:
        move = input(f"Player {env.turn}, what's your move?")
        try:
            move = int(move)
        except:
            print("the move must be a number")
```

```
        if move in env.validinputs:
            return move
        else:
            print("please enter a valid move")
```

The function *ttt_manual()* first prints out the current game state and then asks you to enter a move. If you enter a valid move, the function returns the move you entered. If you enter an invalid move, the function reminds you and asks you to enter your move on the keyboard again, until you select a valid move.

We create a function to play a full Tic Tac Toe game, using two function names as inputs. The function is defined as follows in the local module *ch02util*:

```
[9]:   # Define the one_ttt_game() function
       def one_ttt_game(player1, player2):
           env = ttt()
           env.reset()
           while True:
               action = player1(env)
               state, reward, done, _ = env.step(action)
               if done:
                   break
               action = player2(env)
               state, reward, done, _ = env.step(action)
               if done:
                   break
           return reward
```

The function *one_ttt_game()* simulates one full Tic Tac Toe game: it takes two function names as the two arguments. For example, if we use *ttt_random* and *ttt_manual* as the two arguments and in that order, Player 1 will make moves based on the function *ttt_random()* while Player 2 will make moves based on the function *ttt_manual()*. We skip the *render()* method in the function to speed up game simulation. As a result, you won't see game windows. The function returns the reward of the game. We can infer the outcome from the reward: if the reward is 1, Player X has won; if the reward is −1, Player O has won the game; the game is tied if the reward is 0.

2.2.2 Test the Think-One-Step-Ahead AI in Tic Tac Toe

To test the agents we just created in the last subsection, we first play a game manually against the look-one-step-ahead AI agent:

```
[10]:  from utils.ch02util import one_ttt_game, ttt_think1, ttt_manual

       reward=one_ttt_game(ttt_think1, ttt_manual)
       print(f"the game outcome is {reward}")
```

```
game state is
[[0 0 0]
 [0 1 0]
 [0 0 0]]
Player O, what's your move?1
game state is
[[ 0  0  1]
 [ 0  1  0]
 [-1  0  0]]
Player O, what's your move?2
game state is
[[ 0  0  1]
 [ 0  1  1]
 [-1 -1  0]]
Player O, what's your move?4
the game outcome is 1
```

In the above game, the look-one-step-ahead AI agent moves first. I created an opportunity for the agent to win by occupying cell 3. The AI player indeed took the winning move and won the game. This indicates that the AI agent can look one step ahead. The game outcome is 1, which indicates that the first player, in this case, the look-one-step-ahead AI agent, has won.

As an exercise, call the *one_ttt_game()* function and use *ttt_manual* as the first argument and *ttt_think1* the second argument. Play a game with the AI manually. Be sure to create an opportunity for the AI to win and see if it takes the winning move.

Next, we simulate 1000 games. Half the time, the look-one-step-ahead AI moves first and the remaining half the time, the random-mover goes first. Whenever the random-mover goes first, we multiply the outcome by −1 so that an outcome of 1 indicates a win for the AI player.

```
[11]: from utils.ch02util import ttt_random

results=[]
for i in range(1000):
    # AI moves first if i is an even number
    if i%2==0:
        result=one_ttt_game(ttt_think1,ttt_random)
        # record game outcome
        results.append(result)
    # AI moves second if i is an odd number
    else:
        result=one_ttt_game(ttt_random,ttt_think1)
```

```
        # record negative of the game outcome
        results.append(-result)
```

We first create an empty list *results* to record game outcomes. We iterate i from 0 to 999. When i is an even number, we simulate a game and let the AI player move first. The outcome is added to the list *results*: 1 means the AI player wins and -1 means the random player wins. Whenever i is an odd number, we simulate a game and let the random player move first. We then multiply the outcome by -1 so that 1 means the AI player has won.

Next, we count how many times the AI player has won by counting the number of 1s in the list *results*. The number of -1s is the number of times the AI player has lost:

```
[12]:  # count how many times AI player has won
       wins=results.count(1)
       print(f"the AI player has won {wins} games")
       # count how many times AI player has lost
       losses=results.count(-1)
       print(f"the AI player has lost {losses} games")
       # count tie games
       ties=results.count(0)
       print(f"the game was tied {ties} times")
```

```
the AI player has won 653 games
the AI player has lost 272 games
the game was tied 75 times
```

Results show that the AI player has won 653 out of the 1000 games; it has lost to the random player 272 times. There are a total of 75 tie games. This indicates that the think-one-step-ahead AI is clearly more intelligent than a random player.

2.3   THINK TWO STEPS AHEAD IN TIC TAC TOE

To think two steps ahead, the AI player first checks if any of the next moves leads to a win right away. If yes, the AI player takes the move. If not, the AI player checks if there is a combination of two moves (one by the AI player and one by the opponent) that leads to a win for the opponent. If yes, the AI player blocks the opponent's winning move. Otherwise, the AI player randomly selects an action from available valid moves.

We'll first code in such an AI player who thinks two steps ahead. We'll then test the efficacy of the game strategy by letting it play against the look-one-step-ahead AI we developed in the last section and see how often the new AI wins.

2.3.1 A Tic Tac Toe Agent Who Thinks Two Steps Ahead

We define a function *ttt_think2()* in the local module *ch02util*. The function first checks if there is a move that wins the game for the current player right away. If yes, it returns the move. If not, the function checks if the opponent has a winning move two steps ahead. If yes, it blocks the opponent's move. Otherwise, it returns a random move.

The function *ttt_think2()* is defined as follows in the file *ch02util.py*:

```
[13]:  def ttt_think2(env):
           # iterate through all possible next moves
           for m in env.validinputs:
               # make a hypothetical move
               env_copy=deepcopy(env)
               state,reward,done,_=env_copy.step(m)
               # if reward is 1 or -1, current player wins
               if done and abs(reward)==1:
                   # take the winning move
                   return m
           # otherwise, look two moves ahead
           for m1 in env.validinputs:
               for m2 in env.validinputs:
                   if m1!=m2:
                       env_copy=deepcopy(env)
                       s,r,done,_=env_copy.step(m1)
                       s,r,done,_=env_copy.step(m2)
                       # block opponent's winning move
                       if done and r!=0:
                           return m2
           # otherwise, return a random move
           return env.sample()
```

The function can be applied to both Player X and Player O. When looking two steps ahead, the function examines all possible combinations of move *m1* by the current player and move *m2* by the opponent. If the opponent wins, the function returns *m2* to block the opponent's winning move.

Next, we'll manually play against the think-two-steps-ahead AI and check if it can indeed block the opponent's winning moves.

2.3.2 Test the Think-Two-Steps-Ahead AI in Tic Tac Toe

We first play a game manually against the look-two-steps-ahead AI agent. We'll use *ttt_think2* as the first argument and *ttt_manual* as the second argument in the *one_ttt_game()* function:

[14]:
```
from utils.ch02util import ttt_think2

reward=one_ttt_game(ttt_think2, ttt_manual)
print(f"the game outcome is {reward}")
```

```
game state is
[[0 1 0]
 [0 0 0]
 [0 0 0]]
Player 0, what's your move?5
game state is
[[ 0  1  0]
 [ 0 -1  0]
 [ 1  0  0]]
Player 0, what's your move?3
game state is
[[ 1  1  0]
 [ 0 -1  0]
 [ 1  0 -1]]
Player 0, what's your move?2
the game outcome is 1
```

As you can see above, when I have pieces in cells 5 and 3, the AI player blocks cell 7 to prevent me from winning the game. Further, the AI player takes the winning opportunity by placing a game piece in cell 9 to win the game (by having three Xs in the top row). Looks like the look-two-steps-ahead AI can indeed think two steps ahead and block the opponent's winning move.

Below, we'll use the *one_ttt_game()* function to test the efficacy of the think-two-steps-ahead AI against the think-one-step-ahead AI.

We again create an empty list *results* to store game outcomes. We simulate 1000 games. Half the time, the think-one-step-ahead AI moves first and half of the time, the think-two-steps-ahead AI moves first. This way, no player has a first-mover advantage. Whenever the think-two-steps-ahead AI moves second, we multiple the outcome by −1 so that a value of 1 in the list *results* indicates a win for the think-two-steps-ahead AI.

[15]:
```
results=[]
for i in range(1000):
    # think-two-steps-ahead AI moves first at even i
    if i%2==0:
        result=one_ttt_game(ttt_think2, ttt_think1)
        # record game outcome
        results.append(result)
    # think-two-steps-ahead AI moves second at odd i
```

```
    else:
        result=one_ttt_game(ttt_think1, ttt_think2)
        # record negative of game outcome
        results.append(-result)
```

We iterate i from 0 to 999. Whenever i is an even number, we simulate a game and let the think-two-steps-ahead AI move first. The outcome is added to the list *results*. Whenever i is an odd number, we simulate a game and let the think-one-step-ahead AI move first. We then multiply the outcome by -1 so that 1 indicates a win for the think-two-steps-ahead AI.

Run the above code cell and then count the game outcome as follows:

```
[16]: # count how many times think-two-steps-ahead AI won
      wins=results.count(1)
      print(f"think-two-steps-ahead AI won {wins} games")
      # count how many times it lost
      losses=results.count(-1)
      print(f"think-two-steps-ahead AI lost {losses} games")
      # count tie games
      ties=results.count(0)
      print(f"the game was tied {ties} times")
```

```
think-two-steps-ahead AI won 778 games
think-two-steps-ahead AI lost 77 games
the game was tied 145 times
```

Results show that the think-two-steps-ahead AI has won 778 out of the 1000 games; it has lost to the think-one-step-ahead player 77 times. There are a total of 145 tie games. This indicates that the think-two-steps-ahead AI is indeed more intelligent than the think-one-step-ahead AI.

2.4 THINK THREE STEPS AHEAD IN TIC TAC TOE

This section will allow the AI player to think up to three steps ahead when making a move. If the AI player has no winning move in the next step and the opponent has no winning move two steps ahead, the AI player will look three steps ahead. It will take the next move that most likely leads to a win in three steps. In particular, if there's a next move that guarantees the AI player to win in three steps, the AI player will select that next move.

Let's use an example to demonstrate.

2.4.1 A Think-Three-Steps-Ahead AI in Tic Tac Toe

Consider the example as illustrated in Figure 2.2 below. It's Player X's turn to move, and if it chooses cell 2 as its next move, it can create a double attack and guarantee

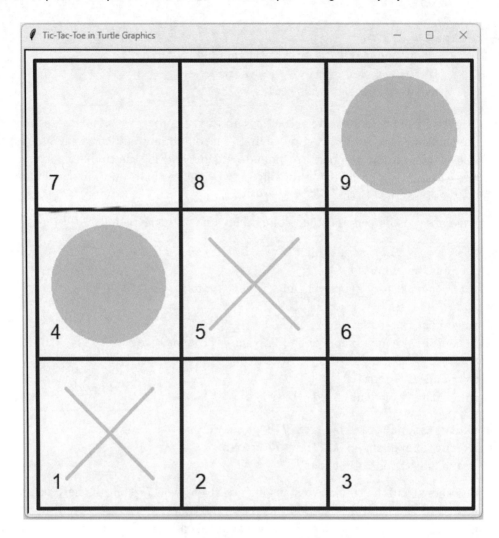

Figure 2.2 Player X can occupy cell 2 to create a double attack

a win in three steps: Player X can win by placing a piece in cell 3 or cell 8 in three steps and win the game. Player O can block either cell 3 or cell 8, but not both.

We define a function *ttt_think3()* in the local module *ch02util*. Take a look at the function *ttt_think3()* in the file *ch02util.py*. In particular, the following lines of code allows the agent to look three steps ahead:

```
def ttt_think3(env):
    ...
    # look three steps ahead
    w3=[]
    for m1 in env.validinputs:
        for m2 in env.validinputs:
            for m3 in env.validinputs:
                if m1!=m2 and m1!=m3 and m2!=m3:
```

```
            env_copy=deepcopy(env)
            s,r,done,_=env_copy.step(m1)
            s,r,done,_=env_copy.step(m2)
            s,r,done,_=env_copy.step(m3)
            if done and r!=0:
                w3.append(m1)
    # Choose the most frequent winner
    if len(w3)>0:
        return max(w3,key=w3.count)
    # Return random move otherwise
    return env.sample()
```

The function applies to both Player X and player O. When looking three steps ahead, the function examines all possible combinations of moves *m1* and *m3* by the current player and move *m2* by the opponent. The function returns the move *m1* that leads to the most wins for the current player.

Next, we'll let the think-three-steps-ahead AI play against the think-two-steps-ahead AI and see which one is more intelligent.

2.4.2   Test the Think-Three-Steps-Ahead AI in Tic Tac Toe

We'll first manually play against the think-three-steps-ahead AI and see if it can indeed look three steps ahead. In particular, we want to see if the agent takes the move that guarantees a win in three steps.

```
[17]: from utils.ch02util import ttt_think3

reward=one_ttt_game(ttt_think3, ttt_manual)
print(f"the game outcome is {reward}")
```

```
game state is
[[0 0 0]
 [0 1 0]
 [0 0 0]]
Player O, what's your move?4
game state is
[[ 0  0  0]
 [-1  1  0]
 [ 1  0  0]]
Player O, what's your move?9
game state is
[[ 0  0 -1]
 [-1  1  0]
 [ 1  1  0]]
Player O, what's your move?3
the game outcome is 1
```

As you can see above, when the AI player places a piece in cell 2, it has created a double attack: it can win through cells 1, 2, and 3, or through cells 2, 5, and 8. I can only block cell 3 or cell 8, but not both. So the think-three-steps-ahead AI wins in three steps.

Below, we'll use the *one_ttt_game()* function to test the efficacy of the think-three-steps-ahead AI against the think-two-steps-ahead AI.

[18]:
```python
results=[]
for i in range(1000):
    # think-three-steps-ahead AI moves first at even i
    if i%2--0:
        result=one_ttt_game(ttt_think3, ttt_think2)
        # record game outcome
        results.append(result)
    # think-three-steps-ahead AI moves second otherwise
    else:
        result=one_ttt_game(ttt_think2, ttt_think3)
        # record negative game outcome
        results.append(-result)
```

Whenever the iterator *i* is an even number, we simulate a game and let the think-three-steps-ahead AI move first. The game outcome is added to the list *results*. Whenever the iterator *i* is an odd number, we simulate a game and let the think-three-steps-ahead AI move second. We then multiply the outcome by −1 so that 1 signals a win for the think-three-steps-ahead AI.

The results are as follows:

[19]:
```python
# count how many times think-three-steps-ahead AI won
wins=results.count(1)
print(f"think-three-steps-ahead AI won {wins} games")
# count how many times it lost
losses=results.count(-1)
print(f"think-three-steps-ahead AI lost {losses} games")
# count tie games
ties=results.count(0)
print(f"the game was tied {ties} times")
```

```
think-three-steps-ahead AI won 270 games
think-three-steps-ahead AI lost 179 games
the game was tied 551 times
```

Results show that the think-three-steps-ahead AI won 270 out of the 1000 games; it has lost to the think-two-steps-ahead player 179 times. There are a total of 551 tie games. This indicates that the think-three-steps-ahead AI is indeed more intelligent than the think-two-steps-ahead AI in the Tic Tac Toe game.

You have learned the rules of the second of the three games that we use in this book: Tic Tac Toe. You also learned how to play Tic Tac Toe by using the custom-made game environment in the local module. You designed three rule-based AI game strategies: they think up to one, two, and three steps ahead, respectively. The AI agents become more and more intelligent as they look further and further ahead in gameplays. You'll use the game environment to design other Tic Tac Toe game strategies in later chapters.

2.5 GLOSSARY

- **Tic Tac Toe:** A game in which two players take turns marking a cell with an X or O in a three-by-three grid. The first player to connect three Xs or Os in a row horizontally, vertically, or diagonally wins.

2.6 EXERCISES

2.1 Rerun the first two cells in Section 2.1.2 and make sure you can see the game window and then close it.

2.2 Call the *one_ttt_game()* function and use *ttt_manual* as the first argument and *ttt_think1* as the second argument. Play a game with the AI player manually. Create an opportunity for the AI player to win and see if it takes the winning move.

2.3 Modify the first code cell in Section 2.3.2 by letting the look-two-steps-ahead AI move second. Try to win the game yourself and see if the AI player can block your move.

2.4 Rerun the first cell in Section 2.4.2 and design your moves so that the AI player has an opportunity to create a double attack. See if it takes the opportunity and wins the game.

## CHAPTER 3

Planning Three Steps Ahead in Connect Four

> "Planning is bringing the future into the present so that you can do something about it now."
> – *Alan Lakein*

IN THIS CHAPTER, we're going to dive into the exciting world of Connect Four, the final game featured in this book. It's going to be a fun and educational journey as we explore the game rules, play Connect Four using our local game environment, and finally create our very own AI players!

Just like in Chapter 2, we'll be crafting some clever AI strategies for Connect Four. These AI players will be able to think up to three moves ahead, making the gameplay more interesting and challenging. You'll get to test these strategies against random players or even pit them against each other to see how effective they are.

Remember how we discussed the importance of coding rule-based AI in Chapter 2? Besides mastering rule-based AI, you'll also gain a deep understanding of all the attributes and methods within the Connect Four game environment. Plus, these rule-based AI skills will come in handy when we explore other AI algorithms later in the book, like MiniMax, Monte Carlo Tree Search, and Policy-Gradient. We'll even use rule-based AI as benchmarks to evaluate the effectiveness of other AI methods.

Now, let's get into the nitty-gritty of how our AI players think and strategize. When the AI player looks one step ahead, it examines all possible next moves and selects the one that could lead to an instant victory. It's similar to our earlier strategies in Tic Tac Toe. However, when thinking two steps ahead in Connect Four, things get a tad more complex. The AI player has to decide whether its next move will block the opponent's progress or unintentionally assist them in winning. We've got a plan for both scenarios: if the AI move obstructs the opponent, it takes that move; otherwise,

DOI: 10.1201/9781032722207-3

it avoids a move that could potentially set up the opponent for a win in two moves. When thinking three steps ahead, the AI player follows the path that's most likely to secure a victory after three moves. In some cases, this three-step strategy can even guarantee a win for our AI player.

What You'll Learn in This Chapter

- Learning the rules of Connect Four
- Playing Connect Four in the local game environment
- Planning one, two, or three steps ahead in Connect Four
- Testing the effectiveness of AI agents in Connect Four

3.1 THE CONNECT FOUR GAME ENVIRONMENT

In Connect Four, two players take turns dropping discs into one of seven columns, from the top. The first player who connects four game pieces in a straight line horizontally, vertically, or diagonally wins.

In this section, you'll familiarize yourself with the local custom-made Connect Four game environment. The game environment also creates game windows using the *turtle* library so you can visualize a graphical representation of the game. The game environment has various attributes and methods that a typical OpenAI Gym game environment has.

3.1.1 Methods and Attributes in Connect Four

We abstract away from the implementation of the Connect Four game rules so you can focus on learning rule-based AI and ML and apply them to various real-world situations. Therefore, we'll place the implementation of game rules in a local module *conn_env*. This way, you can focus on designing game strategies with AI without being distracted by the details of game rules.

Our custom-made Connect Four game environment has the following attributes:

- action_space: the collection of all actions that can be taken by an agent. The action space has seven values, 1 to 7. This represents the 7 columns a player can drop discs in.
- observation_space: the collection of all possible states in the environment. We'll use a NumPy array with 7 rows and 6 columns to represent the 42 cells on a game board.
- state: an attribute indicating which state the agent is currently in. Each of the 42 cells can take values -1 (occupied by the yellow player), 0 (empty), or 1 (occupied by the red player).
- action: an attribute indicating the action taken by an agent. The action is a number between 1 and 7.

- reward: an attribute indicating the reward to the agents because of the actions taken and the game outcome. The reward is 0 in each step unless a player has won the game, in which case the winner has a reward of 1 and the loser a reward of -1.
- done: an attribute indicating whether the game has ended. This happens when one player wins or if the game is tied.
- info: an attribute that provides information about the game. We'll set it as an empty string.

Our self-made Connect Four game environment has a few methods as well:

- reset() is a method to set the game environment to the initial (that is, the starting) state. All cells on the board are empty in the initial state.
- render() is a method showing the current state of the environment graphically.
- step() is a method that returns the new state, the reward, the *done* variable, and the variable *info* based on the action taken by an agent.
- sample() is a method to randomly choose a valid action from the action space.
- close() is a method to close the game environment.

The above methods are the same as those in a typical OpenAI Gym game environment. They are also the same as those in the previous two games: the coin game and Tic Tac Toe.

3.1.2 Access the Connect Four Game Environment

We'll check the attributes and methods of the self-made game environment and make sure it has all the elements that are provided by a typical OpenAI Gym game environment.

First, we'll initiate the game environment and show the game board as follows:

```
[1]: from utils.conn_env import conn

env = conn()
env.reset()
env.render()
```

We import the *conn* class from the local *conn_env* module and set it as our game environment. Since we called the *render()* method in the above code cell, you should see a separate *turtle* window as shown in Figure 3.1.

The seven columns on the game board are marked 1 through 7. After each move, a red or yellow disc will drop to the lowest available slot in that column.

If you want to close the game window, use the *close()* method, like so:

```
[2]: env.close()
```

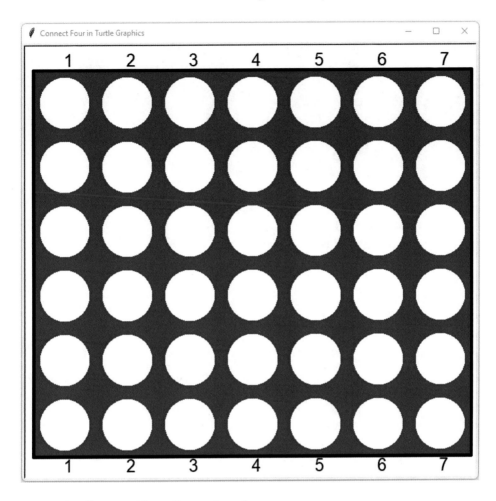

Figure 3.1 The Connect Four Game Board

Next, we'll check the attributes of the environment such as the observation space and action space.

```
[3]:  env=conn()
      # check the action space
      number_actions=env.action_space.n
      print("the number of possible actions is", number_actions)
      # sample the action space ten times
      print("the following are ten sample actions")
      for i in range(10):
          print(env.sample())
      # check the shape of the observation space
      print("the shape of the observation space is",\
            env.observation_space.shape)
```

```
the number of possible actions is 7
the following are ten sample actions
3
4
7
3
5
4
1
6
2
1
the shape of the observation space is (7, 6)
```

The meanings of the actions in this game are as follows

- 1: Placing a game piece in column 1
- 2: Placing a game piece in column 2
- . . .
- 7: Placing a game piece in column 7

The state space is a matrix with 7 columns and 6 rows. Each cell can have a value of −1, 0, or 1, with the following meanings:

- 0 means the cell is empty;
- −1 means the cell is occupied by the yellow player;
- 1 means the cell is occupied by the red player.

3.1.3 Play Games in the Connect Four Environment

Next, we'll play Connect Four games in the custom-made environment. You'll learn to play a full game, either by letting both players select random moves, or by entering moves through your keyboard.

In the code cell below, we'll play a full game by randomly choosing an action from the action space each step.

```
[4]: import time

     # Initiate the game environment
     env=conn()
     env.reset()
     env.render()
     while True:
         action=env.sample()
         time.sleep(1)
         print(f"the {env.turn} player has chosen action={action}")
```

```
        state, reward, done, info = env.step(action)
        env.render()
        print(f"the current state is \n{state.T[::-1]}")
        if done:
            if reward!=0:
                print(f"the {env.turn} player has won!")
            else:
                print("It's a tie!")
            break
env.close()
```

```
the red player has chosen action=4
the current state is
[[0 0 0 0 0 0 0]
 [0 0 0 0 0 0 0]
 [0 0 0 0 0 0 0]
 [0 0 0 0 0 0 0]
 [0 0 0 0 0 0 0]
 [0 0 0 1 0 0 0]]
the yellow player has chosen action=2
the current state is
[[ 0  0  0  0  0  0  0]
 [ 0  0  0  0  0  0  0]
 [ 0  0  0  0  0  0  0]
 [ 0  0  0  0  0  0  0]
 [ 0  0  0  0  0  0  0]
 [ 0 -1  0  1  0  0  0]]
...
the red player has chosen action=4
the current state is
[[ 0  0  0  0  0  0  0]
 [ 0  0  0  0  0  0  0]
 [ 0  0  0  1  0  0  0]
 [ 0  0  0  1  0  0  0]
 [ 0 -1  0  1  1  0  0]
 [ 0 -1  0  1 -1 -1  0]]
the red player has won!
```

In each step, we use the *sample()* method in the game environment, which returns a random valid move. When printing out the game state, we use $T[::-1]$ to first transpose the matrix and then switch the top and bottom row in the NumPy array so that cell positions match those on the game board in the *turtle* game window.

Run the above code cell to play a full game. Your output is likely different because actions are randomly chosen.

3.1.4   Play the Connect Four Game Manually

Next, you'll learn how to manually interact with the Connect Four game. You'll use the keyboard to enter a number between 1 and 7. The following lines of code show you how:

```
[5]:  env=conn()
      state=env.reset()
      env.render()
      print('enter a number between 1 and 7')
      print(f"the current state is \n{state.T[::-1]}")
      # Play a full game manually
      while True:
          action=int(input(f"{env.turn} player, enter your move:"))
          time.sleep(1)
          print(f"{env.turn} player has chosen action={action}")
          state, reward, done, info = env.step(action)
          env.render()
          print(f"the current state is \n{state.T[::-1]}")
          if done:
              if reward!=0:
                  print(f"{env.turn} player has won!")
              else:
                  print("It's a tie!")
              break
      env.close()
```

```
enter a number between 1 and 7
the current state is
[[0 0 0 0 0 0 0]
 [0 0 0 0 0 0 0]
 [0 0 0 0 0 0 0]
 [0 0 0 0 0 0 0]
 [0 0 0 0 0 0 0]
 [0 0 0 0 0 0 0]]
red player, enter your move:4
red player has chosen action=4
the current state is
[[0 0 0 0 0 0 0]
 [0 0 0 0 0 0 0]
 [0 0 0 0 0 0 0]
 [0 0 0 0 0 0 0]
 [0 0 0 0 0 0 0]
 [0 0 0 1 0 0 0]]
yellow player, enter your move:3
yellow player has chosen action=3
...
```

```
the current state is
[[ 0  0  0  0  0  0  0]
 [ 0  0  0  0  0  0  0]
 [ 0  0  0  1  0  0  0]
 [ 0  0  0  1  0  0  0]
 [ 0  0  0  1  0  0  0]
 [ 0  0 -1  1 -1  0 -1]]
red player has won!
```

In each turn, you enter a number between 1 and 7 on your keyboard as your move for the red or yellow player until the game ends. To speed up the game, I have let the red player win in seven steps by connecting four pieces vertically in column 4 in the above example output.

3.2 THINK ONE STEP AHEAD IN CONNECT FOUR

To think one step ahead in Connect Four, the AI player will iterate through all possible next moves and check if any one of them leads to a win right away. If yes, the AI player will take the move. Otherwise, the AI player randomly selects a move.

We'll first code in such an AI player. We'll then test the efficacy of the game strategy by letting it play against random moves and see how often the AI player wins.

3.2.1 A Think-One-Step-Ahead AI in Connect Four

To save space, we'll modularize most functions in this chapter and put them in the *utils* package for this book. This also allows us to use these AI game strategies in later chapters without redefining them: we can simply import the AI agent from the local module every time we need to use the game strategy.

Download the file *ch03util.py* from the book's GitHub repository and place it in the folder /Desktop/ags/utils/ on your computer. Open the file and familiarize yourself with the functions in it. Specifically, we define a function *conn_think1()* in the file to create a look-one-step-ahead agent. The function checks if there is a move that wins the game for the AI player right away. If yes, it returns the move. Otherwise, the function returns a random move.

```python
def conn_think1(env):
    # iterate through all possible next moves
    for m in env.validinputs:
        # make a hypothetical move
        env_copy=deepcopy(env)
        state,reward,done,_=env_copy.step(m)
        # take the winning move
        if done and reward!=0:
            return m
    return env.sample()
```

The function is similar to the function *ttt_think1()* we defined in Chapter 2 for the Tic Tac Toe game. The function takes the current game environment as the input. Both the red and yellow players can use this strategy to think one step ahead.

We'll also define two other agents in the local module to test the look-one-step-ahead agent in Connect Four. The first one selects a move randomly amongst all valid actions. The function, *conn_random()*, is defined as follows in the local module *ch03util*:

```python
def conn_random(env):
    move = env.sample()
    return move
```

The second agent takes the move entered manually through your keyboard. The function, *conn_manual()*, is defined as follows in the local module *ch03util*:

```python
def conn_manual(env):
    print(f"game state is \n{env.state.T[::-1]}")
    while True:
        move=input(f"{env.turn} player, enter your move:")
        try:
            move=int(move)
        except:
            print("the move must be a number")
        if move in env.validinputs:
            return move
        else:
            print("please enter a valid move")
```

The function *conn_manual()* first prints out the current game state and then asks you to enter a move. If you enter a valid move, the function returns the move you made. If you enter an invalid move, the function reminds you and asks you to enter your move on the keyboard again, until you select a valid move.

The following function *one_conn_game()*, defined in the local module *ch03util*, allows two players to play a full Connect Four game:

```python
# Define the one_conn_game() function
def one_conn_game(player1, player2):
    env = conn()
    env.reset()
    while True:
        action = player1(env)
        state, reward, done, _ = env.step(action)
        if done:
            break
        action = player2(env)
        state, reward, done, _ = env.step(action)
```

```
        if done:
            break
    return reward
```

The function takes two function names as the two arguments. For example, if we use *conn_random* and *conn_manual* as the two arguments and in that order, the red player will make moves based on the function *conn_random()* while the yellow player will make moves based on the function *conn_manual()*. We skip the *render()* method to speed up game simulation. As a result, you won't see the game windows. The function returns the reward of the game. We can infer the outcome from the reward: if the reward is 1, the red player has won; if the reward is −1, the yellow player has won the game; the game is tied if the reward is 0.

3.2.2 Test the Think-One-Step-Ahead AI in Connect Four

Next, we'll test the AI player and check if it can indeed think one step ahead. We first play a game manually against the look-one-step-ahead AI agent:

```
[6]: from utils.ch03util import one_conn_game, conn_think1, conn_manual

reward=one_conn_game(conn_think1, conn_manual)
print(f"the game outcome is {reward}")
```

```
game state is
[[0 0 0 0 0 0 0]
 [0 0 0 0 0 0 0]
 [0 0 0 0 0 0 0]
 [0 0 0 0 0 0 0]
 [0 0 0 0 0 0 0]
 [0 1 0 0 0 0 0]]
yellow player, enter your move:7
game state is
[[ 0  0  0  0  0  0  0]
 [ 0  0  0  0  0  0  0]
 [ 0  0  0  0  0  0  0]
 [ 0  0  0  0  0  0  0]
 [ 0  0  0  0  0  0  1]
 [ 0  1  0  0  0  0 -1]]
yellow player, enter your move:7
game state is
[[ 0  0  0  0  0  0  0]
 [ 0  0  0  0  0  0  0]
 [ 0  0  0  0  0  0  0]
 [ 0  0  0  0  0  0 -1]
 [ 0  0  0  0  0  0  1]
 [ 0  1  1  0  0  0 -1]]
```

```
yellow player, enter your move:7
game state is
[[ 0  0  0  0  0  0  0]
 [ 0  0  0  0  0  0  0]
 [ 0  0  0  0  0  0 -1]
 [ 0  0  0  0  0  0 -1]
 [ 0  0  0  0  0  0  1]
 [ 0  1  1  0  0  1 -1]]
yellow player, enter your move:6
game state is
[[ 0  0  0  0  0  0  0]
 [ 0  0  0  0  0  0  0]
 [ 0  0  0  0  0  0 -1]
 [ 0  0  0  0  0  0 -1]
 [ 0  0  0  0  0 -1  1]
 [ 1  1  1  0  0  1 -1]]
yellow player, enter your move:5
the game outcome is 1
```

In the above game, the look-one-step-ahead AI agent moves first. I created an opportunity for the agent to win by dropping a disc in column 4 so that four red discs connect horizontally in a row. The AI player indeed took the winning move and won the game. This indicates that the AI agent can look one step ahead and take a winning move if there is one. The game outcome is 1, which indicates that the first player, in this case, the look-one-step-ahead AI agent, has won.

As an exercise, you can call the *one_conn_game()* function and use *conn_manual* as the first argument and *conn_think1* as the second argument. Play a game with the AI player manually. Be sure to create an opportunity for the agent to win and see if the agent takes the winning move.

Next, we simulate 1000 games to let the look-one-step-ahead AI play against random moves. Half the time, the look-one-step-ahead AI moves first and half the time, the AI player moves second. Whenever the AI player moves second, we multiply the outcome by −1 so that an outcome of 1 indicates a win for the AI player.

```
[7]: from utils.ch03util import conn_random

     results=[]
     for i in range(1000):
         # AI moves first if i is an even number
         if i%2==0:
             result=one_conn_game(conn_think1,conn_random)
             # record game outcome
             results.append(result)
         # AI moves second if i is an odd number
```

```
    else:
        result=one_conn_game(conn_random,conn_think1)
        # record negative game outcome
        results.append(-result)
```

We first create an empty list *results* to record game outcomes. We iterate *i* from 0 to 999. When *i* is an even number, we simulate a game and let the AI player move first. The outcome is added to the list *results*: 1 means the AI player wins and −1 means the random player wins. Whenever *i* is an odd number, we simulate a game and let the random player move first. We then multiply the outcome by −1 so that 1 means the AI player has won.

Run the above code cells so that we simulate 1000 games and collect game results.

Next, we count how many times the AI player has won by counting the number of 1s in the list *results*. Similarly, the number of −1s is the number of times the AI player has lost:

```
[8]: # count how many times AI won
     wins=results.count(1)
     print(f"the AI player has won {wins} games")
     # count how many times AI lost
     losses=results.count(-1)
     print(f"the AI player has lost {losses} games")
     # count tie games
     ties=results.count(0)
     print(f"the game was tied {ties} times")
```

```
the AI player has won 755 games
the AI player has lost 244 games
the game was tied 1 times
```

Results show that the look-one-step-ahead AI has won 755 out of the 1000 games; it has lost to the random player 244 times. There is only one tie game. This indicates that the think-one-step-ahead AI player is clearly better than a random player.

3.3 THINK TWO STEPS AHEAD IN CONNECT FOUR

Thinking two steps ahead in Connect Four is more complicated than that in Tic Tac Toe. While in some cases, the AI player needs to block a move to prevent the opponent from winning in two steps, in other cases, the AI player needs to avoid certain moves to achieve that goal. We'll separate these two cases. Let's first use two examples to demonstrate the two cases.

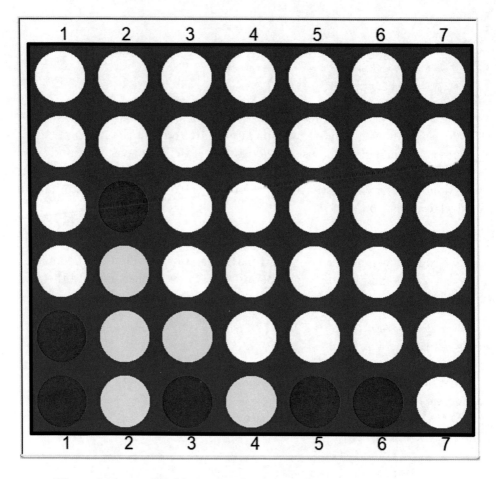

Figure 3.2 The red player should avoid column 1, otherwise the yellow player wins

3.3.1 Moves to Avoid and Moves to Block

In this example, the computer should avoid a move to prevent the opponent from winning. The current state of the game is shown in Figure 3.2 and it's the red player's turn to move. If the red player chooses column 1 as the next move, the opponent can win on the following turn by placing a yellow disc in column 1. Therefore, the red player should avoid move 1.

We therefore define a function *to_avoid()* to collect all moves that the AI player should avoid to prevent the opponent from winning in two steps. The function is included in the file *ch03util.py* and is defined as follows:

```
def to_avoid(env):
    toavoid=[]
    # look for ones you should avoid
    for m in env.validinputs:
        if len(env.occupied[m-1])<=4:
            env_copy=deepcopy(env)
```

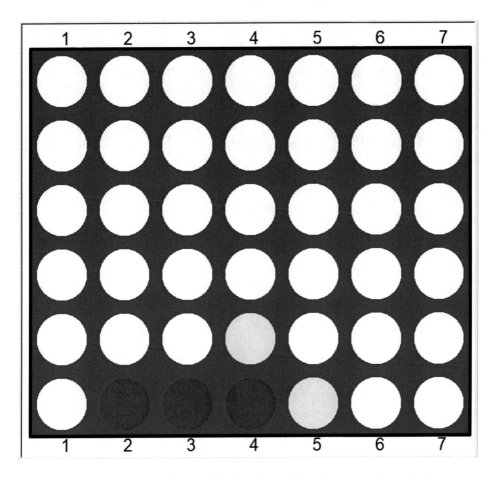

Figure 3.3 The yellow player should block column 1, otherwise the red player wins

```
        s,r,done,_=env_copy.step(m)
        s,r,done,_=env_copy.step(m)
        if done and r==-1:
            toavoid.append(m)
    return toavoid
```

Later when we define the *conn_think2()* function, we'll program in such a way so that the AI player avoids moves generated by the function *to_avoid()*.

In the next case, a player should block a certain move so the opponent won't win in two steps. The game state is shown in Figure 3.3 and it's the yellow player's turn to move. If the yellow player doesn't choose column 1 in the next move, the opponent can choose column 1 and win in two steps. Therefore, the yellow player should block column 1.

Later when we define the *conn_think2()* function, we iterate through all combinations of move *m1* for the AI player and move *m2* for the opponent, where *m1* is different from *m2*. If the next two moves *m1* and *m2* lead to a win for the opponent, the AI player should block the opponent by placing a piece in column *m2* as the next move.

3.3.2   A Think-Two-Steps-Ahead Agent in Connect Four

We define a function *conn_think2()* in the local module. The function first checks if there is a move that wins the game for the AI player right away. If yes, it returns the move. Otherwise, the function checks if there is a move that should be blocked to prevent the opponent from winning two steps ahead. If yes, it blocks the opponent's move. If not, the function checks if there is a move that should be avoided to prevent the opponent from winning two steps ahead. If yes, the AI player randomly picks a valid move that's not one of the moves that should be avoided.

The following function *conn_think2()* is defined in the file *ch03util.py* you just downloaded from the book's GitHub repository:

```
def conn_think2(env):
    ...
    # otherwise, look two moves ahead
    # look for ones you should block
    for m1 in env.validinputs:
        for m2 in env.validinputs:
            if m1!=m2:
                env_copy=deepcopy(env)
                s,r,done,_=env_copy.step(m1)
                s,r,done,_=env_copy.step(m2)
                # block your opponent's winning move
                if done and r!=0:
                    return m2
    # look for ones you should avoid
    toavoid=to_avoid()
    if len(toavoid)>0:
        leftovers=[i for i in env.validinputs if i not in toavoid]
        if len(leftovers)>0:
            return random.choice(leftovers)
    # otherwise, return a random move
    return env.sample()
```

The function applies to both the red and yellow players. Next, we'll play against the think-two-steps-ahead AI and check if it can indeed block the opponent's winning move.

3.3.3   Test the Think-Two-Steps-Ahead AI in Connect Four

We first play a game manually against the look-two-steps-ahead AI agent. We'll use *conn_think2* as the first argument and *conn_manual* as the second argument in the *one_conn_game()* function:

```
[9]: from utils.ch03util import conn_think2

     reward=one_conn_game(conn_think2, conn_manual)
     print(f"the game outcome is {reward}")
```

```
game state is
[[0 0 0 0 0 0 0]
 [0 0 0 0 0 0 0]
 [0 0 0 0 0 0 0]
 [0 0 0 0 0 0 0]
 [0 0 0 0 0 0 0]
 [1 0 0 0 0 0 0]]
yellow player, enter your move:4
game state is
[[ 0  0  0  0  0  0  0]
 [ 0  0  0  0  0  0  0]
 [ 0  0  0  0  0  0  0]
 [ 0  0  0  0  0  0  0]
 [ 0  0  0  0  0  0  0]
 [ 1  0  0 -1  1  0  0]]
yellow player, enter your move:4
game state is
[[ 0  0  0  0  0  0  0]
 [ 0  0  0  0  0  0  0]
 [ 0  0  0  0  0  0  0]
 [ 0  0  0  0  0  0  0]
 [ 1  0  0 -1  0  0  0]
 [ 1  0  0 -1  1  0  0]]
yellow player, enter your move:4
game state is
[[ 0  0  0  0  0  0  0]
 [ 0  0  0  0  0  0  0]
 [ 0  0  0  1  0  0  0]
 [ 0  0  0 -1  0  0  0]
 [ 1  0  0 -1  0  0  0]
 [ 1  0  0 -1  1  0  0]]
yellow player, enter your move:4
game state is
[[ 0  0  0  0  0  0  0]
 [ 0  0  0 -1  0  0  0]
 [ 0  0  0  1  0  0  0]
 [ 0  0  0 -1  0  0  0]
 [ 1  0  0 -1  0  0  0]
 [ 1  0  1 -1  1  0  0]]
yellow player, enter your move:4
```

```
game state is
[[ 0   0   0  -1   0   0   0]
 [ 0   0   0  -1   0   0   0]
 [ 0   0   0   1   0   0   0]
 [ 0   0   0  -1   0   0   0]
 [ 1   0   1  -1   0   0   0]
 [ 1   0   1  -1   1   0   0]]
yellow player, enter your move:7
game state is
[[ 0   0   0  -1   0   0   0]
 [ 0   0   0  -1   0   0   0]
 [ 0   0   0   1   0   0   0]
 [ 0   0   1  -1   0   0   0]
 [ 1   0   1  -1   0   0   0]
 [ 1   0   1  -1   1   0  -1]]
yellow player, enter your move:7
the game outcome is 1
```

As you can see above, the AI player has blocked me from connecting four pieces vertically by placing a piece in column 4. Looks like the think-two-steps-ahead AI can indeed plan two steps ahead and block the opponent's winning moves.

As an exercise, rerun the above code cell. Create a winning opportunity for yourself and see if the AI blocks your winning move.

Next, we let the think-two-steps-ahead AI play against the think-one-step-ahead AI and see if the former is more intelligent than the latter. We again create an empty list *results* to store game outcomes. We simulate 1000 games. Half the time, the think-one-step-ahead AI moves first and the other half, the think-two-steps-ahead AI moves first. This way, no player has a first-mover advantage. Whenever the think-two-steps-ahead AI moves second, we multiply the outcome by −1 so that a value of 1 in the list *results* indicates a win for the think-two-steps-ahead AI.

```
[10]:  results=[]
       for i in range(1000):
           # think-two-steps-ahead AI moves first at even i
           if i%2==0:
               result=one_conn_game(conn_think2, conn_think1)
               # record game outcome
               results.append(result)
           # think-two-steps-ahead AI moves second at odd i
           else:
               result=one_conn_game(conn_think1, conn_think2)
               # record negative game outcome
               results.append(-result)
```

Whenever the iterator i is even, we simulate a game and let the think-two-steps-ahead AI move first. The outcome is added to the list *results*. Whenever the iterator i is odd, we simulate a game and let the think-one-step-ahead AI move first. We then multiply the outcome by -1 before adding it to the list *results*.

We can count how many times the think-two-steps-ahead AI player has won and lost by counting the numbers of 1s and -1s in the list *results*, respectively:

11]:
```
# count how many times think-two-steps-ahead AI won
wins=results.count(1)
print(f"think-two-steps-ahead AI won {wins} games")
# count how many times it lost
losses=results.count(-1)
print(f"think-two-steps-ahead AI lost {losses} games")
# count tie games
ties=results.count(0)
print(f"the game was tied {ties} times")
```

```
think-two-steps-ahead AI won 880 games
think-two-steps-ahead AI lost 120 games
the game was tied 0 times
```

Results show that the think-two-steps-ahead AI has won 880 out of the 1000 games; it has lost to the think-one-step-ahead player 120 times. There is no tie game. This indicates that the think-two-steps-ahead AI is more intelligent than the think-one-step-ahead AI.

3.4 THINK THREE STEPS AHEAD IN CONNECT FOUR

This next section will allow the AI player to think up to three steps ahead before making its move. If the AI player has no winning move in the next step and the opponent has no winning moves two steps ahead, the AI player will look three steps ahead. It will take the next move that most likely leads to a win in three steps. In particular, if there's a next move that guarantees a win in three steps, the AI player will take the move.

Let's use an example to demonstrate.

3.4.1 The Think-Three-Steps-Ahead AI in Connect Four

Consider the example as illustrated in Figure 3.4. The red player is about to move, and if it chooses column 6 as its next move, it can create a double attack and guarantee a win in three steps: the red player can win by placing a piece in column 3 or column 7 in three steps. The yellow player can block either column 3 or column 7, but not both.

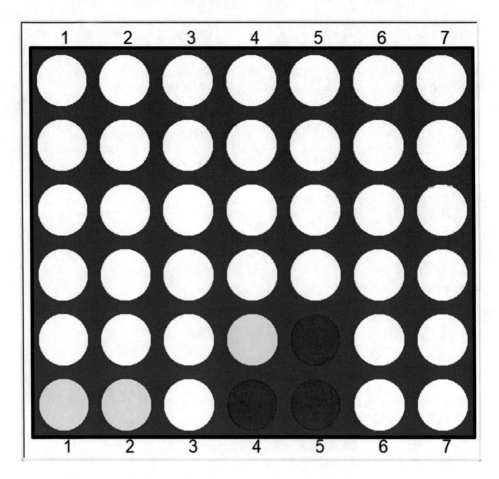

Figure 3.4 The red player can place a game piece in column 6 to create a double attack

We define a function *conn_think3()* in the local module *ch03util*. The function checks if there is a move that wins the game for the AI player right away or if the opponent has a winning move two steps ahead. If not, the player looks three steps ahead and choose the move that most likely leads to a win. The function is defined as follows:

```
def conn_think3(env):
    # if there is only one valid move left
    if len(env.validinputs)==1:
        return env.validinputs[0]
    # take column 4 if it's empty
    if len(env.occupied[3])==0:
        return 4
    ...
    # look 3 steps ahead
    w3=[]
    for m1 in env.validinputs:
        for m2 in env.validinputs:
```

```
        for m3 in env.validinputs:
            try:
                env_copy=deepcopy(env)
                s,r,done,_=env_copy.step(m1)
                s,r,done,_=env_copy.step(m2)
                s,r,done,_=env_copy.step(m3)
                if done and r!=0:
                    w3.append(m1)
            except:
                pass
    # Choose the most frequent winner
    if len(w3)>0:
        return max(w3,key=w3.count)
    # otherwise, return a random move
    return env.sample()
```

To speed up searching for the best moves, we hard coded in two moves: if there is only one valid move left, the function returns the move without searching. If column 4 is empty, the player places a game piece in it since the center column gives both players an advantage at winning. The function applies to both the red and yellow players. When looking three steps ahead, the function examines all possible combinations of moves *m1* and *m3* by the current player and move *m2* by the opponent. The function returns the move *m1* that leads to the most wins for the current player.

Next, we'll let the think-three-steps-ahead AI play against the think-two-steps-ahead AI and see which one is more intelligent.

3.4.2 Test the Think-Three-Steps-Ahead AI in Connect Four

We'll first manually play against the think-three-steps-ahead AI and see if it can indeed look three steps ahead. In particular, we want to see if the agent takes the move that guarantees a win in three steps.

12]:
```
from utils.ch03util import conn_think3

reward=one_conn_game(conn_think3, conn_manual)
print(f"the game outcome is {reward}")
```

```
game state is
[[0 0 0 0 0 0 0]
 [0 0 0 0 0 0 0]
 [0 0 0 0 0 0 0]
 [0 0 0 0 0 0 0]
 [0 0 0 0 0 0 0]
 [0 0 0 1 0 0 0]]
yellow player, enter your move:1
game state is
```

```
[[ 0  0  0  0  0  0  0]
 [ 0  0  0  0  0  0  0]
 [ 0  0  0  0  0  0  0]
 [ 0  0  0  0  0  0  0]
 [ 0  0  0  0  0  0  0]
 [-1  0  1  1  0  0  0]]
yellow player, enter your move:1
game state is
[[ 0  0  0  0  0  0  0]
 [ 0  0  0  0  0  0  0]
 [ 0  0  0  0  0  0  0]
 [ 0  0  0  0  0  0  0]
 [-1  0  0  0  0  0  0]
 [-1  0  1  1  1  0  0]]
yellow player, enter your move:1
the game outcome is 1
```

As you can see above, when the AI player places a piece in column 5, it has created a double attack: it can win by placing a piece in column 2 or column 6. I can block either column 6 or column 2, but not both. So the AI player wins two steps after placing a piece in column 5.

As an exercise, rerun the above code cell. Choose your moves in such a way so that the AI player has an opportunity to create a double attack. See if the think-three-steps-ahead AI indeed takes the opportunity and creates a double attack and wins.

Below, we'll let the think-three-steps-ahead AI play against the think-two-steps-ahead AI and see if the former is more intelligent than the latter.

Game results are stored in the list *results*: a value of 1 indicates a win for the think-three-steps-ahead AI and a loss for the think-two-steps-ahead AI.

```
[13]:  results=[]
       for i in range(1000):
           # think-three-steps-ahead AI moves first at even i
           if i%2==0:
               result=one_conn_game(conn_think3, conn_think2)
               # record game outcome
               results.append(result)
           # think-three-steps-ahead AI moves second otherwise
           else:
               result=one_conn_game(conn_think2, conn_think3)
               # record negative game outcome
               results.append(-result)
```

Whenever the iterator *i* is an even number, we simulate a game and let the think-three-steps-ahead AI move first. The game outcome is added to the list *results*. Whenever the iterator i is an odd number, we simulate a game and let the think-three-steps-ahead AI move second. We then multiply the outcome by -1 so that 1 signals a win for the think-three-steps-ahead AI.

The results are as follows:

```
14]: # count how many times AI player has won
     wins=results.count(1)
     print(f"the think-three-steps-ahead AI won {wins} games")
     # count how many times AI player has lost
     losses=results.count(-1)
     print(f"the think-three-steps-ahead AI lost {losses} games")
     # count tie games
     ties=results.count(0)
     print(f"the game was tied {ties} times")
```

```
the think-three-steps-ahead AI won 625 games
the think-three-steps-ahead AI lost 311 games
the game was tied 64 times
```

Results show that the think-three-steps-ahead AI won 625 out of the 1000 games; it has lost to the think-two-steps-ahead AI 311 times. There are a total of 64 tie games. This indicates that the think-three-steps-ahead AI is indeed more intelligent than the think-two-steps-ahead AI in Connect Four.

You have learned the rules of the last of the three games that we use in this book: Connect Four. You also learned how to play Connect Four by using the custom-made game environment in the local module. You designed three rule-based AI game strategies: they plan moves up to three steps ahead. The AI agents become more and more intelligent as they look further and further ahead in gameplay. You'll use the game environment to design other game strategies in later chapters.

3.5 GLOSSARY

- **Connect Four:** A game in which two players take turns dropping discs into one of seven columns. One player has red discs and the other yellow. The seven columns are on a six-row, vertically suspended grid. When a disc is dropped into a column from the top, it will fall to the lowest available space in the column. The first player who connects four pieces of the same color in a row, either horizontally, vertically, or diagonally, wins the game.

3.6 EXERCISES

3.1 Rerun the first two cells in Section 3.1.2 to see the Connect Four game window and then close it.

3.2 Call the *one_conn_game()* function and use *conn_manual* as the first argument and *conn_think1* as the second argument. Play a game with the AI player manually. Create an opportunity for the AI player to win and see if it takes the winning move.

3.3 Modify the first code cell in Section 3.3.3 by letting the look-two-steps-ahead AI move second. Try to win the game yourself and see if the AI player can block your move.

3.4 Rerun the first cell in Section 3.4.2 and design your moves so that the AI player has an opportunity to create a double attack. See if it takes the opportunity and wins the game.

## CHAPTER 4

Recursion and MiniMax Tree Search

"In another thirty years people will laugh at anyone who tries to invent a language without closures, just as they'll laugh now at anyone who tries to invent a language without recursion."

– Mark Jason Dominus, in 2005

IN CHAPTERS 2 and 3, you learned how to use look-ahead search to design intelligent game strategies in Tic Tac Toe and Connect Four. However, the search process was hard coded. If we look ahead beyond three steps, the coding becomes tedious and error-prone. You may wonder if there is a systematic and more efficient way of conducting look-ahead search. The answer is yes: MiniMax tree search does exactly that. The MiniMax algorithm is a decision rule in artificial intelligence and game theory. The algorithm assumes that each player in the game makes the best possible decisions at each step. Further, each player knows that other players make fully rational decisions as well, and so on.

In this chapter, you'll learn to implement MiniMax tree search in the coin game. Specifically, you'll use recursion to call a function inside the function itself. This creates an infinite loop: all command lines in the function are executed iteration after iteration until a certain condition is met. The recursive algorithm allows the MiniMax agent to search ahead until the end of the game.

You'll create a MiniMax agent in the coin game by using the game environment that we developed in Chapter 1. The algorithm makes hypothetical future moves and exhausts all possible future game paths. The algorithm then uses backward induction to calculate the best move in each step of the game. The MiniMax agent solves the coin game and plays perfectly: it always wins when it plays second. The MiniMax agent makes moves very quickly as well: each move takes a fraction of a second.

DOI: 10.1201/9781032722207-4

After this chapter, you'll understand the logic behind MiniMax tree search and be able to design game strategies for any game based on the algorithm. You'll apply the algorithm to Tic Tac Toe and Connect Four as well in the next few chapters and find ways to overcome or mitigate drawbacks associated with MiniMax tree search.

What You'll Learn in This Chapter

- The logic behind MiniMax tree search
- Understanding recursion and applying it in MiniMax tree search
- Implementing MiniMax tree search in the coin game
- Testing the effectiveness of the MiniMax agent

4.1 INTRODUCING MINIMAX AND RECURSION

This section introduces MiniMax tree search and explains the concept of recursion in programming languages.

4.1.1 What Is MiniMax Tree Search?

MiniMax tree search is a decision rule in artificial intelligence and game theory. It's also called the minimax or MinMax algorithm.

In a nutshell, the algorithm assumes that:

- Each player in the game makes the best possible moves in each step.
- Further, each player knows that other players make fully rational decisions as well.
- Each player knows that other players know that he/she makes the best possible decisions.
- And so on...

In a two-player game, each player makes moves to maximize his/her own expected payoff and minimize the opponent's payoffs. Hence the name MiniMax.

4.1.2 Backward Induction and the Solution to MiniMax

The solution to MiniMax tree search is achieved through backward induction. It starts with the terminal state of the game. In the coin game, this is when the last coin is taken by a player; in Tic Tac Toe, the terminal state is when the game is tied or when one player has connected three pieces in a straight line. We find out the payoff to each player in the terminal state. In the second to last stage of the game, the player looks one step ahead and makes the best decision for himself/herself, anticipating that the opponent makes the best decision in the next step, and so on.

Let's use the coin game as an example. If both players make the best decisions, the game has seven rounds and 14 steps (in each round, Player 1 and Player 2 each make a move). In round 7, three coins are left in the pile, and Player 1 must decide how many coins to take: one or two? At this point, Player 1 knows that he/she will lose for sure: if he/she takes one coin, Player 2 will take two coins and win; if he/she takes two coins, Player 2 will take one coin and win.

Now, let's go to round 6. Six coins are left in the pile. Player 1 knows that no matter what he/she chooses, Player 2 will leave three coins in the pile. The reasoning goes all the way back to round 1, the beginning of the game. There are 21 coins in the pile. No matter what Player 1 chooses, Player 2 will leave 18 coins in the pile.

If you follow this line of reasoning (that is, backward induction), you'll know that Player 2 wins if both players follow the best strategies.

4.1.3 What Is Recursion?

Recursion is the calling of a function inside the function itself. We'll use recursion to implement MiniMax tree search in this book. Below, I'll show you one example of recursion.

Suppose you want to create a clock to tell time. The normal approach is as follows:

```
[1]: import time

     def clock():
         time_now=time.strftime("%H:%M:%S")
         print(f"The current time is {time_now}")
     clock()
```

```
The current time is 19:41:45
```

The *clock()* function we defined above tells time just once. However, what if you want the clock to be live? That is, you want it to tell time once each second until you tell it to stop? One way is to call the *clock()* function in the function itself. This will create an infinite loop and the lines of code inside the function are executed constantly.

Let's redefine the *clock()* function as follows:

```
[2]: start=time.time()
     def clock():
         time_now=time.strftime("%H:%M:%S")
         print(f"The current time is {time_now}")
         time.sleep(1)
         if time.time()-start<=10:
             clock()
     clock()
```

```
The current time is 19:45:46
The current time is 19:45:47
The current time is 19:45:48
```

```
The current time is 19:45:49
The current time is 19:45:50
The current time is 19:45:51
The current time is 19:45:52
The current time is 19:45:53
The current time is 19:45:54
The current time is 19:45:55
```

In the above cell, we call the *clock()* function in the function itself, unless more than ten seconds have passed. As a result, the function tells time for ten consecutive seconds.

4.2   MINIMAX TREE SEARCH IN THE COIN GAME

We'll use a simplified version of the self-made coin game environment from Chapter 1 to speed up MiniMax tree search. Specifically, the module is saved as *coin_simple_env.py* in the folder *utils* in the book's GitHub repository https://github.com/markhliu/AlphaGoSimplified. Download the file and save it in the folder /Desktop/ags/utils/ on your computer. The file *coin_simple_env.py* is the same as *coin_env.py* that we used in Chapter 1, except that we have deleted the graphical game window functionality. As a result, you cannot use the render() method in the simplified coin game environment. We use the simplified coin game environment to speed up moves by the MiniMax agent.

First, let's define a couple of functions that the MiniMax algorithm will use.

4.2.1   The MiniMax() Function

In the local module *ch04util*, we define a *MiniMax()* function for the player who is about to make a move. The function applies to both Player 1 and Player 2. The function tells the player what's the best next move, anticipating that the opponent will make the best decision in the next step as well, and so on.

Download the file *ch04util.py* from the book's GitHub repository and save it in /Desktop/ags/utils/ on your computer. The file acts as a local module with a few functions in it. The *MiniMax()* function is defined as follows in the file:

[3]:
```python
from copy import deepcopy
from random import choice

def MiniMax(env):
    # create a list to store winning moves
    wins=[]
    # iterate through all possible next moves
    for m in env.validinputs:
        # make a hypothetical move and see what happens
```

```
    env_copy=deepcopy(env)
    new_state, reward, done, info = env_copy.step(m)
    # if move m leads to a win now, take it
    if done and reward==1:
        return m
    # see what's the best response from the opponent
    opponent_payoff=maximized_payoff(env_copy,reward,done)
    # Opponent's payoff is the opposite of your payoff
    my_payoff=-opponent_payoff
    if my_payoff==1:
        wins.append(m)
# pick winning moves if there is any
if len(wins)>0:
    return choice(wins)
# otherwise randomly pick
return env.sample()
```

To search for the best move, the player iterates through all possible next moves. Note that we need to use deep copy here. In Python, when you make a regular copy of an object, you just create a link to the original object. When you make changes to the copy, the original is changed as well. To avoid this, we need to use deep copy. Many Python beginners make mistakes on this and can't figure out what's wrong with their code.

If a player finds a move that allows him/her to win the game right away, the player stops searching and takes the move. Otherwise, the player will see what's the best outcome for the opponent in the next step, knowing full well that the opponent will make the best decision to maximize the opponent's payoff. Since it's a zero-sum game, the opponent's payoff is the opposite of the current player's payoff. The player will pick winning moves if there is one; otherwise, the player randomly picks a move.

We'll use the *maximized_payoff()* function to find the best payoff to the opponent in the next stage. Let's define that function next.

4.2.2 The *maximized_payoff()* Function

Next, we'll define the *maximized_payoff()* function in the local module *ch04util*. The function produces the best possible outcome for the next player in the next step of the game. Note this function applies to any player in any stage of the game so we don't need to define one function for Player 1 and another function for Player 2.

```
[4]:  def maximized_payoff(env, reward, done):
          # if the game has ended after the previous player's move
          if done:
              return -1
          # otherwise, search for action to maximize payoff
```

```
best_payoff=-2
# iterate through all possible next moves
for m in env.validinputs:
    env_copy=deepcopy(env)
    new_state,reward,done,info=env_copy.step(m)
    # what's the opponent's response
    opponent_payoff=maximized_payoff(env_copy, reward, done)
    # opponent's payoff is the opposite of your payoff
    my_payoff=-opponent_payoff
    # update your best payoff
    if my_payoff>best_payoff:
        best_payoff=my_payoff
return best_payoff
```

If the game has ended after the previous player's move, the function calculates the payoff to the next player based on the game outcome. In this case, it means the previous player has won the game, so the payoff to the current player is −1. If the game has not ended, the player searches for the best action by iterating through all possible next moves, knowing full well that the opponent will take the best action in the next stage as well.

Note here that we have used the *maximized_payoff()* function inside the *maximized_payoff()* function itself. This creates an infinite loop. The function keeps on searching to the next level until the game ends. The process exhausts all game scenarios in the coin game.

4.2.3 Human versus MiniMax in the Coin Game

Next, you'll play a game against the MiniMax algorithm. We'll let the MiniMax agent move second and see if it can win the game.

```
[5]: from utils.coin_simple_env import coin_game
     from utils.ch04util import MiniMax

     # Initiate the game environment
     env=coin_game()
     state=env.reset()
     # Play a full game
     while True:
         print(f"there are {state} coins in the pile")
         action=input("Player 1, what's your move (1 or 2)?")
         print(f"Player 1 has chosen action={action}")
         state, reward, done, info=env.step(action)
         if done:
             print(f"there are {state} coins in the pile")
             print(f"Player 1 has won!")
```

```
        break
    print(f"there are {state} coins in the pile")
    start=time.time()
    action=MiniMax(env)
    print(f"time lapse = {time.time()-start:.5f} seconds")
    print(f"Player 2 has chosen action={action}")
    state, reward, done, info=env.step(action)
    if done:
        print(f"there are {state} coins in the pile")
        print(f"Player 2 has won!")
        break
```

```
there are 21 coins in the pile
Player 1, what's your move (1 or 2)?2
Player 1 has chosen action=2
there are 19 coins in the pile
time lapse = 0.31630 seconds
Player 2 has chosen action=1
there are 18 coins in the pile
Player 1, what's your move (1 or 2)?1
Player 1 has chosen action=1
there are 17 coins in the pile
time lapse = 0.12109 seconds
Player 2 has chosen action=2
there are 15 coins in the pile
Player 1, what's your move (1 or 2)?2
Player 1 has chosen action=2
there are 13 coins in the pile
time lapse = 0.02154 seconds
Player 2 has chosen action=1
there are 12 coins in the pile
Player 1, what's your move (1 or 2)?1
Player 1 has chosen action=1
there are 11 coins in the pile
time lapse = 0.00852 seconds
Player 2 has chosen action=2
there are 9 coins in the pile
Player 1, what's your move (1 or 2)?2
Player 1 has chosen action=2
there are 7 coins in the pile
time lapse = 0.00100 seconds
Player 2 has chosen action=1
there are 6 coins in the pile
Player 1, what's your move (1 or 2)?1
Player 1 has chosen action=1
```

```
there are 5 coins in the pile
time lapse = 0.00000 seconds
Player 2 has chosen action=2
there are 3 coins in the pile
Player 1, what's your move (1 or 2)?2
Player 1 has chosen action=2
there are 1 coins in the pile
time lapse = 0.00000 seconds
Player 2 has chosen action=1
there are 0 coins in the pile
Player 2 has won!
```

The MiniMax algorithm wins the game. In every stage of the game, after the MiniMax agent's move, the number of coins in the pile is a multiple of three: 18, 15, 12, 9, 6, and then 3.

In the above output, we also print out the time it took for the MiniMax to search for the best move. In the early stages of the game, it takes longer for the agent to exhaust all game paths. For example, the very first step takes 0.3163 seconds. In the late stages of the game, it takes no time at all for the agent to exhaust all game paths. For example, the very last step takes less than 0.00001 seconds.

4.3   EFFECTIVENESS OF MINIMAX IN THE COIN GAME

Next, we'll test how often the MiniMax Algorithm wins against the rule-based AI game strategy that we developed in Chapter 1. We'll first let the MiniMax agent play against random moves. We'll then test the MiniMax agent against the rule-based AI.

4.3.1   MiniMax versus Random Moves in the Coin Game

Next, we'll see how good the MiniMax algorithm is when it plays against random moves. We'll first import the *random_player()* and *one_coin_game()* functions from the local module *ch01util*.

We simulate 100 games and let the MiniMax agent move first.

```
[6]: from utils.ch01util import random_player, one_coin_game

     env=coin_game()
     results=[]
     for i in range(100):
         # MiniMax moves first
         result=one_coin_game(MiniMax,random_player)
         # record game outcome
         results.append(result)
     # count how many times MiniMax has won
```

```
wins=results.count(1)
print(f"the MiniMax algorithm won {wins} games")
# count how many times MiniMax has lost
losses=results.count(-1)
print(f"the MiniMax algorithm lost {losses} games")
```

```
the MiniMax algorithm won 96 games
the MiniMax algorithm lost 4 games
```

The results above show that the MiniMax agent has won 96 games out of 100.

Since we know that if both players use perfect strategies, the second player always wins, we'll see what happens if the MiniMax agent moves second.

[7]:
```
results=[]
for i in range(100):
    # MiniMax moves second
    result=one_coin_game(random_player,MiniMax)
    # record negative game outcome
    results.append(-result)
# count how many times MiniMax has won
wins=results.count(1)
print(f"the MiniMax algorithm won {wins} games")
# count how many times MiniMax has lost
losses=results.count(-1)
print(f"the MiniMax algorithm lost {losses} games")
```

```
the MiniMax algorithm won 100 games
the MiniMax algorithm lost 0 games
```

We record the negative game outcome so that a value of 1 in the list *results* indicates that the MiniMax agent has won. The output from the above cell shows that the MiniMax agent has won all 100 games.

4.3.2 MiniMax versus Rule-Based AI in the Coin Game

Next, we'll see how intelligent the MiniMax algorithm is when it plays against the rule-based AI that we developed in Chapter 1. Below, we simulate 100 games and let the MiniMax agent move first.

[8]:
```
from utils.ch01util import rule_based_AI

env=coin_game()
results=[]
for i in range(100):
    # MiniMax moves first
    result=one_coin_game(MiniMax,rule_based_AI)
```

```
    # record game outcome
    results.append(result)
# count how many times MiniMax has won
wins=results.count(1)
print(f"the MiniMax algorithm won {wins} games")
# count how many times MiniMax has lost
losses=results.count(-1)
print(f"the MiniMax algorithm lost {losses} games")
```

```
the MiniMax algorithm won 0 games
the MiniMax algorithm lost 100 games
```

The results above show that the MiniMax agent has lost all 100 games. The MiniMax algorithm has lost because if both players use perfect strategies, the second player always wins.

Next, we'll see what happens if the MiniMax agent moves second:

[9]:
```
results=[]
for i in range(100):
    # MiniMax moves second
    result=one_coin_game(rule_based_AI,MiniMax)
    # record negative game outcome
    results.append(-result)
# count how many times MiniMax has won
wins=results.count(1)
print(f"the MiniMax algorithm won {wins} games")
# count how many times MiniMax has lost
losses=results.count(-1)
print(f"the MiniMax algorithm lost {losses} games")
```

```
the MiniMax algorithm won 100 games
the MiniMax algorithm lost 0 games
```

The output from the above cell shows that the MiniMax agent has won all 100 games, even against the perfect player that we developed in Chapter 1.

Taken together, our results show that the MiniMax agent plays the game perfectly in the sense that whenever it plays second, it wins 100% of the time.

In this Chapter, you have learned the idea behind the MiniMax algorithm and applied it to the Coin game. In the next Chapter, you'll apply the algorithm to Tic Tac Toe and Connect Four and address the challenges associated with the algorithm.

4.4 GLOSSARY

- **MiniMax Tree Search:** A decision rule in artificial intelligence and game theory. The algorithm assumes that each player in the game makes the best possible decisions at each step. Further, each player knows that other players make fully rational decisions as well, and so on.

- **Recursion:** Recursion is the calling of a function inside the function itself. It's also called the recursive algorithm.

4.5 EXERCISES

4.1 Modify the second code cell in Section 4.1.3 so that the function tells time for five consecutive seconds.

4.2 Rerun the first cell in Section 4.2.3 to play against the MiniMax agent. See if it wins the game.

## CHAPTER 5

Depth Pruning in MiniMax

"Genius sometimes consists of knowing when to stop."
– Charles De Gaulle

YOU LEARNED HOW MiniMax tree search works in the previous chapter and applied it to the coin game by searching for the best move in the next step recursively until the game ends. The MiniMax agent solves the coin game: it wins 100% of the time when it plays second.

In this chapter, you'll first create a MiniMax agent in Tic Tac Toe by using recursion, as you did in Chapter 4. MiniMax tree search exhausts all possible future game paths and solves the Tic Tac Toe game. However, at the beginning of the game, it takes about 35 seconds for the MiniMax agent to make a move. Later moves take much less time, though.

In more complicated games such as Connect Four, Chess, or Go, the MiniMax algorithm cannot exhaust all possible future game paths in a short amount of time. However, this doesn't mean that MiniMax tree search is useless in these games. One of the answers lies in depth pruning: Instead of searching all the way to the terminal state of the game, you search a certain number of moves ahead and stop searching. You can then evaluate the game outcome by using a position evaluation function. In this chapter, we assume that the game is tied after searching a fixed number of steps ahead and if the game is not in a terminal state. We'll discuss how to apply position evaluation functions in Chapter 7.

In this chapter, you'll learn to create a generic MiniMax agent with depth pruning that can be applied to both Tic Tac Toe and Connect Four. Depth pruning allows the MiniMax agent to come up with intelligent (though not perfect) game strategies in a short amount of time. In fact, the algorithm used by Deep Blue to beat World Chess Champion Gary Kasparov in 1997 was based on MiniMax tree search with depth pruning (along with other strategies).

DOI: 10.1201/9781032722207-5

After that, you'll test the effectiveness of your MiniMax agents against the rule-based AI that you developed in Chapters 2 and 3.

What You'll Learn in This Chapter

- Creating a MiniMax agent in Tic Tac Toe
- Understanding the idea behind depth pruning
- Creating a generic MiniMax agent with depth pruning
- Testing MiniMax with depth pruning in Tic Tac Toe and Connect Four

5.1 MINIMAX TREE SEARCH IN TIC TAC TOE

You have already learned how the MiniMax algorithm works in Chapter 4 and applied it to the coin game. In a nutshell, the algorithm assumes each player in the game makes the best possible decisions at each step. Players know that their opponents make fully rational decisions as well, and so on. In this section, you'll apply the same method to Tic Tac Toe to create a MiniMax agent.

The MiniMax agent in Tic Tac Toe comes up with the best moves through backward induction. It starts with the terminal state of the game (when the game is tied or when Player X or Player O wins) and finds out the payoffs to each player in that state. In the second to last stage of the game, the player looks one step ahead and makes the best decision for himself/herself, anticipating that the opponent makes the best decision in the next stage, and so on.

In Tic Tac Toe, Each game has a maximum of 9 steps. In step 9, Player X has only one choice so no decision is needed. In step 8, Player O looks at the two choices and picks the best one for himself/herself. In step 7, Player X picks the best decision, knowing that Player O will make a fully rational decision in step 8, and so on. The reasoning goes all the way back to the very first step when Player X makes a move.

Since the total number of possible scenarios in a Tic Tac Toe game is small (less than $3^9 = 19,683$), the computer program can exhaust all scenarios in a reasonable amount of time and find the best solution for each player in every stage of the game. We'll discuss how to reduce the amount of time that the agent needs to make a decision through depth pruning in the next section.

5.1.1 The MiniMax Algorithm in Tic Tac Toe

We'll use a simplified version of the self-made Tic Tac Toe game environment from Chapter 2 to speed up MiniMax tree search. Specifically, the module is saved as *ttt_simple_env.py* in the folder *utils* in the book's GitHub repository https://github.com/markhliu/AlphaGoSimplified. Download the file and save it in the folder /Desktop/ags/utils/ on your computer. The file *ttt_simple_env.py* is the same as *ttt_env.py* that we used in Chapter 2, except that we have deleted the graphical game window functionality. As a result, you cannot use the *render()* method in the simplified Tic Tac Toe game environment. We use the simplified game environment to speed up moves: to search ahead, the algorithm makes hypothetical moves by creating a deep copy of the current game environment. Without the *render()* method, the algorithm makes deep copies (hence decisions) faster.

We'll define a *MiniMax_X()* function for Player X and a different function *Mini-Max_O()* for Player O. Potentially, we can define one function for both players, but it's easier to explain the functions when we have one for each player. There is a trade-off between code efficiency and code readability and here we choose the latter. As an exercise, define a function *MiniMax_XO()* to replace *MiniMax_X()* and *Min-iMax_O()*. Make sure the function *MiniMax_XO()* that you have defined applies to both Player X and Player O.

Download the file *ch05util.py* from the book's GitHub repository and save it in /Desktop/ags/utils/ on your computer. The file acts as a local module with a few functions in it. The *MiniMax_X()* function is defined as follows:

```python
def MiniMax_X(env):
    wins=[]
    ties=[]
    losses=[]
    # iterate through all possible next moves
    for m in env.validinputs:
        # make a hypothetical move and see what happens
        env_copy=deepcopy(env)
        state,reward,done,info=env_copy.step(m)
        # If wins right away with move m, take it.
        if done and reward==1:
            return m
        # See what's the best response from the opponent
        opponent_payoff=maximized_payoff(env_copy,reward,done)
        # Opponent's payoff is the opposite of your payoff
        my_payoff=-opponent_payoff
        if my_payoff==1:
            wins.append(m)
        elif my_payoff==0:
            ties.append(m)
        else:
            losses.append(m)
    # pick winning moves if there is any
    if len(wins)>0:
        return choice(wins)
    # otherwise pick tying moves
    elif len(ties)>0:
        return choice(ties)
    return env.sample()
```

At each step, Player X iterates through all possible next moves. If a move allows the current player to win the game right away, the player will stop searching and take the move. Otherwise, the player will see what's the best outcome for the opponent in the next stage, knowing full well that the opponent will make fully rational decisions. Since it's a zero-sum game, the current player's payoff is the opposite of the opponent's payoff. The current player will then pick winning moves if there is one; otherwise, he/she will pick a tying move; otherwise, the current player has no choice but to pick whatever move is left.

In the local module *ch05util*, we also define the *maximized_payoff()* function to find the best payoff for a player in the next stage. This function produces the best possible outcome for the next player in the next stage of the game. Note that this function applies to any stage of the game for any player so we don't need to define one for Player X and one for Player O.

```python
def maximized_payoff(env,reward,done):
    # if the game has ended after the previous player's move
    if done:
        # if it's not a tie
        if reward!=0:
            return -1
        else:
            return 0
    # Otherwise, search for action to maximize payoff
    best_payoff=-2
    # iterate through all possible moves
    for m in env.validinputs:
        env_copy=deepcopy(env)
        state,reward,done,info=env_copy.step(m)
        # If I make this move, what's the opponent's response?
        opponent_payoff=maximized_payoff(env_copy,reward,done)
        # Opponent's payoff is the opposite of your payoff
        my_payoff=-opponent_payoff
        # update your best payoff
        if my_payoff>best_payoff:
            best_payoff=my_payoff
    return best_payoff
```

If the game has ended after the previous player's move, the function calculates the payoff to the current player based on the game outcome. Otherwise, the player searches for the best action by iterating through all possible next moves, knowing full well that the opponent takes a fully rational action in the next stage as well.

Note here that we have used the *maximized_payoff()* function in the *maximized_payoff()* function itself. This creates an infinite loop. The function keeps on searching to the next stage until the game ends. The process exhausts all game scenarios in Tic Tac Toe.

5.1.2 Test the MiniMax Algorithm in Tic Tac Toe

Next, you'll play a game against the MiniMax algorithm. We'll let the MiniMax agent move first and see if it can win the game. We also time how long it takes for the MiniMax agent to come up with a move. A bit of warning here: it takes about 35 seconds on my computer for the MiniMax agent to make the first move. It may take longer depending on your computer. So be patient when you run the following code cell.

```
[1]: from utils.ttt_simple_env import ttt
     from utils.ch05util import MiniMax_X, maximized_payoff
     import time

     # Initiate the game environment
     env=ttt()
     state=env.reset()
     # Play a full game manually
     while True:
         # Mesure how long it takes to come up with a move
         start=time.time()
         action = MiniMax_X(env)
         end=time.time()
         print(f"Player X has chosen action={action}")
         print(f"It took the agent {end-start} seconds")
         state, reward, done, info = env.step(action)
         print(f"Current state is \n{state.reshape(3,3)[::-1]}")
         if done:
             if reward==1:
                 print("Player X has won!")
             else:
                 print("Game over, it's a tie!")
             break
         action = input("Player O, what's your move?\n")
         print(f"Player O has chosen action={action}")
         state, reward, done, info = env.step(int(action))
         print(f"Current state is \n{state.reshape(3,3)[::-1]}")
         if done:
             print("Player O has won!")
             break
```

```
Player X has chosen action=5
It took the agent 34.98157286643982 seconds
Current state is
[[0 0 0]
 [0 1 0]
 [0 0 0]]
```

```
Player O, what's your move?
1
Player O has chosen action=1
Current state is
[[ 0  0  0]
 [ 0  1  0]
 [-1  0  0]]
Player X has chosen action=6
It took the agent 0.4136021137237549 seconds
Current state is
[[ 0  0  0]
 [ 0  1  1]
 [-1  0  0]]
Player O, what's your move?
4
Player O has chosen action=4
Current state is
[[ 0  0  0]
 [-1  1  1]
 [-1  0  0]]
Player X has chosen action=7
It took the agent 0.014605283737182617 seconds
Current state is
[[ 1  0  0]
 [-1  1  1]
 [-1  0  0]]
Player O, what's your move?
3
Player O has chosen action=3
Current state is
[[ 1  0  0]
 [-1  1  1]
 [-1  0 -1]]
Player X has chosen action=2
It took the agent 0.0018301010131835938 seconds
Current state is
[[ 1  0  0]
 [-1  1  1]
 [-1  1 -1]]
Player O, what's your move?
8
Player O has chosen action=8
Current state is
[[ 1 -1  0]
 [-1  1  1]
```

```
 [-1  1 -1]]
Player X has chosen action=9
It took the agent 0.0 seconds
Current state is
[[ 1 -1  1]
 [-1  1  1]
 [-1  1 -1]]
Game over, it's a tie!
```

The game is tied. It took the MiniMax algorithm about 35 seconds to make the very first move. It took the agent a fraction of a second to make later moves. I tried my best to win but couldn't: the game was tied.

5.1.3   Efficacy of the MiniMax Algorithm in Tic Tac Toe

Next, we'll test how often the MiniMax Algorithm wins against the think-three-steps-ahead AI that we developed in Chapter 2.

To do that, we first define a *MiniMax_O()* function in the local module. Open the file *ch05util.py* you just downloaded and have a look at the function. You'll notice that the function *MiniMax_O()* is very similar to the *MiniMax_X()* function we defined before. The only difference is that we changed

```
if done and reward==1:
    return m
```

to

```
if done and reward==-1:
    return m
```

At each step, Player O iterates through all possible next moves. If a move allows Player O to win the game right away, the player will stop searching and take the move. Otherwise, the player will see what's the best outcome for Player X in the next stage, knowing full well that the opponent will make fully rational decisions. Player O then chooses the best next move based on the outcomes associated with choosing different moves.

To test how the MiniMax agent fairs against the think-three-steps-ahead AI in Tic Tac Toe, run the following code cell:

```
[2]:  from utils.ch05util import MiniMax_O
      from utils.ch02util import ttt_think3, one_ttt_game

      # Play 20 games
      results=[]
      for i in range(20):
          # MiniMax moves first if i is an even number
```

```
    if i%2==0:
        result=one_ttt_game(MiniMax_X,ttt_think3)
        # record game outcome
        results.append(result)
    # MiniMax moves second if i is an odd number
    else:
        result=one_ttt_game(ttt_think3,MiniMax_O)
        # record negative game outcome
        results.append(-result)
```

We are testing 20 games. The MiniMax agent goes first in ten games and the think-three-steps-ahead AI goes first in the other ten games so no player has the first-mover advantage. The game outcome is 1 when the first player wins and −1 when the second player wins. The game is tied when the outcome is 0. When the MiniMax agent is playing second, we multiply the outcome by −1 before adding it to the list *results*. A value of 1 in the list *results* indicates that the MiniMax agent has won.

[3]:
```
# count how many times the MiniMax agent has won
wins=results.count(1)
print(f"the MiniMax agent has won {wins} games")
# count how many times the MiniMax agent has lost
losses=results.count(-1)
print(f"the MiniMax agent has lost {losses} games")
# count tie games
ties=results.count(0)
print(f"the game was tied {ties} times")
```

```
the MiniMax agent has won 9 games
the MiniMax agent has lost 0 games
the game was tied 11 times
```

The results show that the MiniMax agent has won 9 games, while the rest 11 games are tied. The MiniMax agent has never lost to the think-three-steps ahead AI. This indicates that the MiniMax agent in Tic Tac Toe is more intelligent than the look-three-steps-ahead AI we developed in Chapter 2.

5.2 DEPTH PRUNING IN TIC TAC TOE

In the last section, you have seen that it took the MiniMax agent 35 seconds to make the first move. While this is tolerable, in more complicated games such as Connect Four, Chess, or Go, it takes forever for the agent to make a move. Therefore, unless we modify the MiniMax algorithm, we cannot apply it to those games.

Depth pruning is one of the solutions: instead of searching all the way to the terminal state of the game, the algorithm stops searching after a fixed number of steps. In this section, you'll learn how to implement depth pruning in the game of Tic Tac Toe.

5.2.1   The max_payoff() Function

We'll define a *max_payoff()* function in the local module *ch05util*. The function is similar to the *maximized_payoff()* function we defined in the last section. However, there are two important differences. First, there is a depth argument in the function to control how many steps the MiniMax agent searches. Second, we'll make the function generic so that it can be applied to Tic Tac Toe as well as the Connect Four game later in this chapter.

Go to the file *ch05util.py* you just downloaded and take a look at the *max_payoff()* function, which is defined as follows:

```python
def max_payoff(env,reward,done,depth):
    # if the game has ended after the previous player's move
    if done:
        # if it's not a tie
        if reward!=0:
            return -1
        else:
            return 0
    # If the maximum depth is reached, assume tie game
    if depth==0:
        return 0
    # Otherwise, search for action to maximize payoff
    best_payoff=-2
    # iterate through all possible moves
    for m in env.validinputs:
        env_copy=deepcopy(env)
        state,reward,done,info=env_copy.step(m)
        # If I make this move, what's the opponent's response?
        opponent_payoff=max_payoff(env_copy,reward,done,depth-1)
        # Opponent's payoff is the opposite of your payoff
        my_payoff=-opponent_payoff
        # update your best payoff
        if my_payoff>best_payoff:
            best_payoff=my_payoff
    return best_payoff
```

In the function, if the variable *depth* reaches 0, we assume the game is tied and the payoff is 0. Later in this book, we'll use a position evaluation function to evaluate the current board position and provide a more accurate assessment of the likely game outcome. But for the moment, we assume the game is tied for simplicity.

When the player makes a hypothetical move and anticipates the best response from the opponent, it uses the function *max_payoff(env_copy,reward,done,depth-1)*. This means that each time the player searches to the next level, the *depth* variable decreases by 1. Once the variable *depth* reaches 0, the agent stops searching.

5.2.2 The MiniMax_depth() Function

We also define a *MiniMax_depth()* function to produce the best move for the Min-iMax agent. There is a *depth* argument in the function to control how many steps the MiniMax agent searches. The default *depth* value is set to 3. Note the function applies to Tic Tac Toe as well as Connect Four.

The *MiniMax_depth()* function is defined as follows. It's saved in the file *ch05util.py* that you just downloaded.

```python
def MiniMax_depth(env,depth=3):
    wins=[]
    ties=[]
    losses=[]
    # iterate through all possible next moves
    for m in env.validinputs:
        # make a hypothetical move and see what happens
        env_copy=deepcopy(env)
        state,reward,done,info=env_copy.step(m)
        if done and reward!=0:
            return m
        # See what's the best response from the opponent
        opponent_payoff=max_payoff(env_copy,reward,done,depth)
        # Opponent's payoff is the opposite of your payoff
        my_payoff=-opponent_payoff
        if my_payoff==1:
            wins.append(m)
        elif my_payoff==0:
            ties.append(m)
        else:
            losses.append(m)
    # pick winning moves if there is any
    if len(wins)>0:
        return choice(wins)
    # otherwise pick tying moves
    elif len(ties)>0:
        return choice(ties)
    return env.sample()
```

The *MiniMax_depth()* function has two arguments: *env*, which is the game environment, which can be either the Tic Tac Toe or the Connect Four game environment. The second argument, *depth*, is how many steps the MiniMax agent searches before making a move.

5.2.3 Speed of the Depth-Pruned MiniMax Agent

Next, we test how fast the depth-pruned MiniMax agent is. We use a default depth of 3 and play a game against the agent manually. We let the agent move first again and measure how long it takes for the depth-pruned MiniMax agent to make a move.

[4]:
```python
from utils.ch05util import MiniMax_depth

# Initiate the game environment
env=ttt()
state=env.reset()
# Play a full game manually
while True:
    # Mesure how long it takes to come up with a move
    start=time.time()
    action = MiniMax_depth(env,depth=3)
    end=time.time()
    print(f"Player X has chosen action={action}")
    print(f"It took the agent {end-start} seconds")
    state, reward, done, info = env.step(action)
    print(f"Current state is \n{state.reshape(3,3)[::-1]}")
    if done:
        if reward==1:
            print("Player X has won!")
        else:
            print("Game over, it's a tie!")
        break
    action = input("Player O, what's your move?\n")
    print(f"Player O has chosen action={action}")
    state, reward, done, info = env.step(int(action))
    print(f"Current state is \n{state.reshape(3,3)[::-1]}")
    if done:
        print("Player O has won!")
        break
```

```
Player X has chosen action=5
It took the agent 0.19032764434814453 seconds
Current state is
[[0 0 0]
 [0 1 0]
 [0 0 0]]
Player O, what's your move?
1
Player O has chosen action=1
Current state is
[[ 0  0  0]
```

```
 [ 0   1   0]
 [-1   0   0]]
Player X has chosen action=7
It took the agent 0.0625150203704834 seconds
Current state is
[[ 1   0   0]
 [ 0   1   0]
 [-1   0   0]]
Player 0, what's your move?
2
Player 0 has chosen action=2
Current state is
[[ 1   0   0]
 [ 0   1   0]
 [-1  -1   0]]
Player X has chosen action=3
It took the agent 0.0010073184967041016 seconds
Current state is
[[ 1   0   0]
 [ 0   1   0]
 [-1  -1   1]]
Player X has won!
```

It took only 0.2 seconds here for the MiniMax agent to make the first move, instead of 35 seconds when there is no depth pruning. That's a huge reduction in the amount of time it takes to come up with a move. Of course, the moves with depth pruning are not as intelligent as the ones without depth pruning.

5.3   DEPTH PRUNING IN CONNECT FOUR

Next, we'll create a MiniMax agent for the Connect Four game. The agent searches for a maximum of three steps.

5.3.1   The MiniMax Agent in Connect Four

We first manually play a game against the MiniMax agent.

[5]:
```python
from utils.conn_simple_env import conn

# Initiate the game environment
env=conn()
state=env.reset()
# Play a full game manually
while True:
    # Mesure how long it takes to come up with a move
```

```
    start=time.time()
    action=MiniMax(env,depth=3)
    end=time.time()
    print(f"The red player has chosen action={action}")
    print(f"It took the agent {end-start} seconds")
    state, reward, done, info = env.step(action)
    print(f"the current state is \n{state.T[::-1]}")
    if done:
        if reward==1:
            print(f"The red player has won!")
        else:
            print("Game over, it's a tie!")
        break
    action=input("Player yellow, what's your move?\n")
    print(f"Player yellow has chosen action={action}")
    state, reward, done, info = env.step(int(action))
    print(f"the current state is \n{state.T[::-1]}")
    if done:
        if reward==-1:
            print(f"The yellow player has won!")
        else:
            print("Game over, it's a tie!")
        break
```

```
The red player has chosen action=5
It took the agent 0.14301228523254395 seconds
...
the current state is
[[ 0  0  0  0  0  0  0]
 [ 0  0  0  0  0  0  0]
 [ 0  0  0  0  0  0  0]
 [ 0  0  0  0  0  0  0]
 [-1  0  0  0  0  0  0]
 [-1  0  0  0  1  1  0]]
The red player has chosen action=4
It took the agent 0.13970661163330078 seconds
the current state is
[[ 0  0  0  0  0  0  0]
 [ 0  0  0  0  0  0  0]
 [ 0  0  0  0  0  0  0]
 [ 0  0  0  0  0  0  0]
 [-1  0  0  0  0  0  0]
 [-1  0  0  1  1  1  0]]
Player yellow, what's your move?
3
```

```
Player yellow has chosen action=3
the current state is
[[ 0  0  0  0  0  0  0]
 [ 0  0  0  0  0  0  0]
 [ 0  0  0  0  0  0  0]
 [ 0  0  0  0  0  0  0]
 [-1  0  0  0  0  0  0]
 [-1  0 -1  1  1  1  0]]
The red player has chosen action=7
It took the agent 0.1260826587677002 seconds
the current state is
[[ 0  0  0  0  0  0  0]
 [ 0  0  0  0  0  0  0]
 [ 0  0  0  0  0  0  0]
 [ 0  0  0  0  0  0  0]
 [-1  0  0  0  0  0  0]
 [-1  0 -1  1  1  1  1]]
The red player has won!
```

The MiniMax agent is able to plan three steps ahead, create a double attack, and win the game. It takes less than 0.15 seconds for the agent to come up with a move in each step.

5.3.2   MiniMax versus Rule-Based AI in Connect Four

We'll test if the MiniMax algorithm that searches for three steps ahead can beat the rule-based think-three-steps-ahead AI that we developed in Chapter 3.

[6]:
```python
from utils.ch03util import one_conn_game, conn_think3

results=[]
for i in range(100):
    # MiniMax moves first if i is an even number
    if i%2==0:
        result=one_conn_game(MiniMax_depth,conn_think3)
        # record game outcome
        results.append(result)
    # MiniMax moves second if i is an odd number
    else:
        result=one_conn_game(conn_think3,MiniMax_depth)
        # record negative game outcome
        results.append(-result)
```

We create a list *results* to store game outcomes. We simulate 100 games and half the time, the MiniMax agent moves first and the other half, the rule-based AI moves first. This way, no player has a first-mover advantage and we have a fair assessment of the intelligence of the MiniMax agent against the rule-based AI. Whenever the MiniMax agent moves second, we multiply the outcome by -1 so that a value of 1 in the list *results* indicates a win for the MiniMax agent.

[7]:
```
# count how many times MiniMax won
wins=results.count(1)
print(f"the MiniMax agent won {wins} games")
# count how many times MiniMax lost
losses=results.count(-1)
print(f"the MiniMax agent lost {losses} games")
# count tie games
ties=results.count(0)
print(f"the game was tied {ties} times")
```

```
the MiniMax agent won 68 games
the MiniMax agent lost 26 games
the game was tied 6 times
```

The above outputs show that the MiniMax agent has won 68 games, lost 26, and the rest 6 games are tied. The results show that the MiniMax agent is more intelligent than a think-three-steps-ahead agent. Even though both agents think three steps ahead, MiniMax tree search provides a more systematic and accurate way of searching three steps ahead, hence more intelligent game strategies.

5.4   GLOSSARY

- **Depth Pruning:** Depth pruning is one of the solutions to the MiniMax algorithm when it takes too long to search to the end of the game. Instead of searching all the way to the terminal state of the game, the algorithm stops searching after a fixed number of steps.

5.5   EXERCISES

5.1   Rerun the first cell in Section 5.1.2 to play against the MiniMax agent. Try your best to win and see if the MiniMax agent can win the game.

5.2   Define a function *MiniMax_XO()* so that it applies to both Player X and Player O. Your goal is to replace *MiniMax_X()* and *MiniMax_O()* with one single function *MiniMax_XO()*.

5.3   Rerun the first cell in Section 5.3.1 to play against the MiniMax agent in Connect Four. Try your best to win and see what happens.

## CHAPTER 6

Alpha-Beta Pruning

"Art is the elimination of the unnecessary."
– Pablo Picasso

AS YOU HAVE seen in Chapter 5, depth pruning makes the MiniMax algorithm possible in complicated games such as Connect Four, Chess, and Go: Without depth pruning, it takes forever for the MiniMax agent to come up with a move. In this chapter, you'll use another method to improve the MiniMax algorithm and make it more efficient. Specifically, alpha-beta pruning allows the agent to skip certain branches that cannot possibly influence the final game outcome. Doing so significantly reduces the amount of time for the MiniMax agent to come up with a move. This, in turn, allows the agent to search more steps ahead and come up with more intelligent moves in a given amount of time.

To implement alpha-beta pruning in a game, we keep track of two numbers: alpha and beta, the best outcomes so far for Players 1 and 2, respectively. Whenever we have $alpha > -beta$, or equivalently $beta > -alpha$, the MiniMax algorithm stops searching a branch.

We implement alpha-beta pruning in both Tic Tac Toe and Connect Four in this chapter. We use a concrete example to explain the logic behind the algorithm: why the agent can skip certain branches and come up with the same best move. We show that the game outcomes are the same with and without alpha-beta pruning. We also show that alpha-beta pruning saves a significant amount of time for the player to find the best moves. For example, in Tic Tac Toe, the amount of time for the MiniMax agent to come up with the first move decreases from 35 seconds without alpha-beta pruning to 1.06 seconds with alpha-beta pruning, a 97% reduction in the amount of time the MiniMax agent needs to come up with a move. In Connect Four, we find that on average, the time spent on a move has reduced from 0.15 seconds to 0.05 seconds after we added in alpha-beta pruning when the agent searches three steps ahead.

DOI: 10.1201/9781032722207-6

What You'll Learn in This Chapter

- The logic behind alpha-beta pruning
- Implementing alpha-beta pruning in Tic Tac Toe and Connect Four
- Calculating time saved by the alpha-beta pruning agent
- Verifying that alpha-beta pruning won't affect game outcomes

---

6.1   WHAT IS ALPHA-BETA PRUNING?

What is the idea behind alpha-beta pruning? Let's first look at a concrete example of alpha-beta pruning in Tic Tac Toe and understand how it works.

We use alpha to record the best outcome so far for Player X, and beta the best outcome for Player O.

To demonstrate the idea behind alpha-beta pruning, let's assume the board in a Tic Tac Toe game is as shown in Figure 6.1.

Both Player X and Player O have made three moves. Now it's Player X's turn. Suppose Player X is using MiniMax tree search to figure out the best next move. Let's count how many branches Player X has to search with and without alpha-beta pruning, respectively.

6.1.1   MiniMax Tree Search without Alpha-Beta Pruning

Without any type of pruning (either depth pruning or alpha-beta pruning), Player X will search over six different scenarios:

- Player X occupies 2; O occupies 3; X occupies 9; payoff to X is 0 and payoff to O is 0;
- Player X occupies 2; O occupies 9; X occupies 3; payoff to X is 1 and payoff to O is −1;
- Player X occupies 3; O occupies 2; payoff to X is −1 and payoff to O is 1;
- Player X occupies 3; O occupies 9; X occupies 2; payoff to X is 1 and payoff to O is −1;
- Player X occupies 9; O occupies 2; payoff to X is −1 and payoff to O is 1;
- Player X occupies 9; O occupies 3; X occupies 2; payoff to X is 0 and payoff to O is 0;

Since Player X knows that Player O chooses moves to maximize Player O's payoff, Player X anticipates the following outcomes by using backward induction:

- Player X occupies 2; O occupies 3; payoff to X is 0 and payoff to O is 0;
- Player X occupies 3; O occupies 2; payoff to X is −1 and payoff to O is 1;
- Player X occupies 9; O occupies 2; payoff to X is −1 and payoff to O is 1;

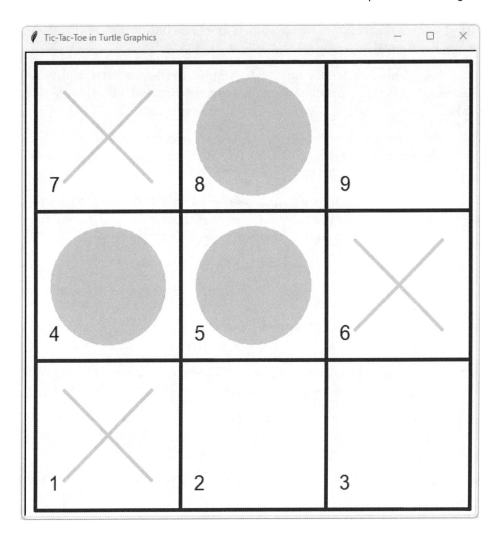

Figure 6.1 Alpha-beta pruning in Tic Tac Toe

Therefore, Player X knows that her payoffs would be 0, −1, or −1, respectively, if she were to choose cell 2, 3, or 9 in the next step. As a result, Player X will choose cell 2 in the next step since doing so has the highest payoff (max{0, −1, −1}=0).

To summarize, without alpha-beta pruning, Player X needs to search for six different branches to come up with the best next move, which is cell 2.

Next, we'll demonstrate that Player X can actually reach the same conclusion by searching only four different branches by using alpha-beta pruning. Therefore, the agent can skip two unnecessary branches and save time.

6.1.2 MiniMax Tree Search with Alpha-Beta Pruning

With alpha-beta pruning, we can exclude certain branches of the game tree to save time. This, in turn, makes the tree search algorithm more powerful because it allows the AI players to search more branches in a fixed amount of time and come up with more intelligent strategies.

We use alpha and beta to denote the best outcomes so far for the first and second players, respectively. At any point in the search process, if $alpha > -beta$ (or equivalently, $beta > -alpha$), we stop searching the branch.

Now, let's go back to the example in the last subsection where Player X needs to decide to place a game piece in cell 2, 3, or 9. With alpha-beta pruning, we can reduce the number of searches.

Before starting the search, let's set alpha and beta to -2. Since the worst outcome for either player is -1 (i.e., losing the game), setting the initial value to -2 guarantees that we keep an accurate record of the two players' best payoffs so far.

After searching over the first two paths

- Player X occupies 2; O occupies 3; X occupies 9; payoff to X is 0 and payoff to O is 0;
- Player X occupies 2; O occupies 9; X occupies 3; payoff to X is 1 and payoff to O is -1;

Player X knows that the outcome of placing a piece in cell 2 is a tie since Player O will respond by placing a piece in cell 3. So we record alpha=0 and beta=0.

Next, player X starts to search for what happens if she places a piece in cell 3 instead. If she were to do that, Player O could place a piece in cell 2 and win. Therefore, after searching over the third path, which is

- Player X occupies 3; O occupies 2; payoff to X is -1 and payoff to O is 1;

we update the value of beta to 1. At this point, since $alpha > -beta$ (alpha is 0 and beta is 1), we don't need to spend time on the fourth scenario. Intuitively, if Player X were to place a piece in cell 3, she doesn't have to consider what would happen if Player O responds by placing a piece in cell 9. Why? Because Player O always chooses moves to maximize Player O's payoff. Choosing cell 2 over cell 9 is in the best interest of Player O.

Similarly, when Player X starts to search for what happens if she places a piece in cell 9 instead, after searching over the fifth path

- Player X occupies 9; O occupies 2; payoff to X is -1 and payoff to O is 1;

we update the value of beta to 1. At this point, since $alpha > -beta$ (or equivalently, $beta > -alpha$), we don't need to spend time on the sixth scenario.

In summary, with alpha-beta pruning, Player X only needs to search for four different branches to come up with the best next move, which is also cell 2.

6.1.3 Math Behind Alpha-Beta Pruning

If we use the payoff to the first player to denote the game outcome, then the first player tries to maximize the game outcome while the second player tries to minimize the game outcome. Hence the name MiniMax tree search.

In the example above, the game outcome as denoted by the payoff to the first player (player X) is as follows:

- Player X occupies 2; O occupies 3; X occupies 9; game outcome is 0;
- Player X occupies 2; O occupies 9; X occupies 3; game outcome is 1;
- Player X occupies 3; O occupies 2; game outcome is -1;
- Player X occupies 3; O occupies 9; X occupies 2; game outcome is 1;
- Player X occupies 9; O occupies 2; game outcome is -1;
- Player X occupies 9; O occupies 3; X occupies 2; game outcome is 0;

Therefore, the MiniMax algorithm comes up with the following solution:

```
Outcome = max{min{0,1},min{-1,1},min{-1,0}}
```

which leads to

```
Outcome = max{0,-1,-1}=0
```

If we use alpha-beta pruning, we can ignore path 4 and path 6, which leads to

```
Outcome = max{min{0,1},min{-1,path4},min{-1,path6}}
```

Since min{-1,path4} cannot be greater than -1, while min{0,1}=0. The game outcome will be 0 no matter what the outcomes from path 4 and path 6 are. That is, we know for sure that

```
Outcome = max{min{0,1},min{-1,path4},min{-1,path6}}=0
```

without knowing the exact values of path4 and path6.

6.2   ALPHA-BETA PRUNING IN TIC TAC TOE

In Chapter 5, you have seen that it took the MiniMax agent 35 seconds to make the first move in Tic Tac Toe. In this section, you'll learn to create a MiniMax agent with alpha-beta pruning and achieve the same results but less time.

We'll modify the functions we used in Chapter 5 for the Tic Tac Toe MiniMax agent to incorporate the idea of alpha-beta pruning.

6.2.1 The maximized_payoff_ttt() Function

We'll define a *maximized_payoff_ttt()* function. The function is similar to the *maximized_payoff()* function we defined in Chapter 5. However, there are two important differences. First, the function keeps track of the best outcomes so far for Players X and O and calls them alpha and beta, respectively. Second, whenever the condition

$alpha > -beta$ (or equivalently $beta > -alpha$) is met, the algorithm stops searching the current branch.

Download the file *ch06util.py* from the book's GitHub repository. The *maximized_payoff_ttt()* function is defined in the file as follows:

```
[1]: def maximized_payoff_ttt(env,reward,done,alpha,beta):
         # if game ended after previous player's move
         if done:
             # if it's not a tie
             if reward!=0:
                 return 1
             else:
                 return 0
         # set initial alpha and beta to -2
         if alpha==None:
             alpha=-2
         if beta==None:
             beta=-2
         if env.turn=="X":
             best_payoff = alpha
         if env.turn=="O":
             best_payoff = beta
         # iterate through all possible moves
         for m in env.validinputs:
             env_copy=deepcopy(env)
             state,reward,done,info=env_copy.step(m)
             # If I make this move, what's the opponent's response?
             opponent_payoff=maximized_payoff_ttt(env_copy,\
                                      reward,done,alpha,beta)
             # Opponent's payoff is the opposite of your payoff
             my_payoff=-opponent_payoff
             if my_payoff > best_payoff:
                 best_payoff = my_payoff
                 if env.turn=="X":
                     alpha=best_payoff
                 if env.turn=="O":
                     beta=best_payoff
                 # skip the rest of the branch
                 if alpha>=-beta:
                     break
         return best_payoff
```

If the game has ended after the previous player's move, the function calculates the payoff to the current player based on the game outcome. Otherwise, the player searches for the best action by iterating through all possible next moves. We use the *maximized_payoff_ttt()* function inside the function itself. This creates an infinite loop. The function keeps on searching to the next stage until the game ends. The process exhausts all game scenarios in Tic Tac Toe, except that we skip branches that won't affect game outcomes.

The function *maximized_payoff_ttt()* applies to both Player X and Player O. Next, we'll use this function to design game strategies.

6.2.2 The MiniMax_ab() Function

We define a *MiniMax_ab()* function to produce the best move for the MiniMax agent. Instead of using one function for Player X and one for Player O, we create one function for both players.

The *MiniMax_ab()* function is defined as follows. It's saved in the file *ch06util.py* that you just downloaded.

```
[2]: def MiniMax_ab(env):
         wins=[]
         ties=[]
         losses=[]
         # iterate through all possible next moves
         for m in env.validinputs:
             # make a hypothetical move and see what happens
             env_copy=deepcopy(env)
             state,reward,done,info=env_copy.step(m)
             # If player X wins right away with move m, take it.
             if done and reward!=0:
                 return m
             # See what's the best response from the opponent
             opponent_payoff=maximized_payoff_ttt(env_copy,\
                                    reward,done,-2,-2)
             # Opponent's payoff is the opposite of your payoff
             my_payoff=-opponent_payoff
             if my_payoff==1:
                 wins.append(m)
             elif my_payoff==0:
                 ties.append(m)
             else:
                 losses.append(m)
         # pick winning moves if there is any
         if len(wins)>0:
             return choice(wins)
         # otherwise pick tying moves
         elif len(ties)>0:
             return choice(ties)
         return env.sample()
```

The *MiniMax_ab()* function takes just one argument: env, which is the current game environment. It's similar to the *MiniMax_X()* or *MiniMax_O()* function we defined in Chapter 5, with the exception that when the agent tries to figure out the opponent's payoff, the function *maximized_payoff_ttt()* is used.

6.2.3 Time Saved by Alpha-Beta Pruning

Next, we test the speed of the alpha-beta-pruned MiniMax agent. We let the agent move first and measure how long it takes for the agent to come up with a move.

[3]:
```python
from utils.ch06util import MiniMax_ab
from utils.ttt_simple_env import ttt
import time

# Initiate the game environment
env=ttt()
state=env.reset()
# Play a full game manually
while True:
    # Mesure how long it takes to come up with a move
    start=time.time()
    action=MiniMax_ab(env)
    end=time.time()
    print(f"Player X has chosen action={action}")
    print(f"It took the agent {end-start} seconds")
    state, reward, done, info = env.step(action)
    print(f"Current state is \n{state.reshape(3,3)[::-1]}")
    if done:
        if reward==1:
            print(f"Player X has won!")
        else:
            print("Game over, it's a tie!")
        break
    action = input("Player O, what's your move?\n")
    print(f"Player O has chosen action={action}")
    state, reward, done, info = env.step(int(action))
    print(f"Current state is \n{state.reshape(3,3)[::-1]}")
    if done:
        print(f"Player O has won!")
        break
```

```
Player X has chosen action=1
It took the agent 1.0604541301727295 seconds
Current state is
[[0 0 0]
 [0 0 0]
```

```
 [1 0 0]]
Player O, what's your move?
9
Player O has chosen action=9
Current state is
[[ 0  0 -1]
 [ 0  0  0]
 [ 1  0  0]]
Player X has chosen action=7
It took the agent 0.06767606735229492 seconds
Current state is
[[ 1  0 -1]
 [ 0  0  0]
 [ 1  0  0]]
Player O, what's your move?
4
Player O has chosen action=4
Current state is
[[ 1  0 -1]
 [-1  0  0]
 [ 1  0  0]]
Player X has chosen action=3
It took the agent 0.006998538970947266 seconds
Current state is
[[ 1  0 -1]
 [-1  0  0]
 [ 1  0  1]]
Player O, what's your move?
5
Player O has chosen action=5
Current state is
[[ 1  0 -1]
 [-1 -1  0]
 [ 1  0  1]]
Player X has chosen action=2
It took the agent 0.0 seconds
Current state is
[[ 1  0 -1]
 [-1 -1  0]
 [ 1  1  1]]
Player X has won!
```

It took only 1.06 seconds for the MiniMax agent to make the first move, instead of
35 seconds when alpha-beta pruning was not used. That's a huge improvement on
the efficiency of the algorithm without affecting the effectiveness of the agent.

6.3 TEST MINIMAX WITH ALPHA-BETA PRUNING

Next, we'll make sure that the MiniMax algorithm with alpha-beta pruning is equally intelligent as the MiniMax algorithm without pruning.

Below, we play ten games between the two algorithms. We let the MiniMax agent with alpha-beta pruning move first in five games and let it move second in the other five games so no player has a first-mover advantage, like so:

```
[4]: from utils.ch05util import MiniMax_X,MiniMax_O
     from utils.ch02util import one_ttt_game

     results=[]
     for i in range(10):
         # MiniMax with pruning moves first if i is an even number
         if i%2==0:
             result=one_ttt_game(MiniMax_ab,MiniMax_O)
             # record game outcome
             results.append(result)
         # MiniMax with pruning moves second if i is an odd number
         else:
             result=one_ttt_game(MiniMax_X,MiniMax_ab)
             # record negative game outcome
             results.append(-result)
```

We now count how many times the MiniMax agent with alpha-beta pruning has won and lost.

```
[5]: # count how many times MiniMax with pruning won
     wins=results.count(1)
     print(f"MiniMax with pruning won {wins} games")
     # count how many times MiniMax with pruning lost
     losses=results.count(-1)
     print(f"MiniMax with pruning lost {losses} games")
     # count tie games
     ties=results.count(0)
     print(f"the game was tied {ties} times")
```

```
MiniMax with pruning won 0 games
MiniMax with pruning lost 0 games
the game was tied 10 times
```

The above results show that all ten games are tied. This indicates that the MiniMax agent with alpha-beta pruning is as intelligent as the MiniMax agent without pruning.

6.4 ALPHA-BETA PRUNING IN CONNECT FOUR

In Connect Four, even with alpha-beta pruning, it still takes forever for the MiniMax agent to make a move if we don't use depth pruning. We therefore combine alpha-beta pruning with depth pruning to make the game faster.

As in Chapter 5, we'll keep the default depth to 3 so that we can compare the speed with and without alpha-beta pruning.

6.4.1 Add Alpha-Beta Pruning in Connect Four

We first create a couple of functions in the local module *ch06util*. The function *max_payoff_conn()*, defined below, is similar to the *max_payoff()* function we defined in Chapter 5, except that there are two more arguments in *max_payoff_conn()*: alpha and beta.

```
[6]: def max_payoff_conn(env,reward,done,depth,alpha,beta):
         # if the game has ended after the previous player's move
         if done:
             # if it's not a tie
             if reward!=0:
                 return -1
             else:
                 return 0
         # If the maximum depth is reached, assume tie game
         if depth==0:
             return 0
         if alpha==None:
             alpha=-2
         if beta==None:
             beta=-2
         if env.turn=="red":
             best_payoff = alpha
         if env.turn=="yellow":
             best_payoff = beta
         # iterate through all possible moves
         for m in env.validinputs:
             env_copy=deepcopy(env)
             state,reward,done,info=env_copy.step(m)
             # If I make this move, what's the opponent's response?
             opponent_payoff=max_payoff_conn(env_copy,\
                             reward,done,depth-1,alpha,beta)
             # Opponent's payoff is the opposite of your payoff
             my_payoff=-opponent_payoff
             if my_payoff > best_payoff:
```

```
            best_payoff = my_payoff
            if env.turn=="red":
                alpha=best_payoff
            if env.turn=="yellow":
                beta=best_payoff
        # Skip the rest of the branch
        if alpha>=-beta:
            break
    return best_payoff
```

The function *max_payoff_conn()* uses both depth pruning and alpha-beta pruning. It's a combination of the function *max_payoff_ttt()* we defined above and the *max_payoff()* function we defined in Chapter 5. The function *max_payoff_ttt()* uses alpha-beta pruning but not depth pruning. The *max_payoff()* function uses depth pruning but not alpha-beta pruning.

In the local module *ch06util*, we also define the function *MiniMax_conn()*, as follows:

```
[7]:  def MiniMax_conn(env,depth=3):
          wins=[]
          ties=[]
          losses=[]
          # iterate through all possible next moves
          for m in env.validinputs:
              # make a hypothetical move and see what happens
              env_copy=deepcopy(env)
              state,reward,done,info=env_copy.step(m)
              # If player X wins right away with move m, take it.
              if done and reward!=0:
                  return m
              # See what's the best response from the opponent
              opponent_payoff=max_payoff_conn(env_copy,\
                              reward,done,depth,-2,-2)
              # Opponent's payoff is the opposite of your payoff
              my_payoff=-opponent_payoff
              if my_payoff==1:
                  wins.append(m)
              elif my_payoff==0:
                  ties.append(m)
              else:
                  losses.append(m)
          # pick winning moves if there is any
          if len(wins)>0:
              return choice(wins)
          # otherwise pick tying moves
```

```
    elif len(ties)>0:
        return choice(ties)
    return env.sample()
```

The function *MiniMax_conn()* is similar to the function *MiniMax_depth()* we defined in Chapter 5. However, we added alpha-beta pruning in addition to the depth pruning. The default depth is 3, but you have the option to change the depth argument to another value.

6.4.2   Time Saved Due to Alpha-Beta Pruning in Connect Four

Next, you'll play a game against the Connect Four MiniMax agent with both depth pruning and alpha-beta pruning by entering moves through the keyboard. We let the MiniMax agent move first and measure how long it takes for the agent to come up with a move.

```
[8]:  from utils.ch06util import MiniMax_conn
      from utils.conn_env import conn
      import time

      # Initiate the game environment
      env=conn()
      state=env.reset()
      # Play a full game manually
      while True:
          # Mesure how long it takes to come up with a move
          start=time.time()
          action=MiniMax_conn(env,depth=3)
          end=time.time()
          print(f"The red player has chosen action={action}")
          print(f"It took the agent {end-start} seconds")
          state, reward, done, info = env.step(action)
          print(f"Current state is \n{state.T[::-1]}")
          if done:
              if reward==1:
                  print(f"The red player has won!")
              else:
                  print("Game over, it's a tie!")
              break
          action=input("Player yellow, what's your move?\n")
          print(f"Player yellow has chosen action={action}")
          state, reward, done, info = env.step(int(action))
          print(f"Current state is \n{state.T[::-1]}")
          if done:
              if reward==-1:
                  print(f"The yellow player has won!")
```

```
        else:
            print("Game over, it's a tie!")
        break
```

The red player has chosen action=6
It took the agent 0.034066200256347656 seconds
Current state is
[[0 0 0 0 0 0 0]
 [0 0 0 0 0 0 0]
 [0 0 0 0 0 0 0]
 [0 0 0 0 0 0 0]
 [0 0 0 0 0 0 0]
 [0 0 0 0 0 1 0]]
Player yellow, what's your move?
1
Player yellow has chosen action=1
Current state is
[[0 0 0 0 0 0 0]
 [0 0 0 0 0 0 0]
 [0 0 0 0 0 0 0]
 [0 0 0 0 0 0 0]
 [0 0 0 0 0 0 0]
 [-1 0 0 0 0 1 0]]
The red player has chosen action=1
It took the agent 0.03681349754333496 seconds
Current state is
[[0 0 0 0 0 0 0]
 [0 0 0 0 0 0 0]
 [0 0 0 0 0 0 0]
 [0 0 0 0 0 0 0]
 [1 0 0 0 0 0 0]
 [-1 0 0 0 0 1 0]]
Player yellow, what's your move?
2
Player yellow has chosen action=2
Current state is
[[0 0 0 0 0 0 0]
 [0 0 0 0 0 0 0]
 [0 0 0 0 0 0 0]
 [0 0 0 0 0 0 0]
 [1 0 0 0 0 0 0]
 [-1 -1 0 0 0 1 0]]
The red player has chosen action=5
It took the agent 0.047269582748413086 seconds
Current state is
[[0 0 0 0 0 0 0]
```
```

```
[ 0  0  0  0  0  0  0]
[ 0  0  0  0  0  0  0]
[ 0  0  0  0  0  0  0]
[ 1  0  0  0  0  0  0]
[-1 -1  0  0  1  1  0]]
Player yellow, what's your move?
1
Player yellow has chosen action=1
Current state is
[[ 0  0  0  0  0  0  0]
 [ 0  0  0  0  0  0  0]
 [ 0  0  0  0  0  0  0]
 [-1  0  0  0  0  0  0]
 [ 1  0  0  0  0  0  0]
 [-1 -1  0  0  1  1  0]]
The red player has chosen action=4
It took the agent 0.049561500549316406 seconds
Current state is
[[ 0  0  0  0  0  0  0]
 [ 0  0  0  0  0  0  0]
 [ 0  0  0  0  0  0  0]
 [-1  0  0  0  0  0  0]
 [ 1  0  0  0  0  0  0]
 [-1 -1  0  1  1  1  0]]
Player yellow, what's your move?
3
Player yellow has chosen action=3
Current state is
[[ 0  0  0  0  0  0  0]
 [ 0  0  0  0  0  0  0]
 [ 0  0  0  0  0  0  0]
 [-1  0  0  0  0  0  0]
 [ 1  0  0  0  0  0  0]
 [-1 -1 -1  1  1  1  0]]
The red player has chosen action=7
It took the agent 0.05922341346740723 seconds
Current state is
[[ 0  0  0  0  0  0  0]
 [ 0  0  0  0  0  0  0]
 [ 0  0  0  0  0  0  0]
 [-1  0  0  0  0  0  0]
 [ 1  0  0  0  0  0  0]
 [-1 -1 -1  1  1  1  1]]
The red player has won!
```

The above results show that it took about 0.05 seconds for the agent to come up with a move. This is about 1/3 of the time the agent spent (about 0.15 seconds) in Chapter 5 when only depth pruning is used.

6.4.3 Effectiveness of Alpha-Beta Pruning in Connect Four

We'll test if the MiniMax algorithm with alpha-beta pruning is as effective as the one without alpha-beta pruning in Connect Four.

```
[9]: from utils.ch05util import MiniMax_depth
     from utils.ch03util import one_conn_game

     results=[]
     for i in range(100):
         # MiniMax with pruning moves first if i is even
         if i%2==0:
             result=one_conn_game(MiniMax_conn,MiniMax_depth)
             # record game outcome
             results.append(result)
         # MiniMax with pruning moves second if i is odd
         else:
             result=one_conn_game(MiniMax_depth,MiniMax_conn)
             # record negative game outcome
             results.append(-result)
```

We create a list *results* to store game outcomes. We simulate 100 games and half the time, the MiniMax agent with alpha-beta pruning moves first and the other half, the MiniMax agent without alpha-beta pruning moves first. This way, no player has a first-mover advantage and we have a fair assessment of the effectiveness of the two algorithms. Whenever the MiniMax agent with alpha-beta pruning moves second, we multiply the outcome by -1 so that a value of 1 in the list *results* indicates that the MiniMax agent with alpha-beta pruning has won.

```
[10]: # count how many times MiniMax with alpha-beta pruning won
      wins=results.count(1)
      print(f"MiniMax with alpha-beta pruning won {wins} games")
      # count how many times MiniMax with pruning lost
      losses=results.count(-1)
      print(f"MiniMax with alpha-beta pruning lost {losses} games")
      # count tie games
      ties=results.count(0)
      print(f"the game was tied {ties} times")
```

```
MiniMax with alpha-beta pruning won 41 games
MiniMax with alpha-beta pruning lost 39 games
the game was tied 20 times
```

The above results show that the MiniMax agent with alpha-beta pruning has won 41 games and lost 39 games. This shows that the MiniMax agent with alpha-beta pruning is as intelligent as the agent without alpha-beta pruning. Note here that since the outcomes are random, you may get results showing that the MiniMax agent with alpha-beta pruning has lost more often than it has won. If that happens, rerun the above two cells and see if the results change.

6.5 GLOSSARY

- **Alpha-Beta Pruning:** A search algorithm that seeks to skip searching certain tree branches that won't affect the game outcome in order to speed up the search process.

6.6 EXERCISES

6.1 Rerun the first cell in Section 6.2.3 and enter moves with your keyboard to play against the MiniMax agent with alpha-beta pruning. Try your best to win and see if you can beat the agent. See how long it takes for the agent to come up with a move on your computer.

6.2 Rerun the two code cells in Section 6.3 to see the game outcomes when the MiniMax agent with alpha-beta pruning plays against the MiniMax agent without alpha-beta pruning in Tic Tac Toe.

6.3 Rerun the first cell in Section 6.4.2 to play against the MiniMax agent with alpha-beta pruning in Connect Four. See how long it takes for the agent to come up with a move on your computer.

6.4 Rerun the two code cells in Section 6.4.3 to see the game outcomes when the MiniMax agent with alpha-beta pruning plays against the MiniMax agent without alpha-beta pruning in Connect Four.

## CHAPTER 7

Position Evaluation in MiniMax

"Part of the improvement between '96 and '97 is we detected more patterns in a chess position and could put values on them and therefore evaluate chess positions more accurately."

– Murray Campbell, Deep Blue team member

THE IBM CHESS engine Deep Blue had two matches with then-world Chess champion Garry Kasparov. In the first match, which was held in Philadelphia in 1996, Deep Blue lost to Kasparov. In the second match in New York City in 1997, Deep Blue defeated Kasparov. What changed, you may wonder? According to Murray Campbell, the team member who programmed Deep Blue's evaluation function, the Chess engine had a more accurate evaluation function in 1997 compared to in 1996 [4].

With depth pruning and alpha-beta pruning to reduce the time it needs to make a move, the MiniMax algorithm can produce fairly powerful agents with advancements in computing hardware. For example, "the 1997 version of Deep Blue searched between 100 million and 200 million positions per second, depending on the type of position. The system could search to a depth of between six and eight pairs of moves—one white, one black—to a maximum of 20 or even more pairs in some situations." According to an article in Scientific America by Larry Greenemeier in 2017 [4].

What made Deep Blue even more powerful was the position evaluation function it used. In Chapter 6, we assume that the game is tied if the number of depth is reached and the game is not over. In many real-world games, however, even when the game is not over, we usually have a good estimate of the outcome of the game based on heuristics. For example, in Chess, we can count the value of each game piece. Whichever side has a higher value of pieces tends to win.

DOI: 10.1201/9781032722207-7

In this chapter, we introduce the concept of the position evaluation function and apply it to the Connect Four game. We show that our evaluation function makes the MiniMax agent much stronger. Specifically, you'll use an evaluation function that we'll develop in Chapter 15: the function takes a game board as the input, and returns an evaluation between -1 and 1. An evaluation of -1 means that the current player will lose for sure, while an evaluation of 1 means that the current player will win for sure. An evaluation of 0 means the game is most likely to be tied.

You'll first use the evaluation function to design a game strategy: an agent armed with this evaluation function will make hypothetical moves and evaluate each future game state. The agent will then select the next move that leads to the highest evaluation of the future game state. We show that the agent beats random moves 97 percent of the time. We then augment the MiniMax algorithm with the position evaluation function. We'll use the evaluation function to evaluate the future game state when the number of depth is reached and the game is not over. The evaluation function provides a more accurate assessment of the game state, hence allowing the MiniMax agent to make more intelligent moves. We show that the augmented MiniMax agent beats the earlier version of the MiniMax agent without position evaluation in seven out of ten games.

We'll also use the concept of position evaluation extensively in later chapters of this book. For example, AlphaGo trained two deep neural networks when designing its game strategies: a policy network and a value network. The value network was used to assess the strength of a board position in game rollouts, and this, in turn, helps AlphaGo select the best next move.

What You'll Learn in This Chapter

- What is a position evaluation function
- Designing a game strategy using an evaluation function in Connect Four
- Adding a position evaluation function to MiniMax with depth pruning
- Assessing the effectiveness of MiniMax augmented by an evaluation function

---

7.1 WHAT ARE POSITION EVALUATION FUNCTIONS?

Position evaluation functions estimate the likelihood of the game outcome. We normalize it to a range between -1 and 1, where -1 means the current player will lose for sure, and 1 means the current player will win for sure. A value of 0 indicates that the game is most likely to be tied. A value of 0.5, for example, indicates that the current player is likely to win but not with certainty.

In this section, you'll use a neural network that we'll develop in Chapter 15 as the position evaluation function. We'll use it to design a game strategy to play against random moves.

7.1.1   A Model to Predict Outcome in Connect Four

We'll add a position evaluation function to the MiniMax algorithm with depth pruning in Connect Four to show how it works. The position evaluation function we use
is generated by a deep neural network in Chapter 15. For now, all you need to know
is that it takes a game board (a matrix with 42 values of −1s, 1s, and 0s) as the
input and generates a value between −1 and 1. The value tells who is likely to win:
−1 means the current player will lose for sure; 0 means it's likely to be a tie game; 1
means the current player will win for sure.

Download the file *value_conn.h5* from the book's GitHub page and save it in the
folder /Desktop/ags/files/ on your computer. Since we need the TensorFlow library
to load the neural network and make predictions, you should install the library by
running the following line of command in a code cell:

```
[1]: !pip install tensorflow
```

After that, load the model using the TensorFlow library as follows:

```
[2]: import tensorflow as tf

model=tf.keras.models.load_model('files/value_conn.h5')
```

If you feed a game board to the model, the output has three numbers in it: the
probability of tying the game, the probability that the current player wins, and the
probability that the opponent wins. Download the file *ch07util.py* from the book's
GitHub repository and place it in the folder /Desktop/ags/utils/ on your computer.
In it, we have defined a *prediction_eval()* function to generate an evaluation of the
game state:

```
def position_eval(env,model):
    # obtain the current state, reshape it
    state=env.state.reshape(-1,7,6,1)
    pred=model.predict(state,verbose=0)
    # prob(current player wins)-prob(opponent wins)
    evaluation=pred[0][1]-pred[0][2]
    return evaluation
```

We obtain the current state of the game and reshape it to a 7 by 6 two-dimensional
game board and feed it to the model. The model has a convolutional layer in it
(which we'll explain later in this book; it treats a game board as a 2D image). Note
the evaluation is from Player 1's point of view. Later, if the current player is Player
2, we'll multiply the position evaluation by −1.

We then feed the game board to the trained model from Chapter 15. The value of
the position is the difference between the probability that Player 1 wins and the
probability that Player 2 wins. Since probabilities are in the range of 0 and 1, our
evaluation ranges from −1 to 1.

What Is A Position Evaluation Function?

A position evaluation function takes in the current game state, and outputs a number between −1 and 1 as the evaluation of the game state. The higher the value, the better the game state hence the greater chance for the current player to win. Here we use a trained deep neural from Chapter 15 to evaluate a game state. We'll explain in detail in Chapter 15 how you should construct and train the neural network. For the moment, all you need to know is that if you feed a game state to the above trained neural network, it returns three numbers: the probability of a tie game, the probability that Player 1 wins, and the probability that Player 2 wins. The evaluation of a game state is the difference between the two probabilities.

We can design game strategies based on the above *prediction_eval()* function, which you'll see in the next subsection.

7.1.2 A Game Strategy Based on the Position Evaluation Function

To have a better understanding of the position evaluation function, we can play a Connect Four game based on its evaluations of different game states.

Specifically, we'll make a hypothetical move and ask the position evaluation function to tell us the value of the hypothetical game state after the move. We then select the next move that leads to the highest value of the future game state. For that purpose, we define the following *eval_move()* function:

```
[3]:  from copy import deepcopy
      from utils.ch07util import position_eval

      def eval_move(env,model):
          # create a dictionary to hold all values
          values={}
          # iteratre through all possible next moves
          for m in env.validinputs:
              # make a hypothetical move
              env_copy=deepcopy(env)
              s,r,d,_=env_copy.step(m)
              # evaluate the hypothetical game state
              value=position_eval(env_copy,model)
              # add value to the dictionary
              if env.turn=="red":
                  values[m]=round(value,5)
              # multiply value by -1 for yellow
              else:
```

```
            values[m]=round(-value,5)
    # choose the move with the highest evaluation
    action = max(values,key=values.get)
    return action, values
```

The *eval_move()* function evaluates a hypothetical future game state after each possible next move. It returns the best next move as well as the evaluations of all possible next moves so that we can better understand the decision-making process of the strategy.

Note here that if it's the yellow player's turn, we need to multiply the evaluation by −1 so that it reflects the fact that the game board has the yellow player's game pieces coded as −1 instead of 1. Again, if this sounds confusing, don't worry and we'll explain in detail in Chapter 15.

For convenience, let's call the player who uses the strategy recommended by the function *eval_move()* the evaluation agent.

Below, we let the evaluation agent play against humans and see how the evaluation agent selects moves step by step:

```
[4]: from utils.conn_simple_env import conn

env=conn()
state=env.reset()
print(f"the current state is \n{state.T[::-1]}")
while True:
    action, values=eval_move(env,model)
    print(f"evaluations of future moves are\n{values}")
    print(f"the red player chose column {action}")
    state, reward, done, info=env.step(action)
    if done:
        print(f"the current state is \n{state.T[::-1]}")
        print("the red player won")
        break
    # the opponent chooses random moves
    action=int(input("what's your move?"))
    print(f"the yellow player chose column {action}")
    state, reward, done, info=env.step(action)
    print(f"the current state is \n{state.T[::-1]}")
    if done:
        if reward==-1:
            print("the yellow player won")
        else:
            print("game over, it's a tie")
        break
```

```
the current state is
[[0 0 0 0 0 0 0]
 [0 0 0 0 0 0 0]
 [0 0 0 0 0 0 0]
 [0 0 0 0 0 0 0]
 [0 0 0 0 0 0 0]
 [0 0 0 0 0 0 0]]
evaluations of future moves are
{1: 0.57383, 2: 0.58247, 3: 0.52876, 4: 0.86937, 5: 0.7459,
6: 0.12794, 7: 0.09338}
the red player chose column 4
what's your move?4
the yellow player chose column 4
the current state is
[[ 0  0  0  0  0  0  0]
 [ 0  0  0  0  0  0  0]
 [ 0  0  0  0  0  0  0]
 [ 0  0  0  0  0  0  0]
 [ 0  0  0 -1  0  0  0]
 [ 0  0  0  1  0  0  0]]
evaluations of future moves are
{1: 0.92464, 2: 0.96153, 3: 0.97883, 4: 0.94346, 5: 0.98155,
6: 0.96366, 7: 0.94616}
the red player chose column 5
what's your move?4
the yellow player chose column 4
the current state is
[[ 0  0  0  0  0  0  0]
 [ 0  0  0  0  0  0  0]
 [ 0  0  0  0  0  0  0]
 [ 0  0  0 -1  0  0  0]
 [ 0  0  0 -1  0  0  0]
 [ 0  0  0  1  1  0  0]]
evaluations of future moves are
{1: 0.91422, 2: 0.9949, 3: 0.99994, 4: 0.95631, 5: 0.97798,
6: 0.99123, 7: 0.97749}
the red player chose column 3
what's your move?2
the yellow player chose column 2
the current state is
[[ 0  0  0  0  0  0  0]
 [ 0  0  0  0  0  0  0]
 [ 0  0  0  0  0  0  0]
 [ 0  0  0 -1  0  0  0]
 [ 0  0  0 -1  0  0  0]
```

```
[ 0 -1  1  1  1  0  0]]
evaluations of future moves are
{1: 0.99909, 2: 0.99899, 3: 0.99689, 4: 0.99205, 5: 0.99792,
6: 1.0, 7: 0.99976}
the red player chose column 6
the current state is
[[ 0  0  0  0  0  0  0]
 [ 0  0  0  0  0  0  0]
 [ 0  0  0  0  0  0  0]
 [ 0  0  0 -1  0  0  0]
 [ 0  0  0 -1  0  0  0]
 [ 0 -1  1  1  1  1  0]]
the red player won
```

At each step, the evaluation agent calculates the values of each future hypothetical game state. It then selects the move that leads to the highest evaluation of the hypothetical future game state. For example, to determine what's the best first move, the agent calculates the values of future game states associated with the seven moves as {1: 0.57383, 2: 0.58247, 3: 0.52876, 4: 0.86937, 5: 0.7459, 6: 0.12794, 7: 0.09338}. Choosing column 4 leads to the highest value (0.86937), therefore, the agent selects 4 as its first move.

The evaluation agent seems to have a very accurate assessment of the values of future game states. When I created a chance for the agent to win, it took the chance and won the game.

Next, we'll let the evaluation agent play against random moves for 100 games and see what the outcomes are.

7.1.3   The Position Evaluation Function versus Random Moves

To have a better understanding of how accurate the position evaluation function is, we simulate 100 games, in which the evaluation agent plays against random moves, as follows:

```
[5]: results=[]
     for i in range(100):
         env=conn()
         state=env.reset()
         if i%2==0:
             action=env.sample()
             state, reward, done, info=env.step(action)
         while True:
             action, values=eval_move(env,model)
             state, reward, done, info=env.step(action)
             if done:
```

```
                results.append(abs(reward))
                break
        action=env.sample()
        state, reward, done, info=env.step(action)
        if done:
                results.append(-abs(reward))
                break
```

We create a list *results* to store game outcomes. We simulate 100 games and half the time, the evaluation agent moves first and the other half, the opponent moves first. This way, no player has a first-mover advantage and we have a fair assessment of the intelligence of the evaluation agent. Whenever the evaluation agent wins, we record a value of 1 in the list *results*. A value of 0 indicates a tie game and a value of −1 in the list *results* indicates that the evaluation agent has lost.

We can count the game outcomes as follows:

[6]:
```
# count how many times the evaluation agent won
wins=results.count(1)
print(f"the evaluation agent won {wins} games")
# count how many times the evaluation agent lost
losses=results.count(-1)
print(f"the evaluation agent lost {losses} games")
# count tie games
ties=results.count(0)
print(f"the game was tied {ties} times")
```

```
the evaluation agent won 97 games
the evaluation agent lost 3 games
the game was tied 0 times
```

The results above show that the evaluation agent is much more intelligent than random moves, winning 97 of the 100 games. This shows that our position evaluation function is fairly accurate (though not perfect).

Next, we'll add a position evaluation function in the MiniMax algorithm with depth pruning in Connect Four.

7.2   MINIMAX WITH POSITION EVALUATION IN CONNECT FOUR

In this section, we'll modify the MiniMax tree search algorithm we used in Chapter 6. Specifically, in the Connect Four game, whenever the agent searches to a certain depth, and if the game has not ended, we'll use the position evaluation function to evaluate the game state, instead of assuming the game is tied. Specifically, we'll use the *position_eval()* function we defined in the local module *ch07util* to evaluate the game state during MiniMax tree search.

Adding the evaluation function to the MiniMax algorithm with depth pruning and alpha-beta pruning in Connect Four will make the algorithm more powerful. The evaluation function provides a more accurate valuation of the game state, instead of assuming the valuation is zero if the game has not ended.

We'll modify the MiniMax algorithm with alpha-beta pruning and depth pruning from Chapter 6. The difference is that once the algorithm reaches a depth of 0, it evaluates the position based on the position evaluation functions we defined in the file *ch07util.py*.

7.2.1 The eval_payoff_conn() Function

We'll define an *eval_payoff_conn()* function in the local module. The function keeps track of the best outcomes so far for the red and yellow players and calls them alpha and beta, respectively. Whenever the condition $alpha > -beta$ or $beta > -alpha$ is met, the algorithm stops searching the current branch. That is, we use alpha-beta pruning here. Second, there is a depth argument in the function and if the depth reaches 0, the function uses the position evaluation function to assess the game board.

The *eval_payoff_conn()* function is defined as follows. It's saved in the file *h07util.py* that you just downloaded.

```
def eval_payoff_conn(env,model,reward,done,depth,alpha,beta):
    # if the game has ended after the previous player's move
    if done:
        # if it's not a tie
        if reward!=0:
            return -1
        else:
            return 0
    # If the maximum depth is reached, assume tie game
    if depth==0:
        if env.turn=="red":
            return position_eval(env,model)
        else:
            return -position_eval(env,model)
    if alpha==None:
        alpha=-2
    if beta==None:
        beta=-2
    if env.turn=="red":
        best_payoff = alpha
    if env.turn=="yellow":
        best_payoff = beta
    # iterate through all possible moves
    for m in env.validinputs:
        env_copy=deepcopy(env)
```

```
        state,reward,done,info=env_copy.step(m)
        # If I make this move, what's the opponent's response?
        opponent_payoff=eval_payoff_conn(env_copy,model,\
                        reward,done,depth-1,alpha,beta)
        # Opponent's payoff is the opposite of your payoff
        my_payoff=-opponent_payoff
        if my_payoff > best_payoff:
            best_payoff = my_payoff
            if env.turn=="red":
                alpha=best_payoff
            if env.turn=="yellow":
                beta=best_payoff
        if alpha>=-beta:
            break
    return best_payoff
```

Next, we'll design a MiniMax algorithm with the position evaluation function.

7.2.2   The MiniMax_conn_eval() Function

We also define a MiniMax_conn_eval() function to produce the best move for the MiniMax agent. The function is similar to the MiniMax_conn() function we used in Chapter 6. However, instead of assuming the game is tied once the search algorithm reaches a depth of 0, the function uses the position evaluation function to assess the game board.

The MiniMax_conn_eval() function is defined as follows. It's saved in the file *ch07util.py* that you just downloaded.

```
def MiniMax_conn_eval(env,model,depth=3):
    values={}
    # iterate through all possible next moves
    for m in env.validinputs:
        # make a hypothetical move and see what happens
        env_copy=deepcopy(env)
        state,reward,done,info=env_copy.step(m)
        # If current player wins with m, take it.
        if done and reward!=0:
            return m
        # See what's the best response from the opponent
        opponent_payoff=eval_payoff_conn(env_copy,\
                        model,reward,done,depth,-2,-2)
        # Opponent's payoff is the opposite of your payoff
        my_payoff=-opponent_payoff
        values[m]=my_payoff
    # pick the move with the highest value
```

```
    best_move=max(values,key=values.get)
    return best_move
```

With this, we have created a MiniMax algorithm with position evaluation.

7.3   TEST MINIMAX WITH POSITION EVALUATIONS IN CONNECT FOUR

In this section, we'll test the MiniMax agent augmented with the position evaluation function.

7.3.1   Play Against the Evaluation-Augmented MiniMax

Next, we manually test a game with the evaluation-augmented MiniMax agent. We let the MiniMax agent play first and the human player move second.

```
[7]:  from utils.ch07util import MiniMax_conn_eval

      # Initiate the game environment
      env=conn()
      state=env.reset()
      # Play a full game manually
      while True:
          action = MiniMax_conn_eval(env,model)
          state, reward, done, info = env.step(action)
          print(f"Current state is \n{state.T[::-1]}")
          if done:
              print("Player red won!")
              break
          action = int(input("What's your move, player yellow?"))
          print(f"Player yellow chose column {action}")
          state, reward, done, info = env.step(action)
          print(f"Current state is \n{state.T[::-1]}")
          if done:
              if reward==-1:
                  print("Player yellow won!")
              else:
                  print("Game over, it's a tie!")
              break
```

```
Current state is
[[0 0 0 0 0 0 0]
 [0 0 0 0 0 0 0]
 [0 0 0 0 0 0 0]
 [0 0 0 0 0 0 0]
 [0 0 0 0 0 0 0]
 [0 0 0 1 0 0 0]]
```

```
What's your move, player yellow?4
Player yellow chose column 4
Current state is
[[ 0   0   0   0   0   0   0]
 [ 0   0   0   0   0   0   0]
 [ 0   0   0   0   0   0   0]
 [ 0   0   0   0   0   0   0]
 [ 0   0   0  -1   0   0   0]
 [ 0   0   0   1   0   0   0]]
Current state is
[[ 0   0   0   0   0   0   0]
 [ 0   0   0   0   0   0   0]
 [ 0   0   0   0   0   0   0]
 [ 0   0   0   0   0   0   0]
 [ 0   0   0  -1   0   0   0]
 [ 0   0   1   1   0   0   0]]
What's your move, player yellow?4
Player yellow chose column 4
Current state is
[[ 0   0   0   0   0   0   0]
 [ 0   0   0   0   0   0   0]
 [ 0   0   0   0   0   0   0]
 [ 0   0   0  -1   0   0   0]
 [ 0   0   0  -1   0   0   0]
 [ 0   0   1   1   0   0   0]]
Current state is
[[ 0   0   0   0   0   0   0]
 [ 0   0   0   0   0   0   0]
 [ 0   0   0   0   0   0   0]
 [ 0   0   0  -1   0   0   0]
 [ 0   0   0  -1   0   0   0]
 [ 0   1   1   1   0   0   0]]
What's your move, player yellow?5
Player yellow chose column 5
Current state is
[[ 0   0   0   0   0   0   0]
 [ 0   0   0   0   0   0   0]
 [ 0   0   0   0   0   0   0]
 [ 0   0   0  -1   0   0   0]
 [ 0   0   0  -1   0   0   0]
 [ 0   1   1   1  -1   0   0]]
Current state is
[[ 0   0   0   0   0   0   0]
 [ 0   0   0   0   0   0   0]
 [ 0   0   0   0   0   0   0]
```

```
[ 0   0   0 -1   0   0   0]
[ 0   0   0 -1   0   0   0]
[ 1   1   1   1 -1   0   0]]
Player red won!
```

The agent has won. It takes longer for the agent to make a move, but the evaluation-augmented MiniMax agent is more sophisticated than the MiniMax agent we created in Chapter 6.

7.3.2 Effectiveness of MiniMax with Position Evaluations in Connect Four

Next, we test the performance improvements of the MiniMax agent due to the use of the position evaluation function. We play ten games. In five games, the MiniMax agent with position evaluation moves first. In the other five games, an earlier version of the MiniMax agent (who assumes that the game is tied when the depth reaches 0) moves first. This way, no agent has a first-mover advantage.

```
[8]:  from utils.ch06util import MiniMax_conn

      results=[]
      for i in range(10):
          state=env.reset()
          if i%2==0:
              action=MiniMax_conn(env,depth=3)
              state,reward,done,_=env.step(action)
          while True:
              action=MiniMax_conn_eval(env,model,depth=3)
              state,reward,done,_=env.step(action)
              if done:
                  results.append(abs(reward))
                  break
              action=MiniMax_conn(env,depth=3)
              state,reward,done,_=env.step(action)
              if done:
                  results.append(-abs(reward))
                  break
```

We create a list *results* to record game outcomes. If the MiniMax agent with position evaluation wins, we record a value of 1 in the list *results*. If the MiniMax agent with position evaluation loses, we record a value of −1 in the list *results*. If the game is tied, we record a value of 0.

Next, we count how many times the MiniMax agent with position evaluation has won and how many times the agent has lost.

```
[9]:  # count how many times MiniMax with evaluation won
      wins=results.count(1)
      print(f"MiniMax with evaluation won {wins} games")
      # count how many times MiniMax with evaluation lost
      losses=results.count(-1)
      print(f"MiniMax with evaluation lost {losses} games")
      # count tie games
      ties=results.count(0)
      print(f"the game is tied {ties} times")
```

```
MiniMax with evaluation won 7 games
MiniMax with evaluation lost 2 games
the game is tied 1 times
```

The above results show that the MiniMax agent with the evaluation function has won seven out of ten games against the MiniMax agent without position evaluation. This indicates that the evaluation function has greatly improved the effectiveness of the MiniMax algorithm.

7.4 GLOSSARY

- **Position Evaluation Function:** A function used by an algorithm to evaluate a game state in a game tree. Higher values mean better chances for the current player to win.

7.5 EXERCISES

7.1 Rerun the second code cell in Section 7.1.2 to play against the evaluation agent. Try your best to win and see if you can beat the evaluation agent.

7.2 Modify the two code cells in Section 7.3.2 so that the depth is 2 in both functions *MiniMax_conn()* and *MiniMax_conn_eval()*. See how often the evaluation-augmented MiniMax agent wins.

## CHAPTER 8

Monte Carlo Tree Search

"Instead, AlphaGo looks ahead by playing out the remainder of the game in its imagination, many times over - a technique known as Monte-Carlo tree search.
– David Silver and Demis Hassabis, Google DeepMind

SO FAR WE have covered one type of tree search: MiniMax tree search. In simple games such as Last Coin Standing or Tic Tac Toe, MiniMax agents solve the game and provide game strategies that are as good as any other intelligent game strategies. In complicated games such as Connect Four or Chess, the number of possibilities is too large and it's infeasible for the MiniMax agent to solve the game in a short amount of time. We therefore use depth pruning and alpha-beta pruning, combined with powerful position evaluation functions, to help MiniMax agents come up with intelligent moves in the allotted time. With such an approach, Deep Blue beat the world Chess champion Garry Kasparov in 1997.

While in games such as Chess, position evaluation functions are relatively accurate, in certain games such as Go, evaluating positions is more challenging. For example, in Chess, if white has an extra rook than black, it's difficult for the black to win or tie the game. We are fairly certain that white will win without following a game tree all the way to the end. In the game of Go, on the other hand, guessing who will eventually win in the mid-game based on board positions is not as simple. Counting the number of stones for each side can provide a clue, but this can change instantly if one side captures a large number of the opponent's stones.

Therefore, in the game of Go, researchers usually use another type of tree search: Monte Carlo Tree Search (MCTS). In depth-pruned MiniMax tree search, the agent searches all possible outcomes to a fixed number of moves ahead, this is sometimes called a *breadth-first approach*. In contrast, in MCTS, the agent simulates games all the way to the terminal state to see the game outcome. It doesn't cover all scenarios. MCTS, therefore, is a *depth-first approach*.

DOI: 10.1201/9781032722207-8

The idea behind MCTS is to roll out random games starting from the current game state and see what the average game outcome is. If you roll out, say 1000 games from this point, and Player 1 wins 99 percent of the time, you know that the current game state must favor Player 1 over Player 2. To select the best next move, the MCTS algorithm uses the Upper Confidence Bounds for Trees (UCT) method. We'll break down the process into four steps: selection, expansion, simulation, and backpropagation. You'll implement an MCTS algorithm that can be applied to the three games in this book: the coin game, Tic Tac Toe, and Connect Four.

As the opening quote of this chapter states, DeepMind uses MCTS to conduct tree search so that "AlphaGo looks ahead by playing out the remainder of the game in its imagination, many times over." [10] Combined with deep reinforcement learning (which you'll learn later in this book), MCTS led to the algorithm's great success. After learning the basics of MCTS in this Chapter, you'll be ready to integrate MCTS with other algorithms to create superhuman agents in various games, as you'll learn to do for the rest of the book.

What You'll Learn in This Chapter

- Monte Carlo Tree Search (MCTS) and Upper Confidence Bounds for Trees (UCT)
- Implementing a naive MCTS algorithm in the Coin game
- Breaking down the four steps in MCTS: select, expand, simulate, and back-propagate
- Designing a generic MCTS game strategy that can apply to the Coin game, Tic Tac Toe, and Connect Four

---

8.1 WHAT IS MONTE CARLO TREE SEARCH?

Monte Carlo Tree Search (MCTS) is a simulation method in AI to evaluate a game state by rolling out a large number of random games and see what the average outcome is.

To help us understand how MCTS works, we'll develop a naive MCTS game strategy and apply it to the coin game that we developed in Chapter 1.

8.1.1 A Thought Experiment

Imagine that you are playing the coin game against a naive MCTS agent, who uses a strategy we'll describe below. You move first and choose to take one coin from the pile. Let's code that in:

```
[1]: from utils.coin_simple_env import coin_game

     # Initiate the game environment
     env = coin_game()
     state=env.reset()
     print(f"the current state is {state}")
     # Player 1 takes one coin from the pile
     player1_move=1
     print(f"Player 1 has chosen action={player1_move}")
     state, reward, done, info = env.step(player1_move)
     print(f"the current state is {state}")
```

```
the current state is 21
Player 1 has chosen action=1
the current state is 20
```

The *coin_simple_env* is a simplified coin game environment. It's the same as the coin game environment we used in Chapter 1 except that we removed the graphical rendering functionality. We do this because, in MCTS, the agent makes deep copies of the game environment many times. Using a simplified game environment can greatly speed up the tree search process. The file *coin_simple_env.py* is in the folder /utils/ of the book's GitHub repository. Download the file and put it in /Desktop/ags/utils/ on your computer.

You have chosen action=1. This leaves 20 coins in the pile. Now the naive MCTS agent needs to make a move. The naive MCTS agent does the following analysis: I'll simulate 100,000 games from this point on. Sometimes I choose action=1 as my next move and other times I choose action=2 as my next move. I'll see which action leads to more wins for me and I'll pick that action as my next move.

To do that, the naive MCTS agent first creates three dictionaries, *counts*, *wins*, and *losses*, to record the total number of games, the number of wins, and the number of losses associated with each next move. Let's code that in as follows:

```
[2]: counts={}
     wins={}
     losses={}
     for move in env.validinputs:
         counts[move]=0
         wins[move]=0
         losses[move]=0
     print(f"the dictionary counts has values {counts}")
     print(f"the dictionary wins has values {wins}")
     print(f"the dictionary losses has values {losses}")
```

```
the dictionary counts has values {1: 0, 2: 0}
the dictionary wins has values {1: 0, 2: 0}
the dictionary losses has values {1: 0, 2: 0}
```

If you run the above code cell, you'll see that the three dictionaries all start with values {1: 0, 2: 0}. The naive MCTS agent will then simulate games and update these three dictionaries accordingly. Below, the agent simulates 100,000 games:

```
[3]: from copy import deepcopy

     # simulate 10,000 games
     for _ in range(100000):
         # create a deep copy of the game environment
         env_copy=deepcopy(env)
         # record moves
         actions=[]
         # play a full game
         while True:
             # randomly select a next move
             move=env.sample()
             actions.append(deepcopy(move))
             state,reward,done,info=env_copy.step(move)
             if done:
                 # see whehter the enxt move is 1 or 2
                 next_move=deepcopy(actions[0])
                 # update total number of simulated games
                 counts[actions[0]] += 1
                 # update total number of wins
                 if (reward==1 and env.turn==1) or \
                     (reward==-1 and env.turn==2):
                     wins[actions[0]] += 1
                 # update total number of losses
                 if (reward==-1 and env.turn==1) or \
                     (reward==1 and env.turn==2):
                     losses[actions[0]] += 1
                 break
```

Next, the MCTS agent counts the total number of games, the number of wins, and the number of losses associated with each next move: action=1 and action=2. Let's code that in as follows:

```
[4]: print(f"the dictionary counts has values {counts}")
     print(f"the dictionary wins has values {wins}")
     print(f"the dictionary losses has values {losses}")
```

```
the dictionary counts has values {1: 49986, 2: 50014}
the dictionary wins has values {1: 25022, 2: 25191}
the dictionary losses has values {1: 24964, 2: 24823}
```

Out of the 100,000 games, the MCTS agent has chosen action=1 49,986 times, and the rest 50,014 times, the agent has chosen action=2. When action=1 is chosen, the agent has won 25,022 times and lost 24,964 times. Every time the agent wins, we assign a value of 1 to the action=1, and every time the agent loses, we assign a value of −1 to the action=1. We scale the score by the total number of games with action=1. Therefore, the score for choosing action=1 is (25022-24964)/49986=0.00116. We do the same for action=2 and find that the score for choosing action=2 is (25191-24823)/50014=0.00734. Therefore, the agent prefers action 2 since doing so leads to a better average outcome (measured by the score). Let's code in that thought process:

[5]:
```
# See which action is most promising
scores={}
for k,v in counts.items():
    scores[k]=(wins.get(k,0)-losses.get(k,0))/v
print(scores)
best_move=max(scores,key=scores.get)
print(f"the best move is {best_move}")
```

```
{1: 0.0011603248909694715, 2: 0.007357939776862479}
the best move is 2
```

Here, the agent first creates a dictionary *scores*. For each possible next move, it assigns a score to it. The score is the number of wins minus the number of losses, scaled by the total number of simulations with that action. This score is a value between −1 and 1: if a move leads to winning 100% of the time, the move has a score of 1; if a move leads to losing 100% of the time, the move has a score of −1; a score of 0 means the move leads to an equal chance of winning and losing.

8.1.2 A Naive MCTS Algorithm

Based on the thought experiment in the last subsection, let's create a naive MCTS algorithm. Whenever it's the MCTS agent's turn. The MCTS agent simulates 100,000 games and makes a decision based on which next action leads to a better outcome.

To do that, we first define a *simulate_a_game()* function in the local package. Download *ch08util.py* from the book's GitHub repository and place it in the folder /Desktop/ags/utils/ on your computer. The function *simulate_a_game()* is defined as follows:

```
def simulate_a_game(env,counts,wins,losses):
    env_copy=deepcopy(env)
    actions=[]
    # play a full game
    while True:
```

```
        #randomly select a next move
        move=random.choice(env_copy.validinputs)
        actions.append(deepcopy(move))
        state,reward,done,info=env_copy.step(move)
        if done:
            counts[actions[0]] += 1
            if (reward==1 and env.turn==1) or \
                (reward==-1 and env.turn==2):
                wins[actions[0]] += 1
            if (reward==-1 and env.turn==1) or \
                (reward==1 and env.turn==2):
                losses[actions[0]] += 1
            break
    return counts, wins, losses
```

This function takes four arguments: the game environment, *env*, and the three dictionaries: *counts*, *wins*, and *losses*. This function simulates a game, all the way to the terminal state, by choosing random moves for both players. After the game, it updates the three dictionaries. If the next move is 1, the number of games associated with action=1 increases by 1 in the dictionary *counts*. Depending on whether the current player has won or lost, one of the two dictionaries, *wins* and *losses*, will update the number of wins or losses associated with action=1. For example, if action 1 is chosen as the next move and the game is lost, then the dictionary *wins* remains unchanged while the number of losses increases by 1 in the dictionary *losses* associated with key 1.

In the file *ch08util.py*, we also define a *best_move()* function as follows:

```
def best_move(counts,wins,losses):
    # See which action is most promising
    scores={}
    for k,v in counts.items():
        if v==0:
            scores[k]=0
        else:
            scores[k]=(wins.get(k,0)-losses.get(k,0))/v
    return max(scores,key=scores.get)
```

This function selects the best move based on the three dictionaries: *counts*, *wins*, and *losses*. It calculates a score for each possible next move: the score is the difference between the number of wins and losses scaled by the total number of moves.

Finally, we define the *naive_mcts()* function in *ch08util.py* as follows:

```
def naive_mcts(env, num_rollouts=10000):
    if len(env.validinputs)==1:
        return env.validinputs[0]
    counts={}
```

```
wins={}
losses={}
for move in env.validinputs:
    counts[move]=0
    wins[move]=0
    losses[move]=0
# roll out games
for _ in range(num_rollouts):
    counts,wins,losses=simulate_a_game(env,counts,\
                                        wins, losses)
return best_move(counts,wins,losses)
```

We set the default number of rollouts to 10000. If there is only one legal move left, we skip searching and select the only move available. Otherwise, we create three dictionaries, *counts*, *wins*, and *losses*, to record the outcomes from simulated games. Once the simulation is complete, we select the best next move based on the simulation results.

8.2 A NAIVE MCTS PLAYER IN THE COIN GAME

In this section, we let the naive MCTS algorithm play against random moves and see how effective it is. We simulate 100 games and let the naive MCTS agent move second.

```
[6]: from utils.ch08util import naive_mcts

results=[]
for i in range(100):
    env=coin_game()
    state=env.reset()
    if i%2==0:
        action=env.sample()
        state, reward, done, info=env.step(action)
    while True:
        action=naive_mcts(env,num_rollouts=1000)
        state, reward, done, info=env.step(action)
        if done:
            # result is 1 if the MCTS agent wins
            results.append(1)
            break
        action=env.sample()
        state, reward, done, info=env.step(action)
        if done:
            # result is -1 if the MCTS agent loses
```

```
        results.append(-1)
        break
```

Half the time, the MCTS agent moves first so that there is a level playing field. We record a result of 1 if the MCTS agent wins and a result of -1 if the MCTS agent loses.

We now count how many times the MCTS agent has won and lost.

[7]:
```
# count how many times the MCTS agent won
wins=results.count(1)
print(f"the MCTS agent has won {wins} games")
# count how many times the MCTS agent lost
losses=results.count(-1)
print(f"the MCTS agent has lost {losses} games")
```

```
the MCTS agent has won 96 games
the MCTS agent has lost 4 games
```

The above results show that the naive MCTS agent is much better than random moves: winning 96% of the time.

8.3 UPPER CONFIDENCE BOUNDS FOR TREES (UCT)

This section introduces the concept of Upper Confidence Bounds for Trees (UCT) method. We'll discuss the intuition behind it and the formula we use for child node selection.

8.3.1 The UCT Formula

The idea behind UCT MCTS is to select the child node based on a formula to balance exploitation and exploration. The Upper Confidence Bounds (UCB) formula is as follows:

$$UCB = v_i + C \times \sqrt{\frac{logN}{n_i}}$$

In the above formula, the value v_i is the estimated value of choosing the child node i. The current game state is called the root, or the parent node. A child node is the subsequent game state if a hypothetical next move is made on the current game state. C is a constant that adjusts how much exploration one wants in child node selection. N is the total number of simulations that have been conducted so far (that is, the number of times the parent node has been visited), whereas n_i is the number of times that child node i has been selected.

The temperature constant, C, controls the balance between exploitation and exploration. When the value of C is large, the formula favors unexplored next moves so that the MCTS agent can examine all moves and consider all possibilities. When C

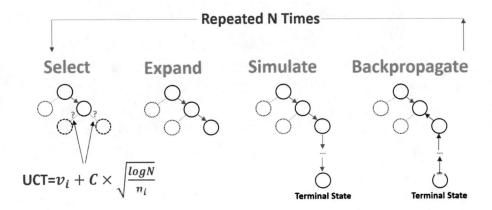

Figure 8.1 The four steps in Monte-Carlo Tree Search and the UCT formula

is small, the agent focuses on the most promising next move so far. The theoretical value of C is $\sqrt{2}$, so you can set the value of C at 1.4 as a starter.

We'll implement the UCT MCTS agent in all three games: the coin game, Tic Tac Toe, and Connect Four. Therefore, we'll create a generic MCTS algorithm that can be applied to all three games.

The MCTS algorithm has four steps: selection, expansion, simulation, and backpropagation. Figure 8.1 provides a diagram of these four steps and the UCT formula used to select the next moves in the first step *select*.

In the first step (on the left of Figure 8.1), we start at the current game state (root node) and select which next child node to choose in one of the current rollouts. The selection process is guided by a strategy that balances exploration (trying out new or less-explored moves) and exploitation (choosing moves known to be effective). Specifically, we'll use the UCT formula we discussed above.

The second step in MCTS is to expand the game tree based on which next child node is selected in the first step.

The third step is to "simulate," also called "playout" or "rollout." This involves simulating a game from the newly expanded node to a terminal state using random moves. The idea is to simulate what could potentially happen in a game after the moves represented by the path from the root to the new node.

In the final step (on the right of Figure 8.1), the results of the simulation are "backpropagated" through the path of the selected nodes to the root. This involves updating the statistical information at each node, such as the number of visits and the win/loss record, which are used in the selection step to guide future explorations of the tree.

The MCTS algorithm iteratively performs these four steps until a computational budget (like time or a set number of iterations) is exhausted, at which point the best move is chosen. This move is typically determined by the node at the root with the highest visit count or the best win/loss ratio.

MCTS is powerful because it can effectively handle extremely large search spaces without requiring domain-specific knowledge. Its performance generally improves with the number of simulations performed, making it a versatile and powerful tool in AI research and application.

8.3.2 An MCTS Agent

We first define a *select()* function to implement the UCB formula so that a child node is selected to simulate a game. The function is defined in the file *ch08util.py* that you just downloaded as follows:

```python
from math import sqrt, log


def select(env,counts,wins,losses,temperature):
    # calculate the uct score for all next moves
    scores={}
    # the ones not visited get the priority
    for k in env.validinputs:
        if counts[k]==0:
            return k
    # total number of simulations conducted
    N=sum([v for k,v in counts.items()])
    for k,v in counts.items():
        if v==0:
            scores[k]=0
        else:
            # vi for each next move
            vi=(wins.get(k,0)-losses.get(k,0))/v
            exploration=temperature*sqrt(log(N)/counts[k])
            scores[k]=vi+exploration
    # Select the next move with the highest UCT score
    return max(scores,key=scores.get)
```

To simulate a game, the MCTS agent selects a child node based on the UCT formula:

$$UCB = v_i + C \times \sqrt{\frac{logN}{n_i}}$$

that we discussed above. It considers the value of each child node and explores child nodes that are not visited frequently enough. It keeps a balance between exploitation and exploration when choosing the child node in each simulation.

Once the MCTS agent selects a child node, it will expand the game tree using a next move to reach the child node. Therefore, we define an *expand()* function in the local module *ch08util* as follows:

```
def expand(env,move):
    env_copy=deepcopy(env)
    state,reward,done,info=env_copy.step(move)
    return env_copy, done, reward
```

The function creates a deep copy of the current game environment and makes a hypothetical move to form a new child node in the game tree. The function returns the hypothetical game environment *env_copy*. The function also returns the variables *done* and *reward* in case the game has ended with the hypothetical move.

The third step in the MCTS algorithm is to simulate a full game based on the expanded game tree, till the game ends. The function then returns the game outcome. The *simulate()* function is defined in the local module as follows:

```
def simulate(env_copy,done,reward):
    # if the game has already ended
    if done==True:
        return reward
    while True:
        move=env_copy.sample()
        state,reward,done,info=env_copy.step(move)
        if done==True:
            return reward
```

The function simulates a game all the way to the terminal state and then returns the game outcome, *reward*.

Finally, the MCTS agent needs to backpropagate the game outcome after each simulation. The *backpropagate()* function below accomplishes that:

```
def backpropagate(env,move,reward,counts,wins,losses):
    # add 1 to the total game counts
    counts[move]=counts.get(move,0)+1
    # if the current player wins
    if reward==1 and (env.turn==1 or \
        env.turn=="X" or env.turn=="red"):
        wins[move]=wins.get(move,0)+1
    if reward==-1 and (env.turn==2 or \
        env.turn=="O" or env.turn=="yellow"):
        wins[move]=wins.get(move,0)+1
    if reward==-1 and (env.turn==1 or \
        env.turn=="X" or env.turn=="red"):
        losses[move]=losses.get(move,0)+1
    if reward==1 and (env.turn==2 or \
        env.turn=="O" or env.turn=="yellow"):
        losses[move]=losses.get(move,0)+1
    return counts,wins,losses
```

The *backpropagate()* function updates the three dictionaries *counts*, *wins*, and *losses* based on the game outcome and which next move was made (i.e., which child node was selected).

After the MCTS agent finishes the fixed number of rollouts, it selects the best next move based on the numbers recorded in the three dictionaries *counts*, *wins*, and *losses*. The function *next_move()* is defined in the local module as follows:

```
def next_move(counts,wins,losses):
    # See which action is most promising
    scores={}
    for k,v in counts.items():
        if v==0:
            scores[k]=0
        else:
            scores[k]=(wins.get(k,0)-losses.get(k,0))/v
    return max(scores,key=scores.get)
```

This function selects the best move based on the numbers in the three dictionaries *counts*, *wins*, and *losses*. It calculates a score for each potential next move: the score is the difference between the number of wins and losses scaled by the total number of moves.

Finally, we define the *mcts()* function in the local module:

```
def mcts(env,num_rollouts=100,temperature=1.4):
    # if there is only one valid move left, take it
    if len(env.validinputs)==1:
        return env.validinputs[0]
    # create three dictionaries counts, wins, losses
    counts={}
    wins={}
    losses={}
    for move in env.validinputs:
        counts[move]=0
        wins[move]=0
        losses[move]=0
    # roll out games
    for _ in range(num_rollouts):
        # selection
        move=select(env,counts,wins,losses,temperature)
        # expansion
        env_copy, done, reward=expand(env,move)
        # simulation
        reward=simulate(env_copy,done,reward)
        # backpropagate
        counts,wins,losses=backpropagate(\
```

```
            env,move,reward,counts,wins,losses)
        # make the move
        return next_move(counts,wins,losses)
```

We follow the four steps outlined earlier in the chapter when creating the MCTS agent: selection, expansion, simulation, and backpropagation. The agent chooses the best next move based on simulation outcomes: whichever next move has the most wins relative to losses is the best next move.

We set the default number of rollouts to 100 and the default temperature to 1.4. If there is only one legal move left, we skip searching and select the only move available.

8.4 TEST THE MCTS AGENT IN TIC TAC TOE

In this section, we'll first play a game manually against the MCTS agent in Tic Tac Toe. We then test 100 games and see how effective the MCTS algorithm is.

8.4.1 Manually Play against the MCTS Agent in Tic Tac Toe

We let the MCTS agent move first in Tic Tac Toe. We use the *input()* function to key in the moves for Player O.

```
[8]: from utils.ttt_simple_env import ttt
     from utils.ch08util import mcts

     env=ttt()
     state=env.reset()
     while True:
         action=mcts(env,num_rollouts=10000)
         print(f"Player {env.turn} has chosen {action}")
         state, reward, done, info = env.step(action)
         print(f"Current state is \n{state.reshape(3,3)[::-1]}")
         if done:
             if reward==1:
                 print(f"Player {env.turn} has won!")
             else:
                 print("Game over, it's a tie!")
             break
         action=int(input("What's your move?"))
         print(f"Player {env.turn} has chosen {action}")
         state, reward, done, info = env.step(action)
         print(f"Current state is \n{state.reshape(3,3)[::-1]}")
         if done:
             print(f"Player {env.turn} has won!")
             break
```

```
Player X has chosen 5
Current state is
[[0 0 0]
 [0 1 0]
 [0 0 0]]
What's your move?1
Player O has chosen 1
Current state is
[[ 0  0  0]
 [ 0  1  0]
 [-1  0  0]]
Player X has chosen 3
Current state is
[[ 0  0  0]
 [ 0  1  0]
 [-1  0  1]]
What's your move?7
Player O has chosen 7
Current state is
[[-1  0  0]
 [ 0  1  0]
 [-1  0  1]]
Player X has chosen 4
Current state is
[[-1  0  0]
 [ 1  1  0]
 [-1  0  1]]
What's your move?6
Player O has chosen 6
Current state is
[[-1  0  0]
 [ 1  1 -1]
 [-1  0  1]]
Player X has chosen 2
Current state is
[[-1  0  0]
 [ 1  1 -1]
 [-1  1  1]]
What's your move?8
Player O has chosen 8
Current state is
[[-1 -1  0]
 [ 1  1 -1]
 [-1  1  1]]
Player X has chosen 9
```

```
Current state is
[[-1 -1  1]
 [ 1  1 -1]
 [-1  1  1]]
Game over, it's a tie!
```

We set the number of rollouts to 10000. It takes a few seconds for the UCT MCTS agent to make a move. The MCTS agent is able to block my winning moves and tie the game. This shows that the MCTS agent is fairly intelligent.

8.4.2 Effectiveness of the Tic Tac Toe MCTS Agent

We will let the MCTS agent play against a random player 100 games and see how many times it wins

[9]:
```python
import random

results=[]
for i in range(100):
    state=env.reset()
    if i%2==0:
        action=env.sample()
        state, reward, done, info=env.step(action)
    while True:
        action=mcts(env,num_rollouts=10000)
        state, reward, done, info=env.step(action)
        if done:
            # result is 1 if the MCTS agent wins
            if reward!=0:
                results.append(1)
            else:
                results.append(0)
            break
        action=env.sample()
        state, reward, done, info=env.step(action)
        if done:
            # result is -1 if the random-move agent wins
            if reward!=0:
                results.append(-1)
            else:
                results.append(0)
            break
```

Half the time, the MCTS agent moves first so that no player has a first mover advantage. We record a result of 1 if the MCTS agent wins and a result of −1 if the UCT MCTS agent loses.

We now count how many times the MCTS agent has won and lost.

```
[10]:  # count how many times the MCTS agent won
       wins=results.count(1)
       print(f"the MCTS agent has won {wins} games")
       # count how many times the MCTS agent lost
       losses=results.count(-1)
       print(f"the MCTS agent has lost {losses} games")
       # count how many tie games
       losses=results.count(0)
       print(f"the game is tied {losses} times")
```

```
the MCTS agent has won 96 games
the MCTS agent has lost 1 games
the game is tied 3 times
```

The above results show that the MCTS agent is much more intelligent than random moves: it won 96 out of the 100 games and lost only once.

8.5   AN MCTS AGENT IN CONNECT FOUR

Next, we test the MCTS agent in Connect Four and see how effective it is. Since the *mcts()* function we defined in the local module applies to all three games, we don't need to create a separate MCTS agent just for Connect Four. All we need is to use the same *mcts()* function that we have imported from the local module.

8.5.1   A Manual Game against the Connect Four MCTS Agent

We first play a game manually against the Connect Four MCTS agent and let it move first, like so:

```
[11]:  from utils.conn_simple_env import conn

       # Initiate the game environment
       env=conn()
       state=env.reset()
       while True:
           action=mcts(env,num_rollouts=5000)
           print(f"Player {env.turn} has chosen {action}")
           state, reward, done, info=env.step(action)
           print(f"Current state is \n{state.T[::-1]}")
           if done:
               print("Player red has won!")
               break
           action=int(input("What's your move?"))
           print(f"Player {env.turn} has chosen {action}")
```

```
    state, reward, done, info=env.step(action)
    print(f"Current state is \n{state.T[::-1]}")
    if done:
        if reward!=0:
            print("Player yellow has won!")
        else:
            print("Game over, it's a tie!")
        break
```

```
Player red has chosen 4
Current state is
[[0 0 0 0 0 0 0]
 [0 0 0 0 0 0 0]
 [0 0 0 0 0 0 0]
 [0 0 0 0 0 0 0]
 [0 0 0 0 0 0 0]
 [0 0 0 1 0 0 0]]
What's your move?4
Player yellow has chosen 4
Current state is
[[ 0  0  0  0  0  0  0]
 [ 0  0  0  0  0  0  0]
 [ 0  0  0  0  0  0  0]
 [ 0  0  0  0  0  0  0]
 [ 0  0  0 -1  0  0  0]
 [ 0  0  0  1  0  0  0]]
Player red has chosen 3
Current state is
[[ 0  0  0  0  0  0  0]
 [ 0  0  0  0  0  0  0]
 [ 0  0  0  0  0  0  0]
 [ 0  0  0  0  0  0  0]
 [ 0  0  0 -1  0  0  0]
 [ 0  0  1  1  0  0  0]]
What's your move?4
Player yellow has chosen 4
Current state is
[[ 0  0  0  0  0  0  0]
 [ 0  0  0  0  0  0  0]
 [ 0  0  0  0  0  0  0]
 [ 0  0  0 -1  0  0  0]
 [ 0  0  0 -1  0  0  0]
 [ 0  0  1  1  0  0  0]]
Player red has chosen 5
Current state is
```

```
[[ 0   0   0   0   0   0   0]
 [ 0   0   0   0   0   0   0]
 [ 0   0   0   0   0   0   0]
 [ 0   0   0  -1   0   0   0]
 [ 0   0   0  -1   0   0   0]
 [ 0   0   1   1   1   0   0]]
What's your move?5
Player yellow has chosen 5
Current state is
[[ 0   0   0   0   0   0   0]
 [ 0   0   0   0   0   0   0]
 [ 0   0   0   0   0   0   0]
 [ 0   0   0  -1   0   0   0]
 [ 0   0   0  -1  -1   0   0]
 [ 0   0   1   1   1   0   0]]
Player red has chosen 2
Current state is
[[ 0   0   0   0   0   0   0]
 [ 0   0   0   0   0   0   0]
 [ 0   0   0   0   0   0   0]
 [ 0   0   0  -1   0   0   0]
 [ 0   0   0  -1  -1   0   0]
 [ 0   1   1   1   1   0   0]]
Player red has won!
```

I set the number of rollouts to 5000. The MCTS agent is able to create a double attack and win the game. This shows that the MCTS agent is fairly intelligent in Connect Four.

8.5.2   Effectiveness of the Connect Four MCTS Agent

We will let the MCTS agent play against a random player 100 games and see how many times it wins.

```
[2]: results=[]
     for i in range(100):
         state=env.reset()
         if i%2==0:
             action=env.sample()
             state, reward, done, info=env.step(action)
         while True:
             action=mcts(env,num_rollouts=5000)
             state, reward, done, info=env.step(action)
             if done:
                 # result is 1 if the MCTS agent wins
```

```
                    results.append(abs(reward))
                    break
            action=env.sample()
            state, reward, done, info=env.step(action)
            if done:
                    # result is -1 if the MCTS agent loses
                    results.append(-abs(reward))
                    break
```

Half the time, the MCTS agent moves first; in the other 50 games, the MCTS agent moves second. Therefore, no player has a first-mover advantage. We record a result of *abs(reward)* if the game ends after the MCTS agent's move and a result of −*abs(reward)* if the game ends after the opponent's move. This ensures that we record a 1 if the MCTS agent wins and a −1 if it loses. A tie game is recorded as 0 in the list *results*.

We now count how many times the MCTS agent has won and lost.

[13]:
```
# count how many times the MCTS agent won
wins=results.count(1)
print(f"the MCTS agent has won {wins} games")
# count how many times the MCTS agent lost
losses=results.count(-1)
print(f"the MCTS agent has lost {losses} games")
# count how many tie games
losses=results.count(0)
print(f"the game is tied {losses} times")
```

```
the MCTS agent has won 100 games
the MCTS agent has lost 0 games
the game is tied 0 times
```

The above results show that the MCTS agent has won all 100 Connect Four games.

Now that you know how MCTS works, you'll integrate the algorithm with deep neural networks in late chapters to create even stronger game strategies in the three games: the coin game, Tic Tac Toe, and Connect Four.

8.6 GLOSSARY

- **Monte Carlo Tree Search (MCTS):** A tree search algorithm for decision processes. It's often used in board games to find the best next move. It simulates a large number of games starting from the current game state to the terminal state. It then chooses whichever next move leads to the most favorable outcome for the current player.
- **Rollout:** A simulation in Monte-Carlo Tree Search till the terminal state of the game.

- **Upper Confidence Bounds for Trees (UCT):** An algorithm to select the child node to roll out games in Monte-Carlo Tree Search. It balances exploration and exploitation. It favors the most promising next move but also explores the next move that hasn't been examined frequently.

8.7 EXERCISES

8.1 Modify the first two cells in Section 8.2 so that the MCTS agent uses the strategy defined in the function *mcts()* instead of the naive strategy. See how many times the MCTS agent has won and lost.

8.2 Modify the first code cell in Section 8.4.1 so that the MCTS agent uses 20000 rollouts when making moves. Try your best to win the game yourself and see if the MCTS agent can win the game.

8.3 Modify the first two code cells in Section 8.4.2 so that the MCTS agent uses 20000 rollouts when making moves. See how many games the MCTS agent has won and lost.

8.4 Modify the first code cell in Section 8.5.1 so that the MCTS agent uses 10000 rollouts when making moves. Try your best to win the game yourself and see if the MCTS agent can win the game.

8.5 Modify the two code cells in Section 8.5.2 so that the MCTS agent uses 10000 rollouts when making moves. See how many games the MCTS agent has won and lost in Connect Four.

II

Deep Learning

## CHAPTER 9

Deep Learning in the Coin Game

"My CPU is a neural net processor, a learning computer. The more contact I have
with humans, the more I learn."
– the Terminator, in Terminator 2: Judgement Day

STARTING FROM THIS chapter, you'll learn a new AI
paradigm: machine learning (ML). Instead of hard
coding in the rules, ML algorithms take in input-output pairs and figure out the
relation between the inputs (which we call features) and outputs (the labels). One
field of ML, deep learning, has attracted much attention recently. The algorithm used
by AlphaGo is based on deep reinforcement learning, which is a combination of deep
learning and reinforcement learning (a type of ML we'll cover later in this book). In
this chapter, you'll learn what deep learning is and how it's related to AI and ML.

Deep learning is a type of ML method that's based on artificial neural networks. A
neural network is a computational model inspired by the structure of neural networks
in the human brain. It's designed to recognize patterns in data, and it contains layers
of interconnected nodes, or neurons. In this chapter, you'll learn to use deep neural
networks to design game strategies for the coin game. In particular, you'll follow the
steps in AlphaGo and create two policy networks. We'll use these networks later in
the book to create an AlphaGo agent to play the coin game.

Specifically, the AlphaGo algorithm follows the following steps. We first gather a
large number of games played by Go experts and use deep learning to train two
policy networks to predict the moves of the Go experts: a fast policy network and
a strong policy network. In the second step, we use self-play deep reinforcement
learning to further train and improve the strong policy network. At the same time,
we train a *value network* to predict game outcomes by using the game experience
data from the self-plays. Finally, we design a game strategy based on an improved

DOI: 10.1201/9781032722207-9

version of MCTS. Instead of using the upper confidence bounds for trees (UCT) formula to select a child node in game rollouts, AlphaGo uses a combination of the recommendations from the improved strong policy network and the average rollout value. Further, instead of randomly selecting moves in game rollouts, AlphaGo uses the fast policy network to roll out games.

In this chapter, you'll implement the first step in the AlphaGo algorithm in the coin game. Specifically, you'll use the rule-based AI we developed in Chapter 1 to generate expert moves. We then create two neural networks and use the generated expert moves to train the two networks to predict moves. You'll then implement policy rollouts in MCTS, where games are played based on the probability distribution from the fast policy network, leading to a more intelligent MCTS agent compared to the traditional one.

What You'll Learn in This Chapter

- The architecture of a neural network
- How deep learning is related to machine learning and artificial intelligence
- Steps and Components of the AlphaGo algorithm
- Building and training a fast policy network and a strong policy network in the Coin game
- Implementing an MCTS game strategy with policy rollouts

9.1 DEEP LEARNING, ML, AND AI

The advancements of AI are quicker than most scientists have imagined. AI has generated much media fanfare and it is redefining the way we live. But exactly what is AI?

In this section, you'll learn what AI is and how ML has emerged as a new paradigm in AI. In particular, deep learning is the most promising area of ML and the most important AI technology to learn nowadays.

9.1.1 What Is Rule-Based AI?

It's widely believed that the term AI was coined by John McCarthy in 1955. The word *artificial* in AI means that it's man-made, instead of naturally occurring in the world. AI is intelligence generated by human-engineered machines. It's different from natural intelligence demonstrated by humans and other animals.

When people hear about AI, the first thing that comes to mind is usually a robot. In reality, AI is much more than that. Nowadays, AI is integrated into every aspect of our lives: examples include recommendation systems, voice assistants, and foreign language translators... AI is based on the idea that human intelligence can be

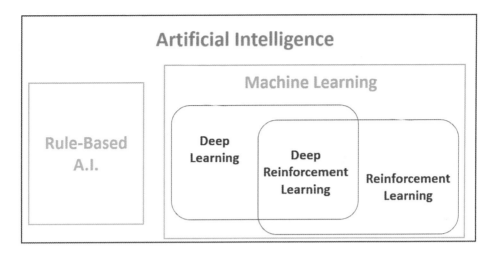

Figure 9.1   How deep learning is related to ML and AI

replicated by machines. Shortly after the computer was invented, scientists have been working on simulating human intelligence in machines to solve complicated problems.

Figure 9.1. is a diagram of how deep learning is related to ML and AI. Broadly speaking, there are two ways to make a machine mimic human intelligence: to program it or to teach it to learn. To program a computer to mimic human intelligence is to lay out the rules and tell the computer what to do in each situation. This is the rule-based AI that we have learned in Chapters 1 to 8 of this book, as shown on the left of Figure 9.1.

Rule-based AI is the traditional AI technique. It is the AI algorithm behind Deep Blue, for example. To implement rule-based AI, humans program all the rules onto a machine and tell it what to do in each situation based on the rules. In the case of Deep Blue, the machine calculates hundreds of billions of chess board positions in the three minutes allotted for a player to make a move, and makes a decision based on which next move has the best chance of winning the game. In other words, in rule-based AI models, we feed rules and input data into the algorithm and ask it to tell us what the output should be.

Rule-based AI achieved great feats in the late 20th century by automating mundane jobs and increasing productivity. According to Forbes, by 1985, corporations spent $1 billion a year on AI systems [7]. Deep Blue brought AI to headline news when it beat world Chess champion Garry Kasparov in 1997.

However, rule-based AI has its limitations. In many situations, rules are not known to humans. In other situations, rules are hard or even impossible to be programmed onto a computer. For example, human beings can tell a dog from a cat at a quick glance. However, if you ask humans to describe all the features that distinguish a dog from a cat, most people will fail. Even if they can articulate a list of features to tell the two apart, it's hard to write a computer program to classify dog and cat images.

This brings us to the new approach in AI, which we'll discuss below.

9.1.2 Machine Learning (ML), A New AI Paradigm

Machine learning (ML) is a new paradigm in AI. The method is very different from the traditional rule-based AI. Instead of programming all the rules onto a computer and telling it what to do in each situation, we feed the computer many different examples and let the computer learn what the rules are.

Arthur Samuel, a pioneer in AI, first coined the term ML in 1959. ML takes a diametrically different approach to AI. Instead of coding in a set of rules and telling the machine what to do, humans give the machine a large number of examples and ask the machine what the rules are. It's a process for machines to infer rules from example data.

This new approach to AI is appealing in situations where coding rules is either too difficult or downright impossible.

In some situations, the rules are clear and relatively easy to code in a computer program, such as in a Tic Tac Toe game. Humans can use a MiniMax algorithm (which is rule-based AI) to find a perfect solution to the game. However, in many other situations, the rules are too complicated or even impossible to code in a computer program. For example, in the game of Go, players usually make a move without explicitly knowing why it's a good move. They only know intuitively it makes sense. This makes it difficult to use rule-based AI to program a Go-player.

If scientists started research in ML since the 1950s, why is it becoming popular only in the last couple of decades? Several factors contributed to the recent rise of ML: advancements in computing power, availability of big data, and breakthroughs in ML research. I'll elaborate on them below.

Advancements in computer power: ML algorithms are computationally costly and time-consuming. For example, OpenAI's GPT-3 model has 175 billion parameters. A model with so many parameters was impossible to train a couple of decades ago. The recent advancements in computing power make the training of many complicated ML systems possible. In particular, nowadays deep learning models can be trained using graphics processing units (GPUs) instead of central processing units (CPUs). Since GPUs devote more transistors to arithmetic units than CPUs, GPUs have greatly reduced the training time. Further, distributed deep learning combines the computing power of multiple machines, which has greatly accelerated ML research.

Availability of data: An article in The Economist in 2017 states that "the worlds' most valuable resource is no longer oil, but data." [5] ML models require a large amount of quality data to train the parameters. In the last couple of decades, the rise of big data has generated a need for ML models to analyze them. At the same time, the availability of big data makes the training of ever more advanced ML models possible.

Breakthroughs in ML research: ML research has seen many breakthroughs in the last decade or two. In particular, the invention of Convolutional Neural Networks (CNNs) has greatly improved the power of deep neural networks (DNNs). CNNs have put deep learning at the cutting edge of artificial intelligence. Because of CNNs, deep learning is now the most promising field in machine learning. CNNs use a different type of layers than regular fully-connected layers of neurons. A convolutional layer treats an image as a two-dimensional object and finds patterns in the image. It then associates these patterns with the image labels. This greatly improves the predictive power of the model. Deep learning is also applied to other types of ML models such as reinforcement learning, which further accelerates the power of ML. Deep reinforcement learning (which is a combination of deep neural networks and reinforcement learning) was the brain behind DeepMind that beat the world Go champion Lee Sedol.

9.1.3 Different Types of ML Algorithms

There are different types of algorithms used in the field of ML to solve complicated problems. Broadly speaking, ML can be classified into three different types: Supervised learning, unsupervised learning, and reinforcement learning. Below, I'll discuss their main characteristics and applications.

Supervised learning uses labeled data to train ML models. Labeled data mean that the output is already known to you. For example, we may have thousands of pictures of dogs and cats. Labeled data tell us whether each picture is a dog or a cat. A supervised learning model learns from the labeled data and extracts the patterns in the input data. Based on these patterns, the trained model then maps inputs (dog or cat images) to outputs (i.e., labels: whether the picture is a dog or a cat). After learning from thousands of picture-label pairs, the trained model then takes an input and makes a prediction on what the output should be. The name supervised training reflects the fact that the training process needs human supervision: human curated data (input-output pairs) need to be prepared before training.

The training process for supervised learning is as follows. The starting point is the human-curated data. The data contain many pairs of inputs and outputs. We then choose a supervised ML model to learn from the input-output pairs. After the training, we feed the model with inputs and the model tells us what the output should be. Supervised learning is used when the human-curated data is relatively easy to obtain. It's widely used in image classifications.

There are different algorithms we can use in supervised learning. Some examples include logit regression, linear regression, random forest, and neural networks. In this book, we'll focus mainly on neural networks as our supervised learning model.

Unsupervised learning doesn't use labeled data. Instead, it uses unlabeled data that have no output variable for each observation. An unsupervised learning model uses the unlabeled data to identify patterns and features and generates the output.

Unsupervised learning doesn't need external supervision in the sense that the model doesn't need human curated and labeled data to train. While in supervised learning, the data we use to train the model are input-output pairs, in reality, we don't know the labels of the data in many situations. Instead, we can use unsupervised learning to generate labels for supervised learning.

Unsupervised learning models find naturally occurring similarities, differences, and other patterns from the training data. Examples of unsupervised learning methods include clustering, principal component analysis, and data visualization (plotting, graphing, and so on). Unsupervised learning is the least powerful of the three types of ML. It has attracted far less attention than the other two types. In this book, we don't cover unsupervised learning in detail.

Reinforcement learning (RL) trains an agent in an environment to choose actions and get rewards accordingly. There is no label or target variable in RL. The training approach is by using trial and error. When a good action is chosen, a positive reward is given to the agent. On the other hand, if a bad action is chosen, a negative reward (i.e., a punishment) is given. The agent learns to choose actions to maximize expected payoff from the actions.

In both supervised and unsupervised learning, we need plenty of data to feed into the model. However, in many situations, the data is hard to come by. All we can observe is the outcome of the actions. In such cases, we need to rely on reinforcement learning.

Deep Learning and Deep reinforcement learning are the coolest buzzwords these days in the AI world. Exactly what are deep learning and deep reinforcement learning?

Deep learning is a special case of the neural networks algorithm we just mentioned above when we discuss supervised learning. As you'll see later in this chapter, a neural network has an input layer, an output layer, and any number of hidden layers. When the number of hidden layers in the neural network is small, say, with 0 or 1 hidden layers, it's called a shallow neural network. On the other hand, if the number of hidden layers is large, we call it a deep neural network. Deep learning is ML with deep neural networks as the training algorithm.

9.2 WHAT ARE NEURAL NETWORKS?

Neural networks have become immensely popular in AI in recent years. The combination of advanced learning capabilities, compatibility with big data, hardware advancements, and wide applicability across numerous fields have made neural networks a cornerstone of contemporary AI development.

This section discusses the basic structure of a neural network.

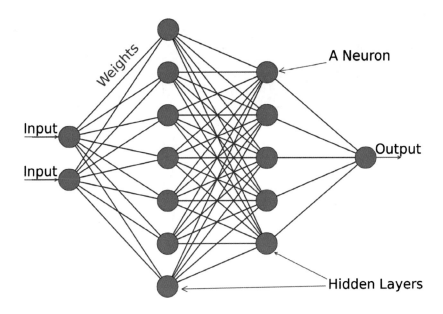

Figure 9.2 A diagram of the architecture of a neural network

9.2.1 Elements of a Neural Network

A neural network is a computational model inspired by the structure of neural networks in the human brain. It's designed to recognize patterns in data. It contains layers of interconnected nodes, or neurons.

Figure 9.2 is a diagram of the architecture of a neural network. A neural network consists of one input layer, one output layer, and a number of hidden layers. Each layer in a neural network has one or more nodes (i.e., neurons). Neural networks with two or more hidden layers are usually called deep neural networks.

The input layer, as shown on the left side of Figure 9.2, is the first layer of the neural network. It receives the input data. Each node in this layer represents one feature of the input data. The hidden layers are shown in the middle of Figure 9.2. These are layers between the input and output layers. They are called "hidden" because they are not directly exposed to the input or output. Each node in these layers represents a learned feature from the input data. There can be one or multiple hidden layers. The neurons in these layers perform complex computations through their weighted connections.

The output Layer is shown on the right of Figure 9.2. This is the final layer, containing one or more neurons. It produces the output of the neural network. The structure of this layer depends on the type of problem being solved (e.g., one node for binary classification, and multiple nodes for multi-category classification).

A neuron is a basic unit in a neural network. It receives input, processes it, and generates an output. Each neuron performs a weighted sum of its inputs, applies an activation function, and outputs the result.

Weights are the parameters of the neural network. They are used to adjust the strength of the input signals. During training, the neural network adjusts these weights based on the error of its predictions, a process known as learning.

There are different types of layers in a neural network. The most common type of layer is the dense layer, in which each neuron is fully connected to the neurons in the next layer. The convolutional layers, in contrast, treat the input as a multi-dimensional object and extract patterns from the input data. We'll discuss more on convolutional layers later in this book.

Training involves adjusting the weights of the neurons. This is typically done using a method called backpropagation, combined with an optimization algorithm like gradient descent. The network learns by comparing its output with the actual output (training data) and minimizing the error.

In summary, a neural network processes input through a series of layers (input, hidden, and output) using interconnected neurons with adjustable weights. The hidden layers allow the network to learn and model complex relationships in the data. The training process involves iteratively adjusting these weights to minimize the difference between the network's predictions and actual outcomes. For detailed discussions on how neural networks learn from training data, see, e.g., my book *Machine Learning, Animated* by CRC press [6].

9.2.2 Activation Functions

In artificial neural networks, activation functions transform inputs into outputs. As the name suggests, the activation functions activate the neuron when the input reaches a certain threshold. Simply put, activation functions are on-off switches in artificial neural networks. These on-off switches play an important role in making artificial neural networks powerful. The activation functions allow a network to learn more complex patterns in the data. Activation functions help us create a nonlinear relationship between the inputs and outputs. Without them, we can only approximate linear relations.

Below are some commonly used activation functions in neural networks.

ReLU is short for rectified linear unit activation function. It returns the original value if it's positive, and 0 otherwise. It has the mathematical formula of

$$ReLU(x) = \begin{cases} x \ if \ x > 0 \\ 0 \ if \ x \leq 0 \end{cases}$$

It's the go-to activation function in neural networks, and you'll see it in this book more often than any other type of activation function. In essence, the ReLU activation function activates the neuron when the value of x reaches the threshold value of zero. When the value of x is below zero, the neuron is switched off. This simple on-off switch is able to create a nonlinear relation between inputs and outputs.

Another commonly used activation function is the sigmoid function. It's widely used in many machine learning models. In particular, it's a must-have in any binary classification problem. The sigmoid function has the form

$$y = \frac{1}{1+e^{-x}}$$

The sigmoid function has an S-shaped curve. It has this nice property: for any value of input x between $-\infty$ and ∞, the output value y is always between 0 and 1. Because of this property, we use the sigmoid activation function to model the probability of an outcome, which also falls between 0 and 1 (0 means there is no chance of the outcome occurring; 1 means that the outcome occurs with a 100% probability).

The third most-used activation function in this book is the softmax function. It's a must-have in any multi-category classification problem. The softmax function has the form

$$y(x) = \frac{e^x}{\sum_{k=1}^{K} e^{x_k}}$$

where $x = [x_1, x_2, ..., x_K]$ and $y = [y_1, y_2, ..., y_K]$ are K-element lists. The i-th element of y is

$$y_i(x) = \frac{e^{x_i}}{\sum_{k=1}^{K} e^{x_k}}$$

The softmax function has a nice property: each element in the output vector y is always between 0 and 1. Further, elements in the output vector y sum up to 1. Because of this property, we use the softmax activation function to model the probability of a multiple outcome event. Therefore, the activation function in the output layer is always the softmax function when we model multi-category classification problems.

Finally, we'll also use the tanh activation function when we train the actor-critic models later in this book. The tanh activation function is similar to the sigmoid activation function in the sense that it is also S-shaped. However, the output from the tanh activation function is in the range of -1 to 1 instead of from 0 to 1. The tanh activation function has the form

$$y = \frac{2}{1+e^{-2x}} - 1$$

In multiplayer games, the game outcome for a player is a number between -1 and 1: -1 means the player has lost the game, 1 means the player has won, and 0 means the game is tied.

9.2.3 Loss Functions

The loss function in ML is the objective function in the mathematical optimization process. Intuitively, the loss function measures the forecasting error of the machine learning algorithm. By minimizing the loss function, the machine learning model finds parameter values that lead to the best predictions.

The most commonly used loss function is mean squared error (MSE). MSE is defined as

$$MSE = \frac{1}{N} \sum_{i=1}^{N} (Y_n - \hat{Y}_n)^2$$

where Y_n is the actual value of the target variable (i.e., the label) and $\hat{Y}_n$ is the predicted value of the target variable. To calculate MSE, we look at the forecasting error: the difference between the model's predictions and the actual values. We then square the forecasting error for each observation and average it across all observations. In short, it is the average squared forecasting error in each observation.

In binary classification problems, the preferred loss function is the binary cross-entropy function, which measures the average difference between the predicted probabilities and the actual labels (1 or 0). If a model makes a perfect prediction and assigns a 100% probability to all observations labeled 1 and a 0% probability to all observations labeled 0, the binary cross-entropy loss function will have a value of 0.

Mathematically, the binary class-entropy loss function is defined as

$$Binary\ Cross\ Entropy = \sum_{n=1}^{N} -[Y_n \times log(\hat{Y}_n) + (1 - Y_n) \times log(1 - \hat{Y}_n)]$$

where $\hat{Y}_n$ is the estimated probability of observation n being class 1, and Y_n is the actual label of observation n (which is either 0 or 1).

The preferred loss function to use in multi-category classifications is the categorical cross-entropy loss function. It measures the average difference between the predicted distribution and the actual distribution.

Mathematically, the categorical class-entropy loss function is defined as

$$Categorical\ Cross\ Entropy = \sum_{n=1}^{N} \sum_{k=1}^{K} -y_{n,k} \times log(\hat{y}_{n,k})$$

where $\hat{y}_{n,k}$ is the estimated probability of observation n being class k, and $y_{n,k}$ is the actual label of observation n belonging to category k (which is either 0 or 1).

9.3 TWO POLICY NETWORKS IN THE COIN GAME

Our goal in this book is to apply the AlphaGo algorithm in the three everyday games: the coin game, Tic Tac Toe, and Connect Four. To do that, we must first know the steps involved in the AlphaGo algorithm.

Therefore, in this section, I'll first provide you with a road map of the AlphaGo algorithm. We'll gradually implement all the steps in AlphaGo in the three games

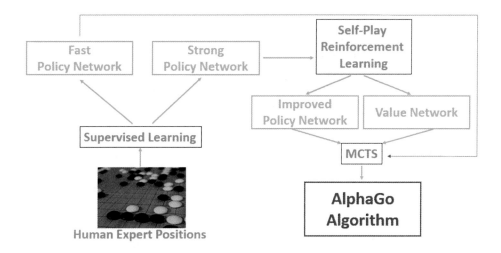

Figure 9.3 Steps and components of the AlphaGo algorithm

in the following chapters. In this chapter, you'll start by building and training two different neural networks for the coin game so that we can use them later in the AlphaGo algorithm.

9.3.1 A High-Level Overview of the AlphaGo Algorithm

AlphaGo, developed by Google DeepMind, represents a significant advancement in the field of artificial intelligence, particularly in the realm of board games. The algorithm that powers AlphaGo involves several key steps and components, which together enabled it to defeat human Go champions. Below is a high-level overview of these steps and components.

Monte Carlo Tree Search (MCTS), which we have discussed in Chapter 8, is the backbone of AlphaGo's decision-making process. MCTS is used to efficiently search through the possible moves in Go, a game known for its vast number of potential moves and board states. The algorithm evaluates the potential future moves and their outcomes, making decisions based on a balance of exploration and exploitation.

Figure 9.3 provides a diagram of the steps and components of the AlphaGo algorithm.

The first step in the AlphaGo algorithm is to gather a large number of games played by human Go experts (bottom left of Figure 9.3). AlphaGo then uses deep learning to train two policy networks to predict the moves of the Go experts by using the gathered data: a fast policy network and a strong policy network (top left of Figure 9.3). The policy networks help in narrowing down the search space. They predict the most promising moves to consider, based on its training from professional human games. The networks significantly reduce the number of moves AlphaGo needs to evaluate at each step.

In the second step, AlphaGo uses self-play deep reinforcement learning to further train and improve the strong policy network. At the same time, it trains a value network to predict game outcomes by using the game experience data from the self-palys (on the right of Figure 9.3). The value network assesses the board positions. It predicts the winner of the game from the current position, providing an estimation of the board position's value without having to simulate the game to the end. AlphaGo employs reinforcement learning in this step, where the system learns by playing games against itself. Through this process, it improves both the policy and value networks, learning from its mistakes and successes.

In the third step, AlphaGo designs a game strategy based on an improved version of MCTS. The combination of MCTS with the policy and value networks is what gives AlphaGo its strength. The policy network guides the MCTS to focus on the most promising areas of the search tree, while the value network evaluates the positions reached by the search. Specifically, instead of using the UCT formula to select the next move in traditional MCTS (as you've seen in Chapter 8), AlphaGo uses a combination of the improved strong policy network and the value network (bottom right of Figure 9.3). Further, instead of randomly selecting moves in game rollouts, AlphaGo uses the fast policy network to roll out games so that the evaluations from the simulations are more accurate and informative.

9.3.2 Fast and Strong Policy Networks in the Coin Game

Now that you have a road map of how the AlphaGo algorithm works, we'll apply the algorithm to the three games (the coin game, Tic Tac Toe, and Connect Four) in later chapters in this book. In this chapter, you'll build and train a fast policy network and a strong policy network in the coin game so that you can use them later to build the AlphaGo algorithm.

In particular, you'll first create a fast policy neural network with just one hidden layer. The advantage of this fast policy network is that later when you use it in MCTS to roll out games, the network recommends a move very fast due to the simple structure of the neural network. You'll also create a strong neural network with three hidden layers. Later in this book, we'll use this strong policy network to generate more accurate game experience data to train a value network.

You'll learn how to prepare data to train the two policy networks, how to interpret the predictions from the networks. Here is a summary of what we'll do to train the two neural networks:

1. We'll create two computer players: an expert and a non-expert. The expert selects moves according to the rule-based AI that we created in Chapter 1. The non-expert computer player selects a random move 50% of the time. In the other 50% of the time, it selects moves according to the rule-based AI strategy. If we let both players select moves according to rule-based AI from Chapter 1, the moves are identical in each game and the game experience data will not cover all game scenarios. By letting the second player choose random moves half the time, we can generate game experience data to cover different game scenarios.

2. We let the two players play a game, and record the board positions and all moves made by the expert player. We'll use the game board positions as features X, and the moves made by the expert as labels y. We'll treat this as a multi-category classification problem since there are two possible moves that the expert can make: removing 1 coin from the pile or removing two coins from the pile.

3. We'll simulate 10,000 games and use the histories of the games and the corresponding moves as Xs and ys. We then feed the data (X, y) into the two neural networks to train them.

In the coin game, there are only two possible game outcomes: a win or a loss. Therefore, we can potentially use a binary classification in the second step above. However, in the other two games used in this book (Tic Tac Toe and Connect Four), there are three possible game outcomes: a win, a loss, and a tie. We therefore use multi-category classifications in all three games to make the strategies consistent across the three games.

9.4 TRAIN TWO POLICY NEURAL NETWORKS IN THE COIN GAME

We'll first use the rule-based AI to generate expert moves as the training data. We'll then use Keras to create two neural networks: a fast policy network and a strong policy network. We'll finally use the generated data (expert moves) to train the two networks.

9.4.1 Generate Data to Train the Networks

You'll learn how to generate data to train the two policy neural networks. Specifically, you'll generate 10,000 games in which an expert plays against a non-expert. You'll then record the board positions and the moves made by the expert.

First, let's define the expert player and the non-expert player.

```
[1]: import numpy as np
     import random

     def expert(env):
         if env.state%3 != 0:
             move = env.state%3
         else:
             move = random.choice([1,2])
         return move

     def non_expert(env):
         if env.state%3 != 0 and np.random.rand()<0.5:
             move = env.state%3
         else:
```

```
            move = random.choice([1,2])
        return move
```

The expert player always tries to make a move so that the number of coins left in the pile is a multiple of three. The non-expert player, however, makes such a move with a 50% probability. With the remaining probability, it randomly selects a move.

First, let's simulate one game. The code in the cell below accomplishes that:

```
[2]:  from utils.coin_simple_env import coin_game
      import time

      # Initiate the game environment
      env=coin_game()
      # Define the one_game() function
      def one_game(episode):
          history=[]
          state=env.reset()
          # The nonexpert moves firsts half the time
          if episode%2==0:
              action=non_expert(env)
              state,reward,done,_=env.step(action)
          while True:
              action=expert(env)
              history.append((state,action))
              state,reward,done,_=env.step(action)
              if done:
                  break
              action=non_expert(env)
              state,reward,done,_=env.step(action)
              if done:
                  break
          return history

      # Simulate one game and print out results
      history=one_game(0)
      print(history)
```

[(20, 2), (17, 2), (13, 1), (11, 2), (8, 2), (5, 2), (1, 1)]

The first element in the above output is (20, 2). This indicates that when there are 20 coins left in the pile, the expert takes two coins from the pile so the number of coins left, 18, is a multiple of three. Similarly, the second element in the above output is (17, 2). This indicates that when there are 17 coins left in the pile, the expert takes two coins from the pile so the number of coins left, 15, is a multiple of three. The last element in the above output is (1,1). This indicates that when there is one coin left in the pile, the expert takes the coin and wins the game.

Next, let's simulate 10,000 games:

```
[3]:  # simulate the game 10000 times
      results = []
      for episode in range(10000):
          history=one_game(episode)
          results+=history
```

Now, let's save the data on your computer for later use:

```
[4]:  import pickle
      # save the simulation data on your computer
      with open('files/games_coin.p', 'wb') as fp:
          pickle.dump(results,fp)
      # read the data and print out the first 10 observations
      with open('files/games_coin.p', 'rb') as fp:
          games = pickle.load(fp)
      print(games[:10])
```

```
[(20, 2), (17, 2), (14, 2), (11, 2), (8, 2), (5, 2), (2, 2),
(21, 1), (18, 1), (15, 1)]
```

The results show ten state-action pairs in the simulated data.

We now have the data we need. You'll learn how to build and train the two policy neural networks next.

9.4.2 Create Two Neural Networks

We first use Keras to create the following neural network with just one hidden layer as our fast policy network.

```
[5]:  from tensorflow.keras.utils import to_categorical
      from tensorflow.keras.layers import Dense
      from tensorflow.keras.models import Sequential

      fast_model = Sequential()
      fast_model.add(Dense(units=32,activation="relu",
                      input_shape=(22,)))
      fast_model.add(Dense(2, activation='softmax'))
      fast_model.compile(loss='categorical_crossentropy',
                      optimizer='adam',
                      metrics=['accuracy'])
```

The input shape is 22 because we'll change the game state to a one-hot variable with 22 values in it. We include a hidden layer with 32 neurons. The output layer has two neurons, representing two possible actions that can be taken by the expert: 1 or 2.

We'll also create a strong policy network, with three hidden layers:

```
[6]:   strong_model = Sequential()
       strong_model.add(Dense(units=64,activation="relu",
                       input_shape=(22,)))
       strong_model.add(Dense(32, activation="relu"))
       strong_model.add(Dense(16, activation="relu"))
       strong_model.add(Dense(2, activation='softmax'))
       strong_model.compile(loss='categorical_crossentropy',
                       optimizer='adam',
                       metrics=['accuracy'])
```

The strong policy network has three hidden layers with 64, 32, and 16 neurons in them respectively. The output layer has also two neurons, representing two possible actions that can be taken by the expert: 1 or 2.

Next, we'll train the two neural networks using the expert moves we just generated.

9.4.3   Train the Two Policy Neural Networks

We'll train the two neural networks we just created in the last subsection. We first pre-process the data so that we can feed them into the models.

We'll convert both the game states and the moves into one-hot variables so that the deep neural network can process them.

```
[7]:   states=[20,1]
       one_hot=to_categorical(states,22)
       print(one_hot)
```

```
[[0. 0. 0. 0. 0. 0. 0. 0. 0. 0. 0. 0. 0. 0. 0. 0. 0. 0. 0. 0. 1. 0.]
 [0. 1. 0. 0. 0. 0. 0. 0. 0. 0. 0. 0. 0. 0. 0. 0. 0. 0. 0. 0. 0. 0.]]
```

In the example above, we have two states: 20 and 1. We use the *to_categorical()* method in TensorFlow to change them into one-hot variables. The second argument in the *to_categorical()* method, 22, indicates the depth of the one-hot variable. This means each one-hot variable will be a vector with a length of 22, with a value 1 in one position and 0 in all others.

The game state 20 now becomes a one-hot label: a 22-value vector with 0 in all positions except in the position indexed as 20, which has a value of 1.

Similarly, we change the actions to one-hot variables with a depth of 2, like so:

```
[8]: actions=[1,2]
     # change actions 1 and 2 to 0 and 1.
     actions=np.array(actions)-1
     # change actions to one-hot actions
     one_hot_actions=to_categorical(actions,2)
     print(one_hot_actions)
```

```
[[1. 0.]
 [0. 1.]]
```

We first change the actions from 1 and 2 to 0 and 1 because Python uses zero-based indexing. We then change 0 and 1 to two one-hot variables with a depth of 2.

Next, we load up the simulated game data and convert them into Xs and ys so that we can feed them to the deep neural networks:

```
[9]: with open('files/games_coin.p','rb') as fp:
         games=pickle.load(fp)

     states = []
     actions = []
     for x in games:
         state=to_categorical(x[0],22)
         action=to_categorical(x[1]-1,2)
         states.append(state)
         actions.append(action)

     X = np.array(states).reshape((-1, 22))
     y = np.array(actions).reshape((-1, 2))
```

We first train the fast policy network for 25 epochs:

```
[10]: # Train the models for 25 epochs
      fast_model.fit(X, y, epochs=25, verbose=1)
      fast_model.save('files/fast_coin.h5')
```

It takes about two minutes to train the model. Once done, we save the trained model in the local folder.

Next, we train the strong policy network for 25 epochs as well.

```
[11]: strong_model.fit(X, y, epochs=25, verbose=1)
      strong_model.save('files/strong_coin.h5')
```

It takes slightly longer to train the strong policy network. The trained model is saved in the local folder as well. Alternatively, you can download both models from the book's GitHub repository.

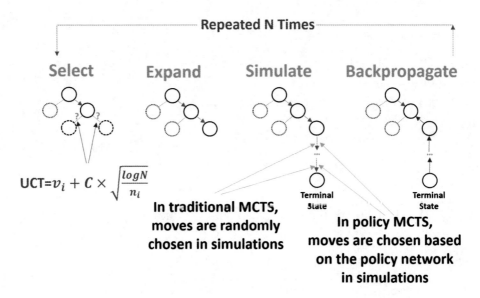

Figure 9.4 Policy-based MCTS algorithm.

9.5   MCTS WITH POLICY ROLLOUTS IN THE COIN GAME

In the original AlphaGo algorithm developed by DeepMind, the purpose of the fast policy network is to roll out games in MCTS. Therefore, in this section, you'll learn how policy rollouts work in MCTS.

Figure 9.4 provides a diagram of the policy-based MCTS algorithm. Compared to the traditional MCTS algorithm that we discussed in Chapter 8, policy-based MCTS rolls out games according to the distribution in the policy network, instead of randomly selecting moves. The other three steps: select, expand, and backpropagate, are the same as those in the traditional MCTS.

9.5.1   Policy-Based MCTS in the Coin Game

Instead of choosing moves randomly each step in game rollouts, we'll use the trained fast policy network earlier in this chapter to guide the moves in each step. Intelligent moves lead to more accurate game outcomes, which in turn lead to more accurate position evaluations from game rollouts. This makes the MCTS algorithm more intelligent.

Go to the book's GitHub repository, download the file *ch09util.py*, and place it in the folder /Desktop/ags/utils/ on your computer. In the file, we define a *DL_stochastic()* function as follows:

```
def onehot_encoder(state):
    onehot=np.zeros((1,22))
    onehot[0,state]=1
    return onehot
```

```
def DL_stochastic(env):
    state = env.state
    onehot_state = onehot_encoder(state)
    action_probs = model(onehot_state)
    return np.random.choice([1,2],
            p=np.squeeze(action_probs))
```

The *DL_stochastic()* function selects the best move based on the trained fast policy network. Note we are using the stochastic policy here, meaning we select the moves randomly based on the probability distribution from the policy network. Another possibility is to use a deterministic policy, meaning you choose the action with the highest probability.

Now that we know how to select the best moves based on the trained policy network, we'll define a *policy_simulate()* function in the local module *ch09util*. The function simulates a game from a certain starting position all the way to the end of the game.

```
def policy_simulate(env_copy,done,reward,model):
    # if the game has already ended
    if done==True:
        return reward
    while True:
        move=DL_stochastic(env_copy,model)
        state,reward,done,info=env_copy.step(move)
        if done==True:
            return reward
```

This function is similar to the *simulate()* function we defined in Chapter 8. However, instead of randomly selecting moves, the above *policy_simulate()* function selects moves based on the probabilities in the trained fast policy network.

Further, we define a *policy_mcts_coin()* function in the local module as follows:

```
def policy_mcts_coin(env,model,num_rollouts=100,temperature=1.4):
    # if there is only one valid move left, take it
    if len(env.validinputs)==1:
        return env.validinputs[0]
    # create three dictionaries counts, wins, losses
    counts={}
    wins={}
    losses={}
    for move in env.validinputs:
        counts[move]=0
        wins[move]=0
        losses[move]=0
    # roll out games
    for _ in range(num_rollouts):
```

```
    # selection
    move=select(env,counts,wins,losses,temperature)
    # expansion
    env_copy, done, reward=expand(env,move)
    # simulation
    reward=policy_simulate(env_copy,done,reward,model)
    # backpropagate
    counts,wins,losses=backpropagate(\
        env,move,reward,counts,wins,losses)
# make the move
return next_move(counts,wins,losses)
```

We set the default number of rollouts to 100. You can change it to a different number when calling the function. We create three dictionaries, *counts*, *wins*, and *losses*, to record the outcomes from the simulated games. Once all game rollouts are complete, we select the best next move based on the simulation results.

9.5.2 The Effectiveness of the Policy MCTS Agent

We'll compare the policy-based MCTS algorithm in the coin game that we defined above with the UCT MCTS algorithm that we defined in Chapter 8. We'll show that the former is stronger than the latter, with the same number of rollouts in both algorithms.

We will let the two MCTS agents play 100 games against each other and see how many times each algorithm wins.

```
[12]: from utils.ch08util import mcts
      from utils.ch09util import policy_mcts_coin

      env=coin_game()
      results=[]
      for i in range(100):
          state=env.reset()
          # Half the time, the UCT MCTS agent moves first
          if i%2==0:
              action=mcts(env,num_rollouts=100)
              state, reward, done, info=env.step(action)
          while True:
              action=policy_mcts_coin(env,fast_model,num_rollouts=100)
              state, reward, done, info=env.step(action)
              if done:
                  # result is 1 if the policy MCTS agent wins
                  results.append(1)
                  break
              action=mcts(env,num_rollouts=100)
              state, reward, done, info=env.step(action)
```

```
    if done:
        # result is -1 if the policy MCTS agent loses
        results.append(-1)
        break
```

Half the time, the UCT MCTS agent moves first and the other half the policy MCTS agent moves first so that no player has an advantage. We record a result of 1 if the policy MCTS agent wins and a result of −1 if the UCT MCTS agent wins.

We now count how many times the policy MCTS agent has won and how many times the UCT MCTS agent has won:

```
[3]: wins=results.count(1)
     print(f"the policy MCTS agent has won {wins} games")
     losses=results.count(-1)
     print(f"the policy MCTS agent has lost {losses} games")
```

```
the policy MCTS agent has won 96 games
the policy MCTS agent has lost 4 games
```

The above results show that the policy MCTS agent has won 96 games and lost 4 games. This indicates that the policy MCTS algorithm is much more intelligent than the UCT MCTS algorithm.

Later in the book when we implement the AlphaGo algorithm in the coin game, we'll use the policy MCTS to help evaluate different moves before selecting the best next move. We'll also utilize a value network based on self-play deep reinforcement learning.

9.6   GLOSSARY

- **Artificial Intelligence (AI):** A branch of computer science dealing with the simulation of intelligent behavior in computers. It is different from the natural intelligence of humans and other animals.
- **Binary Classification** Binary classification is the machine learning algorithm with the task of classifying samples into one of the two categories.
- **Binary Cross Entropy** A loss function used to measure the average difference between the predicted probabilities of an outcome and the actual labels (1 or 0). It's the preferred loss function in binary classifications.
- **Categorical Cross-Entropy** The loss function used in multi-category classifications. It measures the average difference between the predicted distribution and the actual distribution.
- **Convolutional Layer** A layer of neurons that forms the main building block of a convolutional neural network. The convolutional layer uses filters to scan over different parts of the input data to detect patterns.
- **Convolutional Neural Network (CNN)** A class of neural networks with at least one convolutional layer. The network is able to detect spatial patterns in the input data.

- **Deep Learning** A machine learning method based on deep neural networks that are characterized by many hidden layers of neurons, in addition to an input layer and an output layer.
- **Deep Neural Networks:** Neural networks consist of many hidden layers of connected neurons, besides an input layer and an output layer.
- **Hidden Layer** The hidden layer is located between the input layer and the output layer in a neural network. It receives processed data from the input layer, further processes it, and passes them on to the output layer.
- **Input Layer** The input layer is the first layer of neurons in a neural network. It brings the input data into the system for further processing by hidden layers and the output layer.
- **Loss Function:** Also called the cost function. It measures the error between the forecasts from ML models and the actual values. Some commonly used loss functions include mean squared error, mean absolute error, and cross entropy.
- **Machine Learning (ML):** A branch of artificial intelligence (AI) in which humans give computers the ability to learn without being explicitly programmed.
- **Mean Squared Error (MSE) Loss Function** A commonly used loss function in machine learning. It is the average squared value of the difference between the actual value and the predicted value from the model.
- **Multi-Category Classification** A machine learning algorithm to classify instances into one of multiple categories. The number of categories is three or more.
- **Neural Networks:** A type of machine learning model inspired by the biological neural networks of human brains. They are also called artificial neural networks or simply neural nets. Neural networks consist of multiple layers of connected neurons: an input layer, an output layer, and in most cases a number of hidden layers.
- **Output Layer** The output layer is the last layer of neurons in a neural network. It produces the predictions from the model. **Activation Functions** Functions in neural networks that are used to determine the output of neurons in the network. Commonly used activation functions include ReLU, sigmoid, and softmax.
- **ReLU Activation Function** ReLU is short for rectified linear unit activation function. It returns the original value if the input is positive, and 0 otherwise.
- **Reinforcement Learning (RL):** A type of ML in which agents interact with an environment to explore different actions. Agents learn to choose actions to maximize the cumulative rewards through trial and error.
- **Sigmoid Activation Function** The sigmoid function has the form

$$y = \frac{1}{1 + e^{-x}}$$

It has this nice property: for any value of input x between $-\infty$ and ∞, the output value y is always between 0 and 1. Because of this property, it is used to model the probability of an outcome.

- **Softmax Activation Function:** The softmax function has the form

$$y(x) = \frac{e^x}{\sum_{k=1}^{K} e^{x_k}}$$

where $x = [x_1, x_2, ..., x_K]$ and $y = [y_1, y_2, ..., y_K]$ are K-element lists. Each element in the output vector has a value between 0 and 1. The elements in the output vector add up to 1. Because of these properties, we use the softmax activation function to model the probability distribution of a multiple-category outcome.
- **Supervised Learning:** A type of ML in which the model uses labeled data to learn the relation between the input variables and the output variables.
- **Unsupervised Learning:** A type of ML in which the model uses unlabeled data to learn the similarities, differences, and other patterns among the input variables to generate the output variables.

9.7 EXERCISES

9.1 What is artificial intelligence (AI)? What is rule-based AI?

9.2 What is machine learning (ML)? How is it different from rule-based AI?

9.3 What are the three types of ML?

9.4 What is supervised learning? What is unsupervised learning? What is reinforcement learning?

9.5 What are deep learning and deep reinforcement learning?

9.6 What is an input layer? an output layer? and a hidden layer?

9.7 What is the mean squared error (MSE) loss function?

9.8 What is an activation function? Give three examples of commonly used activation functions.

9.9 What is the ReLU activation function? The sigmoid activation function?

9.10 What is the softmax activation function? Why do we use it as the activation function when we model multi-category classification problems?

9.11 What is binary classification? What is the binary cross-entropy loss function?

9.12 What is a convolutional neural network? A dense layer? A convolutional layer?

9.13 What is multi-category classification? What is the categorical class-entropy loss function?

9.14 Modify the two code cells in Section 9.5.2 so that both MCTS agents use 200 rollouts when making moves. See how many games the policy MCTS agent wins.

## CHAPTER 10

Policy Networks in Tic Tac Toe

"All you need is lots and lots of data and lots of information about what the right answer is, and you'll be able to train a big neural net to do what you want."
– *Geoffrey Hinton*

IN THE PREVIOUS chapter, you learned the basics of deep learning and applied it to the coin game. Specifically, you generated expert moves in the game and used them to train two policy networks: a fast policy network with just one hidden layer and a strong policy network with three hidden layers.

In this chapter, you'll learn to use deep learning to train a fast policy network and a strong policy network in Tic Tac Toe. Different from those in the previous chapter, the two neural networks in this chapter include a new type of layers, convolutional layers, which are different from fully-connected dense layers. While dense layers treat inputs as one-dimensional vectors, convolutional layers treat images or game boards as multi-dimensional objects and extract spatial features from them. Convolutional layers can greatly improve the predictive power of neural networks. This, in turn, makes the game strategies that use these policy networks more intelligent.

To generate expert moves in Tic Tac Toe, you'll use the MiniMax algorithm with alpha-beta pruning that we developed in Chapter 6. You'll use the board positions as inputs (Xs) and the expert moves as targets (ys). Since there are nine potential next moves for a player in each step, we'll treat this as a multi-category classification problem and use supervised learning to train the two policy neural networks. The two trained policy networks will be used in the AlphaGo algorithm later in this book.

We'll use the trained fast policy network later in the book to roll out games in MCTS when implementing the AlphaGo algorithm. In contrast, we'll use the trained strong policy network to help select which child node (i.e., next move) to select when

DOI: 10.1201/9781032722207-10

expanding the game tree in MCTS. To gain insight on how the strong policy network can be used in the final AlphaGo algorithm, you'll learn to augment MCTS with the trained strong policy network in this chapter. Specifically, instead of selecting child nodes based on upper confidence bounds for trees (UCT) scores, you'll select them based on both rollout values and the probability distribution from the trained strong policy network. We call the agent who selects child nodes this way the mixed MCTS agent. You'll show that the mixed MCTS agent is more intelligent than the traditional MCTS agent that you developed in Chapter 8.

What You'll Learn in This Chapter

- What is a convolutional neural network
- Building a fast policy network and a strong policy network in Tic Tac Toe
- Generating expert moves to train the two policy networks in Tic Tac Toe
- Implementing a mixed MCTS game strategy in Tic Tac Toe

10.1 WHAT ARE CONVOLUTIONAL LAYERS?

This section discusses the basic structure of a convolutional layer.

Convolutional layers use filters (also called kernels) to find patterns in the input data. A convolutional layer can automatically detect a large number of patterns and associate these patterns with the target label. This is useful in both image classifications and game strategy developments in machine learning.

In particular, we'll use the Tic Tac Toe game board, something everyone knows, as our example in this chapter to explain how convolutional layers work. Game boards have far fewer pixels than images and we can focus on certain patterns that we know are associated with game outcomes (vertical, horizontal, or diagonal lines in Tic Tac Toe and Connect Four games, for example). Using game boards instead of actual images greatly simplifies the explanation on how convolutional neural networks (CNNs) work.

Let's say that the input data is the Tic Tac Toe game board, as shown in Figure 10.1.

We use the NumPy array below to represent the game board:

```
import numpy as np

board = np.array([[1,0,0],
                  [1,-1,-1],
                  [1,0,0]]).reshape(-1,3,3,1)
```

A value of 1 indicates the cell is occupied by Player X; a value of -1 indicates that the cell is occupied by Player O; a value of 0 indicates the cell is empty. In the game board above, the three cells in the left column are occupied by Player X. We

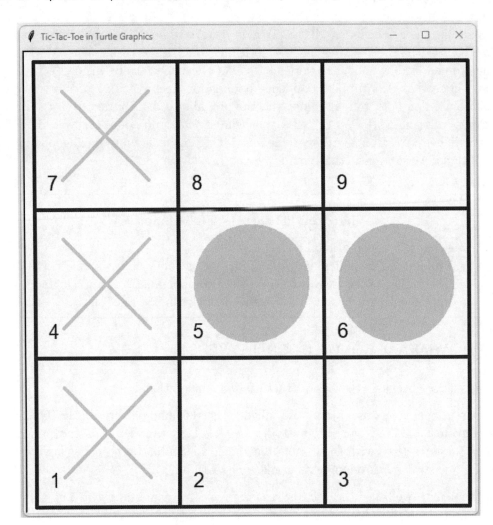

Figure 10.1   An example game board position in Tic Tac Toe

use $reshape(-1, 3, 3, 1)$ to change the matrix to a four-dimensional array: the first dimension represents how many images we have in the batch (that is, the batch size); the second and third dimensions are the width and height of the image. The last dimension is the color channel. A color picture has three channels (RGB, i.e., red, green, and blue). Here the game board has just one color channel.

Below, we'll create a vertical filter with a size of 3 by 3. The middle column has values 1, while the other two columns have 0s.

```
[2]: # Create a vertical filter
vertical_filter = np.array([[0,1,0],
                [0,1,0],
                [0,1,0]]).reshape(3,3,1,1)
```

A vertical filter highlights the vertical features in the image and blurs the rest. We'll apply the 3 by 3 vertical filter on the Tic Tac Toe game board as follows:

```
[3]: import tensorflow as tf

     # Apply the filter on the game board
     result=tf.nn.conv2d(board,vertical_filter,strides=1,padding="SAME")
     # Print out results
     print(result.numpy().reshape(3,3))
```

```
[[ 2 -1 -1]
 [ 3 -1 -1]
 [ 2 -1 -1]]
```

The values in the first column are much larger than the values in other cells. This indicates that the vertical filter has detected the vertical pattern in the first column on the game board. The *strides=1* argument means the filter shifts one pixel to the right or down at a time on the image during the convolutional operation. The *padding="SAME"* argument in the *conv2d()* function means the network adds 0s around the input image. For more details on how convolutional operations work, see, e.g., my book *Machine Learning, Animated* [6].

10.2 DEEP LEARNING IN TIC TAC TOE

In this section, you'll train deep neural networks in Tic Tac Toe so that you can use them later in the book when implementing the AlphaGo algorithm. In particular, you'll first create a fast neural network with one convolutional layer and two hidden dense layers. The advantage of this fast neural network is that later when you use it in MCTS to roll out games, the network recommends a move fast due to its simple structure. Second, you'll create a strong neural network with a convolutional layer and three hidden dense layers. Later in this book, you'll use self-play deep reinforcement learning to improve the strong policy network. At the same time, you'll use the game experience data in self-plays to train a value network to estimate game outcomes. The improved strong policy network and the value network will be used to augment child node selection in tree search.

10.2.1 Steps to Train Neural Networks in Tic Tac Toe

In this chapter, you'll build and train a fast policy network and a strong policy network in Tic Tac Toe so that you can use them later to build the AlphaGo algorithm. The two policy networks are similar, but the fast policy network has one fewer hidden dense layer.

You'll learn how to prepare data to train the two policy networks, how to interpret the predictions from the networks. Here is a summary of what we'll do to train the two neural networks:

1. We'll create two computer players: an expert and a non-expert. The expert selects moves based on the MiniMax algorithm with alpha-beta pruning we discussed in in Chapter 6. The non-expert computer player selects a random move 50% of the time. In the other 50% of the time, it selects moves the same way as the expert player (i.e., based on the MiniMax algorithm with alpha-beta pruning). If we let both players use expert moves, the moves are identical in each game and the game experience data will not cover all game scenarios. By letting the non-expert player choose random moves half the time, we can generate game experience data to cover different game scenarios. This, in turn, allows us to train more intelligent policy networks.

2. We let the two players play a game, and record board positions and all moves made by the expert player. We'll use game board positions as features X, and moves made by the expert as labels y. We'll treat this as a multi-category classification problem since there are nine possible moves that the expert can make: occupying cells 1, 2, ..., or 9.

3. We'll simulate 10,000 games and use the board positions and the corresponding moves as Xs and ys. We then feed the data (X, y) into the two neural networks to train them.

10.2.2 Generate Expert Moves in Tic Tac Toe

You'll first generate data to train the two policy neural networks. The logic is as follows: you'll generate 10,000 games in which an expert player plays against a non-expert. You'll then record the board positions and moves made by the expert.

We define the expert player and the non-expert player as follows:

```
[4]: from utils.ch06util import MiniMax_ab

def expert(env):
    move = MiniMax_ab(env)
    return move

def non_expert(env):
    if np.random.rand()<0.5:
        move = MiniMax_ab(env)
    else:
        move = env.sample()
    return move
```

The expert player selects moves based on the MiniMax algorithm with alpha-beta pruning that we developed in Chapter 6. The non-expert player, however, makes such a move with a 50% probability. With the remaining probability, it randomly selects a legal move.

The following *one_game()* function simulates one game and records game board positions and expert moves:

```
[5]:  from utils.ttt_simple_env import ttt
      from copy import deepcopy

      # Initiate the game environment
      env=ttt()
      # Define the one_game() function
      def one_game(episode):
          history = []
          state=env.reset()
          # The nonexpert moves firsts half the time
          if episode%2==0:
              action=non_expert(env)
              state,reward,done,_=env.step(action)
          while True:
              action=expert(env)
              if episode%2==0:
                  statei=deepcopy(-state)
              else:
                  statei=deepcopy(state)
              actioni=deepcopy(action)
              # record board position and the move
              history.append((statei,actioni))
              state,reward,done,_=env.step(action)
              if done:
                  break
              action=non_expert(env)
              state,reward,done,_=env.step(action)
              if done:
                  break
          return history

      # Simulate one game and print out results
      history=one_game(0)
      print(history)
```

```
[(array([ 0,  0,  0,  0,  0,  0,  0, -1,  0]), 9),
 (array([ 0, -1,  0,  0,  0, 0,  0, -1,  1]), 5),
 (array([-1, -1,  0,  0,  1,  0,  0, -1,  1]), 3),
 (array([-1, -1,  1,  0,  1, -1,  0, -1,  1]), 7)]
```

The above output has four state-action pairs. The state is the game board before the expert makes a move, and the action is the move chosen by the expert. Note that if the expert is Player O, we multiply the game board by -1 so that -1 means a cell occupied by the opponent while 1 means a cell occupied by the current player. Therefore, the best move is from the current player's point of view. We do this to make the state-action pair player-independent.

Now, let's simulate 10,000 games and save the data.

```
[6]:  # simulate the game 10000 times and record all games
      results = []
      for episode in range(10000):
          history=one_game(episode)
          results+=history
```

The data are saved on your computer for later use, as follows:

```
[7]:  import pickle

      # save the simulation data on your computer
      with open('files/games_ttt.p', 'wb') as fp:
          pickle.dump(results,fp)
      # read the data and print out the first 10 observations
      with open('files/games_ttt.p', 'rb') as fp:
          games = pickle.load(fp)
      print(games[:10])
```

```
[(array([ 0, -1,  0,  0,  0,  0,  0,  0,  0]), 5),
 ...,
 (array([ 0,  0, -1,  0,  1, 0, -1,  0,  0]), 2)]
```

We now have the data we need to train two policy networks. Next, we'll create two policy networks in Tic Tac Toe.

10.3   TWO POLICY NETWORKS IN TIC TAC TOE

We'll use Keras to create two neural networks: a fast policy network and a strong policy network. We'll then use the data generated in the last section to train the two networks.

10.3.1   Create Two Neural Networks for Tic Tac Toe

We first use Keras to create the following neural network with one convolutional layer and two hidden dense layers as the fast policy network in Tic Tac Toe:

```
[8]:  from tensorflow.keras.utils import to_categorical
      from tensorflow.keras.layers import Dense
      from tensorflow.keras.models import Sequential
      from tensorflow.keras.layers import Conv2D, Flatten
```

```
fast_model = Sequential()
fast_model.add(Conv2D(filters=128,
     kernel_size=(3,3),padding="same",activation="relu",
                input_shape=(3,3,1)))
fast_model.add(Flatten())
fast_model.add(Dense(units=64, activation="relu"))
fast_model.add(Dense(units=64, activation="relu"))
fast_model.add(Dense(9, activation='softmax'))
fast_model.compile(loss='categorical_crossentropy',
                optimizer='adam',
                metrics=['accuracy'])
```

The input shape is 3 by 3 by 1 because the convolutional layer treats the game board as a multi-channel two-dimensional image and extracts spatial features from it. The first hidden layer is a convolutional layer with 128 filters. The kernel size is 3 by 3. We then flatten the output from the convolutional layer. The flattened one-dimensional vector is then fed to the two hidden dense layers (each with 64 neurons in it). The output layer has nine neurons, representing the nine possible actions: occupying cell 1 through 9. The softmax activation ensures that the output can be interpreted as the probability distribution of a multiple-outcome event: each value in the output is between 0 and 1; and the values add up to 100%.

We'll also create a strong policy network, with a similar structure to the fast policy network but with an extra hidden dense layer:

[9]:
```
strong_model = Sequential()
strong_model.add(Conv2D(filters=128,
     kernel_size=(3,3),padding="same",activation="relu",
                input_shape=(3,3,1)))
strong_model.add(Flatten())
strong_model.add(Dense(units=64, activation="relu"))
strong_model.add(Dense(units=64, activation="relu"))
strong_model.add(Dense(units=64, activation="relu"))
strong_model.add(Dense(9, activation='softmax'))
strong_model.compile(loss='categorical_crossentropy',
                optimizer='adam',
                metrics=['accuracy'])
```

In simple games such as Tic Tac Toe, even training a strong network is not so time-consuming. In complicated games such as Chess or Go, a strong network can be extremely complicated: it will take a long time for the strong policy network to spit out a move for a given board position. Therefore, the fast policy network tends to be much simpler than the strong network in complicated games. Here we just add one single layer to the fast network to create a strong network, for demonstration purposes. The goal is for you to learn the steps involved in the AlphaGo algorithm.

10.3.2 Train the Two Policy Networks in Tic Tac Toe

We'll train the two policy networks we just created in the last subsection. We first pre-process the data so that we can feed them to the models.

Specifically, we first change the actions from numbers between 1 and 9 to numbers between 0 and 8 because Python uses zero-based indexing. Next, we load up the simulated game data and convert them into Xs and ys so that we can feed them into the deep neural networks:

```
[10]: import pickle
      import numpy as np
      with open('files/games_ttt.p','rb') as fp:
          games=pickle.load(fp)

      states=[]
      actions=[]
      for x in games:
          state=x[0]
          action=to_categorical(x[1]-1,9)
          states.append(state)
          actions.append(action)

      X=np.array(states).reshape((-1, 3, 3, 1))
      y=np.array(actions).reshape((-1, 9))
```

We reshape X into NumPy arrays with a shape of $(-1, 3, 3, 1)$. The first dimension indicates the number of observations in the batch: a value of -1 allows the program to automatically detect the batch size. This is needed since the number of observations in each batch is different due to the leftovers in the last batch. The values 3, 3, and 1 represent the width, height, and number of color channels in the input data.

We first train the fast policy network for 100 epochs:

```
[11]: # Train the fast policy network for 100 epochs
      fast_model.fit(X, y, epochs=100, verbose=1)
      fast_model.save('files/fast_ttt.h5')
```

```
Epoch 1/100
1194/1194 [==============================] - 1s 951us/step -
loss: 1.2428 - accuracy: 0.5271
Epoch 2/100
1194/1194 [==============================] - 1s 936us/step -
loss: 0.9380 - accuracy: 0.6098
...
Epoch 99/100
1194/1194 [==============================] - 1s 935us/step -
```

```
loss: 0.7557 - accuracy: 0.6475
Epoch 100/100
1194/1194 [==============================] - 1s 922us/step -
loss: 0.7565 - accuracy: 0.6461
```

It takes about five minutes to train the model. Once done, we save the trained model in the local folder.

Next, we train the strong policy network for 100 epochs as well.

```
2]: strong_model.fit(X, y, epochs=100, verbose=1)
    strong_model.save('files/strong_ttt.h5')
```

```
Epoch 1/100
1194/1194 [==============================] - 2s 980us/step -
loss: 1.2319 - accuracy: 0.5284
...
Epoch 99/100
1194/1194 [==============================] - 1s 973us/step -
loss: 0.7553 - accuracy: 0.6472
Epoch 100/100
1194/1194 [==============================] - 1s 964us/step -
loss: 0.7568 - accuracy: 0.6473
```

It takes slightly longer to train the strong policy network. The trained model is saved in the local folder as well. Alternatively, you can download both trained models from the book's GitHub repository.

10.4 A MIXED MCTS ALGORITHM IN TIC TAC TOE

As we mentioned in Chapter 9, our goal in this book is to apply the AlphaGo algorithm in the three everyday games. We have discussed the main steps and components of the AlphaGo algorithm in Figure 9.1. In particular, Monte Carlo Tree Search (MCTS) serves as the backbone of AlphaGo's decision-making process. MCTS is used to efficiently search through possible moves in Go, a game known for its vast number of potential moves and board states. The algorithm evaluates the potential future moves and their outcomes, making decisions based on a balance of exploration and exploitation.

However, the MCTS algorithm used in AlphaGo is different from the traditional MCTS algorithm that we discussed in Chapter 8, which uses the UCT formula to select potential future moves. In contrast, AlphaGo augments the UCT formula with an improved strong policy network and a value network.

In this section, you'll learn how to augment the UCT formula with the strong policy network you trained in the last section to create an improved MCTS algorithm.

10.4.1 Augment the UCT Formula with a Strong Policy Network

If you recall, in Chapter 8, we discussed the formula for the Upper Confidence Bounds for Trees (UCT), which is defined as follows:

$$UCB = v_i + C\sqrt{\frac{logN}{n_i}}$$

In the above formula, the value v_i is the estimated value of choosing child node (i.e., next move) i. C is a constant that adjusts how much exploration one wants in move selection. N is the total number of times the parent node (i.e., the root, or the current game state) has been visited (i.e., how many simulations have been conducted so far), whereas n_i is the number of times child node i has been selected among the N simulations.

Now, let's modify the selection rule by adding the prior from the strong policy network to the UCT score as follows:

$$mix\_score = v_i + C\sqrt{\frac{logN}{n_i}} + \gamma\frac{p_i}{1+n_i}$$

The last term in the above formula takes into account the recommendation from the strong policy network on how to select the next move i. γ is a constant used to determine how much weight to put on the recommendation from the strong policy network. If you are confident that the policy network provides intelligent moves, you use a high value of γ (e.g, set it to 10 or 20); on the other hand, if the policy network is not as intelligent, you can use a low value of γ (e.g, set it to 0.25 or 0.5). We set it to 10 in this chapter but you can experiment with other values. p_i is the probability of choosing the next move i based on the policy network. Further, we scale p_i by $1 + n_i$: if the child node i (that is, the future move i) is visited only a few times in simulations so far, the formula gives a large weight on the prior from the policy network. On the other hand, if the child node i is visited many times, whether to select the child node i depends mainly on the outcomes from simulations (i.e., v_i).

Figure 10.2 provides a diagram of the difference between the mixed MCTS versus the traditional MCTS that we used in Chapter 8. As you can see, the difference lies in how the child node i (that is, the future move i) is selected to expand the game tree. Other steps (expand, simulate, and backpropagate) are the same in the two MCTS algorithms.

10.4.2 Mixed MCTS in Tic Tac Toe

To show exactly how mixed MCTS works, we'll implement it in the Tic Tac Toe game. Instead of selecting the child node using the UCT score alone in tree search, we'll use a combination of the UCT score and the prior from the strong policy network. This way, the algorithm benefits from both UCT scores and the priors from the trained strong policy network.

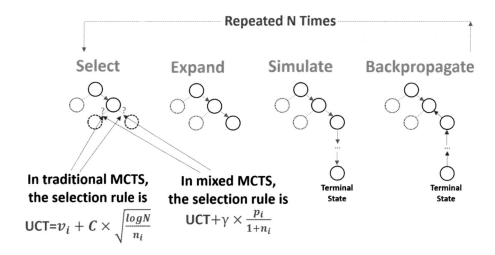

Figure 10.2   A diagram of the difference between mixed MCTS versus UCT MCTS

Download the file *ch10util.py* from the book's GitHub repository and save it in /Desktop/ags/utils/ on your computer.

In the local module *ch10util*, we define a *mix_select()* function as follows:

```
gamma=10
def mix_select(env,ps,counts,wins,losses,temperature):
    # a dictionary of mixed scores for all next moves
    scores={}
    # the ones not visited get the priority
    for k in env.validinputs:
        if counts[k]==0:
            return k
    # total number of simulations conducted
    N=sum([v for k,v in counts.items()])
    # calculate scores
    for k,v in counts.items():
        # the third term based on policy network
        weighted_pi=gamma*ps[k]/(1+counts[k])
        if v==0:
            scores[k]=weighted_pi
        else:
            # vi for each next move
            vi=(wins.get(k,0)-losses.get(k,0))/v
            # exploratoin term
            exploration=temperature*sqrt(log(N)/counts[k])
            # mixed score
            scores[k]=vi+exploration+weighted_pi
```

```
    # Select the next move with the highest UCT score
    return max(scores,key=scores.get)
```

The above function *mix_select()* determines which next move i to select to expand the game tree in each simulation. It has two parts: the first part is based on the UCT formula $v_i + C\sqrt{\frac{logN}{n_i}}$, and the second part is the weighted probability from the trained strong policy network $\gamma\frac{p_i}{1+n_i}$.

We also define a *next_move()* function in the file *ch10util.py*, which selects the best next move based on the numbers of wins and losses associated with each next move. The function is defined as follows:

```
def next_move(ps,counts,wins,losses):
    # See which action is most promising
    scores={}
    # calculate scores
    for k,v in counts.items():
        # the third term based on policy network
        weighted_pi=gamma*ps[k]/(1+counts[k])
        # vi for each next move
        vi=(wins.get(k,0)-losses.get(k,0))/v
        # mixed score
        scores[k]=vi+weighted_pi
    # Select the next move with the score
    return max(scores,key=scores.get)
```

Several other functions are defined in the local module and they are the same as those in Chapter 8: *expand()*, *simulate()*, and *backpropagate()*. Finally, in the local module *ch10util*, we define a *mix_mcts()* function as follows:

```
def mix_mcts(env,model,num_rollouts=100,temperature=1.4):
    # if there is only one valid move left, take it
    if len(env.validinputs)==1:
        return env.validinputs[0]
    # create three dictionaries counts, wins, losses
    counts={}
    wins={}
    losses={}
    for move in env.validinputs:
        counts[move]=0
        wins[move]=0
        losses[move]=0
    # priors from the policy network
    state = env.state.reshape(-1,3,3,1)
    if env.turn=="X":
        action_probs= model(state)
    else:
```

```
    action_probs= model(-state)
ps={}
for a in sorted(env.validinputs):
    ps[a]=np.squeeze(action_probs)[a-1]
# roll out games
for _ in range(num_rollouts):
    # selection
    move=mix_select(env,ps,counts,wins,losses,temperature)
    # expansion
    env_copy, done, reward=expand(env,move)
    # simulation
    reward=simulate(env_copy,done,reward)
    # backpropagate
    counts,wins,losses=backpropagate(\
        env,move,reward,counts,wins,losses)
# make the move
return next_move(ps,counts,wins,losses)
```

We set the default number of rollouts to 100. If there is only one legal move left, we skip searching and select the only move available. Otherwise, we create three dictionaries, *counts*, *wins*, and *losses*, to record the outcomes from simulated games. Once all rollouts are completed, we select the best next move based on simulation results.

10.5 MIXED MCTS VERSUS UCT MCTS

In this section, we will let the mixed MCTS agent play against the UCT MCTS agent for 100 games and see which agent is stronger.

```
3]:  from utils.ttt_simple_env import ttt
     from utils.ch10util import mix_mcts
     from utils.ch08util import mcts
     from tensorflow.keras.models import load_model

     # load the trained strong policy network
     model=load_model("files/strong_ttt.h5")

     # Initiate the game environment
     env=ttt()
     state=env.reset()
     num_rollouts=200
     results=[]
     for i in range(100):
         state=env.reset()
         if i%2==0:
```

```
        action=mcts(env,num_rollouts=num_rollouts)
        state, reward, done, info = env.step(action)
    while True:
        action=mix_mcts(env,model,num_rollouts=num_rollouts)
        state, reward, done, info = env.step(action)
        if done:
            # result is 1 if mixed MCTS wins
            if reward!=0:
                results.append(1)
            else:
                results.appond(0)
            break
        action=mcts(env,num_rollouts=num_rollouts)
        state, reward, done, info = env.step(action)
        if done:
            # result is -1 if mixed MCTS loses
            if reward!=0:
                results.append(-1)
            else:
                results.append(0)
            break
```

We choose 200 rollouts in both algorithms. You can change the number of rollouts and see how results change. I'll leave that as an exercise for you.

Half the time, the mixed MCTS agent moves first and the other half the UCT MCTS agent moves first so that no player has the first-mover advantage. We record a result of 1 if the mixed MCTS agent wins and a result of −1 if the UCT MCTS agent wins. If the game is tied, we record a result of 0.

We now count how many times the mixed MCTS agent has won and lost:

[14]:
```
# count how many times mixed MCTS won
wins=results.count(1)
print(f"mixed MCTS won {wins} games")
# count how many times mix MCTS lost
losses=results.count(-1)
print(f"mixed MCTS lost {losses} games")
# count how many tie games
ties=results.count(0)
print(f"the game is tied {ties} times")
```

```
mixed MCTS won 30 games
mixed MCTS lost 7 games
the game is tied 63 times
```

The above results show that the mixed MCTS agent is better than the UCT MCTS agent: the mixed MCTS agent has won 30 games and lost 7 games. The rest 63 games were tied.

Later in this book, you'll use the two trained policy networks in this chapter to implement the AlphaGo algorithm in Tic Tac Toe.

10.6 GLOSSARY

- **Filter:** Also called a kernel. A matrix with a certain size that moves over the input data to extract features.
- **Policy Network:** A policy network takes the current game board as the input and produces the probability distribution of possible next moves.
- **Stride:** The number of pixels to move in each step when the filter moves over the input data.
- **Value Network:** A value network takes the current game board as the input and produces a value indicating which side is likely to win: for example, 1 means the current player will win for sure while -1 means the current player will lose for sure. A 0 indicates the game is likely to be tied.
- **Zero-Padding:** The process of adding zeros around the edges of the input matrix.

10.7 EXERCISES

10.1 Modify the two code cells in Section 10.5 so that the number of rollouts is 250 in both MCTS algorithms. Run the code cells and see how many times the mixed MCTS agent has won and lost.

## CHAPTER 11

A Policy Network in Connect Four

"We first trained the policy network on 30 million moves from games played by human experts, until it could predict the human move 57% of the time (the previous record before AlphaGo was 44%)."

– David Silver and Demis Hassabis, Google DeepMind

IN THIS CHAPTER, you'll continue with what you learned in Chapters 9 and 10 and apply deep learning to another game: Connect Four.

Since the coin game and Tic Tac Toe are solved games, generating expert moves is relatively straightforward: the moves made by the game-solving agent are considered expert moves. Connect Four is also a solved game, but implementing a game-solving rule-based algorithm involves too many steps. It probably takes a whole book to explain the logic and the steps in such an algorithm. Interested readers can look into, for example, Victor Allis' 1988 master thesis [1]. Further, machine learning is most useful in unsolved games such as Chess or Go that cannot rely on rule-based algorithms alone. Therefore, it's important to master machine learning skills to help unsolved games, as the DeepMind team did. As a result, we treat Connect Four as an unsolved game and use the AlphaGo algorithm to create intelligent game strategies.

To generate expert moves in Connect Four, we first design a computer player who chooses moves by using the MCTS algorithm 50% of the time. It chooses moves by using the MiniMax algorithm with alpha-beta pruning the other 50% of the time. By randomizing between two algorithms, we avoid identical games in simulations so we can cover different game scenarios. We let the above computer player play against itself for 10,000 games. In each game, the winner's moves are considered expert moves while the loser's moves are discarded.

DOI: 10.1201/9781032722207-11

You'll use these expert moves to train a deep neural network. To save time, we train one network to serve as both the fast policy network and the strong policy network. The output layer has seven neurons, representing the seven possible moves the expert can take: column 1 through column 7. Essentially we are conducting a multi-category classification, predicting which one of the seven moves to choose based on the current game state. The neural network we create includes both dense layers and a convolutional layer. You'll learn to treat the Connect Four game board as a two-dimensional image and extract spatial features from the board (several game pieces in a row horizontally, vertically, or diagonally, for example) and associate these features with expert moves.

After the policy network is trained, you'll use it to design a game strategy to play Connect Four by using the mixed MCTS algorithm (similar to what we did in Chapter 10 in Tic Tac Toe). Specifically, instead of selecting moves based on UCT scores, you'll select child nodes based on both rollout values and the probability distribution from the policy network we just trained. We call the agent who selects child nodes this way the mixed MCTS agent. Finally, you'll show that the mixed MCTS agent is more intelligent than the UCT MCTS agent that we developed in Chapter 8.

What You'll Learn in This Chapter

- How to generate expert moves in Connect Four
- Building a policy network in Connect Four
- Training the policy network to predict expert moves
- Implementing a mixed MCTS game strategy in Connect Four

11.1 DEEP LEARNING IN CONNECT FOUR

In this section, you'll learn how to train a policy neural network in Connect Four to prepare you for the AlphaGo algorithm in the game later in the book. In particular, you'll create a deep neural network with dense layers and a convolutional layer. To save time, we use the network as both the fast policy network and the strong policy network. Later in the book, we'll use self-play deep reinforcement learning to further improve this policy network. At the same time, we'll use the game experience data in self-plays to train a value network to estimate the final outcome of the game. The trained value network will help implement the AlphaGo agent in Connect Four to evaluate game states in rollouts so we don't need to simulate all games to a terminal state.

11.1.1 Steps to Train a Policy Network in Connect Four

Here is a summary of the steps involved in this chapter to train a policy neural network in Connect Four:

1. We design a computer player who chooses moves by using the MCTS algorithm 50% of the time. It chooses moves by using the MiniMax algorithm with alpha-beta pruning the other 50% of the time. The reason we randomize between two algorithms is to avoid identical games in simulations so we can have different game board positions to train the neural networks. We let the computer player play against itself for 10,000 games. In each game, the winner's moves are considered expert moves while the loser's moves are discarded.

2. We create a deep neural network with an input layer, some hidden layers, and an output layer. The output layer has seven neurons, representing the seven possible moves the expert can take: column 1 through column 7. The neural network includes both dense layers and a convolutional layer. You'll learn to treat the Connect Four game board as a two-dimensional image and extract spatial features from the board and associate these features with expert moves.

3. After the policy network is trained, we'll use it to design a game strategy to play Connect Four by using a mixed MCTS algorithm: instead of selecting child nodes based on the UCT scores, you'll select moves based on both rollout values and the probability distribution from the policy network we trained.

Now that you have a blueprint on how to train the policy neural network, let's implement the steps we just outlined.

11.1.2 Generate Expert Moves in Connect Four

You'll learn how to generate data to train the policy neural network. The logic is as follows: you'll generate 10,000 games in which two players play against each other. Whoever wins the game is considered the expert and you'll keep the board positions before the winner's move as well as the move made by the winner.

First, let's create a computer player to simulate games:

```
[1]:  from utils.conn_simple_env import conn
      from utils.ch08util import mcts
      import numpy as np
      from utils.ch06util import MiniMax_conn

      # Initiate the game environment
      env=conn()
      # Define a player
      def player(env):
          if len(env.occupied[3])==0:
              action=4
          elif len(env.validinputs)==1:
              action=env.validinputs[0]
          else:
              # Use Minimax 50% of the time
              if np.random.uniform(0,1,1)<=0.5:
```

```
            action=MiniMax_conn(env,depth=3)
        # Use MCTS 50% of the time
        else:
            action=mcts(env,num_rollouts=1000)
    return action
```

The computer player selects moves based on the MiniMax algorithm with alpha-beta pruning 50% of the time. It selects moves based on the UCT MCTS algorithm the other 50% of the time. We use two different algorithms to avoid identical game board positions in simulations so that the game outcomes cover different scenarios to effectively train our neural network.

To strike a balance between the speed and effectiveness of moves by the computer player, we let the player look three steps ahead when using the MiniMax algorithm with alpha-beta pruning. The player rolls out 1000 games in each step when using the UCT MCTS algorithm to generate the best moves. As an exercise, you'll modify the computer player by letting it look *four* steps ahead when using the MiniMax algorithm and roll out *10,000* games in each step when using the UCT MCTS algorithm.

Below, we'll simulate one game and record the game outcome, board positions, and the moves made by the player in each step:

```
2]: # Define the one_game() function
    def one_game():
        history = []
        state=env.reset()
        while True:
            action=player(env)
            history.append([np.array(state).reshape(7,6),
                            action, env.turn])
            state, reward, done, info = env.step(action)
            if done:
                break
        return history, reward

    # Simulate one game and print out results
    history,reward=one_game()
    print(history)
    print(reward)
```

```
...
[array([[ 1,  0,  0,  0,  0,  0],
        [ 0,  0,  0,  0,  0,  0],
        [-1,  1,  1,  1, -1,  0],
        [ 1,  1, -1, -1, -1,  1],
        [-1,  1, -1, -1, -1,  1],
```

```
         [ 0,  0,  0,  0,  0,  0],
         [ 1,  0,  0,  0,  0,  0]]), 6, 'yellow'],
        [array([[ 1,  0,  0,  0,  0, 0],
         [ 0,  0,  0,  0,  0,  0],
         [-1,  1,  1,  1, -1,  0],
         [ 1,  1, -1, -1, -1,  1],
         [-1,  1, -1, -1, -1,  1],
         [-1,  0,  0,  0,  0,  0],
         [ 1,  0,  0,  0,  0,  0]]), 6, 'red']]
```
1

The *one_game()* function simulates a full Connect Four game till a player wins or the game ties. The function returns a list *history*, which contains all the steps in the game. In each game step, three pieces of information are recorded in a list: the game board before the player makes a move, the move made by the player, and the player's color (red or yellow). The function also returns an integer *reward*, which indicates the game outcome: 1 means the red player has won, −1 means the yellow player has won, and 0 means the game is tied.

We then simulate 10,000 games as follows and save the data in the local folder on your computer:

[3]:
```
# simulate 10000 games; take hours to run
# as an exercise, change the depth in Minimax and rollouts in MCTS
results = []
for episode in range(10000):
    history,reward=one_game()
    results.append((reward, history))

import pickle
# save the simulation data on your computer
with open('files/games_conn.p', 'wb') as fp:
    pickle.dump(results,fp)
# read the data and print out the first 10 observations
with open('files/games_conn.p', 'rb') as fp:
    games = pickle.load(fp)
print("the first game is", games[0])
```

```
the first game is (1,
[[array([[0, 0, 0, 0, 0, 0],
         [0, 0, 0, 0, 0, 0],
         [0, 0, 0, 0, 0, 0],
         [0, 0, 0, 0, 0, 0],
         [0, 0, 0, 0, 0, 0],
         [0, 0, 0, 0, 0, 0],
         [0, 0, 0, 0, 0, 0]]), 4, 'red'],
```

```
. . .
[array([[-1, -1,  1,  1,  0,  0],
        [ 1,  0,  0,  0,  0,  0],
        [-1, -1, -1,  1,  0,  0],
        [ 1,  1, -1,  1,  1,  0],
        [-1,  0,  0,  0,  0,  0],
        [-1,  1, -1, -1,  1,  0],
        [ 1,  1, -1, -1,  1, -1]]), 5, 'red']])
```

It takes several hours to generate the 10,000 games in the above code cell. You can alter the depth in the MiniMax algorithm or the number of rollouts in MCTS to adjust how long it takes to generate the simulated games.

Now that you have the expert moves, you'll learn how to train the policy neural network next.

11.2   A POLICY NETWORK IN CONNECT FOUR

We'll use Keras to create a neural network and use the data generated in the last section to train it.

11.2.1   Create a Neural Network for Connect Four

We first use the Keras API in TensorFlow to create the following policy neural network with a convolutional layer and three dense layers.

```
[4]:  from tensorflow.keras.utils import to_categorical
      from tensorflow.keras.layers import Dense
      from tensorflow.keras.models import Sequential
      from tensorflow.keras.layers import Conv2D, Flatten

      fast_model = Sequential()
      fast_model.add(Conv2D(filters=128,
          kernel_size=(4,4),padding="same",activation="relu",
                      input_shape=(7,6,1)))
      fast_model.add(Flatten())
      fast_model.add(Dense(units=64, activation="relu"))
      fast_model.add(Dense(units=64, activation="relu"))
      fast_model.add(Dense(7, activation='softmax'))
      fast_model.compile(loss='categorical_crossentropy',
                      optimizer='adam',
                      metrics=['accuracy'])
```

The input shape is 7 by 6 by 1 because the convolutional layer treats the game board as a two-dimensional image with one color channel and extracts spatial features from it. We first include a convolutional layer with 128 filters. The kernel size is 4 by 4.

We then flatten the output from the convolutional layer to a one-dimensional tensor and feed it to two hidden dense layers, each with 64 neurons in it. The output layer has seven neurons, representing the seven possible actions: dropping a game piece in columns 1 through 7. The softmax activation ensures that the output represents a probability distribution: each value in the output is between 0 and 1, and the seven values in the output add up to 100%.

The network serves as both the strong policy network and the fast policy network in the AlphaGo algorithm. We do this to save time so that we don't need to train different neural networks (which you already know how to do in the previous two chapters). Later in the book, we'll use self-play deep reinforcement learning to further improve the policy network.

11.2.2 Train the Neural Network in Connect Four

We'll train the neural network we just created in the last subsection. We first pre-process the data so that we can feed them into the model.

We first change the actions from a number between 1 and 7 to a number between 0 and 6 because Python uses zero-based indexing.

Next, we load up the simulated game data and convert them into Xs and ys so that we can feed them into the deep neural network to train it:

```
[5]: import pickle
     import numpy as np
     with open('files/games_conn.p','rb') as fp:
         games=pickle.load(fp)

     X=[]
     y=[]
     for reward, history in games:
         # games in which the red won the game
         if reward>0:
             for state, action, turn in history:
                 # we only use actions taken by red
                 if turn=="red":
                     X.append(state)
                     y.append(action-1)
         # games in which the yellow won the game
         if reward<0:
             for state, action, turn in history:
                 # we only use actions taken by red
                 if turn=="yellow":
                     # multiply the board by -1
                     X.append(-state)
```

```
                y.append(action-1)

X=np.array(X).reshape((-1,7,6,1))
y=to_categorical(y,7)
print(X.shape, y.shape)
```

(129776, 7, 6, 1) (129776, 7)

We look at the outcome of each game. If the red player has won the game, the red player is considered the expert and we'll use all moves made by the red player in the game as expert moves. The game board positions before the red player's move are considered features (Xs in a multi-category classification) and the moves made by the red player are considered labels or targets (ys in a multi-category classification).

On the other hand, if the yellow player has won the game, the yellow player is considered the expert and we'll use all its moves in the game as expert moves. The game board positions before the yellow player's move are used as Xs and the moves made by the yellow player are used as ys. Note that when the game is tied, we'll consider neither player as the expert and discard the whole game.

Further, we multiply the game board by -1 if we use the yellow player's moves. This way, the game board is coded from the current player's perspective: 1 means the current player has a game piece in a cell, -1 means the opponent has a game piece in a cell, and 0 means the cell is empty.

We first train the policy network for 100 epochs:

6]:
```
# Train the policy network for 100 epochs
fast_model.fit(X, y, epochs=100, verbose=1)
fast_model.save('files/policy_conn.h5')
```

```
Epoch 1/100
4056/4056 [==============================] - 17s 4ms/step -
loss: 1.5642 - accuracy: 0.4046
Epoch 2/100
4056/4056 [==============================] - 15s 4ms/step -
loss: 1.4327 - accuracy: 0.4617
...
Epoch 100/100
4056/4056 [==============================] - 15s 4ms/step -
loss: 0.7238 - accuracy: 0.7515
```

It takes about half an hour to train the model. Once done, we save the trained model in the local folder. Alternatively, you can download the trained model from the book's GitHub repository.

11.3 MIXED MCTS IN CONNECT FOUR

We'll use the same formula to select moves in MCTS for Connect Four games, as we did in Chapter 10 for Tic Tac Toe games. Specifically, in mixed MCTS, the agent selects moves based on a combination of the UCT score and the probability distribution from the policy network:

$$mix\_score = v_i + C\sqrt{\frac{logN}{n_i}} + \gamma\frac{p_i}{1+n_i}$$

If the child node i is visited only a few times so far in rollouts, the formula places a high weight on the probability distributed from the trained policy network. On the other hand, if the child node i is visited many times, whether to select child node i as the next move in the next rollout depends mainly on the outcomes from the previous rollouts, v_i.

Instead of choosing moves using the UCT score alone or the prior from the trained policy network alone when selecting moves in rollouts in Connect Four, we'll use a combination of the two criteria. This way, the algorithm benefits from the advantages of both UCT scores and the trained policy network.

We create a local module for the mixed MCTS algorithm. Download the file *ch11util.py* from the book's GitHub repository and save it in /Desktop/ags/utils/ on your computer.

In the local module *ch11util*, we define a *mix_mcts_conn()* function as follows:

```python
def mix_mcts_conn(env,model,num_rollouts=100,temperature=1.4):
    # if there is only one valid move left, take it
    if len(env.validinputs)==1:
        return env.validinputs[0]
    # create three dictionaries counts, wins, losses
    counts={}
    wins={}
    losses={}
    for move in env.validinputs:
        counts[move]=0
        wins[move]=0
        losses[move]=0
    # priors from the policy network
    state = env.state.reshape(-1,7,6,1)
    if env.turn=="red":
        action_probs= model(state)
    else:
        action_probs= model(-state)
    ps={}
    for a in sorted(env.validinputs):
```

```
        ps[a]=np.squeeze(action_probs)[a-1]
    # roll out games
    for _ in range(num_rollouts):
        # selection
        move=mix_select(env,ps,counts,wins,losses,temperature)
        # expansion
        env_copy, done, reward=expand(env,move)
        # simulation
        reward=simulate(env_copy,done,reward)
        # backpropagate
        counts,wins,losses=backpropagate(\
            env,move,reward,counts,wins,losses)
    # make the move
    return next_move(ps,counts,wins,losses)
```

The above function relies on the same *mix_select()* function that we defined in Chapter 10, which determines which next move to select when rolling out games. It has two parts: the first part is based on the UCT formula $v_i + C \times \sqrt{\frac{logN}{n_i}}$, and the second part is the discounted probability from the trained fast policy network $\frac{p_i}{1+n_i}$.

We set the default number of rollouts to 100. If there is only one legal move left, we skip searching and select the only move available. Otherwise, we create three dictionaries, *counts*, *wins*, and *losses* to record the outcomes from simulated games. Once the simulation is complete, we select the best next move based on the simulation results.

11.4   THE EFFECTIVENESS OF THE MIXED MCTS IN CONNECT FOUR

In this section, we'll test the effectiveness of the mixed MCTS relative to the traditional UCT MCTS that we developed in Chapter 8.

11.4.1   Manually Play Against the Mixed MCTS Agent in Connect Four

We first play a game manually against the mixed MCTS agent in Connect Four, as follows:

```
from utils.conn_simple_env import conn
from utils.ch11util import mix_mcts_conn
from tensorflow.keras.models import load_model
model=load_model("files/policy_conn.h5")

env=conn()
state=env.reset()
while True:
    action=mix_mcts_conn(env,model,num_rollouts=10000)
```

```
    print(f"Player {env.turn} has chosen {action}")
    state, reward, done, info = env.step(action)
    print(f"Current state is \n{state.T[::-1]}")
    if done:
        if reward==1:
            print(f"Player {env.turn} has won!")
        else:
            print("Game over, it's a tie!")
        break
    action=int(input("What's your move?"))
    print(f"Playor {cnv.turn} has chosen {action}")
    state, reward, done, info = env.step(action)
    print(f"Current state is \n{state.T[::-1]}")
    if done:
        print(f"Player {env.turn} has won!")
        break
```

```
Player red has chosen 4
Current state is
[[0 0 0 0 0 0 0]
 [0 0 0 0 0 0 0]
 [0 0 0 0 0 0 0]
 [0 0 0 0 0 0 0]
 [0 0 0 0 0 0 0]
 [0 0 0 1 0 0 0]]
What's your move?4
Player yellow has chosen 4
Current state is
[[ 0  0  0  0  0  0  0]
 [ 0  0  0  0  0  0  0]
 [ 0  0  0  0  0  0  0]
 [ 0  0  0  0  0  0  0]
 [ 0  0  0 -1  0  0  0]
 [ 0  0  0  1  0  0  0]]
Player red has chosen 5
Current state is
[[ 0  0  0  0  0  0  0]
 [ 0  0  0  0  0  0  0]
 [ 0  0  0  0  0  0  0]
 [ 0  0  0  0  0  0  0]
 [ 0  0  0 -1  0  0  0]
 [ 0  0  0  1  1  0  0]]
What's your move?4
Player yellow has chosen 4
Current state is
```

```
[[ 0   0   0   0   0   0   0]
 [ 0   0   0   0   0   0   0]
 [ 0   0   0   0   0   0   0]
 [ 0   0   0  -1   0   0   0]
 [ 0   0   0  -1   0   0   0]
 [ 0   0   0   1   1   0   0]]
```
Player red has chosen 6
Current state is
```
[[ 0   0   0   0   0   0   0]
 [ 0   0   0   0   0   0   0]
 [ 0   0   0   0   0   0   0]
 [ 0   0   0  -1   0   0   0]
 [ 0   0   0  -1   0   0   0]
 [ 0   0   0   1   1   1   0]]
```
What's your move?3
Player yellow has chosen 3
Current state is
```
[[ 0   0   0   0   0   0   0]
 [ 0   0   0   0   0   0   0]
 [ 0   0   0   0   0   0   0]
 [ 0   0   0  -1   0   0   0]
 [ 0   0   0  -1   0   0   0]
 [ 0   0  -1   1   1   1   0]]
```
Player red has chosen 7
Current state is
```
[[ 0   0   0   0   0   0   0]
 [ 0   0   0   0   0   0   0]
 [ 0   0   0   0   0   0   0]
 [ 0   0   0  -1   0   0   0]
 [ 0   0   0  -1   0   0   0]
 [ 0   0  -1   1   1   1   1]]
```
Player red has won!

I let the mixed MCTS agent move first. I created an opportunity for the agent to place a game piece in either column 3 or column 6 so that there is a double attack. The agent seized the opportunity and placed a game piece in column 6 and won the game. As an exercise, play a game manually with the mixed MCTS agent; design a double attach opportunity for the agent and see if it seizes the opportunity.

11.4.2   Mixed MCTS versus UCT MCTS in Connect Four

We let the mixed MCTS agent play 100 games against the traditional UCT MCTS agent. We use 100 rollouts in both MCTS algorithms. To make sure no agent has a first mover advantage, we let the traditional UCT MCT agent move first in half the time. We let the mixed MCTS agent move first the other 50% of the time.

[8]:
```
num_rollouts=100
results=[]
for i in range(100):
    print(i)
    state=env.reset()
    if i%2==0:
        action=mcts(env,num_rollouts=num_rollouts)
        state, reward, done, info = env.step(action)
    while True:
        action=mix_mcts_conn(env,model,num_rollouts=num_rollouts)
        state, reward, done, info = env.stop(action)
        if done:
            # result is 1 if mixed MCTS wins
            if reward!=0:
                results.append(1)
            else:
                results.append(0)
            break
        action=mcts(env,num_rollouts=num_rollouts)
        state, reward, done, info = env.step(action)
        if done:
            # result is -1 if mixed MCTS loses
            if reward!=0:
                results.append(-1)
            else:
                results.append(0)
            break
```

We create a list *results* to record game outcomes. If the mixed MCTS agent wins, we record a result of 1 in the list. If the traditional UCT MCTS agent wins, we record a result of −1 in the list. A value of 0 in the list *results* means the game is tied.

After running the above code cell, we count how many times the mix MCTS agent has won.

[9]:
```
# count how many times mixed MCTS won
wins=results.count(1)
print(f"mixed MCTS won {wins} games")
# count how many times mix MCTS lost
losses=results.count(-1)
print(f"mixed MCTS lost {losses} games")
# count how many tie games
ties=results.count(0)
print(f"the game was tied {ties} times")
```

```
mixed MCTS won 66 games
mixed MCTS lost 32 games
the game was tied 2 times
```

The above results show that the mixed MCTS agent is better than the traditional UCT MCTS agent: it has won 66 games and lost 32 games. The remaining two games are tied. We choose 100 rollouts in both MCTS algorithms. If you change the number to 90 or 120, you should get similar results. However, if you change the number of rollouts to a number much larger than 100, say 1000, the two MCTS algorithms may have similar performance. The mixed MCTS is most useful when it's time-consuming to roll out games so the number of rollouts is small.

Starting in the next Chapter, you'll learn how reinforcement learning works. In particular, you'll use deep reinforcement learning to further train the policy networks you created in the three games to improve their performance so that you can use them later in the AlphaGo algorithm.

11.5 EXERCISES

11.1 Modify the first code cell in Section 11.1.2 so that the number of rollouts is 10,000 in MCTS and the agent looks four steps ahead in the MiniMax algorithm with alpha-beta pruning.

11.2 Modify the last code cell in Section 11.1.2 so that you generate 1000 games using the computer player you modified in the previous exercise.

11.3 Rerun the code cells in Section 11.2.2, but with the generated games from the previous two exercises. Save the trained model as *policy_conn2.h5* on your computer.

11.4 Modify the first code cell in Section 11.4.1 so that you use the trained model *policy_conn2.h5* from the previous exercise. Choose your moves so that the mixed MCTS agent has an opportunity to create a double attack. See if the agent seizes the opportunity and wins the game.

11.5 Rerun the first code cell in Section 11.4.1 by using the trained model *policy_conn.h5* (which can be downloaded from the book's GitHub page). Choose your moves so that the mixed MCTS agent has an opportunity to create a double attack. See if the agent seizes the opportunity and wins the game.

11.6 Modify the two code cells in Section 11.4.2 so that the number of rollouts is 500 in both MCTS algorithms. Run the code cells and see how many times the mixed MCTS agent has won.

III

Reinforcement Learning

## CHAPTER 12

Tabular Q-Learning in the Coin Game

"Reinforcement learning is the idea of being able to assign credit or blame to all the actions you took along the way while you were getting that reward signal."
– Jeff Dean, Chief Scientist at Google

THIS CHAPTER INTRODUCES you to the basics of reinforcement learning. You'll use one type of reinforcement learning, namely tabular Q-learning, to solve the coin game. Along the way, you'll learn the concepts of dynamic programming and the Bellman equation. You'll also learn how to train and use Q-tables in tabular Q-learning.

Machine learning can be classified into three areas: Supervised learning, unsupervised learning, and reinforcement learning. The deep learning method we covered in the last few chapters belongs to supervised learning. Generally, supervised learning models learn from examples of input-output pairs. In the process, the model extracts features from the input data (dog and cat pictures, for example) and associates them with the output labels (this image is a dog and that one is a cat). In contrast, in unsupervised learning, the model doesn't have access to pre-assigned target variables (labels) in the training data. Instead, unsupervised learning models discover naturally occurring patterns in the data without human supervision. Methods used in unsupervised learning include clustering, principal component analysis, and data visualization.

The third type of machine learning, reinforcement learning (RL), uses trial and error to achieve optimal outcomes. Typically, an agent operates in an environment and selects different actions. The environment provides feedback in the form of rewards and punishments. The agent learns to select actions leading to high rewards to maximize cumulative payoffs. This chapter covers one type of RL, tabular Q-learning. Later in the book, you'll learn other types of RL such as the policy gradient method.

In this chapter, you'll use the coin game as an example to learn how RL works. You'll learn to train a Q-table by trial and error: the agent plays the coin game many times and adjusts the values in the Q-table based on the rewards: increase the Q-value if an action leads to positive rewards and decrease the Q-value otherwise. Once the Q-table is trained, you'll use it to play and win the coin game. You'll win 100% of the time when you move second, even when playing against the perfect rule-based AI that we developed in Chapter 1.

What You'll Learn in This Chapter

- The idea behind reinforcement learning,
- What is tabular Q-learning
- Winning the coin game by using a trained Q-table
- Creating and training a Q-table in the coin game

12.1 WHAT IS REINFORCEMENT LEARNING?

Reinforcement Learning (RL) is one type of Machine Learning (ML). In a typical RL problem, an agent decides how to choose among a list of actions in an environment step by step to maximize the cumulative payoff from all the steps that it has taken.

RL is widely used in many different fields, from control theory, operations research, to statistics. The optimal actions are solved by using a Markov Decision Process (MDP). We'll use trial and error to interact with the environment and see what the rewards from those actions are. We then adjust the decision based on the outcome: reward good choices and punish bad ones. Hence the name reinforcement learning.

12.1.1 Basics of Reinforcement Learning

Before we train the RL agent in the coin game, we should first discuss some basic concepts related to RL.

In RL, an agent lives in an *environment*. The agent interacts with the environment and possibly other agents who also live in it. The agent explores and learns the best strategies to maximize its cumulative payoff. The OpenAI Gym library provides many game environments for machine learning enthusiasts to design game strategies and learn AI. Popular game environments in OpenAI Gym include the Frozen Lake game, the Cart Pole game, and a suite of Atari games such as Breakout, Space Invaders, Pong... In this book, we'll explore different RL game strategies in three self-made environments: the coin game, Tic Tac Toe, and Connect Four.

The *agent* in RL is the player in the game environment. In most OpenAI Gym games, there is only one player and the opponent is embedded into the environment. The three games in this book are all two-player games. In the coin game, the two agents are Player 1 and Player 2. In Tic Tac Toe, the two agents are Player X and Player O. In Connect Four, the two agents are the red player and the yellow player, respectively.

The *state* of the game is the current situation of the game. In the coin game, the state is the number of coins left on the table. Therefore, the game state is an integer between 0 and 21. In Tic Tac Toe, the state is the game board, represented by a NumPy array with nine elements. Each element has a value of -1, 0, or 1. In Connect Four, the game state is a NumPy array with seven columns and six rows, filled with values of -1, 0, or 1.

An *action* is a move made by an agent. The agent in the coin game can take one of the two actions: 1 or 2. In Tic Tac Toe, there are nine possible actions: placing a game piece in one of the nine cells. In Connect Four, the agent can take seven different actions: dropping a disc in one of the seven columns.

The *reward* is the payoff to an agent as a result of moves made by itself and its opponent(s). A reward is assigned to each agent at each time step of the game. Positive values are rewards and negative values are penalties. However, rewards are affected not only by the actions in the current time step but also by actions in previous time steps. Therefore, rewards can be delayed and can be sparse. We'll discuss the credit assignment problem in RL later in the book.

12.1.2 The Bellman Equation and Q-Learning

Q-learning is one way to solve the optimization problem in RL. Q-learning is a value-based approach. Another approach is policy gradients, which is a policy-based approach. We'll discuss both in this book.

The agent is trying to learn the best strategy in order to maximize its expected payoff over time. A strategy (also called a policy) maps a certain state to a certain action. A strategy is a decision rule that tells the agent what to do in a certain situation.

The Q-value, $Q(s, a)$, measures how good a strategy is. You can interpret the letter Q as quality. The better the strategy, the higher the payoff to the agent, and the higher the Q-value. The agent is trying to find the best strategy that maximizes the Q-value.

An agent's action in time step t not only affects the reward in this period, but also rewards in future periods (t+1, t+2, ...). Therefore, finding the best strategy can be complicated and involves dynamic programming. For details of dynamic programming and the Bellan equation, see, e.g., https://en.wikipedia.org/wiki/Bellman_equation.

In the case of Q-learning, the Bellman equation is as follows:

$$Q(s, a) = Reward + DiscountFactor * maxQ(s', a')$$

where $Q(s, a)$ is the Q-value to the agent in the current state s when an action a is taken. *Reward* is the payoff to the agent as a result of this action. *DiscountFactor* is a constant between 0 and 1, and it measures how much the agent discounts future reward as opposed to current reward. Lastly, $maxQ(s', a')$ is the maximized future reward, assuming optimal strategies will be applied in the future as well.

In order to find out the Q-values, we'll try different actions in each state multiple times. We'll adjust the Q-values based on the outcome, increase the Q-value if the reward is high and decrease the Q-value if the reward is low. Hence the name reinforcement learning.

Rather than providing you with a lot of abstract technical jargon, I will use a simple example to show you how reinforcement learning works.

12.2   USE Q-VALUES TO PLAY THE COIN GAME

Imagine you have a Q-table to guide your actions in the coin game. You'll learn how to consult the Q-table step by step to select moves to play the game and win the game 100% of the time when you are Player 2. The strategy works even if you are playing against the perfect AI player that we designed in Chapter 1.

12.2.1   The Logic Behind Q Learning

What if you have a Q-table to guide you to successfully play the coin game? The Q-table is a 22 by 2 matrix, with the rows representing the 22 states: 0 means there is no coin left on the table (that is, the game is over), 1 means there is one coin left on the table..., and 21 means all 21 coins are in the pile on the table. The two columns represent the two actions that the agent can take in any state: 0 means taking one coin from the pile and 1 means taking two coins from the pile.

The Q table, which is stored in a CSV file *coin_Qs.csv*, can be downloaded from the book's GitHub repository. If you open the file, you'll see a table as shown in Figure 12.1 (I added two rows and one column for explanation purposes):

With the guidance of the Q-table, winning the game (i.e., taking the last coin in the pile) when playing second is easy for a computer program. Here are the steps:

1. The computer first checks how many coins are left in the pile. Let's call the number *state*.
2. It looks at the above Q-table and consults the row corresponding to *state*. If the number under action 0 is greater than that under action 1, the computer takes one coin from the pile. Otherwise, the computer takes two coins from the pile. For example, if Player 1 has taken one coin in the first step, there are *state=20* coins left. The computer looks at the row corresponding to *state=20* and the two numbers under action 0 and action 1 are −0.7249 and 0.7350, respectively. The computer therefore takes two coins from the pile since the value under action 1 is greater. On the other hand, if Player 1 has taken two coins in the first step, there are *state=19* coins left. The computer looks at the row corresponding to *state=19* and the two numbers under action 0 and action

	A	B	C
1		action 0	action 1
2		remove one coin	remove two coins
3	state 0	0.0000	0.0000
4	state 1	1.0000	1.0000
5	state 2	-1.0000	1.0000
6	state 3	-1.0000	-1.0000
7	state 4	0.9500	-1.0000
8	state 5	-0.8811	0.9500
9	state 6	-0.9500	-0.9500
10	state 7	0.9025	-0.9262
11	state 8	-0.8709	0.9025
12	state 9	-0.9025	-0.9025
13	state 10	0.8573	-0.8849
14	state 11	-0.8399	0.8573
15	state 12	-0.8574	-0.8574
16	state 13	0.8145	-0.8554
17	state 14	-0.8113	0.8145
18	state 15	-0.8145	-0.8145
19	state 16	0.7737	-0.8141
20	state 17	-0.7730	0.7737
21	state 18	-0.7684	-0.7686
22	state 19	0.7350	-0.7737
23	state 20	-0.7249	0.7350
24	state 21	0.0000	0.0000

Figure 12.1   A Q-table to win the coin game

1 are 0.7350 and −0.7737, respectively. The computer therefore takes one coin from the pile since the value under action 0 is greater.

3. The computer repeats the previous step until the game ends.

Based on the above rules, we'll let the computer play a game and see what happens.

12.2.2 A Python Program to Win the Coin Game

We'll implement the rules we outlined in the last subsection. The computer player will play second. The opponent is the rule-based AI that we designed in Chapter 1:

```
[1]: import random

     def AI(state):
         if state%3 != 0:
             move = state%3
         else:
             move = random.choice([1,2])
         return move
```

The AI player looks at the current state of the game. If the number of coins left on the table is not a multiple of 3, it will make a move so that the number of coins left on the table is a multiple of 3. For example, if there are seven coins left, it will remove one coin; if there are eight coins left, it will remove two coins. On the other hand, if the number of coins left on the table is a multiple of 3, it will randomly pick an action: remove one coin with a 50% probability and or remove two coins with a 50% probability.

Now that we know how the two players make moves, we'll play a full game as follows:

```
[2]: from utils.coin_env import coin_game
     import numpy as np
     import time

     # initiate the game environment
     env=coin_game()
     # create a Q-table by using values from the CSV file
     file="files/coin_Qs.csv"
     Q=np.loadtxt(file, delimiter=",")

     # play a full game
     state=env.reset()
     # turn on the graphical rendering
     env.render()
     while True:
         # Rule-based AI moves first
         m1=AI(state)
```

```
    print(f"state is {state}; Player 1 chooses action {m1}")
    state, reward, done, _ = env.step(m1)
    env.render()
    time.sleep(1)
    if done==True:
        print('Player 1 won!')
        break
    # pick the action with the higher Q value
    m2=np.argmax(Q[state, :])+1
    print(f"state is {state}; Player 2 chooses action {m2}")
    state, reward, done, _ = env.step(m2)
    env.render()
    time.sleep(1)
    if done==True:
        print('Player 2 won!')
        break
time.sleep(5)
env.close()
```

```
state is 21; Player 1 chooses action 1
state is 20; Player 2 chooses action 2
state is 18; Player 1 chooses action 2
state is 16; Player 2 chooses action 1
state is 15; Player 1 chooses action 1
state is 14; Player 2 chooses action 2
state is 12; Player 1 chooses action 1
state is 11; Player 2 chooses action 2
state is 9; Player 1 chooses action 2
state is 7; Player 2 chooses action 1
state is 6; Player 1 chooses action 2
state is 4; Player 2 chooses action 1
state is 3; Player 1 chooses action 1
state is 2; Player 2 chooses action 2
Player 2 won!
```

The Q values are saved in a CSV file. We use the *loadtxt()* method in NumPy to load up the Q table.

The *state=env.reset()* command resets the game so that the initial state is 21. We then use a *while* loop to play the game. In each iteration, the rule-based AI player moves first. The tabular Q player chooses the action that leads to the higher Q value in that state. Note here the *argmax()* method in NumPy returns the argument that leads to the highest value. This is different from the *max()* method in NumPy, which returns the highest value among a group of values.

We then print out the current state and the action taken by the player so that we can keep track of the moves taken by the computer.

The *env.step()* method returns the new state and the reward based on the action taken. It also tells us whether the game has ended. If the game has not ended, we go to the next iteration to repeat the process. If the game has ended, the program prints out who the winner is and the *while* loop stops.

We have turned on the graphical rendering of the game, so you should see a game window with coins in it. As the game progresses, the number of coins gradually decreases until the game ends.

The tabular Q player has won the game. You probably have noticed that the tabular Q player always takes an action so that the number of coins left in the pile is a multiple of three.

You can run the above code cell multiple times, and the tabular Q player wins every time.

Amazing, right? You may wonder, how did you come up with the numbers in the Q-table to play the game? That's what we'll discuss next.

12.3 TRAINING THE Q-TABLE

In this section, we'll first discuss what Q-learning is and the logic behind it. We then code in the logic and use a program to train the Q-values that we have just used in the last section.

12.3.1 What Is Q-Learning?

The Q-values form a table of S rows and A columns, where S is the number of states and A is the number of actions. We call it the Q-table. We need to find out the Q-values in the table so that the player can use these values to figure out the optimal strategies in every situation.

Before Q-learning starts, we set all the values in the Q-table to 0.

At each iteration during training, we'll use one type of reinforcement learning (specifically, Q-learning) to update Q-values as follows:

$$NewQ(s,a) = lr * [Reward + DiscountFactor * maxQ(s',a')] + (1 - lr) * OldQ(s,a)$$

The learning rate, lr, has a value between 0 and 1. It controls how fast you update the Q-values. The updated $Q(s,a)$ is a weighted average of the Q-value based on Bellman's equation and the previous $Q(s,a)$. Here is when the updating (i.e., learning) happens.

After many rounds of trial and error, the updating will be minimal, which means the Q-values converge to the equilibrium values.

If you look at the above equation, when

$$Q(s,a) = Reward + DiscountFactor * maxQ(s',a')$$

There is no update, and we have

$$NewQ(s,a) = OldQ(s,a)$$

And that is the equilibrium state we are looking for.

12.3.2 Let the Learning Begin

We'll write a Python program and let the agent randomly select moves to play the game many rounds. Unavoidably, there will be many mistakes along the way. But we'll assign a low reward if the agent fails so that it assigns a low Q-value to actions taken in that state. On the other hand, if the agent makes right choices and wins the game, we'll assign a high reward so that the agent assigns high Q-values to actions taken.

It's through such repeated rewards and punishments that the agent learns the correct Q-values.

The code cell below trains the Q-table.

```
[3]:  # the learning rate
      lr=0.01
      # discount rate
      gamma=0.95
      # parameters to control exploration
      max_exp=0.9
      min_exp=0.1
      # maximum steps in a game
      max_steps=50
      # number of episodes to train Q-values
      max_episode=10000

      # Set Q-values to zeros at first
      Q=np.zeros((22, 2))
      # Train the Q-table
      for episode in range(max_episode):
          # The initial state is the starting position (state 0)
          state=env.reset()
          # AI moves first
          AIaction=AI(state)
          state, reward, done, _ = env.step(AIaction)
          # The cutoff value for exploration
          cutoff=min_exp+(max_exp-min_exp)*episode/max_episode
          # Play a game
```

```
    for _ in range(max_steps):
        # Exploitation
        if np.random.uniform(0,1,1)>cutoff:
            action=np.argmax(Q[state, :])
        # Exploration
        else:
            action=random.choice(range(2))
        # Use the selected action to make the move
        # Important: convert 0 and 1 to 1 and 2
        new_state,reward,done,_=env.step(action+1)
        # Update Q values
        if done==True:
            # Q-agent moves second, -1 means winning
            reward=-reward
            Q[state,action]=reward
            break
        else:
            # AI player's turn
            AIaction=AI(new_state)
            new_state,reward,done,_=env.step(AIaction)
            # Q-agent moves second, -1 means winning
            reward=-reward
            if done:
                Q[state,action]=reward
                break
            else:
                Q[state,action]=lr*(reward+gamma*np.max(\
                    Q[new_state,:]))+(1-lr)*Q[state,action]
                state=new_state

# Print out and save the trained Q-table
Q=np.round(Q,4)
print(Q)
np.savetxt("files/coin_Qs.csv",Q,delimiter=',')
```

```
[[ 0.      0.    ]
 [ 1.      1.    ]
 [-1.      1.    ]
 [-1.     -1.    ]
 [ 0.95   -1.    ]
 [-0.8804  0.95  ]
 [-0.95   -0.95  ]
 [ 0.9025 -0.921 ]
 [-0.8678  0.9025]
 [-0.9025 -0.9025]]
```

```
[ 0.8573 -0.8945]
[-0.8368  0.8573]
[-0.8574 -0.8574]
[ 0.8144 -0.8541]
[-0.8104  0.8144]
[-0.8145 -0.8145]
[ 0.7737 -0.8142]
[-0.7728  0.7737]
[-0.77   -0.7701]
[ 0.735  -0.7737]
[-0.7278  0.735 ]
[ 0.      0.    ]]
```

We set the learning rate to 0.01. This parameter can take different values in this simple case. You can set it to a smaller value such as 0.005 or a higher value such as 0.02. As long as you train the model many times, the Q values will converge.

The discount rate we use here is 0.95. This parameter will directly affect the Q values. Remember in the last subsection, we discussed that in equilibrium when the Q values converge, we have

$$Q(s, a) = Reward + DiscountFactor * maxQ(s', a')$$

You can see that the converged Q value is a function of discount factor. In our case, as long as you set it anywhere between 0.9 and 1, the resulting Q values will work in the sense that it will successfully guide the agent to win the game.

Exploration versus Exploitation

Another important parameter in the process of training the Q-table is the exploration rate. Exploration means that the agent will randomly selects an action in that given state. This is important for training the Q values because without it, the Q-values may be trapped in the wrong equilibrium and cannot get out of it. With exploration, it gives the agent the chance to explore new strategies and see if they lead to higher Q-values.

Exploitation is the opposite of exploration: it means the agent chooses the action based on the values in the current Q-table. This ensures that the final Q table converges.

At each iteration, the Q values are updated. If the agent wins the game, the action earns a reward of 1. If the agent fails, the action earns a reward of −1. The updating rule follows the equation we specified earlier

$$NewQ(s, a) = lr * [Reward + DiscountFactor * maxQ(s', a')] + (1 - lr) * OldQ(s, a)$$

12.3.3   Test the Trained Q-Table

Next, we test the tabular Q agent ten times and see the game outcomes.

[4]:
```
# test trained Q
for t in range(10):
    print(f"game {t+1}")
    # The initial state is the starting position (state 0)
    state=env.reset()
    # AI move first
    AIaction=AI(state)
    state, reward, done, _ = env.step(AIaction)
    # Play a full game
    for _ in range(max_steps):
        action=np.argmax(Q[state, :])
        # Use the selected action to make the move
        new_state,reward,done,_=env.step(action+1)
        if done==True:
            print("Player 2 wins the game!")
            break
        else:
            AIaction=AI(new_state)
            new_state, reward, done, _ = env.step(AIaction)
            if done:
                print("Player 1 wins the game!")
                break
            else:
                state=new_state
```

```
game 1
Player 2 wins the game!
game 2
Player 2 wins the game!
game 3
Player 2 wins the game!
game 4
Player 2 wins the game!
game 5
Player 2 wins the game!
game 6
Player 2 wins the game!
game 7
Player 2 wins the game!
game 8
Player 2 wins the game!
game 9
```

Player 2 wins the game!
game 10
Player 2 wins the game!

We have tested ten games. In each game, the AI player moves first and the tabular Q agent moves second. The tabular Q agent consults the Q-table at each step of the game and selects the action with a higher Q-value. In all ten games, the second player (i.e., the tabular Q agent) has won.

In this chapter, you have learned the basics of reinforcement learning. You have also implemented a value-based approach, namely, tabular Q-learning, in the coin game. In the next few chapters, you'll learn a policy-based approach in reinforcement learning. You'll apply the approach to the three games in this book: the coin game, Tic Tac Toe, and Connect Four.

12.4 GLOSSARY

- **Discount Factor:** In reinforcement learning, the discount factor determines how much the agent cares about future rewards relative to current rewards. The discount factor is a value between 0 and 1. The higher the value, the more the agent cares about future rewards.
- **Dynamic Programming:** A method to optimize the cumulative payoff by choosing a sequence of actions through recursion.
- **Exploitation:** In RL, exploitation is when the agent selects a move based on Q-values in the current Q-table. It's the opposite of exploration. It's necessary in Q-learning to make the Q-table converge.
- **Exploration:** In RL, exploration is when the agent randomly selects a move to explore new strategies and checks if they lead to higher Q values. It's the opposite of exploitation. It's necessary in Q-learning to make sure that the Q-values don't get stuck in the wrong equilibrium.
- **Learning Rate:** A hyperparameter in machine learning models to govern how fast the model parameters should be updated during the learning process.
- **Q-Learning:** A value-based reinforcement learning algorithm. The agent learns the value of an action a in a state s, $Q(s, a)$ through trial and error.

12.5 EXERCISES

12.1 What is reinforcement learning? How is it related to machine learning?

12.2 What is Q-learning? How is it related to reinforcement learning?

12.3 Is Q-learning a value-based or policy-based approach in reinforcement learning?

12.4 Rerun the second code cell in Section 12.2.2 and see which player wins, the rule-based AI or the tabular Q agent.

12.5 Modify the first cell in Section 12.3.2 and change the value of the discount factor, *gamma*, to 0.98. Retrain the Q-table and compare the Q-values to those in the old Q-table (Hint, they should be different). Save the new Q-table as *new_coin_Qs.csv* on your computer.

12.6 Continue the previous question. Modify the first code cell in 12.3.3 by using the newly trained Q-table, *new_coin_Qs.csv*, from the previous question to play the coin game. See how often the tabular Q agent wins.

## CHAPTER 13

Self-Play Deep Reinforcement Learning

"Play is our brain's favorite way of learning."
– Diane Ackerman

ALPHAGO EMPLOYS SELF-PLAY and deep reinforcement learning to enhance its policy network, making it even more intelligent. During self-play, AlphaGo accumulates game experience data, which is then used to train a powerful value network. This network predicts the outcome of the game, a critical component in AlphaGo's strategy when competing against the renowned Go player, Lee Sedol. This chapter will guide you through understanding and implementing deep reinforcement learning, particularly the policy gradient method, in a coin game context. You'll explore the concept of a policy and how deep neural networks can be utilized to train a policy for intelligent gameplay.

Previously, in Chapter 12, the focus was on value-based reinforcement learning for mastering the coin game. This involved learning the Q-value for each action in a state, denoted as $Q(a|s)$. After training the reinforcement model, decisions in the game were made based on choosing actions with the highest $Q(a|s)$ value in a given state s.

Now, this chapter introduces policy-based reinforcement learning, where decisions are driven by a policy $\pi(a|s)$, directing the agent on which actions to take in each state s. Policies can be deterministic, prescribing actions with absolute certainty, or stochastic, offering a probability distribution for possible actions.

In the policy gradients method, the agent engages in numerous game sessions to learn the optimal policy. The agent bases its actions on the model's predictions, observes the resulting rewards, and adjusts the model parameters to align the predicted action probabilities with desired probabilities. If a predicted action probability is lower than desired, the model weights are tweaked to increase the prediction, and vice versa.

Additionally, this chapter delves into self-play, a technique to strengthen the deep reinforcement learning agent by pitting it against an incrementally stronger version of itself. The self-play generates a wealth of game experiences, which are then used to train a value network that predicts game outcomes based on current game states. You'll also learn how to leverage the trained value network for strategic gameplay.

What You'll Learn in This Chapter

- What is a policy? What is deep reinforcement learning?
- Implementing policy gradients in the coin game
- Using self-play deep reinforcement learning to strengthen the policy network
- Training a value network using game experience data in the coin game

---

13.1 THE POLICY GRADIENT METHOD

This section introduces you to policy-based reinforcement learning. We'll first discuss what a policy is. We'll then briefly discuss the idea behind the policy gradient (PG) method.

13.1.1 What Is a Policy?

In the context of reinforcement learning, a policy, denoted as $\pi(a, s)$, is essentially a strategy or set of rules that guides an agent's decision-making in a given state. It specifies the action the agent should take in a particular state s. Let's consider the example of the coin game to understand this concept better.

In this game, we design a deep neural network that inputs the current state of the game. The network's output layer features two neurons, employing a softmax activation function. The softmax function ensures that the output is a vector of numbers between 0 and 1, and these numbers sum up to 1. This output can be interpreted as the probability distribution of actions that the agent should take in that state.

For instance, if the output vector is [0.3, 0.7], the policy dictates the following:

- Remove one coin from the pile (action 0) with a 30% probability;
- Remove two coins from the pile (action 1) with a 70% probability.

This type of policy is known as a stochastic policy, where the agent's actions are determined based on a probability distribution. The benefit of a stochastic policy is that it naturally incorporates both exploitation and exploration. Exploitation occurs as the agent is more likely to choose an action with a higher assigned probability. Exploration is facilitated because the policy does not always dictate a single course of action with absolute certainty; there's always a chance of choosing a different action.

On the other hand, a deterministic policy would involve the agent taking a specific action with 100% certainty when in a given state. In the context of this book, mainly stochastic policies are used. Typically, during the training phase of a model, a stochastic policy is preferred to balance exploration and exploitation. This approach allows the model to learn more effectively by experiencing a wider range of scenarios and responses.

13.1.2 What Is the Policy Gradient Method?

The policy gradient method is a technique used in reinforcement learning (RL) to optimize the parameters of a model, aiming to maximize the expected reward for an agent.

In policy-based RL, the agent's goal is to learn the most effective policy to maximize its expected payoff over time. A policy, in this context, is a decision rule that maps a given state to a specific action.

Consider a policy denoted as $\pi_\theta(a_t|s_t, \theta)$, where θ represents the model parameters (such as the weights in a neural network). In this framework, the agent selects an action a_t at time t based on the current state s_t and as a function of model parameters θ. The agent aims to choose a sequence of actions $(a_0, a_1, \ldots, a_{T-1})$ to maximize its expected accumulated rewards. At each time period t, after observing the state s_t and taking action a_t, the agent receives a reward of $r(a_t, s_t)$. If the discount rate is γ, the expected cumulative reward is given by:

$$R(s_0, a_0, \ldots, a_{T-1}, s_T) = \sum_{t=0}^{T-1} \gamma^t r(s_t, a_t) + \gamma^T r(s_T)$$

where s_T is the terminal state.

The agent's objective is to find the optimal parameter values θ that maximize the expected cumulative payoff:

$$\max_\theta E[R(s_0, a_0, \ldots, a_{T-1}, s_T)|\pi_\theta]$$

This maximization problem can be approached using a gradient ascent algorithm. Here, the model parameters θ are updated iteratively using the following formula until convergence:

$$\theta \leftarrow \theta + lr * \nabla_\theta E[R|\pi_\theta]$$

where lr is the learning rate, a hyperparameter that controls how fast we update the model parameters. Essentially, this process involves training the model to predict the probability of the correct action based on the state. The solution can be expressed as:

$$\theta \leftarrow \theta + lr \times E[\sum_{t=0}^{T-1} \nabla_\theta log\pi_\theta(a_t|s_t)R|\pi_\theta]$$

For a detailed proof and further explanation, interested readers can refer to the documentation provided by OpenAI at:

https://spinningup.openai.com/en/latest/spinningup/extra_pg_proof1.html.

13.2 USE POLICY GRADIENTS TO PLAY THE COIN GAME

Using policy gradients to play the coin game involves several steps. Here's a high-level overview:

The first step is to define the policy, which is a strategy that the agent (the player using policy gradients) follows to decide its actions based on the current state of the environment. This policy is represented by a neural network, where the inputs are the states of the environment and the outputs are the probabilities of taking each possible action.

In the second step, we let the agent play the game multiple times against the strong policy network we trained in Chapter 9. In each of these games, we record the states, actions taken, and rewards (whether the current player wins or loses). After each game, we calculate the total reward. In the coin game, the total reward is 1 for a win and -1 for a loss.

The third step involves using the collected data to update the policy network. This is where policy gradients come into play. The objective is to maximize the expected reward. The update is performed using gradient ascent on the expected reward by using the equations we outlined in the last section.

Finally, we repeat the process of playing the game, collecting data, calculating rewards, and updating the policy. Over multiple iterations, the policy should improve, leading to better decisions (actions) in the game.

13.2.1 Use a network to define the policy

We first create a neural network to represent the policy as follows:

```
[1]: from tensorflow import keras
     from tensorflow.keras import layers

     num_inputs = 22
     num_actions = 2
     # The input layer
     inputs = layers.Input(shape=(22,))
     # The common layer
     common = layers.Dense(32, activation="relu")(inputs)
     common = layers.Dense(32, activation="relu")(common)
     # The policy layer (the output layer)
     action = layers.Dense(num_actions, activation="softmax")(common)
```

```
# Put together the policy network
model = keras.Model(inputs=inputs, outputs=action)
```

The input layer of the neural network has 22 neurons in it: number 22 comes from the fact that we'll convert the game state into a one-hot variable with a depth of 22 (since the number of coins left in the pile can range from 0 to 21). There are two possible actions for the agent: the agent can take either 1 or 2 coins from the pile in each turn. Therefore, there are two neurons in the output layer. We apply the softmax activation function on the output layer so the two values in the output add up to one. We can interpret the two values as the probabilities of taking actions 1 and 2, respectively.

We define the optimizer as follows:

```
[2]: optimizer = keras.optimizers.Adam(learning_rate=0.01)
```

We use the Adam optimizer with a learning rate of 0.01.

13.2.2 Calculate Gradients and Discounted Rewards

We'll let the agent play against a version of itself. For that purpose, we first define an *opponent()* function as follows:

```
[3]: import numpy as np

def onehot_encoder(state):
    onehot=np.zeros((1,22))
    onehot[0,state]=1
    return onehot
# the trained strong policy model
trained=keras.models.load_model('files/strong_coin.h5')
def opponent(state):
    onehot_state=onehot_encoder(state)
    policy=trained(onehot_state)
    return np.random.choice([1,2],p=np.squeeze(policy))
```

We first define a *onehot_encoder()* function to convert the game state to a one-hot variable with a depth of 22. We then load the strong policy network, *strong_coin.h5*, we trained in Chapter 9 and select moves based on the probability distribution recommended by *strong_coin.h5*. The *opponent()* function returns a move randomly based on this probability distribution, and the move serves as the opponent's move against the self-play deep reinforcement learning agent.

Next, we define a *playing()* function to simulate a full game. The strong policy network agent is the first player, and the policy-gradient (PG) agent is the second player. The *playing()* function is defined as follows:

```
[4]: from utils.coin_simple_env import coin_game
     import tensorflow as tf

     env=coin_game()
     def playing():
         # create lists to record game history
         action_probs_history = []
         rewards_history = []
         state = env.reset()
         episode_reward = 0
         # the strong policy network agent moves first
         state, reward, done, _ = env.step(opponent(state))
         # record all game states
         states = []
         while True:
             # convert state to onehot to feed to model
             onehot_state = onehot_encoder(state)
             # estimate action probabilities
             action_probs = model(onehot_state)
             # select action based on the policy distribution
             action=np.random.choice(num_actions,
                                 p=np.squeeze(action_probs))
             # record log probabilities
             action_probs_history.append(
                 tf.math.log(action_probs[0, action]))
             # Apply the sampled action in our environment
             # Remember to add 1 to action (change 0 or 1 to 1 or 2)
             state, reward, done, _ = env.step(action+1)
             states.append(state)
             if done:
                 # PG player is player 2, -1 means PG player wins
                 reward = -reward
                 rewards_history.append(reward)
                 episode_reward += reward
                 break
             else:
                 state, reward, done, _ = env.step(opponent(state))
                 reward = -reward
                 rewards_history.append(reward)
                 episode_reward += reward
                 if done:
                     break
         return action_probs_history,\
             rewards_history, episode_reward, states, reward
```

The *playing()* function simulates a full game, and it records all the intermediate steps made by the PG agent. The function returns five values:

- a list *action_probs_history* with the natural logarithm of the recommended probability of the action taken by the agent from the policy network;
- a list *rewards_history* with the rewards for each action taken by the agent in the game;
- a number *episode_reward* showing the total rewards to the agent during the game;
- a list *states* to record game states after the PG agent makes a move;
- a number *reward* indicating the outcome of the game; 1 means the PG agent has won and −1 means the PG agent has lost.

In particular, we record all game states after the PG agent makes a move and place them in a list *states*. Note that the list *states* doesn't include game states after the move made by the opponent. The function also returns the game outcome indicator *reward*: if the value of *reward* is 1, the PG agent has won the game; if the value of *reward* is −1, the PG agent has lost the game. We collect the list *states* and the game outcome indicator *reward* so that in the next section, we can use them as game experience data to train a value network.

In reinforcement learning, actions affect not only the current period rewards, but also future rewards. We therefore use discounted rewards to assign credits properly as follows:

```
5]: def discount_rs(r):
        discounted_rs = np.zeros(len(r))
        running_add = 0
        for i in reversed(range(0, len(r))):
            running_add = gamma*running_add + r[i]
            discounted_rs[i] = running_add
        return discounted_rs.tolist()
```

13.2.3 Update Parameters

Instead of updating model parameters after one episode, we update after a certain number of episodes to make the training stable. Here we update parameters after every ten games, as follows:

```
6]: batch_size=10
    allstates=[]
    alloutcome=[]
    def create_batch(batch_size):
        action_probs_history = []
        rewards_history = []
        episode_rewards = []
        for i in range(batch_size):
```

```
        aps,rs,er,ss,outcome = playing()
        returns = discount_rs(rs)
        action_probs_history += aps
        rewards_history += returns
        episode_rewards.append(er)
        # record game history for the next section
        allstates.append(ss)
        alloutcome.append(outcome)
    return action_probs_history,\
        rewards_history,episode_rewards
```

We'll train the model and update the parameters until the average episode reward to the PG agent in the last 100 games reaches 0.999. Since in each episode, the total reward to the PG agent is either −1 or 1, this amounts to the PG agent winning all 100 games against the opponent.

```
[7]: from collections import deque

running_rewards=deque(maxlen=100)
gamma = 0.95
episode_count = 0
# Train the model
while True:
    with tf.GradientTape() as tape:
        action_probs_history,\
        rewards_history,episode_rewards=create_batch(batch_size)
        # Calculating loss values to update our network
        history = zip(action_probs_history, rewards_history)
        actor_losses = []
        for log_prob, ret in history:
            # Calculate actor loss
            actor_losses.append(-log_prob * ret)
        # Adjust model parameters
        loss_value = sum(actor_losses)
    grads = tape.gradient(loss_value, model.trainable_variables)
    optimizer.apply_gradients(zip(grads,
                                model.trainable_variables))


    # Log details
    episode_count += batch_size
    for r in episode_rewards:
        running_rewards.append(r)
    running_reward=np.mean(np.array(running_rewards))
    # print out progress
    if episode_count % 100 == 0:
```

```
        template = "running reward: {:.6f} at episode {}"
        print(template.format(running_reward, episode_count))
    # Stop if the game is solved
    if running_reward > 0.999 and episode_count>100:
        print("Solved at episode {}!".format(episode_count))
        break
model.save("files/PG_coin.h5")
```

```
running reward: -0.980000 at episode 100
running reward: -0.940000 at episode 200
running reward: -0.960000 at episode 300
running reward: -1.000000 at episode 400
running reward: -0.980000 at episode 500
running reward: -0.920000 at episode 600
running reward: -0.840000 at episode 700
running reward: 0.100000 at episode 800
running reward: 0.920000 at episode 900
Solved at episode 960!
```

Note here we adjust the parameters by the product of the log probability and the discounted reward. This is related to the solution to the rewards maximization problem in the PG method that we outlined in the last section.

The above output shows that the model is trained after 960 episodes (your result is likely different) and the PG agent is able to beat the strong policy agent in all 100 games.

13.3 TRAIN A VALUE NETWORK IN THE COIN GAME

The game experience data we collected through self-play in the last section will be used to train a value network for the coin game, as the AlphaGo algorithm did for the Go game. In this section, you'll create a neural network to predict the outcome of the coin game based on the game state. First, you'll process the game experience data we gathered in the last section when training the PG agent. We'll use the game states after the PG agent's moves as the input to the neural network (i.e., Xs when training the model) and the final game outcome for the PG agent as the output of the neural network (i.e., ys when training the model).

Once the value network is trained, we'll design game strategies based on the value network in the next section.

13.3.1 Plans to Train a Value Network in the Coin Game

Here is a summary of what we'll do to train a value network to design intelligent game strategies in the coin game:

1. We'll collect the game experience data we gathered in the last section when training the PG agent: the game states after the PG agent's moves and the final game outcome (the PG agent has won or lost the game).
2. We then associate each game state with the final game outcome for the PG agent. We'll use the game state as features X, and the outcome for the agent as labels y. We'll treat this as a multi-category classification problem since there are two possible outcomes associated with each game state: a win or a loss.
3. We'll feed the processed data (Xs and ys) into a deep neural network to train the model to predict the game outcome based on the game state. After the training is done, we have a trained value network.
4. We can now use the trained model to play a game. At each step of the game, the player looks at all possible next moves, and makes hypothetical moves to create hypothetical game states in the next step. We then feed the hypothetical game states into the trained value network. The network tells the agent the probabilities of a win and a loss.
5. The agent selects the move that the model predicts with the highest chance of winning the game.

13.3.2 Process the Game Experience Data

The data we gathered in the last section are not ready to be fed into the deep neural network. We'll first change both game states and game outcomes into one-hot vectors.

Changing game states into one-hot variables is easy: we have already defined the *one-hot_encoder()* function above. To change the game outcomes into one-hot variables, we manually encode them. The game outcome is either 1 or −1, with 1 indicating the PG agent has won the game and −1 indicating a loss. We'll change the outcome to [1, 0] as winning and [0, 1] as losing. That is, we use a one-hot variable with a depth of 2 to indicate the game outcome.

In the code cell below, we process the game experience data and make them ready for training.

```
[8]:  Xs=[]
      ys=[]
      for states, result in zip(allstates,alloutcome):
          for state in states:
              onehot_state=onehot_encoder(state)
              Xs.append(onehot_state)
              if result==1:
                  # player 2 wins
                  ys.append(np.array([1,0]))
              if result==-1:
                  # player 2 loses
                  ys.append(np.array([0,1]))
```

```
Xs=np.array(Xs).reshape(-1,22)
ys=np.array(ys).reshape(-1,2)
```

Now the game states, Xs, are one-hot variables with a depth of 22 and the game outcomes, ys, are one-hot variables with a depth of 2.

Next, we create a deep neural network as the value network and use the above data to train it.

13.3.3 Train a Value Network Using Game Experience Data

We'll use Keras API in TensorFlow to create a deep neural network to represent the value network in the coin game. In particular, the network will include two dense layers as hidden layers, plus an input layer and an output layer. Since there are two possible game outcomes (a win or a loss), we'll treat the learning process as a multi-category classification problem. Therefore, we'll have two neurons in the output layer. We'll use softmax as our activation function in the output layer.

```
9]: from tensorflow.keras.layers import Dense
    from tensorflow.keras.models import Sequential

    value_network = Sequential()
    value_network.add(Dense(units=64,activation="relu",
                     input_shape=(22,)))
    value_network.add(Dense(32, activation="relu"))
    value_network.add(Dense(16, activation="relu"))
    value_network.add(Dense(2, activation='softmax'))
    value_network.compile(loss='categorical_crossentropy',
        optimizer=keras.optimizers.Adam(learning_rate=0.0001),
        metrics=['accuracy'])
```

We use the Adam optimizer with a learning rate of 0.0001 to ensure that the model converges. The loss function is categorical cross-entropy since this is a multi-category classification problem. Because there are only two outcomes here, we can potentially change it to a binary classification problem by including only one neuron in the output layer. Since in the other two games in the book (Tic Tac Toe and Connect Four), there are three game outcomes (a win, a loss, and a tie), we use multi-category classification here to make models consistent across the three games in the book.

Next, we train the value network for 100 epochs, as follows:

```
)]: # Train the model for 100 epochs
    value_network.fit(Xs, ys, epochs=100, verbose=1)
    value_network.save('files/value_coin.h5')
```

```
Epoch 1/100
195/195 [==============================] - 1s 631us/step
- loss: 0.6507 - accuracy: 0.7284
...
Epoch 98/100
195/195 [==============================] - 0s 649us/step
- loss: 0.1800 - accuracy: 0.9023
Epoch 99/100
195/195 [==============================] - 0s 619us/step
- loss: 0.1799 - accuracy: 0.9023
Epoch 100/100
195/195 [==============================] - 0s 590us/step
- loss: 0.1802 - accuracy: 0.9023
```

The above training takes just a couple of minutes. After the value network is trained, we save the trained model in the local folder on your computer as *value_coin.h5*. Next, we'll design game strategies using the trained value network in the coin game.

13.4 PLAY THE COIN GAME WITH THE VALUE NETWORK

First, we'll define a *best_move()* function for Player 2. The function will return the best move based on the value network we just trained. We'll test it against the rule-based AI player we created in Chapter 1. We'll also let the value network agent move first to play against random moves.

13.4.1 Best Moves Based on the Value Network in the Coin Game

To find the best move for Player 2, we'll go over each next move hypothetically and use the trained value network to predict the probability of Player 2 winning the game if the move were taken. The function then compares which next move has the highest probability of Player 2 winning the game.

Below, we define a *best_move()* function for the computer to find the best move. What the function does is as follows:

- Look at the game state.
- Look at all possible next moves; make a hypothetical move and to reach a hypothetical next state.
- Use the trained model to predict the chance of winning in the hypothetical next state.
- Choose the move that produces the highest chance of Player 2 winning.

```
[11]: # design game strategy
      from copy import deepcopy

      def best_move(env):
```

```
# Set the initial value of bestoutcome
bestoutcome=-2;
bestmove=None
#go through all possible moves hypothetically
for move in env.validinputs:
    env_copy=deepcopy(env)
    state,reward,done,info=env_copy.step(move)
    onehot_state=onehot_encoder(state)
    ps=value_network.predict(onehot_state,verbose=0)
    # output is prob(2 wins)
    win_prob=ps[0][0]
    if win_prob>bestoutcome:
        # Update the bestoutcome
        bestoutcome = win_prob
        # Update the best move
        bestmove = move
return bestmove
```

We'll test the game strategy next.

13.4.2 Value Network Agent Against the Rule-Based AI

We'll see how the above game strategy based on the value network fairs against the rule-based AI. We test 10 games. The rule-based AI moves first and the value network agent moves second.

First, let's define a function rule_based_AI() to represent the rule-based AI agent:

```
2]: import random

def rule_based_AI(env):
    if env.state%3 != 0:
        move = env.state%3
    else:
        move = random.choice([1,2])
    return move
```

The rule-based AI agent will make a move so that the number of coins left on the table is a multiple of three, if possible. Otherwise, it randomly picks 1 or 2.

Next, we see how many times the value network agent has won:

```
3]: # test ten games
for i in range(10):
    state=env.reset()
    # The AI player moves firsts
    action=rule_based_AI(env)
```

```
state,reward,done,_=env.step(action)
while True:
    # move recommended by the value network
    action=best_move(env)
    state,reward,done,_=env.step(action)
    if done:
        print("The value network wins!")
        break
    # The AI player moves
    action=rule_based_AI(env)
    state,reward,done,_=env.step(action)
    if done:
        print("The value network loses!")
        break
```

```
The value network wins!
The value network wins!
The value network wins!
The value network wins!
The value network wins!
The value network wins!
The value network wins!
The value network wins!
The value network wins!
The value network wins!
```

In each game, if the value network agent wins, the output says "the value network wins!" Otherwise, the output says "the value network loses!" The above output shows that the value network agent has won all ten games.

13.4.3 Value Network Agent Against Random Moves

Even though we trained the value network assuming that the value network agent plays second, the game strategy works for Player 1 as well. The game state is player-independent. That is, once the game has started, no matter whether you are Player 1 or Player 2, if you can make sure the number of coins left in the pile is a multiple of three, you'll win the game for sure. We'll test what happens when the value network agent moves first against random moves.

```
[14]:  # does the strategy work if the agent moves first?
       # test ten games against random moves
       for i in range(10):
           state=env.reset()
           while True:
               # move recommended by the value network
               action=best_move(env)
```

```
        state,reward,done,_=env.step(action)
        if done:
            print("The value network wins!")
            break
        # The random player moves
        action=random.choice(env.validinputs)
        state,reward,done,_=env.step(action)
        if done:
            print("The value network loses!")
            break
```

```
The value network wins!
The value network wins!
The value network wins!
The value network wins!
The value network wins!
The value network wins!
The value network wins!
The value network wins!
The value network wins!
The value network wins!
```

The value network agent has won all ten games even when it moves first against random moves. However, it's possible that the random moves may win a game just by chance.

In this chapter, you have learned how deep reinforcement learning works. Specifically, you used a deep neural network to create a policy for the agent to decide which moves to take in a given situation. You then use self-play to train the agent to learn the optimal policy. The agent bases its actions on the model's predictions, observes the resulting rewards, and adjusts the model parameters to align predicted action probabilities with desired probabilities. You use the self-play deep reinforcement learning to further train the strong policy network that you created in Chapter 9. The self-play also generated game experience data, and you used them to train a value network that predicts game outcomes based on current game states. The value network was then used to design game strategies.

In the next chapter, you'll apply self-play deep reinforcement learning to another game: Tic Tac Toe. You'll further train the strong policy network and train a value network in Tic Tac Toe.

13.5 GLOSSARY

- **Policy:** In reinforcement learning, a policy is a decision rule to map the current state to an action. It tells the agent what to do in every situation.

- **Policy Gradients:** A reinforcement learning algorithm in which a policy is adjusted to maximize the expected payoff.
- **Self-Play:** An algorithm to improve the performance of an agent in reinforcement learning. An agent plays against a variant of itself and adjusts its strategies in the process.
- **Value Network:** A deep neural network to predict the game outcome.

13.6 EXERCISES

13.1 What is a policy? What's the difference between a stochastic policy and a deterministic policy?

13.2 Explain how policy gradients work.

13.3 Rerun the second code cell in Section 13.4.2 and see how many times the value network agent wins.

13.4 Rerun the first code cell in Section 16.3.2 and see how many times the value network agent wins.

13.5 Modify the first code cell in Section 16.3.2 so that the value network agent moves second. See how many times the value network agent wins.

## CHAPTER 14

Vectorization to Speed Up Deep Reinforcement Learning

> "Mathematics is the art of reducing any problem to linear algebra."
>
> – *William Stein*

IN CHAPTER 13, we explored self-play deep reinforcement learning and its application to the coin game. Now, we're extending this approach to two additional games, Tic Tac Toe and Connect Four, in this and the following chapter. This transition raises three key challenges.

Firstly, unlike the coin game, where illegal moves are non-existent as players simply choose to remove one or two coins per turn, Tic Tac Toe and Connect Four have a decreasing number of legal moves as the game advances. For example, Tic Tac Toe starts with nine possible moves, which reduces to eight in the next turn, and so on. To address this, we'll penalize illegal moves by assigning negative rewards. However, we'll also differentiate between poorly chosen legal moves that lead to a loss and outright illegal moves. To assign credit properly, we penalize a bad legal move and all preceding moves. In contrast, we'll only penalize the specific illegal move, not moves before illegal moves.

Secondly, the computational demands of training for Tic Tac Toe and Connect Four are significantly higher than for the coin game. To tackle this, we'll shift from using loops to vectorization, a method that significantly speeds up the training process. You'll understand the concept of vectorization, and learn how it facilitates rapid execution. The implementation of vectorization in various functions will be a key focus in this and the next chapter.

DOI: 10.1201/9781032722207-14

Finally, this chapter will guide you through the process of encoding the game board in a player-independent manner. In the coin game, the strategy remains the same regardless of the player, as it's independent of whether Player 1 or Player 2 is playing. However, in games like Tic Tac Toe and Connect Four, the strategies vary significantly depending on the player's turn and the existing layout of game pieces on the board. You'll learn to encode the board in such a way that the current player's pieces are represented as 1 and the opponent's as −1, effectively transforming a player-dependent board into a player-independent format. This conversion to player-independent encoding allows the use of the same neural network for training both players.

More specifically, this chapter focuses on developing a single model for both Player X and Player O in Tic Tac Toe. With the game board cells represented as 1 for Player X's pieces, −1 for Player O's, and 0 for empty spaces, we'll invert the board (multiply by −1) when it's Player O's turn. This ensures consistent board encoding when fed into the deep neural network: 1 for the current player's cells, −1 for the opponent's, and 0 for vacant cells. Such an approach enables the same model to make predictions for both Player X and Player O.

With the above challenges properly handled, you'll implement self-play deep reinforcement learning in Tic Tac Toe, mirroring the approach used in the coin game. By allowing the agent to play against itself, the self-play process generates a wealth of game data, which is then used to train a value network. This network predicts game outcomes based on current game states. You'll also learn how to employ this trained value network to devise intelligent game strategies in Tic Tac Toe.

What You'll Learn in This Chapter

- Training a policy network to avoid illegal moves in Tic Tac Toe
- Encoding the Tic Tac Toe game board so that it's player-independent
- Using vectorization to speed up training in Tic Tac Toe
- Training a policy gradient network in Tic Tac Toe
- Train a value network using game experience data in Tic Tac Toe

---

14.1 HOW TO HANDLE ILLEGAL MOVES IN TIC TAC TOE?

In the coin game we discussed in Chapter 13, the deep reinforcement learning agent (specifically, the policy gradient agent) makes one of the two moves each step: taking one or two coins from the pile. The number of legal moves is the same in every step: two. This is not the case in more complicated games such as Tic Tac Toe or Connect Four.

In Tic Tac Toe, the first player has nine legal moves in the first step: cells 1 through 9. After that, it's Player O's turn and there are only eight legal moves left: if Player X has taken cell 1 in the first move, for example, cell 1 is not a legal move for Player

O anymore. How to train the model so that the agent avoids illegal moves? The answer is to assign a negative reward each time the agent makes an illegal move. However, this relates to the credit assignment problem in reinforcement learning and we need to handle the negative rewards with a little more care. Specifically, we need to differentiate between illegal moves and bad legal moves that lead to a loss.

14.1.1   The Credit Assignment Problem in Reinforcement Learning

In reinforcement learning, agents learn the best actions through feedback from rewards (which can be either positive or negative). However, rewards are sparse and delayed and the agent needs to figure out how to assign proper credits to a sequence of actions that lead to a good or a bad outcome. The discounted rewards are the solution.

To illustrate the point, let's assume that in a Tic Tae Toe game, the sequence of moves are the following:

- Player X takes cell 1;
- Player O takes cell 2;
- Player X takes cell 5;
- Player O takes cell 3;
- Player X takes cell 9.

At this point, Player X has connected three game pieces in a row diagonally in cells 1, 5, and 9, as shown in Figure 14.1.

The undiscounted rewards for the three moves made by Player X are 0, 0, and 1, respectively. However, the third step alone didn't win the game, so we should give credits to the first two moves as well by discounting rewards. Assuming the discount rate is 0.9, the discounted rewards for the three steps made by Player X are 0.81, 0.9, and 1, respectively. The discounted rewards to the three steps made by Player X are shown in their corresponding cells in the figure. We have also calculated the discounted rewards to the two moves made by Player O.

14.1.2   The Credit Assignment Problem in Illegal Moves

To train the policy gradient agent to avoid illegal moves, we can assign negative rewards to the agent each time the agent makes an illegal move. However, we should make sure that only the illegal move gets the blame, not the moves before it. That is, we need to distinguish between illegal moves and bad legal moves that lead to a loss for the agent.

To make the point clear, let's consider two different scenarios. In scenario 1, the following sequence of moves are made by the two players:

- Player X takes cell 1;
- Player O takes cell 5;
- Player X takes cell 2;
- Player O takes cell 3;

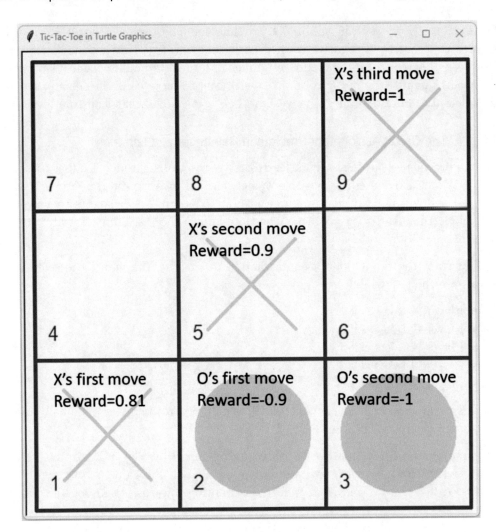

Figure 14.1 Credit assignments in a Tic Tac Toe game in which X has won

- Player X takes cell 4.
- Player O takes cell 7.

The resulting game board is shown in Figure 14.2.

At this point, Player O has connected three game pieces in a row diagonally in cells 3, 5, and 7. The undiscounted rewards for the three moves made by Player X are 0, 0, and −1, respectively. Assuming a discount rate of 0.9, the discounted rewards to the three moves made by Player X are −0.81, −0.9, and −1, respectively. This is appropriate because the third step alone didn't lose the game for Player X: the first two moves should get penalized as well. This scenario shows us how to assign credits to bad legal moves by a player.

Now let's consider a separate situation in which a player has made an illegal move. Imagine that the following sequence of moves are made by the two players:

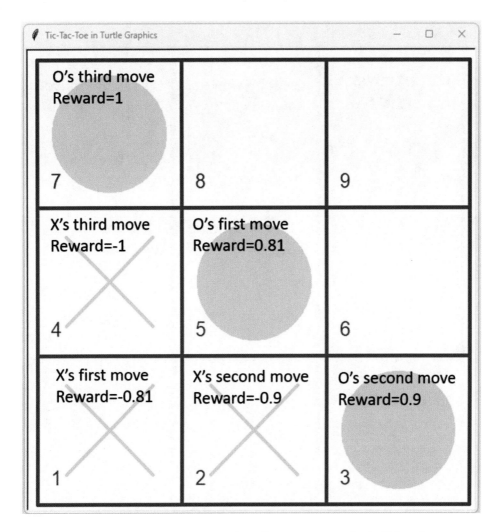

Figure 14.2 Credit assignments in a Tic Tac Toe game in which X has lost

- Player X takes cell 1;
- Player O takes cell 7;
- Player X takes cell 5;
- Player O takes cell 9;
- Player X takes cell 7;
- Player X takes cell 6;
- Player O takes cell 8.

Player X made an illegal move in cell 7 since cell 7 was already taken by Player O. So we should assign a reward of -1 to the move. However, the two previous moves made by Player X (occupying cells 1 and 5), should not get punished for the illegal move. We should treat the illegal move by X (occupying cell 7) and the three bad moves (1, 5, and 6) that lead to a loss differently as follows: the move to occupy cell 7 should be assigned a reward of -1; this reward is final and should not be discounted. Moves to occupy cells 1, 5, and 6 should be assigned undiscounted rewards of 0, 0, and -1,

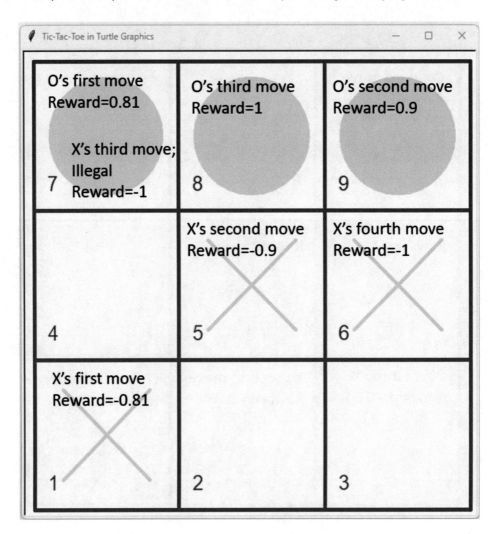

Figure 14.3 Credit assignments in a Tic Tac Toe game to an illegal move

respectively. Assuming the discount rate is 0.9, the discounted rewards to the three moves made by Player X (occupying cells 1, 5, and 6) should be −0.81, −0.9, and −1, respectively. The resulting game board is shown in Figure 14.3.

To summarize, we should assign a negative reward each time the policy gradient agent makes an illegal move, but we don't punish moves before the illegal move.

14.2 USE VECTORIZATION TO SPEED UP TRAINING

Training deep neural networks often requires significant computational resources. For instance, when DeepMind trained AlphaGo for the match with Lee Sedol, they utilized a substantial setup of 1920 CPUs and 280 GPUs, as reported by the Economist in their article "Showdown" dated March 12, 2016 [8].

In contrast, the games we develop are less complex than Go, yet they still demand considerable computing power. Hence, enhancing the efficiency of our code is vital for reducing computational costs. A key method for achieving this is through vectorization, which streamlines computations.

Vectorization is faster than loops for several reasons, primarily due to the way modern computers and their processors are designed and how they handle operations. Modern processors are equipped with Single Instruction, Multiple Data (SIMD) capabilities. This means they can perform the same operation on multiple data points simultaneously. Vectorized operations take advantage of SIMD by processing multiple elements of an array in parallel, whereas loops process elements one at a time.

Vectorization can also improve memory access patterns. In a loop, each iteration may involve fetching data from memory, which is slower than processing it. With vectorization, larger chunks of data are processed at once, leading to more efficient use of the memory hierarchy, like caching.

Loops in high-level languages often come with overhead, such as loop counter management and condition checking at each iteration. Vectorized operations eliminate this overhead, as they involve applying a single operation to a whole set of data. Many vectorized operations use highly optimized library routines that are fine-tuned for specific hardware architectures. These routines are often more efficient than a general-purpose loop written in a high-level programming language.

Vectorization can also avoid interpreter overhead: In interpreted languages like Python, each iteration of a loop can involve interpreter overhead. Vectorized operations are usually implemented in a compiled language like C, avoiding this overhead.

Beyond SIMD, some systems can distribute vectorized operations across multiple cores or even different machines, whereas loops are typically executed on a single core unless explicitly parallelized.

In summary, vectorization leverages advanced hardware capabilities and optimized software routines to process data more efficiently than traditional loop-based approaches.

To illustrate the time-saving benefits of vectorization, let's consider an example where we aim to sum all natural numbers from 1 to 10,000,000. This task can be performed using a loop, as demonstrated below:

```
import time

start=time.time()
total=0
for i in range(1,10000001):
    total += i
print(f"the sum is {total}")
```

```
end=time.time()
print(f"the calculation took {end-start} seconds to finish")
```

```
the sum is 50000005000000
the calculation took 0.5736210346221924 seconds to finish
```

The computation was completed in approximately 0.57 seconds. It's important to remember that the duration might vary for you, as it is influenced by the specific hardware configurations of your computer.

Next, we'll apply vectorization to perform the same calculation and observe the time required for its completion.

```
[2]: import numpy as np

start=time.time()
constant=np.ones(10000000)
numbers=np.arange(10000000)+1
total=np.matmul(constant,numbers)
print(f"the sum is {total}")
end=time.time()
print(f"the calculation took {end-start} seconds to finish")
```

```
the sum is 50000005000000.0
the calculation took 0.06393122673034668 seconds to finish
```

In this instance, we have constructed two vectors: *constant*, a vector filled entirely with 1s, and *numbers*, a vector containing values ranging from 1 to 10,000,000. We employ NumPy's *matmul()* function to execute matrix multiplication for sum calculation. Although the result is the same, the process took merely around 0.06 seconds. Through this method, we've managed to reduce the computational time by about 90 percent.

For the remainder of this book, as we develop game strategies, we will adopt similar approaches, utilizing vectors instead of loops to expedite the training process.

14.3 SELF-PLAY DEEP REINFORCEMENT LEARNING IN TIC TAC TOE

You have learned how to play the coin game using the policy gradient approach in Chapter 13. Specifically, you have adjusted the model parameters proportional to the product of log probability and the discounted reward. In this section, we'll apply the same technique to Tic Tac Toe.

14.3.1 Combine Two Networks into One as Inputs

Below, we'll create two separate input networks first: one is a dense layer with 9 neurons and the other network has a convolutional layer that can detect the spatial features on the Tic Tac Toe board. We'll then combine the two networks together using the *concat()* method in TensorFlow. We'll use the combined network as the input to our policy gradient model. The model has one output network with 9 neurons in it. We apply softmax activation on the output so they can be interpreted as the probability of choosing the next move (i.e., a policy network).

The code in the cell below creates such a model:

```
import tensorflow as tf
from tensorflow import keras
from tensorflow.keras import layers


num_inputs = 9
num_actions = 9
num_hidden = 32
# The convolutional input layer
conv_inputs = layers.Input(shape=(3,3,1))
conv = layers.Conv2D(filters=64, kernel_size=(3,3),padding="same",
    input_shape=(3,3,1), activation="relu")(conv_inputs)
# Flatten the output from the conv layer
flat = layers.Flatten()(conv)
# The dense input layer
inputs = layers.Input(shape=(9,))
# Combine the two into a single input layer
two_inputs = tf.concat([flat,inputs],axis=1)
# two hidden layers
common = layers.Dense(128, activation="relu")(two_inputs)
action = layers.Dense(32, activation="relu")(common)
# Policy output network
action = layers.Dense(num_actions, activation="softmax")(action)
# The final model
model = keras.Model(inputs=[inputs, conv_inputs],\
                    outputs=action)
```

The model has two input networks. The first one takes in the game board as a three by three image and uses a convolutional layer to extract the spatial features on the game board. The output is then flattened into a one-dimensional vector. The second input network is a dense layer with nine neurons. We combine the two input layers together by using the *concat()* method in TensorFlow. The combined layer is then fed into two hidden layers sequentially. We also create an output layer: a policy layer telling the agent which moves to choose.

Below, we specify the optimizer we use to train the model.

```
optimizer=keras.optimizers.Adam(learning_rate=0.0005)
```

We use the Adam optimizer with a learning rate of 0.0005.

14.3.2 Play Against the Strong Policy Agent in Tic Tac Toe

In Chapter 10, you have trained a fast policy network and a strong policy work for the Tic Tac Toe game. In this chapter, you'll use the strong policy network as the opponent when training the policy gradient agent in Tic Tac Toe. For that purpose, we define an *opponent()* function as follows:

```
[5]: import numpy as np

     # load the trained strong policy model
     trained=keras.models.load_model('files/strong_ttt.h5')
     # define an opponent for the policy gradient agent
     def opponent(env):
         state = env.state.reshape(-1,3,3,1)
         if env.turn=="X":
             action_probs=trained(state)
         else:
             action_probs=trained(-state)
         aps=[]
         for a in sorted(env.validinputs):
             aps.append(np.squeeze(action_probs)[a-1])
         ps=np.array(aps)/np.array(aps).sum()
         return np.random.choice(sorted(env.validinputs),p=ps)
```

To train Player X, we define a *playing_X()* function. Player X moves first to play against the opponent (defined above). The function simulates a full self-play game as follows:

```
[6]: from utils.ttt_simple_env import ttt

     # allow a maximum of 50 steps per game
     max_steps=50
     env=ttt()

     def playing_X():
         # create lists to record game history
         action_probs_history = []
         wrongmoves_history = []
         rewards_history = []
         state = env.reset()
         episode_reward = 0
         states=[]
         for step in range(max_steps):
             state = state.reshape(-1,9,)
             conv_state = state.reshape(-1,3,3,1)
             # Predict action probabilities and future rewards
             action_probs = model([state,conv_state])
```

```
    # select action based on the policy network
    action=np.random.choice(num_actions,\
                            p=np.squeeze(action_probs))
    # record log probabilities
    action_probs_history.append(\
                tf.math.log(action_probs[0, action]))
    # punish the agent if there is an illegal move
    if action+1 not in env.validinputs:
        rewards_history.append(0)
        wrongmoves_history.append(-1)
    # otherwise, place the move on the game board
    else:
    # Apply the sampled action in our environment
        state, reward, done, _ = env.step(action+1)
        states.append(state)
        if done:
            wrongmoves_history.append(0)
            rewards_history.append(reward)
            episode_reward += reward
            break
        else:
            state,reward,done,_=env.step(opponent(env))
            rewards_history.append(reward)
            wrongmoves_history.append(0)
            episode_reward += reward
            if done:
                break
return action_probs_history,\
        wrongmoves_history,rewards_history, \
        episode_reward,states,reward
```

The *playing_X()* function plays a full game and records all the intermediate steps made by the policy gradient agent. The function returns six values:

- a list *action_probs_history* with the natural logarithm of the recommended probability of the action taken by the agent from the policy network;
- a list *wrongmoves_history* with the rewards to each action associated with illegal moves;
- a list *rewards_history* with the rewards for each action taken by the agent in the game associated with legal moves;
- a number *episode_reward* showing the total rewards to the agent during the game;
- a list *states* recording the game board after each of the policy gradient agent's moves;
- a number *reward* indicating the game outcome: 1 means Player X has won, −1 means Player X has lost, and 0 means the game is tied.

The *playing_X()* function calculates the gradients and rewards from the game. Since in reinforcement learning, actions affect not only current period rewards, but also future rewards, we therefore use discounted rewards to assign credits properly to legal moves. Note that every time there is an illegal move, we skip the discounting in that step since we'll penalize illegal moves separately. The following function reflects such discounting of rewards:

```
[7]: def discount_rs(r,wrong):
         discounted_rs = np.zeros(len(r))
         running_add = 0
         for i in reversed(range(0, len(r))):
             if wrong[i]==0:
                 running_add = gamma*running_add + r[i]
                 discounted_rs[i] = running_add
         return discounted_rs.tolist()
```

The function takes two lists, *r* and *wrong*, as inputs, where *r* stores the undiscounted rewards related to legal moves while *wrong* stores rewards related to illegal moves. We discount *r* but not *wrong*. The output is the properly discounted reward in each step when a legal move is made. Note that if an illegal move is made in a step, the reward is 0 from the output. We'll add in a reward of -1 for illegal moves later separately.

To train Player O, we define a *playing_O()* function, which is similar to the *playing_X()* function we defined before. The function simulates a full game, with the opponent makes the first move and the policy gradient agent makes the second move, as follows:

```
[8]: def playing_O():
         # create lists to record game history
         action_probs_history = []
         wrongmoves_history = []
         rewards_history = []
         state = env.reset()
         episode_reward = 0
         states=[]
         # the opponent moves first
         state, reward, done, _ = env.step(opponent(env))
         for step in range(max_steps):
             state = state.reshape(-1,9,)
             conv_state = state.reshape(-1,3,3,1)
             # predict action probabilities; multiply the board by -1
             action_probs = model([-state,-conv_state])
             # select action based on the policy network
             action=np.random.choice(num_actions,\
                             p=np.squeeze(action_probs))
             # record log probabilities
```

```
action_probs_history.append(\
                tf.math.log(action_probs[0, action]))
# punish the agent if there is an illegal move
if action+1 not in env.validinputs:
    rewards_history.append(0)
    wrongmoves_history.append(-1)
# otherwise, place the move on the game board
else:
# apply the sampled action in our environment
    state, reward, done, _ = env.step(action+1)
    states.append(-state)
    if done:
        wrongmoves_history.append(0)
        rewards_history.append(-reward)
        episode_reward += -reward
        break
    else:
        state,reward,done,_=env.step(opponent(env))
        rewards_history.append(-reward)
        wrongmoves_history.append(0)
        episode_reward += -reward
        if done:
            break
return action_probs_history,\
        wrongmoves_history,rewards_history, \
        episode_reward,states,-reward
```

The *playing_O()* function plays a complete Tic Tac Toe game and records all intermediate moves made by the policy gradient agent. The function returns six values, which are defined the same as those in the function *playing_X()*.

Most importantly, we use $[-state, -conv\_state]$ instead of $[state, conv\_state]$ when we feed the game board to the model. This is because the game board has a value 1 in a cell if Player X has placed a game piece in it, and -1 if Player O has placed a game piece in it. To use the same network for both players, we multiply the input by -1 so that the model treats 1 as occupied by the current player and -1 as occupied by the opponent. This is how we make the model player-independent.

The second most important thing is to change the rewards. Instead of using 1 and -1 to denote a win by Players X and O, respectively, we'll use a reward of 1 to indicate that the current player has won and a reward of -1 to indicate that the current player has lost. We accomplish this by using $-reward$ instead of $reward$ in the above function. Therefore, after Player O makes a move, the reward is now 1 if Player O wins and -1 if Player O loses.

14.3.3 Train Players X and O

Instead of updating model parameters after one episode, we update after a certain number of episodes to make the training stable. Here we update parameters every ten games to train Player X, as follows:

```
[9]: batch_size=10
     allstates=[]
     alloutcome=[]
     def create_batch_X(batch_size):
         action_probs_history = []
         wrongmoves_history - []
         rewards_history = []
         episode_rewards = []
         for i in range(batch_size):
             aps,wms,rs,er,ss,outcome = playing_X()
             # rewards are discounted
             returns = discount_rs(rs,wms)
             action_probs_history += aps
             # punishments for wrong moves are not discounted
             wrongmoves_history += wms
             # combine discounted rewards with punishments
             combined=np.array(returns)+np.array(wms)
             # add combined rewards to rewards history
             rewards_history += combined.tolist()
             episode_rewards.append(er)
             # record game history for the next section
             allstates.append(ss)
             alloutcome.append(outcome)
         return action_probs_history,\
             rewards_history,episode_rewards
```

We discount the rewards associated with wins and losses, but not the rewards associated with wrong moves, due to the credit assignment problem we discussed earlier. We then combine the discounted rewards with punishments associated with wrong moves and put the combined values in the list *rewards_history*. We'll use the combined values when deciding how much to adjust the model parameters later.

Similarly, we simulate ten games to train Player O, as follows:

```
[10]: def create_batch_O(batch_size):
          action_probs_history = []
          critic_value_history = []
          wrongmoves_history = []
          rewards_history = []
          episode_rewards = []
```

```
    for i in range(batch_size):
        aps,cvs,wms,rs,er,ss,outcome = playing_0()
        # reward related to legal moves are discounted
        returns = discount_rs(rs,wms)
        action_probs_history += aps
        critic_value_history += cvs
        # punishments for wrong moves are not discounted
        wrongmoves_history += wms
        # combine discounted rewards with punishments
        combined=np.array(returns)+np.array(wms)
        # add combined rewards to rewards history
        rewards_history += combined.tolist()
        episode_rewards.append(er)
        # record game history for the next section
        allstates.append(ss)
        alloutcome.append(outcome)
    return action_probs_history,critic_value_history,\
        rewards_history,episode_rewards
```

We'll train the model and update parameters until the policy gradient agent wins or ties the opponent in each of the last 100 games.

```
[]: from collections import deque

running_rewards=deque(maxlen=100)
gamma = 0.95
episode_count = 0
batches=0
# Train the model
while True:
    with tf.GradientTape() as tape:
        if batches%2==0:
            action_probs_history,\
    rewards_history,episode_rewards=create_batch_X(batch_size)
        else:
            action_probs_history,\
    rewards_history,episode_rewards=create_batch_0(batch_size)

        # Calculating loss values to update our network
        rets=tf.convert_to_tensor(rewards_history,\
                                dtype=tf.float32)
        alosses=-tf.multiply(tf.convert_to_tensor(\
          action_probs_history,dtype=tf.float32),rets)
        # Backpropagation
        loss_value = tf.reduce_sum(alosses)
```

```
    grads = tape.gradient(loss_value, model.trainable_variables)
    optimizer.apply_gradients(zip(grads,\
                                  model.trainable_variables))
    # Log details
    episode_count += batch_size
    batches += 1
    running_rewards+=episode_rewards
    running_reward=np.mean(np.array(running_rewards))
    # print out progress
    if episode_count % 1000 == 0:
        template = "running reward: {:.6f} at episode {}"
        print(template.format(running_reward, episode_count))
    # Stop if the game is solved
    if min(running_rewards)>=0 and episode_count>100:
        print("Solved at episode {}!".format(episode_count))
        break
model.save("files/pg_ttt.h5")
```

Here is where the vectorization happens. If you recall, in Chapter 3, when we calculate the total loss, we iterate through the values in lists *action_probs_history* and *rewards_history* by using a loop. Instead of using a loop, we convert the lists into vectors and conduct vector multiplication, which significantly speeds up the training process.

Even with vectorization, it takes about an hour to train the model. The exact amount of time depends on your computer hardware. Alternatively, you can download the trained model from the book's GitHub repository https://github.com/markhliu/AlphaGoSimplified.

Once done, we also save the game experience data during the above self-plays in the local folder so we can use them in the next section to train the value network:

[12]:
```
import pickle

with open("files/PG_games_ttt.p","wb") as f:
    pickle.dump((allstates,alloutcome),f)
```

The trained policy network *pg_ttt.h5* will be used in the AlphaGo algorithm later in the book. Specifically, it will be used to select the next move in MCTS, along with the UTC formula and a value network that we'll train in the next section.

14.4 TRAIN A VALUE NETWORK IN TIC TAC TOE

In this section, you'll create a neural network to predict the game outcome in Tic Tac Toe based on the board position. First, you'll process the game experience data we gathered in the last section when training the policy gradient agent. We'll use the game states after the policy gradient agent's moves as the input to the neural network (i.e., the Xs when training the model) and the final game outcome as the output of the neural network (i.e., the ys when training the model).

Once the value network is trained, we'll design game strategies based on the network in the next section.

14.4.1 The Plan to Train a Value Network in Tic Tac Toe

Here is a summary of what we'll do to train a value network to design intelligent game strategies in Tic Tac Toe:

1. We'll process the game experience data we gathered in the last section when training the policy gradient model: the game states after the agent's moves and the final game outcome (the agent has won or lost the game).
2. We then associate each game state with the final game outcome for the policy gradient agent. We'll use the game state as features X, and the outcome for the agent as labels y. We'll treat this as a multi-category classification problem since there are three possible outcomes associated with each game state: a win, a loss, or a tie.
3. We'll feed the processed data (Xs and ys) into a deep neural network to train the model to predict the game outcome based on the game state. After the training is done, we have a trained value network.
4. We can now use the trained model to play a game. At each move of the game, the player looks at all possible next moves, and makes hypothetical moves. Each hypothetical move leads to a hypothetical game state. We feed the hypothetical game state into the pre-trained value network and ask the network to tell us the probability of the agent winning the game.
5. The agent selects the hypothetical move with the highest chance of winning the game.

14.4.2 Process the Game Experience Data

The data we gathered in the last section are not ready to be fed into the deep neural network. We'll first change the game states into three by three matrices. We also encode the game outcomes into one-hot variables. The game outcome can be 1, 0, or −1. A value of 1 indicates the policy gradient agent has won the game; −1 indicates the agent has lost the game; 0 means a tie game. We'll change the outcome to [0, 1, 0] as winning, [1, 0, 0] as tying, and [0, 0, 1] as losing. That is, we use a one-hot variable with a depth of 3 to indicate the game outcome.

In the code cell below, we process the game experience data and make them ready for training.

```
with open("files/PG_games_ttt.p","rb") as f:
    history,results=pickle.load(f)
```

```
Xs=[]
ys=[]
for states, result in zip(history,results):
    for state in states:
        Xs.append(state)
        if result==1:
            ys.append(np.array([0,1,0]))
        elif result==-1:
            ys.append(np.array([0,0,1]))
        elif result==0:
            ys.append(np.array([1,0,0]))

Xs=np.array(Xs).reshape(-1,3,3,1)
ys=np.array(ys).reshape(-1,3)
```

Next, we create a deep neural network as the value network and use the above data to train it.

14.4.3 Build and Train a Value Network in Tic Tac Toe

We'll use Keras to create a deep neural network to represent the value network in Tic Tac Toe. In particular, the network will include one convolutional layer and two hidden dense layers, plus an input layer and an output layer. Since there are three possible game outcomes (a win, a tie, or a loss), we'll treat the learning process as a multi-category classification problem. Therefore, we'll have three neurons in the output layer. We'll use softmax as our activation function in the output layer.

[14]:
```
from tensorflow.keras.layers import Dense,Conv2D,Flatten
from tensorflow.keras.models import Sequential

value_model = Sequential()
value_model.add(Conv2D(filters=128,
    kernel_size=(3,3),padding="same",activation="relu",
                input_shape=(3,3,1)))
value_model.add(Flatten())
value_model.add(Dense(units=64, activation="relu"))
value_model.add(Dense(units=64, activation="relu"))
value_model.add(Dense(3, activation='softmax'))
value_model.compile(loss='categorical_crossentropy',
                optimizer='adam',
                metrics=['accuracy'])
```

We use the Adam optimizer with the default learning rate of 0.001. The loss function is categorical cross-entropy since this is a multi-category classification problem. Next, we train the value network for 50 epochs, as follows:

```
5]: # Train the model for 50 epochs
    value_model.fit(Xs, ys, epochs=50, verbose=1)
    value_model.save('files/value_ttt.h5')
```

The value network is now trained and saved in the local folder on your computer. Alternatively, you can download the trained model in the book's GitHub repository.

Next, we'll design game strategies using the value network in Tic Tac Toe.

14.5   PLAY TIC TAC TOE WITH THE VALUE NETWORK

First, we'll define a *best_move()* function for the value network agent. The function will return the best move based on the value network we just trained. We'll test it against the strong policy agent we trained in Chapter 10.

14.5.1   Game Strategies Based on the Value Network

To find the best move for the value network agent, we'll go over each next move hypothetically and use the trained value network to predict the probability of winning the game if the move were taken. The function then compares these probabilities and selects the hypothetical move with the highest probability of winning.

Below, we define a *best_move()* function for the computer to find the best move. What the function does is as follows:

1. Looks at the current game board.
2. Looks at all possible next moves; makes a hypothetical move and records the hypothetical game board position as a result.
3. Uses the pre-trained model to predict the chance of winning with the hypothetical board position.
4. Choose the move that leads to the highest chance of winning.

```
5]: # design game strategy
    from copy import deepcopy

    def best_move(env):
        # Set the initial value of bestoutcome
        bestoutcome=-2;
        bestmove=None
        #go through all possible moves hypothetically
        for move in env.validinputs:
            env_copy=deepcopy(env)
            state,reward,done,info=env_copy.step(move)
            state=state.reshape(-1,3,3,1)
            if env.turn=="X":
                ps=value_model.predict(state,verbose=0)
```

```
    else:
        ps=value_model.predict(-state,verbose=0)
    # output is prob(win) - prob(lose)
    win_lose_dif=ps[0][1]-ps[0][2]
    if win_lose_dif>bestoutcome:
        # Update the bestoutcome
        bestoutcome = win_lose_dif
        # Update the best move
        bestmove = move
return bestmove
```

We'll test the game strategy next against the strong policy network that we trained in Chapter 10.

14.5.2   Test the Value Network Agent Against the Strong Policy Agent

We test the effectiveness of the above game strategy based on the value network. The opponent makes moves based on the *opponent()* function we defined earlier in the chapter. Recall that the function selects moves based on the trained strong policy network from Chapter 10. Therefore, we are effectively pitting the value network agent against the strong policy agent.

Below, we test ten games and let the value network agent move first. The strong policy agent moves second.

[17]:
```
# test ten games when the value network agent moves first
for i in range(10):
    state=env.reset()
    while True:
        # move recommended by the value network
        action=best_move(env)
        state,reward,done,_=env.step(action)
        # print game outcome
        if done:
            if reward==0:
                print("It's a tie!")
            else:
                print("The value network wins!")
            break
        # The strong policy agent moves second
        action=opponent(env)
        state,reward,done,_=env.step(action)
        # print game outcome if the game ends
        if done:
            if reward==0:
                print("It's a tie!")
```

```
        else:
            print("The value network loses!")
        break
```

```
It's a tie!
It's a tie!
It's a tie!
It's a tie!
It's a tie!
It's a tie!
It's a tie!
It's a tie!
It's a tie!
It's a tie!
```

All ten games are tied. Since the strong policy agent already makes perfect moves, the value network agent makes perfect moves as well: it's able to tie all ten game when playing against perfect moves. We know that in Tic Tac Toe, if both player makes perfect moves, the game is always tied. Therefore, our training strategy seems to work.

Just to be sure, we test another ten games. This time, we let the strong policy agent move first.

```
[3]: # test against the strong policy agent
     # test ten games when move second
     for i in range(10):
         state=env.reset()
         # The AI player moves firsts
         action=opponent(env)
         state,reward,done,_=env.step(action)
         while True:
             # move recommended by the value network
             action=best_move(env)
             state,reward,done,_=env.step(action)
             # if value network wins, record 1
             if done:
                 if reward==0:
                     print("It's a tie!")
                 else:
                     print("The value network wins!")
                 break
             # The AI player moves
             action=opponent(env)
             state,reward,done,_=env.step(action)
             # if value network wins, record 1
```

```
if done:
    if reward==0:
        print("It's a tie!")
    else:
        print("The value network loses!")
    break
```

```
It's a tie!
It's a tie!
It's a tie!
It's a tie!
It's a tie!
It's a tie!
It's a tie!
It's a tie!
It's a tie!
It's a tie!
```

All ten games are tied as well. This shows that we have trained an agent who can make perfect moves in Tic Tac Toe.

Now that you learned how to handle illegal moves and how to speed up training with vectorization, you'll apply these skills to another game, Connect Four, in the next chapter.

14.6 GLOSSARY

- **Credit Assignment Problem:** The credit assignment problem in reinforcement learning involves determining which actions are responsible for observed outcomes and to what extent.
- **Illegal Move:** In the context of games, an illegal move refers to an action taken by a player that is not allowed according to the rules of the game.
- **Player-Independent Game State** The concept of a player-independent game state in the context of games refers to a representation of the game's state that is not specific to any particular player. This means that the game state is described in a way that is neutral and does not vary based on which player's perspective is being considered.
- **Vectorization:** Vectorization refers to a process in computer science and mathematics where operations are applied to an entire array of values or a set of values simultaneously, rather than applying the operation to each value individually.

14.7 EXERCISES

14.1 What is vectorization? Why does it speed up training?

14.2 Modify the two code cells in Section 14.2 and see how long it takes to add up the values from 1 to 20,000,000 with and without vectorization.

14.3 Modify the first code cell in Section 14.5.1 so that the agent chooses an action to maximize the probability of winning, instead of the difference between probabilities of winning and losing. Call the new function *best_move2()*.

14.4 Modify the two code cells in Section 14.5.2 so the value network agent uses the new function *best_move2()* you defined in the previous question to select the best moves.

## CHAPTER 15

A Value Network in Connect Four

"One neural network — known as the "policy network" — selects the next move to play. The other neural network — the "value network" — predicts the winner of the game."

– Demis Hassabis, CEO and Co-Founder, DeepMind

IN CHAPTER 14, we applied the policy gradient method to Tic Tac Toe. Specifically, you learned how to handle illegal moves and use vectorization to speed up training. After several hours of training, the policy gradient agent becomes as effective as the strong policy agent that we trained in Chapter 10: it ties all games when playing against perfect moves.

In this chapter, you'll apply the policy gradient method to Connect Four. You'll handle illegal moves the same way you did in Chapter 14: assigning a reward of -1 every time the agent makes an illegal move. You'll also use vectorization to speed up training. You'll create one single model to train both the red player and the yellow player in Connect Four. We'll train the model as follows: in the first ten games, we'll let the policy gradient agent move first. The strong policy agent acts as the opponent. We'll then collect information such as the natural logarithms of the predicted probabilities and discounted rewards to update model parameters (i.e., train the model). In the second ten games, the policy gradient agent moves second and selects actions based on recommendations from the policy network in the model to play against the strong policy agent. We'll also collect information from gameplays to train the model. We'll alternate between training the red player and training the yellow player after every ten games. After the policy gradient agent beats or ties the strong policy agent at least 90% of the time, we stop the training process.

We also use the game experience data from the above training process to train a value network: the network will predict the game outcome based on the board position. You

DOI: 10.1201/9781032722207-15

also learn how to use the trained value network to design a game strategy in Connect Four. Since the strong policy agent we trained in Chapter 11 doesn't make perfect moves, the trained value network generates better game strategies than the strong policy agent.

What You'll Learn in This Chapter

- Training a policy network to avoid illegal moves in Connect Four
- Training a policy gradient network in Connect Four
- Training a value network using game experience data in Connect Four
- Designing game strategies based on the trained value network

---

15.1 THE POLICY GRADIENT METHOD IN CONNECT FOUR

You have learned how to play the coin game and Tic Tac Toe using the policy gradient approach in the previous two chapters. Specifically, you have adjusted the model parameters proportional to the product of the gradients and the discounted rewards. In this section, we'll apply the same technique to Connect Four to train a policy gradient agent.

15.1.1 Create the Policy Gradient Model in Connect Four

Below, we'll create two separate input networks first: one is a dense layer with 42 neurons and the other network has a convolutional layer that can detect the spatial features on the Connect Four game board. We'll then combine the two networks using the *concat()* method in TensorFlow. We'll use the combined network as the input to our policy gradient model. The model's output layer has seven values in it, each representing a potential next move.

The code in the cell below creates such a model:

```
import tensorflow as tf
from tensorflow import keras
from tensorflow.keras import layers


num_inputs=42
num_actions=7
# The convolutional input layer
conv_inputs=layers.Input(shape=(7,6,1))
conv=layers.Conv2D(filters=128, kernel_size=(4,4),padding="same",
     input_shape=(7,6,1), activation="relu")(conv_inputs)
flat=layers.Flatten()(conv)
# The dense input layer
inputs = layers.Input(shape=(42,))
```

```
# Combine the two into a single input layer
two_inputs = tf.concat([flat,inputs],axis=1)
# hidden layers
common = layers.Dense(256, activation="relu")(two_inputs)
common = layers.Dense(64, activation="relu")(common)
# Policy output network
action = layers.Dense(num_actions, activation="softmax")(common)
# The final model
model = keras.Model(inputs=[inputs, conv_inputs],\
                    outputs=action)
```

The model has two input networks. The first one takes in the game board as a seven by six image and uses a convolutional layer to extract the spatial features on the game board. The output is then flattened into a one-dimensional vector. The second input network is a dense layer with 42 neurons. We combine the two input layers together by using the *concat()* method from TensorFlow. The combined layer is then passed through two hidden layers. The output layer is a policy network that outputs the probabilities of each action.

Below, we specify the optimizer we use to train the model.

```
[2]: optimizer=keras.optimizers.Adam(learning_rate=0.00025)
```

The optimizer is Adam with a learning rate of 0.00025.

15.1.2   Use the Strong Policy Agent as the Opponent

In Chapter 11 we have trained a strong policy work in Connect Four. In this chapter, we'll use the strong policy network as the opponent when training the policy gradient agent in Tic Tac Toe. For that purpose, we define an *opponent()* function as follows:

```
[3]: # use the trained strong policy model as opponent
     trained=keras.models.load_model('files/policy_conn.h5')
     def opponent(env):
         state = env.state.reshape(-1,7,6,1)
         if env.turn=="red":
             action_probs=trained(state)
         else:
             action_probs=trained(-state)
         aps=[]
         for a in sorted(env.validinputs):
             aps.append(np.squeeze(action_probs)[a-1])
         ps=np.array(aps)/np.array(aps).sum()
         return np.random.choice(sorted(env.validinputs),p=ps)
```

To train the red player to choose moves based on the policy gradient method, we define a *playing_red()* function. We let the policy gradient agent move first as the red player and the strong policy agent move second as the opponent. The function simulates a full self-play game as follows:

```python
from utils.conn_simple_env import conn

# allow a maximum of 50 steps per game
max_steps=50
env=conn()

def playing_red():
    # create lists to record game history
    action_probs_history = []
    wrongmoves_history = []
    rewards_history = []
    state = env.reset()
    episode_reward = 0
    states=[]
    for step in range(max_steps):
        state = state.reshape(-1,42,)
        conv_state = state.reshape(-1,7,6,1)
        # Predict action probabilities and future rewards
        action_probs = model([state,conv_state])
        # select action based on the policy network
        action=np.random.choice(num_actions,\
                                p=np.squeeze(action_probs))
        # record log probabilities
        action_probs_history.append(\
                    tf.math.log(action_probs[0, action]))
        # punish the agent if there is an illegal move
        if action+1 not in env.validinputs:
            rewards_history.append(0)
            wrongmoves_history.append(-1)
            #episode_reward += -1
        # otherwise, place the move on the game board
        else:
        # Apply the sampled action in our environment
            state, reward, done, _ = env.step(action+1)
            states.append(state)
            if done:
                wrongmoves_history.append(0)
                rewards_history.append(reward)
                episode_reward += reward
                break
            else:
                state,reward,done,_=env.step(opponent(env))
```

```
                    rewards_history.append(reward)
                    wrongmoves_history.append(0)
                    episode_reward += reward
                    if done:
                        break
        return action_probs_history,\
                wrongmoves_history,rewards_history, \
                episode_reward,states,reward
```

The *playing_red()* function simulates a full game and records all the intermediate steps made by the policy gradient agent. The function returns six values, the first four of which are:

- a list *action_probs_history* with the natural logarithm of the recommended probability of the action taken by the agent from the policy network;
- a list *rewards_history* with the rewards for each action taken by the agent in the game;
- a list *wrongmoves_history* with the rewards for each action associated with illegal moves;
- a variable *episode_reward* showing the total rewards to the agent during the game.

We also collect game board positions after the policy gradient agent makes a move; we put them in a list *states*. The game outcome is recorded in the variable *reward*: 1 indicates the policy gradient agent has won; −1 means the policy gradient agent has lost; 0 signals a tie game.

The *playing_red()* function calculates the gradients and rewards from the game. Since in reinforcement learning, actions affect not only current period rewards, but also future rewards, we therefore use discounted rewards to assign credits properly to all legal moves in a game. The following function reflects such discounting of rewards:

```
[5]: def discount_rs(r,wrong):
         discounted_rs = np.zeros(len(r))
         running_add = 0
         for i in reversed(range(0, len(r))):
             if wrong[i]==0:
                 running_add = gamma*running_add + r[i]
                 discounted_rs[i] = running_add
         return discounted_rs.tolist()
```

The function takes two lists, *r* and *wrong*, as inputs, where *r* is the list of undiscounted rewards related to legal moves while *wrong* is the list of rewards related to illegal moves in the game. If a move is legal, the value is 0 in the list *wrong*; if a move is illegal, the value is −1 in the list. We discount *r* but not *wrong*, for reasons we discussed in Chapter 14. The output is a list of discounted rewards associated with legal moves in the game. Note that if an illegal move is made in a time step, the discounted reward is 0. We'll add in a reward of −1 for illegal moves later at training.

Similarly, to train the yellow player, we define a *playing_yellow()* function. The function simulates a full game, with the strong policy agent as the first player, and the policy gradient agent as the second player, as follows:

```python
def playing_yellow():
    # create lists to record game history
    action_probs_history = []
    wrongmoves_history = []
    rewards_history = []
    state = env.reset()
    episode_reward = 0
    states=[]
    state, reward, done, _ = env.step(opponent(env))
    for step in range(max_steps):
        state = state.reshape(-1,42,)
        conv_state = state.reshape(-1,7,6,1)
        # Predict action probabilities and future rewards
        action_probs = model([-state,-conv_state])
        # select action based on the policy network
        action=np.random.choice(num_actions,\
                            p=np.squeeze(action_probs))
        # record log probabilities
        action_probs_history.append(\
                    tf.math.log(action_probs[0, action]))
        # punish the agent if there is an illegal move
        if action+1 not in env.validinputs:
            rewards_history.append(0)
            wrongmoves_history.append(-1)
            #episode_reward += -1
        # otherwise, place the move on the game board
        else:
        # Apply the sampled action in our environment
            state, reward, done, _ = env.step(action+1)
            states.append(-state)
            if done:
                wrongmoves_history.append(0)
                rewards_history.append(-reward)
                episode_reward += -reward
                break
            else:
                state,reward,done,_=env.step(opponent(env))
                rewards_history.append(-reward)
```

```
                wrongmoves_history.append(0)
                episode_reward += -reward
                if done:
                    break
      return action_probs_history,\
            wrongmoves_history,rewards_history, \
            episode_reward,states,-reward
```

The *playing_yellow()* function simulates a full game and records all the intermediate steps made by the policy gradient agent. The function returns six values, the same as those from the function *playing_red()*.

Most importantly, we use $[-state, -conv\_state]$ instead of $[state, conv\_state]$ when we feed the game board to the model. This is because the game board has a value of 1 in a cell if the red player has placed a game piece in it, -1 if the yellow player has placed a game piece in it. To use the same network for both players, we multiply the input by -1 when it's the yellow player's turn so that the model treats 1 as occupied by the current player and -1 as occupied by the opponent.

The second most important thing is to change the rewards. Instead of using 1 and -1 to denote a win by the red player and the yellow player, respectively, we'll use a reward of 1 to denote the current player has won and a reward of -1 to denote that the current player has lost. We accomplish this by using $-reward$ instead of $reward$ in the above *playing_yellow()* function. Therefore, after the yellow player makes a move, the reward is now 1 if the yellow player wins and -1 if the yellow player loses.

15.1.3 Train the Red and Yellow Players Iteratively

Instead of updating model parameters after one episode, we update after a certain number of episodes to make the training stable. Here we update parameters every ten games to train the red player, as follows:

[7]:
```
batch_size=10
allstates=[]
alloutcome=[]
def create_batch_red(batch_size):
    action_probs_history = []
    wrongmoves_history = []
    rewards_history = []
    episode_rewards = []
    for i in range(batch_size):
        aps,wms,rs,er,ss,outcome = playing_red()
        # rewards are discounted
        returns = discount_rs(rs,wms)
        action_probs_history += aps
        # punishments for wrong moves are not discounted
```

```
        wrongmoves_history += wms
        # combined discounted rewards with punishments
        combined=np.array(returns)+np.array(wms)
        # add combined rewards to rewards history
        rewards_history += combined.tolist()
        episode_rewards.append(er)
        # record game history for the next section
        allstates.append(ss)
        alloutcome.append(outcome)
    return action_probs_history,\
        rewards_history,episode_rewards
```

Here we discount the rewards associated with wins and losses, but not the rewards associated with illegal moves, due to the credit assignment problem we discussed in Chapter 14. We then combine the discounted rewards with punishments associated with illegal moves and put the combined values in the list *rewards_history*.

Similarly, we simulate ten games to train the yellow player, as follows:

```
[3]: def create_batch_yellow(batch_size):
        action_probs_history = []
        wrongmoves_history = []
        rewards_history = []
        episode_rewards = []
        for i in range(batch_size):
            aps,wms,rs,er,ss,outcome = playing_yellow()
            # reward related to legal moves are discounted
            returns = discount_rs(rs,wms)
            action_probs_history += aps
            # punishments for wrong moves are not discounted
            wrongmoves_history += wms
            # combined discounted rewards with punishments
            combined=np.array(returns)+np.array(wms)
            # add combined rewards to rewards history
            rewards_history += combined.tolist()
            episode_rewards.append(er)
            # record game history for the next section
            allstates.append(ss)
            alloutcome.append(outcome)
        return action_probs_history,\
            rewards_history,episode_rewards
```

We'll train the model and update the parameters until the policy gradient agent wins or ties the strong policy agent at least 90% of the time in the last 100 games.

```
[9]: from collections import deque
     import numpy as np

     running_rewards=deque(maxlen=100)
     gamma = 0.95
     episode_count = 0
     batches=0
     # Train the model
     while True:
         with tf.GradientTape() as tape:
             if batches%2==0:
                 action_probs_history,rewards_history,\
                     episode_rewards=create_batch_red(batch_size)
             else:
                 action_probs_history,rewards_history,\
                     episode_rewards=create_batch_yellow(batch_size)


             # Calculating loss values to update our network
             rets=tf.convert_to_tensor(rewards_history,\
                                       dtype=tf.float32)
             alosses=-tf.multiply(tf.convert_to_tensor(\
               action_probs_history,dtype=tf.float32),rets)
             # Backpropagation
             loss_value = tf.reduce_sum(alosses)
         grads = tape.gradient(loss_value, model.trainable_variables)
         optimizer.apply_gradients(zip(grads,\
                                       model.trainable_variables))

         # Log details
         episode_count += batch_size
         batches += 1
         for r in episode_rewards:
             running_rewards.append(r)
         running_reward=np.mean(np.array(running_rewards))
         # print out progress
         if episode_count % 100 == 0:
             template = "running reward: {:.6f} at episode {}"
             print(template.format(running_reward, episode_count))
         # Stop if the game is solved
         if running_reward>=0.9 and episode_count>100:
             print("Solved at episode {}!".format(episode_count))
             break
     model.save("files/PG_conn.h5")
```

It takes about ten hours to train the model. The exact amount of time depends on your computer hardware. Alternatively, you can download the trained model from the book's GitHub repository.

After training, we also save the game experience data in the local folder so that we can use them in the next section to train a value network:

```
import pickle

with open("files/PG_games_conn.p","wb") as f:
    pickle.dump((allstates,alloutcome),f)
```

15.2 TRAIN A VALUE NETWORK IN CONNECT FOUR

In this section, you'll create a neural network to predict the outcome in Connect Four based on board positions (i.e., game states). First, you'll process the game experience data we gathered in the last section when training the policy gradient model. We'll use the game states after the policy gradient agent's moves as the input to the neural network (i.e., the Xs when training the model) and the final game outcome for the policy gradient agent as the output of the neural network (i.e., the ys when training the model).

Once the value network is trained, we'll design game strategies based on the network in the next section.

15.2.1 How to Train a Value Network in Connect Four

Here is a summary of what we'll do to train a value network to design intelligent game strategies in Connect Four:

1. We'll process the game experience data we gathered in the last section when training the policy gradient model: the game states after the policy gradient agent's moves and the final game outcomes.
2. We then associate each game state with the final game outcome for the policy gradient agent. We'll use game states as features X, and the outcomes for the agent as labels y. We'll treat this as a multi-category classification problem since there are three possible outcomes associated with each game state: a win, a tie, or a loss.
3. We'll feed the processed data (Xs and ys) into a deep neural network to train the model to predict the game outcome based on the game state. After the training is done, we have a trained value network.
4. We can now use the trained value network to play a game. At each move of the game, the player looks at all possible next moves and imagines what the hypothetical game board looks like after a hypothetical next move. We feed the hypothetical game state into the pertained value network. The network tells the agent the probabilities of a win, a tie, and a loss.

5. The agent selects the move that the model predicts with the highest value $Prob(win) - Prob(loss)$.

15.2.2 Process the Game Experience Data in Connect Four

The data we gathered in the last section are not ready to be fed into a deep neural network. We'll first change the game states to seven by six matrices and game outcomes into one-hot vectors with a depth of three. To change the game outcomes into one-hot variables, we manually encode them. The game outcome can be 1, 0, or -1. A value of 1 indicates the policy gradient agent has won the game; -1 indicates the agent has lost the game; 0 means a tie game. We'll change the outcome to $[0, 1, 0]$ as winning, $[1, 0, 0]$ as tying, and $[0, 0, 1]$ as losing. That is, we use a one-hot variable with a depth of three to indicate the game outcome.

In the code cell below, we process the game experience data and make them ready for training.

```
[11]:   with open("files/PG_games_conn.p","rb") as f:
            history,results=pickle.load(f)

        Xs=[]
        ys=[]
        for states, result in zip(history,results):
            for state in states:
                Xs.append(state)
                if result==1:
                    ys.append(np.array([0,1,0]))
                elif result==-1:
                    ys.append(np.array([0,0,1]))
                elif result==0:
                    ys.append(np.array([1,0,0]))

        Xs=np.array(Xs).reshape(-1,7,6,1)
        ys=np.array(ys).reshape(-1,3)
```

Next, we create a deep neural network as the value network and use the above data to train it.

15.2.3 Train a Value Network in Connect Four

We'll use Keras to create a deep neural network to represent the value network in Connect Four. In particular, the network will include one convolutional layer and two hidden dense layers, plus an input layer and an output layer. Since there are three possible game outcomes (a win, a tie, or a loss), we'll treat the learning process as a multi-category classification problem. Therefore, we'll have three neurons in the output layer. We'll use softmax as our activation function in the output layer so the output can be interpreted as probabilities of three different outcomes.

```
2]: from tensorflow.keras.layers import Dense,Conv2D,Flatten
    from tensorflow.keras.models import Sequential

    value_model = Sequential()
    value_model.add(Conv2D(filters=128,
       kernel_size=(4,4),padding="same",activation="relu",
                    input_shape=(7,6,1)))
    value_model.add(Flatten())
    value_model.add(Dense(units=64, activation="relu"))
    value_model.add(Dense(units=64, activation="relu"))
    value_model.add(Dense(3, activation='softmax'))
    value_model.compile(loss='categorical_crossentropy',
        optimizer=keras.optimizers.Adam(learning_rate=0.0005),
        metrics=['accuracy'])
```

We use the Adam optimizer with a learning rate of 0.0005 to make sure that the parameters converge. The loss function is categorical cross-entropy since this is a multi-category classification problem. Next, we train the value network for 100 epochs, as follows:

```
3]: # Train the model for 100 epochs
    value_model.fit(Xs, ys, epochs=100, verbose=1)
    value_model.save('files/value_conn.h5')
```

The value network is now trained and saved in the local folder on your computer. Next, we'll design game strategies using the value network in Connect Four.

15.3   PLAY CONNECT FOUR WITH THE VALUE NETWORK

First, we'll define a *best_move()* function for the value network agent. The function will return the best move based on the value network we just trained. We'll test it against the policy agent we created in Chapter 11.

15.3.1   Best Moves Based on the Value Network in Connect Four

To find the best move for the value network agent, we'll go over each next move hypothetically and use the trained value network to predict the probability of the agent winning the game if the move were taken. The function then compares which next move has the highest probability of the agent winning.

Below, we define a *best_move()* function for the computer to find the best move. What the function does is as follows:

- Look at the current game board.
- Look at all possible next moves; make a hypothetical move to create a hypothetical game board position.

- Use the pertained model to predict the probabilities of winning, tying, and losing with the hypothetical board position.
- Choose the move with the highest value of $Prob(win) - Prob(loss)$.

```
[14]:  # design game strategy
       from copy import deepcopy
       from tensorflow.keras.models import load_model


       value_model=load_model('files/value_conn.h5')

       def best_move(env):
           # Set the initial value of bestoutcome
           bestoutcome=-2;
           bestmove=None
           #go through all possible moves hypothetically
           for move in env.validinputs:
               env_copy=deepcopy(env)
               state,reward,done,info=env_copy.step(move)
               state=state.reshape(-1,7,6,1)
               if env.turn=="red":
                   ps=value_model.predict(state,verbose=0)
               else:
                   ps=value_model.predict(-state,verbose=0)
               # output is prob(win) - prob(lose)
               win_lose_dif=ps[0][1]-ps[0][2]
               if win_lose_dif>bestoutcome:
                   # Update the bestoutcome
                   bestoutcome = win_lose_dif
                   # Update the best move
                   bestmove = move
           return bestmove
```

We'll test the game strategy next.

15.3.2 Play Against the Strong Policy Agent in Connect Four

We test the effectiveness of the above game strategy based on the value network. We let the value network agent play against the policy agent for 100 games:

```
[15]:  # test ten games when move first
       results=[]
       for i in range(100):
           state=env.reset()
           # half the time, the policy network agent moves first
           if i%2==0:
               action=opponent(env)
```

```
            state,reward,done,_=env.step(action)
        while True:
            # move recommended by the value network
            action=best_move(env)
            state,reward,done,_=env.step(action)
            # if value network wins, record 1
            if done:
                if reward==0:
                    results.append(0)
                    print("It's a tie!")
                else:
                    results.append(1)
                    print("The value network wins!")
                break
            # The policy network agent moves
            action=opponent(env)
            state,reward,done,_=env.step(action)
            # if value network loses, record -1
            if done:
                if reward==0:
                    results.append(0)
                    print("It's a tie!")
                else:
                    results.append(-1)
                    print("The value network loses!")
                break
```

```
The value network wins!
The value network wins!
The value network wins!
The value network loses!
The value network wins!
...
...
The value network wins!
The value network wins!
The value network wins!
The value network wins!
The value network loses!
```

Half the time, the policy network agent moves first. The other half of the time, the value network agent moves first, so no player has a first-mover advantage. We let the two players play 100 games. If the value network agent wins, we add a value of 1 to the list *results*. If the value network agent loses, we add a value of -1 to the list *results*. If the game ties, we add a value of 0 to the list *results*.

We can check how often the value network agent has won:

```
[16]:  # count how many times the value network agent won
       wins=results.count(1)
       print(f"the value network agent has won {wins} games")
       # count how many times the value network agent lost
       losses=results.count(-1)
       print(f"the value network agent has lost {losses} games")
       # count how many tie games
       ties=results.count(0)
       print(f"the game is tied {ties} times")
```

```
the value network agent has won 67 games
the value network agent has lost 33 games
the game is tied 0 times
```

The above results show that the value network agent is better than the policy network agent that we trained in Chapter 11: it has won 67 games and lost 33 games. There is no tie game. This indicates that self-play deep reinforcement learning has improved the intelligence of the game strategy.

We now have all the pieces needed to implement the AlphaGo algorithm. Starting from the next chapter, you'll learn how to implement AlphaGo in the three games: the coin game, Tic Tac Toe, and Connect Four.

15.4 EXERCISES

15.1 Modify the first code cell in Section 15.3.1 so that the agent chooses an action to maximize the probability of winning, instead of the difference between probabilities of winning and losing. Call the new function *best_move2()*.

15.2 Modify the two code cells in Section 15.3.2 so the value network agent uses the new function *best_move2()* you defined in the previous question to select the best moves.

IV

AlphaGo Algorithms

## CHAPTER 16

Implementing AlphaGo in the Coin Game

"I thought AlphaGo was based on probability calculation and that it was merely a machine. But when I saw this move, I changed my mind. Surely, AlphaGo is creative. "

– Lee Sedol, winner of 18 world Go titles

THE ALPHAGO ALGORITHM combines deep reinforcement learning (namely, the policy gradient method) with traditional rule-based AI (specifically, Monte Carlo Tree Search or MCTS) to generate intelligent game strategies in Go. Now that you have learned both deep reinforcement learning and MCTS, you'll learn to combine them together as the DeepMind team did and apply the algorithm to the three games in this book: the coin game, Tic Tac Toe, and Connect Four.

In this chapter, you'll implement AlphaGo in the coin game. First, we'll go over the AlphaGo algorithm and see how it brings various pieces together to create a powerful AI player. After that, you'll apply the same logic to the coin game to create your very own AlphaGo agent.

MCTS is the core of AlphaGo's decision-making process. MCTS is used to find the most promising moves by building a search tree. Each node in the tree represents a game position, and branches represent possible moves. The search through this tree is guided by statistical analysis of the moves. AlphaGo also uses three deep neural networks – a fast policy network, a strengthened policy network through self-play deep reinforcement learning, and a value network. The fast policy network helps in narrowing down the selection of moves to consider in game rollouts. It's trained on expert games and learns to predict their moves. This network is used to guide the tree search to more promising paths. The strengthened policy network is used to select child nodes in game rollouts so that the most valuable child nodes are selected to roll out games. The value network evaluates board positions and predicts the winner of the game from that position. It's crucial for looking ahead and evaluating future positions without having to play out the entire game.

AlphaGo's success lies in the effective combination of traditional tree search methods with powerful machine-learning techniques. This allowed it to tackle the immense complexity of Go, a game with more possible positions than atoms in the observable universe.

The three games we consider in this book are much simpler than the game of Go. Nonetheless, we'll mimic the strategies used by the DeepMind team and implement the AlphaGo algorithm in these games. Along the way, you'll pick up valuable skills in both rule-based AI and cutting-edge developments in deep learning.

To implement AlphaGo in the coin game, we'll utilize the skills and the trained networks earlier in this book. Specifically, we'll use the skills you learned about MCTS from Chapter 8. However, instead of rolling out games with random moves, you'll roll out games by letting both players choose moves based on the fast policy network we trained in Chapter 9. More intelligent moves in rollouts lead to more informative game outcomes. Further, instead of playing out the entire game during rollouts, you'll use the value network we trained in Chapter 13 to evaluate game states after a fixed number of moves (that is, after a certain depth). Finally, to select a child node to roll out games in MCTS, instead of using the UCT formula from Chapter 8, you'll use a weighted average of the rollout values and the prior probabilities recommended by the strengthened policy network from Chapter 13.

After creating the AlphaGo agent in the coin game, you'll test it against both random moves and the perfect rule-based AI player from Chapter 1. You'll see that when moving second, the AlphaGo agent beats the ruled-based AI player in all ten games. When moving first, the AlphaGo agent wins all ten games against random moves. This shows that the AlphaGo algorithm is as strong as any possible game strategy we could have designed for the coin game.

What You'll Learn in This Chapter

- Selecting child nodes in the AlphaGo algorithm
- Rolling out games and updating the game tree in the AlphaGo algorithm
- Creating an AlphaGo agent in the coin game
- Testing the effectiveness of AlphaGo in the coin game

16.1 THE ALPHAGO ARCHITECTURE

In this section, we'll introduce the detailed network architecture of AlphaGo. We'll then provide a blueprint on how we'll implement the algorithm in the coin game. To make the AlphaGo algorithm easy to understand, we'll use a concrete example to

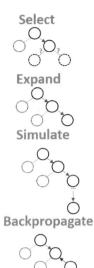

Select

The agent selects the child node L={L1,L2}, to maximize
$$value(L) = \lambda * prior(L) + (1 - \lambda) * rollout\_value(L)$$

Expand

Expand the game tree to reach the selected child node L

Simulate

Roll out a game till a terminal state or the maximum depth is reached; moves are guided by the fast policy network trained in Chapter 9; If the maximum depth is reached, use the value network trained in Chapter 13 to evaluate game state

Backpropagate

The agent updates the current move sequence as well as values of $prior(L)$ and $rollout\_value(L)$

Figure 16.1   Steps of tree search when implementing the AlphaGo algorithm in the coin game

illustrate how the algorithm works: assuming that you are Player 2 in the coin game and there are 20 coins left on the table. That is, Player 1 just made a move and took one coin from the pile. You'll have to come up with a move with the AlphaGo algorithm. What are the steps you have to take to come up with the best move? This thought experiment will explain in detail all the steps involved in the AlphaGo algorithm.

Figure 16.1 is a diagram of the steps in MCTS when implementing the AlphaGo algorithm in the coin game.

To make a move in a real game, the AlphaGo algorithm combines MCTS with deep reinforcement learning. Specifically, it follows the four steps involved in MCTS that we outlined in Chapter 8: select, expand, simulate, and backpropagate.

1. **Select.** The current game state is called the root node. In each rollout during tree search, the agent needs to select one of the child nodes of the root node by taking a hypothetical next move. Specifically, the AlphaGo agent chooses the child node L among all possible child nodes, $L_1, L_2, ..., L_S$, by selecting the child node that leads to the highest value, defined by the following formula:

$$value(L) = \lambda \times prior(L) + (1 - \lambda) \times rollout\_value(L)$$

That is, the agent selects a child node to maximize the expected value of the next game state:

$$L' = argmax_L \ value(L)$$

To calculate $prior(L)$, the agent uses the strengthened strong policy network from Chapter 13, while $rollout\_value(L)$ is the average game outcome in roll-outs in which the child node L is reached. If you recall, in Chapter 9 we have trained a strong policy network for the coin game. Then in Chapter 13, we have used self-play deep reinforcement learning to further train the strong policy network. The self-play has also generated game experience data. We trained a value network for the coin game based on the game experience data to predict game outcomes based on current game states. This value network will be used in Step 3 (simulate) below.

2. **Expand.** Make a hypothetical move to expand the game tree to reach the selected child node L.

3. **Simulate.** Roll out a game till a terminal state or the maximum depth is reached. Moves are guided by the fast policy network trained in Chapter 9 during rollouts. If you recall, in Chapter 9 we have trained a fast policy network for the coin game. The advantage of the fast policy network is its simple architecture: as a result, it can recommend a move based on the game state very quickly. This allows the AlphaGo algorithm to roll out as many games as possible in a short period of time. If the maximum depth is reached at the end of the rollout, we'll use the value network trained in Chapter 13 to evaluate the game state. If a terminal state is reached at the end of the rollout, we'll evaluate the outcome of the simulation as follows: if Player 1 wins the game, the evaluation is 1; if Player 1 loses the game, the evaluation is -1; if the game is tied, the evaluation is 0.

4. **Backpropagate.** The agent updates the current move sequence, as well as the values of $prior(L)$ and $rollout\_value(L)$ based on the simulated outcome. Specifically, if the rollout passes through child node L, we'll update the value of $rollout\_value(L))$ based on the evaluation in step 3 above. Further, update the value of $prior(L)$ as follows:

$$prior(L) = \frac{P(L)}{1 + N(L)}$$

The idea is that if very few rollouts have passed through the game state L, we'll rely heavily on the prior distribution $P(L)$. Once we have many rollouts through child node L, we rely more on the actual game outcomes and less on the prior distribution.

16.2   IMPLEMENT THE ALPHAGO ALGORITHM IN THE COIN GAME

In the local module *ch16util*, we'll implement the AlphaGo algorithm in the coin game. Download the file *ch16util.py* from the book's GitHub repository and place it in the folder /utils/ on your computer. Take some time to go through the details of the module. Below, I'll explain the logic behind the algorithm in the sequence of four steps in MCTS: select, expand, simulate, and backpropagate.

16.2.1   Select the Best Child Node and Expand the Game Tree

We'll place all functions related to the AlphaGo algorithm in the coin game in the local module *ch16util*, where we first load up the pre-trained networks from the previous chapters, as follows:

```
from copy import deepcopy
import numpy as np
from tensorflow import keras
```

```
# Load the trained fast policy network from Chapter 9
fast_net=keras.models.load_model("files/fast_coin.h5")
# Load the strengthend strong net from Chapter 13
PG_net=keras.models.load_model("files/PG_coin.h5")
# Load the trained value network from Chapter 13
value_net=keras.models.load_model("files/value_coin.h5")
```

The above code block loads three pre-trained networks. The first one is the fast policy network from Chapter 9. We'll use this network to roll out games: this way, the game outcome is more informative compared to rollouts with random moves. The second network is the policy gradient network from Chapter 13, where we used self-play deep reinforcement learning to further strengthen the strong policy network we trained in Chapter 9. The policy gradient network will help select child nodes in the first step of MCTS. The third network is the value network we trained in Chapter 13. Whenever the game is not over in a rollout, we'll use the trained value network to assess the game state and estimate which player will win the game.

As we did in Chapters 1, 9, and 13, we define a *onehot_encoder()* function in the local module to convert the game state into a onehot variable with 22 values so we can feed it to neural networks. We then define a *best_move_fast_net()* to recommend moves in rollouts based on the fast policy network:

```
def onehot_encoder(state):
    onehot=np.zeros((1,22))
    onehot[0,state]=1
    return onehot

def best_move_fast_net(env):
    state = env.state
    onehot_state = onehot_encoder(state)
    action_probs = fast_net(onehot_state)
    return np.random.choice([1,2],
        p=np.squeeze(action_probs))
```

To select a child node, the AlphaGo agent looks at all possible child nodes. The current game state represents the root node. The agent chooses a child node L, which can be either L_1 or L_2, to maximize the following objective function:

$$value(L) = \lambda \times prior(L) + (1 - \lambda) \times rollout\_value(L)$$

where λ is a constant weight between 0 and 1. We'll assign a high value such as 0.9 to it in this chapter since the policy gradient agent solves the coin game. The value of the prior is defined as

$$prior(L) = \frac{PG\_action\_prob}{1 + N(L)}$$

To calculate $prior(L)$, the agent uses the strengthened strong policy network from Chapter 13 (i.e., the policy gradient network). Further, we scale the action probability recommended by the policy gradient agent by the term $1 + N(L)$, where $N(L)$ is the number of times the child node L has been visited in rollouts so far. The idea is that the AlphaGo agent relies more on the prior at the early stages of rollouts since the average rollout outcome is not informative. In contrast, after many rounds of rollouts, the average outcome is a good indicator of the value of the child node so the AlphaGo agent should rely more on it, compared to the prior.

We define a *select()* function in the local module to reflect how the AlphaGo agent selects a child node L based on the prior and the average rollout value, as follows:

```
def select(priors,env,results,weight):
    # weighted average of priors and rollout_value
    scores={}
    for k,v in results.items():
        # rollout_value for each next move
        if len(v)==0:
            vi=0
        else:
            vi=sum(v)/len(v)
        # scale the prior by (1+N(L))
        prior=priors[0][k-1]/(1+len(v))
        # calculate weighted average
        scores[k]=weight*prior+(1-weight)*vi
    # select child node based on the weighted average
    return max(scores,key=scores.get)
```

The *select()* function takes four arguments: *priors*, *env*, *results*, and *weight*. The list *priors* contains the recommended probabilities from the trained policy-gradient network from Chapter 13, which we'll calculate later; *env* is the current game environment. The argument *results* is a dictionary whose keys are possible next child nodes (i.e., next moves). The value corresponding to each key is a list of rewards from rollouts following each child node. We'll define the dictionary *results* later and update the dictionary during the tree search process. To give you an idea on the dictionary *results*, just know that we'll initiate the dictionary as follows in the coin game:

```
results={1:[], 2:[]}
```

The dictionary has two keys: 1 and 2, representing the two possible child nodes (the two hypothetical game states after removing either one or two coins from the pile). The value for each key is an empty list. After each rollout, we add the outcome to one of the two lists. For example, if child node 1 is selected and the outcome is −1 for the current player, we update the dictionary to

```
results={1:[-1], 2:[]}
```

The argument *weight* is a number between 0 and 1. When selecting a child node, the AlphaGo agent relies on both the priors recommended by the policy gradient network we trained in Chapter 13 and the average rollout results. The parameter *weight* is how much weight we place on the priors and the rest of the weight is placed on the average rollout outcome. In this chapter, we set the value of *weight* to say, 0.9. This weight is high since the coin game is a solved game and the priors recommend perfect moves. Later in Chapter 18 when we design an AlphaGo agent for Connect Four, we'll set a much lower value for *weight* because the policy gradient agent in Connect Four doesn't make perfect moves. As a result, we place more weight on actual rollout outcomes and less weight on the priors.

The *select()* function first calculates the rollout value for each child node. The rollout value ranges from −1 to 1, where −1 means the child node leads to a loss for the AlphaGo agent and 1 means the child node leads to a win. The function then calculates the scaled prior for each child node. The agent selects a node based on the weighted average of the prior and the rollout value: the child node with the highest weighted average is chosen.

In order to roll out games to evaluate different child nodes, we'll expand the game tree. To expand the game tree, the AlphaGo agent takes a hypothetical next move so that the selected child node is reached. To implement this, we define a *expand()* function in the local module *ch16util* as follows:

```
# expand the game tree by taking a hypothetical move
def expand(env,move):
    env_copy=deepcopy(env)
    state,reward,done,info=env_copy.step(move)
    return env_copy, done, reward
```

The function *expand()* function takes two arguments: the current game environment, *env*, and the recommended hypothetical move generated by the *select()* function above, *move*. Make sure you use the *deepcopy()* method to make a deep copy of the current game environment to create a hypothetical game environment.

The *expand()* function returns three objects: the hypothetical game environment if the selected child node is reached, *env_copy*; a variable *done* indicating if the game is over; and a variable *reward* indicating the game outcome. The variable *reward* can take one of three values: −1, 0, and 1, where −1 means Player 2 has won the game, 1 means Player 1 has won the game, and 0 means the game is not over yet.

16.2.2 Roll Out a Game and Backpropagate

Next, we roll out a game, starting from the child node, until the terminal state or the maximum depth is reached. After that, we evaluate the child node. If the terminal state is reached, we evaluate the child node with the actual game outcome. If the maximum depth is reached but the game is not over, we evaluate the node with the trained value network from Chapter 13.

In the local module *ch16util*, we define the *simulate()* function as follows:

```
# roll out a game till terminal state or depth reached
def simulate(env_copy,done,reward,depth):
    # if the game has already ended
    if done==True:
        return reward
    # select moves based on fast policy network
    for _ in range(depth):
        move=best_move_fast_net(env_copy)
        state,reward,done,info=env_copy.step(move)
        # if terminal state is reached, returns outcome
        if done==True:
            return reward
    # depth reached but game not over, evaluate
    onehot_state=onehot_encoder(state)
    # use the trained value network to evaluate
    ps=value_net.predict(onehot_state,verbose=0)
    # output is prob(1 wins)-prob(2 wins)
    reward=ps[0][1]-ps[0][0]
    return reward
```

The *simulate()* function first checks if the child node is in a terminal state. If yes, the function returns the game outcome. If not, the function makes hypothetical moves to roll out a game. The moves are selected based on the function *best_move_fast_net()* we defined earlier; that is, the moves are recommended by the trained fast policy network we trained in Chapter 9. The function *simulate()* makes a maximum number of moves, defined by the argument *depth*, during the game rollout. If a terminal state is reached before the maximum depth is reached, we evaluate the child node based on the game outcome: 1 means Player 1 has won and −1 means Player 2 has won. Here we record the game outcome from Player 1's point of view and we'll adjust that based on who the current player is later in the function *backpropagate()*.

The argument *depth* is the maximum number of hypothetical moves we allow in a rollout. The idea is to save time in rollouts: if we roll out games to the terminal state, it may take a long time to finish a game. By stopping the tree search after a fixed number of steps, we can allow the AlphaGo agent to utilize the trained value network to assess the game state. That way, the agent can roll out more games in the allotted time limit. Setting a depth is especially valuable in complicated games such as Chess or Go, where a complete game may take a long time to finish.

Finally, the function *simulate()* uses the trained value network from Chapter 13 to evaluate the game state if the game is not over when the maximum depth is reached. The value of a game state is defined as the probability of Player 1 winning minus the probability of Player 2 winning. Again, we evaluate a game state from Player 1's point of view. We'll make adjustments later in the function *backpropagate()*.

The final step in the tree search is to update the game tree after each rollout. Specifically, if the current player is Player 2, we'll multiply the game outcome by −1 so that everything is from the current player's point of view, not from Player 1's point of view.

We define the *backpropagate()* function in the local module, as follows:

```python
def backpropagate(env,move,reward,results):
    # if current player is Player 1, update results
    if env.turn==1:
        results[move].append(reward)
    # if current player is Player 2, multiply outcome with -1
    elif env.turn==2:
        results[move].append(-reward)
    return results
```

The main purpose of the *backpropagate()* function is to update the dictionary *results* so that we have a complete record of all rollout outcomes. Recall that the rollout outcome is from Player 1's point of view. We make adjustments as follows: if the current player is Player 1, we keep the outcome as it is; if the current player is Player 2, we multiply the outcome by −1 so that the outcome is from the current player's point of view. The function *backpropagate()* returns the updated dictionary *results*.

16.2.3 Create an AlphaGo Agent in the Coin Game

Now we are ready to create our AlphaGo agent in the coin game, by using the four functions defined above: *select()*, *expand()*, *simulate()*, and *backpropagate()*.

Specifically, we define the *alphago_coin()* function in the local module as follows:

```python
def alphago_coin(env,weight,depth,num_rollouts=100):
    # if there is only one valid move left, take it
    if len(env.validinputs)==1:
        return env.validinputs[0]
    # get the prior from the PG policy network
    priors = PG_net(onehot_encoder(env.state))
    # create a dictionary results
    results={}
    for move in env.validinputs:
        results[move]=[]
```

```
# roll out games
for _ in range(num_rollouts):
    # select
    move=select(priors,env,results,weight)
    # expand
    env_copy, done, reward=expand(env,move)
    # simulate
    reward=simulate(env_copy,done,reward,depth)
    # backpropagate
    results=backpropagate(env,move,reward,results)
# select the most visited child node
visits={k:len(v) for k,v in results.items()}
return max(visits,key=visits.get)
```

The AlphaGo agent first checks if there is only one valid move left. If yes, the agent takes the move without searching. Otherwise, the agent calculates the prior probabilities of choosing each next child node, based on the trained policy gradient network from Chapter 13. These priors will help the agent to select child nodes in the *select()* function we defined earlier.

The agent also initiates a dictionary *results* to record the rollout results. Before a rollout starts, the dictionary looks like this:

`results={1:[], 2:[]}`

The dictionary *results* records the rollout outcomes for each child node. The value corresponding to each child node is a list containing rewards to Player 1 after a rollout is finished.

The argument *num_rollouts* specifies how many rollouts the AlphaGo agent conducts before making a move in the real game. We set the default value of *num_rollouts* to 100 but you can change it when calling the *alphago_coin()* function. In each rollout, we follow the four steps as defined in the four functions *select()*, *expand()*, *simulate()*, and *backpropagate()*. The dictionary *results* updates the rollout outcome after each rollout.

Once the specified number of rollouts are finished, the AlphaGo agent makes an actual move to play in the real game, by selecting the most visited child node.

16.3   TEST THE ALPHAGO ALGORITHM IN THE COIN GAME

Next, we'll test the AlphaGo algorithm in the coin game. We set the number of rollouts to 100. Since Player 2 always wins if it makes perfect moves, we'll first let Player 2 use the moves recommended by the AlphaGo algorithm. Player 1 will use the rule-based AI strategy that we developed in Chapter 1.

16.3.1   When the AlphaGo Agent Moves Second

Since each game takes about half a minute to finish, we'll test only 10 games. In each game, the rule-based AI moves first and the AlphaGo agent moves second.

First, let's define a function *rule_based_AI()* to represent the rule-based AI agent that we developed in Chapter 1:

```
import random

def rule_based_AI(env):
    if env.state%3 != 0:
        move = env.state%3
    else:
        move = random.choice([1,2])
    return move
```

The rule-based AI agent will make a move so that the number of coins left on the table is a multiple of three, if possible. Otherwise, it randomly picks 1 or 2.

Next, we let the two players play ten games. After each game, we print out the winner of the game, as follows:

```
from utils.coin_simple_env import coin_game
from utils.ch16util import alphago_coin

# initiate game environment
env=coin_game()
# test ten games
for i in range(10):
    state=env.reset()
    while True:
        # The rule-based AI player moves first
        action=rule_based_AI(env)
        state,reward,done,_=env.step(action)
        if done:
            # print out the winner
            print("Rule-based AI wins!")
            break
        # The AlphaGo agent moves second
        action=alphago_coin(env,0.9,10,num_rollouts=100)
        state,reward,done,_=env.step(action)
        if done:
            # print out the winner
            print("AlphaGo wins!")
            break
```

```
AlphaGo wins!
AlphaGo wins!
AlphaGo wins!
AlphaGo wins!
AlphaGo wins!
AlphaGo wins!
AlphaGo wins!
AlphaGo wins!
AlphaGo wins!
AlphaGo wins!
```

When calling the function *alphago_coin()*, we set the value of the argument *weight* to 0.9. This means we rely mainly on the trained policy gradient agent when selecting child nodes. We set the value of the argument *depth* to 10. This means in rollouts, we search ahead for at most ten steps. Given that a coin game can have a maximum of 21 steps, our choice of the value of *depth* is about half of that value. This means in the early stages of the game in each rollout, we use the trained value network to assess the final game state before the game is over.

In each of the above ten games, if the AlphaGo agent wins, the output says "AlphaGo wins!". Otherwise, the output says "Rule-based AI wins!" The above output shows that the AlphaGo Algorithm has won all ten games. This shows that our AlphaGo algorithm makes perfect moves: it beats the perfect rule-based AI agent that we designed in Chapter 1.

16.3.2 Against Random Moves in the Coin Game

Even though we trained the AlphaGo algorithm assuming that the AlphaGo agent plays second, the coin game is player-independent. That is, once the game has started, no matter whether the current player is Player 1 or Player 2, the game strategy is the same. A player will win if it makes sure the number of coins left in the pile is a multiple of three.

As a result, we'll test what happens if Player 1 uses the AlphaGo algorithm in the coin game. Below, we'll play ten games and let the AlphaGo agent move first. The opponent will make random moves.

```
[3]: # test ten games against random moves
     for i in range(10):
         state=env.reset()
         while True:
             # The AlphaGo agent moves first
             action=alphago_coin(env,0.9,10,num_rollouts=100)
             state,reward,done,_=env.step(action)
             if done:
                 print("AlphaGo wins!")
```

```
            break
    # The random player moves second
    action=random.choice(env.validinputs)
    state,reward,done,_=env.step(action)
    if done:
        print("AlphaGo loses!")
        break
```

```
AlphaGo wins!
AlphaGo wins!
AlphaGo wins!
AlphaGo wins!
AlphaGo wins!
AlphaGo wins!
AlphaGo wins!
AlphaGo wins!
AlphaGo wins!
AlphaGo wins!
```

The AlphaGo agent has won all ten games even when it moves first against random moves. However, it's possible that the random-move agent may win a game just by chance. Of course, if the rule-based AI moves second against AlphaGo, rule-based AI will win all games.

The results show that the AlphaGo algorithm we designed is really powerful. It solves the coin game and is as powerful as the rule-based AI agent that we developed in Chapter 1.

16.4 REDUNDANCY IN THE ALPHAGO ALGORITHM

The AlphaGo algorithm uses three neural networks to strengthen the tree search, and this is needed in complicated games such as Go or Chess. In a simple game such as the coin game, any one of these three neural networks solves the game and provides a perfect game strategy.

In this section, we'll first that the value network is redundant in the AlphaGo algorithm for the coin game: even if we don't use it, the AlphaGo agent is just as effective. This has implications for how we develop the AlphaZero algorithm for the coin game in Chapter 19: we'll omit the value network altogether. Instead, we'll design an algorithm based on two policy networks only, which are trained from scratch without any human expert moves as training data.

To demonstrate that the value network is redundant, we'll set the maximum depth to 22. Since there are only 21 coins in the pile and a player must take at least one coin from the pile in each turn, setting a maximum depth of 22 means the value network is never used in the AlphaGo algorithm we designed in this chapter.

Next, we let two players play ten games: the rule-based AI moves first and the AlphaGo agent moves second. We set the maximum depth to 22 and the weight to 0.8. We keep the number of rollouts to 100, as follows:

```
[4]: from utils.coin_simple_env import coin_game
     from utils.ch16util import alphago_coin

     # initiate game environment
     env=coin_game()
     # test ten games
     for i in range(10):
         state=env.reset()
         while True:
             # The rule-based AI player moves first
             action=rule_based_AI(env)
             state,reward,done,_=env.step(action)
             if done:
                 # print out the winner
                 print("Without value network, rule-based AI wins!")
                 break
             # The AlphaGo agent moves second
             action=alphago_coin(env,0.8,22,num_rollouts=100)
             state,reward,done,_=env.step(action)
             if done:
                 # print out the winner
                 print("Without value network, AlphaGo wins!")
                 break
```

```
Without value network, AlphaGo wins!
Without value network, AlphaGo wins!
Without value network, AlphaGo wins!
Without value network, AlphaGo wins!
Without value network, AlphaGo wins!
Without value network, AlphaGo wins!
Without value network, AlphaGo wins!
Without value network, AlphaGo wins!
Without value network, AlphaGo wins!
Without value network, AlphaGo wins!
```

The results above show that even without using the value network, the AlphaGo agent still wins all ten games.

We also test if the AlphaGo algorithm without the value network can beat random moves when acting as Player 1. Below, we set the maximum depth to 22 and the weight to 0.8. We let the AlphaGo agent move first and the random-move agent move second. We simulate a total of ten games, as follows:

```
5]: # test ten games against random moves
    for i in range(10):
        state=env.reset()
        while True:
            # The AlphaGo agent moves first
            action=alphago_coin(env,0.8,22,num_rollouts=100)
            state,reward,done,_=env.step(action)
            if done:
                print("Without value network, AlphaGo wins!")
                break
            # The random player moves second
            action=random.choice(env.validinputs)
            state,reward,done,_=env.step(action)
            if done:
                print("Without value network, AlphaGo loses!")
                break
```

```
Without value network, AlphaGo wins!
Without value network, AlphaGo wins!
Without value network, AlphaGo wins!
Without value network, AlphaGo wins!
Without value network, AlphaGo wins!
Without value network, AlphaGo wins!
Without value network, AlphaGo wins!
Without value network, AlphaGo wins!
Without value network, AlphaGo wins!
Without value network, AlphaGo wins!
```

We have kept the number of rollouts at 100. The AlphaGo agent once again has won all ten games when it moves first against random moves. However, when you run the above code block, there is a small chance that the random-move agent may win a game. This is due to the nature of the coin game: the second player always wins if it makes perfect moves.

Now that you know how to create an AlphaGo agent in the coin game, you'll apply the same logic to the other two games in the book and create AlphaGo agents in Tic Tac Toe and Connect Four in the next two chapters.

16.5 EXERCISES

16.1 Modify the second code cell in Section 16.3.1 so that the AlphaGo agent chooses a *weight* value of 0.8 instead of 0.9. Rerun the code cell and see what happens.

16.2 Modify the first code cell in Section 16.3.2 so that the AlphaGo agent chooses a *depth* value of 9 instead of 10. Rerun the code cell and see what happens.

16.3 Modify the first code cell in Section 16.4 so that the AlphaGo agent chooses a *weight* value of 0.85 instead of 0.8. Keep the maximum depth at 22. Rerun the code cell and see what happens.

16.4 Modify the second code cell in Section 16.4 so that the AlphaGo agent chooses a *weight* value of 0.85 instead of 0.8. Keep the maximum depth at 22. Rerun the code cell and see what happens when the AlphaGo agent plays against random moves without using the value network.

## CHAPTER 17

AlphaGo in Tic Tac Toe and Connect Four

"We also introduce a new search algorithm that combines Monte Carlo simulation with value and policy networks. Using this search algorithm, our program AlphaGo achieved a 99.8% winning rate against other Go programs."
– *Google DeepMind Team, Nature (2016)*

IN CHAPTER 16, you have learned the basic architecture of the AlphaGo algorithm, which combines Monte Carlo tree search with deep neural networks, as outlined in the open quote in an article published in the journal *Nature* in 2016 [2]. Specifically, you have implemented a basic version of the AlphaGo algorithm for the coin game, combining deep reinforcement learning with conventional rule-based AI. In this chapter, you'll expand this approach, creating an AlphaGo agent adaptable to various games.

The AlphaGo agent you create features two main enhancements. Firstly, it will be versatile, capable of handling two games, Tic Tac Toe and Connect Four. This flexibility reduces code redundancy and simplifies the application of the AlphaGo algorithm to a broader range of games. Secondly, the agent's game simulation strategy includes a choice between random moves and those suggested by the fast policy network. This decision involves a trade-off: the network's moves provide more insight but require more processing time due to the complex neural network. In contrast, random moves accelerate game simulations, enabling more game rollouts within a given time frame and potentially smarter move selection in actual gameplay.

Monte Carlo Tree Search (MCTS) remains the core of the agent's decision process, involving selection, expansion, simulation, and backpropagation, as outlined in Chapter 8. However, now three deep neural networks, introduced in previous chapters, will enhance the tree search. During real games, a large number of simulations will start from the current game state. Each simulation involves choosing a child node for expansion, not based on the upper confidence bounds applied to trees (UCT) formula from Chapter 8, but on a weighted average of each node's rollout value and its prior probability from the trained policy-gradient network. Additionally, players can choose between random moves or those from the fast policy network for rollouts. Instead of playing to a terminal state, the game state will be evaluated at a certain depth using the trained value networks, allowing more simulations within the time limit.

You'll evaluate the AlphaGo algorithm's effectiveness in Tic Tac Toe. Against the perfect rule-based AI from Chapter 6, the AlphaGo agent consistently draws, indicating its ability to solve the game.

Given Tic Tac Toe's simplicity compared to Chess or Go, we'll also explore an AlphaGo version without the value network, rolling out games to their end. Another variant will use random moves instead of those from the fast policy network. Both versions will be shown to effectively solve Tic Tac Toe, setting the stage for Chapter 20, where we implement AlphaZero in Tic Tac Toe, omitting the value network and relying solely on one policy network.

What You'll Learn in This Chapter

- Creating an AlphaGo algorithm that can be applied to multiple games
- Rolling out games using either random moves or a fast policy network.
- Testing the effectiveness of the AlphaGo algorithm in Tic Tac Toe
- Implementing AlphaGo without the value network

17.1 AN ALPHAGO ALGORITHM FOR MULTIPLE GAMES

In the local module *ch17util*, we'll implement the AlphaGo algorithm that can be applied to both Tic Tac Toe and Connect Four. Download the file *ch17util.py* from the book's GitHub repository and place it in the folder /utils/ on your computer. Take some time to go through the details of the module.

Since MCTS is the core of AlphaGo's decision-making process, I'll explain the logic behind the algorithm in the sequence of the four steps of MCTS we outlined in Chapter 8: selection, expansion, simulation, and backpropagation.

17.1.1 Functions to Select and Expand

In the local module *ch17util*, we first define a *select()* function to select a child node to expand the game tree, as follows:

```
def select(priors,env,results,weight):
    # weighted average of priors and rollout_value
    scores={}
```

```
for k,v in results.items():
    # rollout_value for each next move
    if len(v)==0:
        vi=0
    else:
        vi=sum(v)/len(v)
    # scale the prior by (1+N(L))
    prior=priors[0][k-1]/(1+len(v))
    # calculate weighted average
    scores[k]=weight*prior+(1-weight)*vi
# select child node based on the weighted average
return max(scores,key=scores.get)
```

The *select()* function in this context works similarly to its counterpart introduced in Chapter 16 for the coin game. It uses the argument *priors*, which contains probabilities suggested by the policy-gradient agent trained in previous chapters (specifically, Chapter 14 for Tic Tac Toe and Chapter 15 for Connect Four). Another argument, *results*, is a dictionary mapping potential next child nodes (essentially, upcoming moves) to a list of rewards obtained from each node's rollout. We will elaborate on the structure of *results* later, as it gets populated and updated during the tree search process. The *weight* argument is a value between 0 and 1, balancing the influence of priors and rollout results in the node selection process.

The *select()* function first computes the rollout value for each child node, with values ranging from -1 to 1. Here, a -1 indicates a loss for the AlphaGo agent when selecting that node, while a 1 signifies a win. It also calculates a scaled version of the priors for each child node. The AlphaGo agent then selects a node by considering the weighted average of these priors and the rollout values. The node with the highest weighted average is chosen, reflecting a balance between the trained policy gradient's recommendations and the empirical results of the rollouts.

To assess various child nodes through game simulations, we need to grow the game tree. This expansion is accomplished by the AlphaGo agent performing a hypothetical next move, thereby reaching the chosen child node. To facilitate this, we introduce an *expand()* function within the *ch17util* local module, outlined as follows:

```
# expand the game tree by taking a hypothetical move
def expand(env,move):
    env_copy=deepcopy(env)
    state,reward,done,info=env_copy.step(move)
    return env_copy, done, reward
```

Next, we'll define functions to allow the agent to roll out games and backpropagate the simulation results.

17.1.2 Functions to Simulate and Backpropagate

Following the selection of a child node, we simulate a game beginning from that node. This simulated game continues until it either reaches a terminal state or hits a predefined maximum depth. Subsequently, we appraise the chosen child node. In cases where the terminal state is reached, the node's evaluation is based on the real outcome of the game. However, if the maximum depth is reached without concluding the game, we assess the node using a trained value network from earlier chapters.

Within the local module, we establish a function named *best_move_fast_net()*. This function is designed to suggest moves during rollouts, leveraging a fast policy network that has been previously trained:

```python
def best_move_fast_net(env, fast_net):
    # priors from the policy network
    if env.turn=="X":
        state = env.state.reshape(-1,3,3,1)
        action_probs=fast_net(state)
    elif env.turn=="O":
        state = env.state.reshape(-1,3,3,1)
        action_probs=fast_net(-state)
    elif env.turn=="red":
        state = env.state.reshape(-1,7,6,1)
        action_probs=fast_net(state)
    elif env.turn=="yellow":
        state = env.state.reshape(-1,7,6,1)
        action_probs=fast_net(-state)
    ps=[]
    for a in sorted(env.validinputs):
        ps.append(np.squeeze(action_probs)[a-1])
    ps=np.array(ps)
    return np.random.choice(sorted(env.validinputs),
        p=ps/ps.sum())
```

The *best_move_fast_net()* function, as defined above, requires two arguments: *env*, representing the current game environment, and *fast_net*, which is the trained fast policy network from the previous chapters. Specifically, we'll utilize the fast policy network for Tic Tac Toe developed in Chapter 10 or the one for Connect Four from Chapter 11. This function is designed to suggest the optimal next move during game simulations and is applicable to both Tic Tac Toe and Connect Four games.

To roll out a game, we define a *simulate()* function in the local module *ch17util* as follows:

```python
# roll out a game till terminal state or depth reached
def simulate(env_copy,done,reward,depth,value_net,
            fast_net, policy_rollout=True):
    # if the game has already ended
```

```
        if done==True:
            return reward
    # select moves based on fast policy network
    for _ in range(depth):
        if policy_rollout:
            move=best_move_fast_net(env_copy, fast_net)
        else:
            move=env_copy.sample()
        state,reward,done,info=env_copy.step(move)
        # if terminal state is reached, returns outcome
        if done==True:
            return reward
    # depth reached but game not over, evaluate
    if env_copy.turn=="X":
        state=state.reshape(-1,3,3,1)
        ps=value_net.predict(state,verbose=0)
        # reward is prob(X win) - prob(O win)
        reward=ps[0][1]-ps[0][2]
    elif env_copy.turn=="O":
        state=state.reshape(-1,3,3,1)
        ps=value_net.predict(-state,verbose=0)
        # reward is prob(X win) - prob(O win)
        reward=ps[0][2]-ps[0][1]
    elif env_copy.turn=="red":
        state=state.reshape(-1,7,6,1)
        ps=value_net.predict(state,verbose=0)
        # reward is prob(red win) - prob(yellow win)
        reward=ps[0][1]-ps[0][2]
    elif env_copy.turn=="yellow":
        state=state.reshape(-1,7,6,1)
        ps=value_net.predict(-state,verbose=0)
        # reward is prob(red win) - prob(yellow win)
        reward=ps[0][2]-ps[0][1]
    return reward
```

The function starts by determining if the selected child node signifies a terminal state. If it does, it directly returns the outcome of the game. If not, the function proceeds to simulate hypothetical moves to advance the game. This *simulate()* function is versatile, applicable to both Tic Tac Toe and Connect Four. Additionally, the parameter *policy_rollout* within the function offers a choice between random moves and those advised by the trained policy network. When *policy_rollout* is set to *True*, the function opts for moves as per the trained policy network, specifically using the *best_move_fast_net()* function defined earlier in this chapter. Conversely, when *policy_rollout* is set to *False*, it uses random moves to roll out games.

During the simulation, there's a cap on the number of moves, dictated by the *depth* argument. This limit can be potentially beneficial for time efficiency in rollouts: fully playing out a game to its terminal state might be too time-consuming. By halting the simulation after a predetermined number of steps, the AlphaGo agent can then employ the trained value network to evaluate the current game state. This strategy enables the agent to simulate a higher number of games within the given time limit. The concept of setting a depth is particularly beneficial in complex games like Chess or Go, where completing a game could be quite lengthy.

Finally, if the maximum depth is reached without concluding the game, the *simulate()* function uses the trained value network to assess the game state. The value here is defined as the likelihood of the first player winning minus that of the second player. This assessment is initially from the perspective of the first player. Adjustments to account for the current player's perspective are made later in the *backpropagate()* function.

The concluding phase in the tree search involves updating simulation results after each rollout. Particularly, if the current player is the second player, we invert the reward by multiplying it by −1. This adjustment ensures that the evaluation and subsequent decisions are based on the current player's perspective, rather than defaulting to the perspective of the first player.

To implement this, we introduce the *backpropagate()* function within our local module, outlined as follows:

```
def backpropagate(env,move,reward,results):
    # update results
    if env.turn=="X" or env.turn=="red":
        results[move].append(reward)
    # if current player is player 2, multiply outcome with -1
    if env.turn=="0" or env.turn=="yellow":
        results[move].append(-reward)
    return results
```

The primary goal of *backpropagate()* is to modify the *results* dictionary, ensuring it encompasses a comprehensive record of all outcomes from the rollouts. It's important to remember that these outcomes are initially from the perspective of the first player. Within the *backpropagate()* function, we adjust for this: if the current player is the second player, we invert the outcome by multiplying it by −1. This alteration ensures that the recorded outcome reflects the viewpoint of the current player. The *backpropagate()* function then returns this updated *results* dictionary.

17.1.3   An AlphaGo Agent for Tic Tac Toe and Connect Four

We're now equipped to construct our AlphaGo agent for both Tic Tac Toe and Connect Four, utilizing the four functions we've defined: *select()*, *expand()*, *simulate()*, and *backpropagate()*.

To achieve this, we have created the *alphago()* function within the *ch17util* local module, structured as follows:

```python
def alphago(env,weight,depth,PG_net,value_net,
        fast_net, policy_rollout=True,num_rollouts=100):
    # if there is only one valid move left, take it
    if len(env.validinputs)==1:
        return env.validinputs[0]
    # get the prior from the PG policy network
    if env.turn=="X" or env.turn=="O":
        state = env.state.reshape(-1,9)
        conv_state = state.reshape(-1,3,3,1)
        if env.turn=="X":
            priors = PG_net([state,conv_state])
        elif env.turn=="O":
            priors = PG_net([-state,-conv_state])
    if env.turn=="red" or env.turn=="yellow":
        state = env.state.reshape(-1,42)
        conv_state = state.reshape(-1,7,6,1)
        if env.turn=="red":
            priors = PG_net([state,conv_state])
        elif env.turn=="yellow":
            priors = PG_net([-state,-conv_state])
    # create a dictionary results
    results={}
    for move in env.validinputs:
        results[move]=[]
    # roll out games
    for _ in range(num_rollouts):
        # select
        move=select(priors,env,results,weight)
        # expand
        env_copy, done, reward=expand(env,move)
        # simulate
        reward=simulate(env_copy,done,reward,depth,value_net,
                    fast_net, policy_rollout)
        # backpropagate
        results=backpropagate(env,move,reward,results)
    # select the most visited child node
    visits={k:len(v) for k,v in results.items()}
    return max(visits,key=visits.get)
```

The AlphaGo agent begins by determining if only one valid move remains. If that's the case, it proceeds with that move directly, bypassing any tree search. If there are multiple options, the agent computes the prior probabilities for selecting each potential child node, drawing upon the trained policy gradient network. These priors are then used to guide the agent in choosing child nodes through the *select()* function we previously defined.

The agent also sets up a dictionary, *results*, to keep track of the outcomes from the rollouts. Initially, this dictionary lists all valid moves as keys, with corresponding empty lists as values. During game rollouts, the list *results* is updated with the outcomes for each child node. The value linked to each child node is a list of rewards for the first player following the completion of a rollout.

The parameter *num_rollouts* dictates the number of rollouts the AlphaGo agent performs before executing a move in the actual game. While the default value for *num_rollouts* is set to 100, it can be adjusted when invoking the *alphago()* function. In each rollout, the agent systematically follows the four steps defined in the functions *select()*, *expand()*, *simulate()*, and *backpropagate()*, with *results* being updated after each rollout.

After completing the designated number of rollouts, the AlphaGo agent finalizes its move in the real game. This decision is based on selecting the child node that was visited the most during the rollouts.

17.2 TEST THE ALPHAGO AGENT IN TIC TAC TOE

Next, we'll conduct a trial of the AlphaGo algorithm in Tic Tac Toe, setting the number of rollouts to 100. To account for the inherent advantage of the first player, we will initially have Player X employ the strategies suggested by AlphaGo. Following this, Player O will then adopt the AlphaGo algorithm as well. The opponent in these games is a rule-based AI that employs the MiniMax algorithm specifically for Tic Tac Toe, enhanced with alpha-beta pruning to expedite the tree search process.

17.2.1 The Opponent in Tic Tac Toe Games

First, let's define a function *rule_based_AI()* to represent the rule-based AI agent that we developed in Chapter 6:

[1]:
```
from utils.ch06util import MiniMax_ab

def rule_based_AI(env):
    move = MiniMax_ab(env)
    return move
```

We begin by importing the *MiniMax_ab()* function from the *ch06util* module. As you might remember from Chapter 6, we created a rule-based AI agent that employs the MiniMax algorithm for solving the Tic Tac Toe game. Additionally, this agent incorporates alpha-beta pruning to expedite the tree search procedure.

Next, we import the three neural networks that will be used by the AlphaGo agent in Tic Tac Toe:

```
2]: from copy import deepcopy
    import numpy as np
    from tensorflow import keras

    # Load the trained fast policy network from Chapter 10
    fast_net=keras.models.load_model("files/fast_ttt.h5")
    # Load the policy gradient network from Chapter 14
    PG_net=keras.models.load_model("files/pg_ttt.h5")
    # Load the trained value network from Chapter 14
    value_net=keras.models.load_model("files/value_ttt.h5")
```

We have imported three networks that were trained in earlier chapters. The first is the fast policy network from Chapter 10, which we'll utilize for game rollouts. This approach ensures that the outcome of the game is more insightful than rollouts with random moves. The second network is the policy gradient network from Chapter 14. There, we enhanced a strong policy network from Chapter 10 using self-play and deep reinforcement learning. This network will aid in selecting child nodes during the initial phase of Monte Carlo Tree Search (MCTS). Lastly, the third network is the value network developed in Chapter 14. In cases where a game doesn't conclude during a rollout, this trained value network will evaluate the game's current state and predict the likely winner.

17.2.2 AlphaGo versus Rule-Based AI in Tic Tac Toe

To save time, we will conduct only 10 games for testing. In these games, the AlphaGo agent moves first and the rule-based AI agent moves second, as follows:

```
3]: from utils.ttt_simple_env import ttt
    from utils.ch17util import alphago

    weight=0.75
    depth=5
    # initiate game environment
    env=ttt()
    # test ten games
    for i in range(10):
        state=env.reset()
        while True:
            # AlphaGo moves first
            action=alphago(env,weight,depth,PG_net,value_net,
                    fast_net, policy_rollout=True,num_rollouts=100)
            state,reward,done,_=env.step(action)
            if done:
                if reward==0:
                    print("The game is tied!")
```

```
        else:
            print("AlphaGo wins!")
        break
    # move recommended by rule-based AI
    action=rule_based_AI(env)
    state,reward,done,_=env.step(action)
    if done:
        print("Rule-based AI wins!")
        break
```

```
The game is tied!
The game is tied!
The game is tied!
The game is tied!
The game is tied!
The game is tied!
The game is tied!
The game is tied!
The game is tied!
The game is tied!
```

When invoking the *alphago()* function, we assign a value of 0.75 to the *weight* parameter. This indicates a primary reliance on the trained policy gradient agent for selecting child nodes. We set the *depth* parameter to 5, signifying that during rollouts, we make a maximum of five moves. Considering that a Tic Tac Toe game can span up to 9 steps, our chosen depth value roughly equates to half of this maximum. This means that in the early stages of each rollout, we depend on the trained value network to evaluate the game states.

In each of the ten games played, the output is determined as follows: if the AlphaGo agent emerges victorious, the result displays "AlphaGo wins!". If the game ends in a draw, it states "The game is tied!" Otherwise, the message "Rule-based AI wins!" is shown. The results indicate that all ten games end in a tie, demonstrating that our AlphaGo algorithm is on par with the rule-based AI algorithm we developed in Chapter 6 that has solved the Tic Tac Toe game.

In Tic Tac Toe, the initial player possesses a significant advantage due to being the first to move. Therefore, we want to see if the AlphaGo agent is indeed as strong as the rule-based AI if it plays second. We test ten games in which the rule-based AI moves first and the AlphaGo agent moves second, as follows:

```
[4]: # test ten games
    for i in range(10):
        state=env.reset()
        while True:
            # Rule-based AI moves first
```

```
        action=rule_based_AI(env)
        state,reward,done,_=env.step(action)
        if done:
            if reward==0:
                print("The game is tied!")
            else:
                print("Rule-based AI wins!")
            break
        # AlphaGo moves second
        action=alphago(env,weight,depth,PG_net,value_net,
                fast_net, policy_rollout=True,num_rollouts=100)
        state,reward,done,_=env.step(action)
        if done:
            print("AlphaGo wins!")
            break
```

```
The game is tied!
The game is tied!
The game is tied!
The game is tied!
The game is tied!
The game is tied!
The game is tied!
The game is tied!
The game is tied!
The game is tied!
```

Once again, all ten games are tied. This indicates that the AlphaGo agent is indeed as strong as rule-based AI, even when it doesn't have the first mover advantage.

17.3 REDUNDANCY IN ALPHAGO

The AlphaGo algorithm incorporates three neural networks to enhance its tree search capabilities, a necessity for complex games like Go or Chess. However, in a straightforward game like Tic Tac Toe, any one of these networks is sufficient to solve the game and provide an optimal strategy.

In this section, we will demonstrate that the value network is not needed in the AlphaGo algorithm for Tic Tac Toe. We'll illustrate that the AlphaGo algorithm, as we have configured it, can still effectively solve the game without the value network. Furthermore, we'll show that if we remove both the value network and the fast policy network, the AlphaGo agent is still capable of solving the game. This finding has significant implications for the development of the AlphaZero algorithm in Chapter 20. We will exclude both the value network and the fast policy network from AlphaZero. Instead, we will design an algorithm solely based on the policy gradient network, which will be trained from the ground up without using any human expert moves as training data.

To prove the redundancy of the value network, we'll adjust the maximum search depth to 10. Given that a Tic Tac Toe game consists of at most nine moves, setting the depth to 10 ensures that the value network is not utilized in the AlphaGo algorithm.

We then arrange for the two players to compete in 20 games. In half of these games, the rule-based AI will make the first move, followed by the AlphaGo agent. In the remaining ten games, the roles are reversed, with the AlphaGo agent moving first and the rule-based AI second. This setup neutralizes the first mover advantage for either player. The maximum depth is set to 10 and the weight to 0.8, with the number of rollouts set at 100, as detailed below:

```
[5]: weight=0.8
     depth=10
     # create a list to record game outcome
     results=[]
     # test ten games
     for i in range(20):
         state=env.reset()
         if i%2==0:
             # Ruled-based AI moves
             action=rule_based_AI(env)
             state,reward,done,_=env.step(action)
         while True:
             # AlphaGo moves
             action=alphago(env,weight,depth,PG_net,value_net,
                     fast_net, policy_rollout=True,num_rollouts=100)
             state,reward,done,_=env.step(action)
             if done:
                 results.append(abs(reward))
                 break
             # Rule-based AI moves
             action=rule_based_AI(env)
             state,reward,done,_=env.step(action)
             if done:
                 results.append(-abs(reward))
                 break
```

We set up a list named *results* to track the outcomes of the games. In our simulation of 20 games, the AlphaGo agent moves first in half of them, and in the other half, the rule-based AI takes the first move. Whenever a game concludes following a move by the AlphaGo agent, we add the absolute value of the reward, *abs(reward)*, to *results*. Conversely, if the game ends after a move by the rule-based AI, we record −*abs(reward)* in *results*. In this arrangement, a value of −1 in *results* signifies a defeat for the AlphaGo agent, 1 indicates a victory for AlphaGo, and 0 represents a tie.

We tally the game outcomes as follows:

```
6]: # count how many times AlphaGo won
    wins=results.count(1)
    print(f"AlphaGo won {wins} games")
    # count how many times AlphaGo lost
    losses=results.count(-1)
    print(f"AlphaGo lost {losses} games")
    # count tie games
    ties=results.count(0)
    print(f"the game was tied {ties} times")
```

```
AlphaGo won 0 games
AlphaGo lost 0 games
the game was tied 20 times
```

The above results show that all 20 games are tied. This indicates that the value network is indeed redundant in the AlphaGo algorithm for Tic Tac Toe. Without it, the algorithm is just as effective.

Furthermore, the *simulate()* function we defined in this chapter has an optional *policy_rollout* argument. If we set the value of the argument to *False*, the AlphaGo agent uses random moves in rollouts. Below, we test if the AlphaGo agent is just as effective if we don't use the fast policy network.

```
]: weight=0.9
   depth=10
   # create a list to record game outcome
   results=[]
   # test ten games
   for i in range(20):
       state=env.reset()
       if i%2==0:
           # Ruled-based AI moves
           action=rule_based_AI(env)
           state,reward,done,_=env.step(action)
       while True:
           # AlphaGo moves, setting policy_rollout=False
           action=alphago(env,weight,depth,PG_net,value_net,
                   fast_net, policy_rollout=False,num_rollouts=100)
           state,reward,done,_=env.step(action)
           if done:
               results.append(abs(reward))
               break
```

```
# Rule-based AI moves
action=rule_based_AI(env)
state,reward,done,_=env.step(action)
if done:
    results.append(-abs(reward))
    break
```

We test 20 games by setting the *policy_rollout* argument to *False* and the *depth* argument to 10. This means we use neither the value network nor the fast policy network in the AlphaGo algorithm. Only the policy gradient network is used to select child nodes. Below, we tally the game outcomes by counting the number of −1s, 1s, and 0s in results:

[8]:
```
# count how many times AlphaGo won
wins=results.count(1)
print(f"AlphaGo won {wins} games")
# count how many times AlphaGo lost
losses=results.count(-1)
print(f"AlphaGo lost {losses} games")
# count tie games
ties=results.count(0)
print(f"the game was tied {ties} times")
```

```
AlphaGo won 0 games
AlphaGo lost 0 games
the game was tied 20 times
```

Once again, all 20 games are tied. This indicates that the AlphaGo algorithm in Tic Tac Toe is just as effective with just one neural network: the policy gradient network. As a result, in Chapter 20 when we create an AlphaZero agent in Tic Tac Toe, we'll rely on just one neural network, and we'll train it from scratch without relying on any human expert moves.

In the next chapter, you'll apply the AlphaGo algorithm we developed in this chapter to another game: Connect Four. Since this book doesn't provide a strategy that solves the Connect Four game, we'll focus on selecting the best hyperparameters to create the most powerful AlphaGo agent in Connect Four.

17.4 EXERCISES

17.1 Modify the first code cell in Section 17.2.2 so that the AlphaGo agent chooses a weight value of 0.7 instead of 0.75 and a depth of 4 instead of 5. Rerun the code cell and see what happens.

17.2 Modify the second code cell in Section 17.2.2 so that the AlphaGo agent chooses a weight value of 0.8 instead of 0.75 and a depth of 6 instead of 5. Rerun the code cell and see what happens.

17.3 Modify the first two code cells in Section 17.3 so that the AlphaGo agent chooses a weight of 0.7 instead of 0.8. Rerun the code cells and see what happens.

17.4 Modify the last two code cells in Section 17.3 so that the AlphaGo agent chooses a weight of 0.85 instead of 0.9. Rerun the code cells and see what happens.

## CHAPTER 18

Hyperparameter Tuning in AlphaGo

"Currently, most of the job of a deep-learning engineer consists of munging data with Python scripts and then tuning the architecture and hyperparameters of a deep network at length to get a working model—or even to get a state-of-the-art model, if the engineer is that ambitious."

– Francois Chollet, creator of the Keras deep-learning library

IN CHAPTER 16 and 17, we applied a simplified version of the AlphaGo algorithm to the Coin game and Tic Tac Toe. This integration of Monte Carlo Tree Search (MCTS) with deep reinforcement learning enabled the AlphaGo-based agent to effectively solve both games. Notably, in the Coin game, the AlphaGo agent consistently won when playing second, even against opponents employing flawless strategies. In Tic Tac Toe, it consistently achieved draws against the MiniMax agent, which made perfect moves in each game.

The focus of this chapter is on adapting the AlphaGo algorithm for Connect Four. Unlike in the previous games, creating expert-level moves in Connect Four is a more complex task. Consequently, the AlphaGo agent, trained within a constrained time frame and with limited computational resources, won't achieve perfection. Nevertheless, it impressively outperforms the agent that plans three moves ahead. This achievement underscores a key takeaway: the adaptability of the AlphaGo algorithm to various games. Given sufficient training and computational power, the AlphaGo algorithm has the potential to reach superhuman performance levels, a feat demonstrated by the DeepMind team in 2016.

In the coin game and Tic Tac Toe, fine-tuning hyperparameters is less critical: the majority of hyperparameter configurations result in the development of optimal game strategies. However, in the case of Connect Four, where the AlphaGo agent does

DOI: 10.1201/9781032722207-18

not fully solve the game, it becomes crucial to identify the optimal combination of hyperparameters that yields the most effective game strategy.

Grid search is a common approach for hyperparameter tuning. This process involves experimenting with different permutations of hyperparameters in the model to determine empirically which combination offers the best performance. However, this technique can be quite resource-intensive and time-consuming, particularly when dealing with a large number of hyperparameters.

In this chapter, to streamline the process and save time, we'll limit ourselves to testing only a few values per hyperparameter. The optimal parameters identified here should be regarded as a basic benchmark and a lower bound for the model's capabilities. Specifically, you'll explore 18 different hyperparameter combinations using grid search to determine which leads to the strongest game strategy.

We focus on four key hyperparameters for the AlphaGo agent: *weight* (ranging from 0 to 1), which balances the impact of priors (suggested probabilities by the policy-gradient agent) and rollout outcomes in node selection; *policy_rollout* (either *True* or *False*), determines whether to use the policy network to roll out games; *depth*, defining the maximum search steps ahead in a rollout; and *num_rollouts*, the number of rollouts performed in MCTS for each move in actual gameplay.

We also impose a one-second time limit per move. This constraint effectively reduces the number of hyperparameters to three, as we will determine the maximum *num_rollouts* that can fit within this limit for each combination of *weight*, *policy_rollout*, and *depth*. The most effective combination identified is *weight=0.75*, *policy_rollout=False*, and *depth=45*. The maximum number of rollouts the AlphaGo agent can perform within a second is *num_rollouts=584*. This optimized AlphaGo agent can defeat an AI that plans three steps ahead. If we relax the one-second-per-move time constraint and increase the number of rollouts to 5000, the AlphaGo agent becomes even stronger: it surpasses a rule-based AI that looks four steps ahead.

What You'll Learn in This Chapter

- Applying the multi-game AlphaGo algorithm to Connect Four
- Tuning hyperparameters in AlphaGo for Connect Four
- Determining the maximum number of rollouts under a one-second-per-move constraint
- Testing the optimized AlphaGo agent in Connect Four

18.1 TEST THE ALPHAGO AGENT IN CONNECT FOUR

Next, we'll conduct a trial of the AlphaGo algorithm in Connect Four, setting the number of rollouts to 100. To account for the inherent advantage of the first player, we will initially have the red player employ the strategies suggested by AlphaGo.

Following this, the yellow player will then adopt the AlphaGo algorithm as well. The opponent in these games is a rule-based AI that employs the MiniMax algorithm specifically for Connect Four, enhanced with both alpha-beta pruning and depth pruning to expedite the tree search process.

18.1.1 The Opponent in Connect Four Games

First, we need to create an opponent when testing the AlphaGo agent in Connect Four. For that purpose, let's define a function *rule_based_AI()* to represent the rule-based AI agent that we developed in Chapter 6:

```
[1]: from utils.ch06util import MiniMax_conn

     def rule_based_AI(env,depth=3):
         move = MiniMax_conn(env,depth=depth)
         return move
```

We begin by importing the *MiniMax_conn()* function from the *ch06util* module. As you might remember from Chapter 6, we created a rule-based AI agent that employs the MiniMax algorithm for Connect Four. Additionally, this agent incorporates both alpha-beta pruning and depth pruning to expedite the tree search procedure.

Next, we import the three neural networks that we have trained in previous chapters. These networks will be used by the AlphaGo agent in Connect Four:

```
[2]: from copy import deepcopy
     import numpy as np
     from tensorflow import keras

     # Load the trained fast policy network from Chapter 11
     fast_net=keras.models.load_model("files/policy_conn.h5")
     # Load the policy gradient network from Chapter 15
     PG_net=keras.models.load_model("files/PG_conn.h5")
     # Load the trained value network from Chapter 15
     value_net=keras.models.load_model("files/value_conn.h5")
```

In the above code snippet, We have imported three networks that were trained in earlier chapters. The first is the fast policy network from Chapter 11, which we'll utilize for game rollouts. This approach ensures that the outcome of the game is more insightful than rollouts with random moves, even though the model also allows random moves if doing so leads to better game strategies. The second network is the policy gradient network from Chapter 15. There, we enhanced a strong policy network from Chapter 11 using self-play and deep reinforcement learning. This network will aid in selecting child nodes during the initial phase of Monte Carlo tree search (MCTS). Lastly, the third network is the value network developed in Chapter 15. In cases where a game doesn't end during a rollout, this trained value network will evaluate the game's current state and predict the likely winner.

18.1.2 AlphaGo versus Rule-Based AI in Connect Four

To save time, we will conduct only ten games for testing. In these games, the AlphaGo agent will make the first move, and the rule-based AI agent moves second, as follows:

```
from utils.conn_simple_env import conn
from utils.ch17util import alphago

weight=0.75
depth=20
# initiate game environment
env=conn()
# test ten games
for i in range(10):
    state=env.reset()
    while True:
        # AlphaGo moves first
        action=alphago(env,weight,depth,PG_net,value_net,
                fast_net, policy_rollout=True,num_rollouts=100)
        state,reward,done,_=env.step(action)
        if done:
            print("AlphaGo wins!")
            break
        # move recommended by rule-based AI
        action=rule_based_AI(env)
        state,reward,done,_=env.step(action)
        if done:
            if reward==0:
                print("The game is tied!")
            else:
                print("Rule-based AI wins!")
            break
```

```
AlphaGo wins!
AlphaGo wins!
Rule-based AI wins!
Rule-based AI wins!
AlphaGo wins!
AlphaGo wins!
Rule-based AI wins!
AlphaGo wins!
AlphaGo wins!
Rule-based AI wins!
```

Note here that there is a difference between Tic Tac Toe and Connect Four: a game can be tied only after the first player's move in Tic Tac Toe (since there are a maximum of nine moves). If the game ends after Player O's move, Player O must have won. In contrast, in Connect Four, the game can be tied only after the second player's move since there are a maximum of 42 moves. If the game ends after the red player's move, the red player must have won. On the other hand, if the game ends after the yellow player's move, either the yellow player has won or the game is tied.

When calling the function *alphago()*, we set the value of argument *weight* to 0.75. This means we rely mainly on the trained policy gradient agent when selecting child nodes. We set the value of the argument *depth* to 20. This means in rollouts, we search ahead for at most 20 steps. Given that a Connect Four game can have a maximum of 42 steps, our choice of the value of *depth* is about half of that value. This means in the early stages of the game in each rollout, we rely on the trained value network to assess game states.

In each of the ten games played, the output is determined as follows: if the AlphaGo agent emerges victorious, the result displays "AlphaGo wins!". If the game ends in a draw, it states "The game is tied!" Otherwise, the message "Rule-based AI wins!" is shown. The results indicate that the AlphaGo agent has won six games while the rule-based AI has won the rest four games. This shows that our AlphaGo algorithm is slightly better than the rule-based AI algorithm we developed in Chapter 6.

In Connect Four, the first player has a significant advantage due to being the first to move. Therefore, we want to see if the AlphaGo agent can beat the rule-based AI if it plays second. We test ten games in which the rule-based AI moves first and the AlphaGo agent moves second, as follows:

```
[4]:  # test ten games
      for i in range(10):
          state=env.reset()
          while True:
              # Rule-based AI moves first
              action=rule_based_AI(env)
              state,reward,done,_=env.step(action)
              if done:
                  print("Rule-based AI wins!")
                  break
              # AlphaGo moves second
              action=alphago(env,weight,depth,PG_net,value_net,
                      fast_net, policy_rollout=True,num_rollouts=100)
              state,reward,done,_=env.step(action)
              if done:
                  if reward==0:
                      print("The game is tied!")
                  else:
                      print("AlphaGo wins!")
                  break
```

```
Rule-based AI wins!
AlphaGo wins!
AlphaGo wins!
The game is tied!
Rule-based AI wins!
AlphaGo wins!
Rule-based AI wins!
AlphaGo wins!
Rule-based AI wins!
Rule-based AI wins!
```

The above results show that the AlphaGo agent has won four games while the rule-based AI has won five games. There is one tie game. This shows that our AlphaGo algorithm is on par with the rule-based AI algorithm when playing second.

Overall, results show that our AlphaGo is not that much stronger than the MiniMax agent who looks three steps ahead.

18.2 HYPERPARAMETER TUNING

There are four parameters that we can choose when designing the AlphaGo agent:

- *weight*, which is a value between 0 and 1, balancing the influence of priors (probabilities suggested by the policy-gradient agent) and rollout results in the node selection process.
- *policy_rollout*, which can be either *True* or *False*. The AlphaGo agent rolls out games using probabilities suggested by the fast policy network if *policy_rollout=True*; otherwise, the AlphaGo agent rolls out games using random moves.
- *depth*, the maximum number of steps to search ahead in a rollout. If the maximum depth is reached and the game is not over, the AlphaGo agent uses the trained value network to evaluate the game state.
- *num_rollouts*, the number of rollouts to conduct in MCTS before making a move in a real game.

Since our AlphaGo agent solves both the coin game and Tic Tac Toe, hyperparameter tuning is not important. Most combinations of the above four parameters lead to perfect game strategies. However, in Connect Four, since the AlphaGo agent doesn't solve the game, it's important to investigate which combination of the above four hyperparameters leads to the best game strategy.

The usual method in hyperparameter tuning is grid search. We explore various combinations of different hyperparameters in the model and empirically test which combination is the best. This method can be extremely time-consuming, especially when the number of hyperparameters is large.

In this chapter, we'll simplify things and use only a few different values in each hyperparameter to save time. You may consider the performance of our optimized AlphaGo agent as a lower bound for the model's capabilities.

18.2.1 A Time Limit to Reduce the Number of Hyperparameters

In complex games like Chess and Go, specific rules exist to cap the time a player can take to decide on a move.

Take Chess as an example: there's no time limit for a single move. Instead, players are allotted a total amount of time for the entire game, which can vary from 10 to 90 minutes (or longer). In Go, players commonly adhere to several established time constraints. A prevalent method is "byo-yomi," wherein players initially have a main time for all their moves. Following this, they enter "byo-yomi" or "overtime," during which they must complete a set number of moves within a fixed time, often about 30 seconds per move.

Leveraging this real-world limitation allows us to reduce the hyperparameters from four to three. For ease of understanding, let's set a rule that the maximum time a player takes for a move is one second. Consequently, we'll focus on selecting just three hyperparameters: *weight*, *policy_rollout*, and *depth*. The hyperparameter *num_rollouts* will be determined as the highest number of rollouts feasible within one second, after setting the values for the other three hyperparameters.

To streamline the grid search, we'll evaluate the following permutations of three hyperparameters: *weight* (with values 0.25, 0.5, 0.75), *policy_rollout* (options *True* or *False*), and *depth* (set at 25, 35, or 45). In Connect Four, a game can have up to 42 moves. Therefore, a depth of 45 ensures that the value network is bypassed, leading all games to conclude at the terminal state during rollouts.

In the code cell below, we create a list to store different permutations of the three hyperparameters, as follows:

```
[5]: grid=[]
     weights=[0.25, 0.5, 0.75]
     policy_rollouts=[True, False]
     depths=[25, 35, 45]
     for x in weights:
         for y in policy_rollouts:
             for z in depths:
                 parameters={"weight":x,"policy_rollout":y,"depth":z}
                 grid.append(parameters)
     print(f"there are {len(grid)} combinations of hyperparameters")
```

there are 18 combinations of hyperparameters

As you can see from the output, there are 18 different combinations of hyperparameters in our grid search. Next, we'll figure out how many rollouts the AlphaGo agent can perform in a second with each of the above 18 combinations of hyperparameters in the list *grid*.

18.2.2 The Maximum Number of Rollouts in a Second

With each combination of hyperparameters, we'll let the AlphaGo agent make the first move in a Connect Four game and count the maximum number of rollouts the agent can make within a second.

First, we obtain the list *priors* from the trained policy gradient network so that we can use it to select a child node in each rollout, as follows:

```
# get the priors from the PG policy network
state=env.reset()
state=env.state.reshape(-1,42)
conv_state=state.reshape(-1,7,6,1)
priors=PG_net([state,conv_state])
```

Next, we iterate through different combinations of hyperparameters in the list *grid* to calculate the maximum number of rollouts in each case, like this:

```
# create a new list of hyperparameters
new_grid=[]

import time
from utils.ch17util import (select, expand,
            simulate, backpropagate)
# iterate through different combinations of hyperparameters
for parameters in grid:
    # reset the Connect Four game
    state=env.reset()
    # create a dictionary results
    results={}
    for move in env.validinputs:
        results[move]=[]
    # extract hyperparameters
    weight=parameters["weight"]
    policy_rollout=parameters["policy_rollout"]
    depth=parameters["depth"]
    # start counting
    start=time.time()
    n=0
    # roll out games
    while True:
        n += 1
        # select
```

```
        move=select(priors,env,results,weight)
        # expand
        env_copy, done, reward=expand(env,move)
        # simulate
        reward=simulate(env_copy,done,reward,depth,value_net,
                    fast_net, policy_rollout)
        # backpropagate
        results=backpropagate(env,move,reward,results)
        # stop rollouts if it lasts more than a second
        if time.time()-start>=1:
            parameters["num_rollouts"]=n
            new_grid.append(parameters)
            break
```

We have created a new list *new_grid* to store different combinations of hyperparameters. We iterate through values in the old list *grid*. In each iteration, we ask the AlphaGo agent to make the first move in a Connect Four game. The agent will follow the four steps in MCTS: selection, expansion, simulations, and backpropagation. We calculate how many rollouts the agent can make in a second, and use that number as the hyperparameter *num_rollouts*. The new dictionary *parameters* now contains four hyperparameters: *weight*, *policy_rollout*, *depth*, and *num_rollouts*. This new dictionary is added to the new list *new_grid*.

Below, we print out the values in the new list *new_grid*, like so:

[8]:
```
from pprint import pprint
pprint(new_grid)
```

```
[{'depth': 25, 'num_rollouts': 31, 'policy_rollout': True,
  'weight': 0.25},
 {'depth': 35, 'num_rollouts': 32, 'policy_rollout': True,
  'weight': 0.25},
 {'depth': 45, 'num_rollouts': 34, 'policy_rollout': True,
  'weight': 0.25},
 {'depth': 25, 'num_rollouts': 107, 'policy_rollout': False,
  'weight': 0.25},
 {'depth': 35, 'num_rollouts': 464, 'policy_rollout': False,
  'weight': 0.25},
 {'depth': 45, 'num_rollouts': 575, 'policy_rollout': False,
  'weight': 0.25},
 {'depth': 25, 'num_rollouts': 29, 'policy_rollout': True,
  'weight': 0.5},
 {'depth': 35, 'num_rollouts': 32, 'policy_rollout': True,
  'weight': 0.5},
 {'depth': 45, 'num_rollouts': 34, 'policy_rollout': True,
  'weight': 0.5},
```

```
{'depth': 25, 'num_rollouts': 128, 'policy_rollout': False,
 'weight': 0.5},
{'depth': 35, 'num_rollouts': 387, 'policy_rollout': False,
 'weight': 0.5},
{'depth': 45, 'num_rollouts': 577, 'policy_rollout': False,
 'weight': 0.5},
{'depth': 25, 'num_rollouts': 27, 'policy_rollout': True,
 'weight': 0.75},
{'depth': 35, 'num_rollouts': 32, 'policy_rollout': True,
 'weight': 0.75},
{'depth': 45, 'num_rollouts': 37, 'policy_rollout': True,
 'weight': 0.75},
{'depth': 25, 'num_rollouts': 165, 'policy_rollout': False,
 'weight': 0.75},
{'depth': 35, 'num_rollouts': 405, 'policy_rollout': False,
 'weight': 0.75},
{'depth': 45, 'num_rollouts': 584, 'policy_rollout': False,
 'weight': 0.75}]
```

The results clearly show a significant variation in the number of rollouts, ranging from as few as 27 to as many as 584. When the hyperparameter *depth* is set to 25 and *policy_rollout* is *True*, the AlphaGo agent utilizes the policy network to simulate games and frequently employs the value network for assessing game states. The process of feeding game states through an intricate neural network is time-consuming, which explains why using both policy and value networks results in a reduced number of rollouts within the given time frame. This accounts for the lower *num_rollouts* values, like 27 or 29, observed in these cases.

Conversely, with a *depth* setting of 45 and *policy_rollout* set to *False*, the AlphaGo agent resorts to random moves for game simulations. Moreover, it completely bypasses the value network for evaluating game states because a Connect Four game is limited to 42 moves. Omitting the use of policy and value networks allows for a greater number of rollouts within the same time limit. Hence, we observe significantly higher *num_rollouts* values, such as 584 or 575, in these scenarios.

18.3 SEARCH FOR THE BEST HYPERPARAMETER COMBINATION

With 18 different hyperparameter sets at your disposal, you'll engage in a grid search to identify which hyperparameter combination yields the most effective game strategy.

For simplicity, let's label these 18 hyperparameter sets as s_1, s_2, ..., s_{18}. We'll have each strategy, denoted as s_i (where s_i is one of $\{s_1, s_2, \ldots, s_{18}\}$), compete in 20 games against a distinct strategy s_j, ensuring s_j is always different from s_i. To level the playing field, in half of these 20 games, s_i will make the first move, while in the other half, s_j will make the first move. This arrangement eliminates any first-mover advantage for any player. During each game, the scoring is straightforward:

the winner earns 1 point, the loser gets −1 point, and in the event of a tie, both players score 0. The strategy that accumulates the highest total score following the grid search will be selected as the most effective.

18.3.1 Grid Search to Find the Best Strategy

We first define a function, *one_game()*, to play a complete Connect Four game between two strategies.

```
[9]: def one_game(si,sj):
         # parameters in strategy i
         weight_i=si["weight"]
         policy_rollout_i=si["policy_rollout"]
         depth_i=si["depth"]
         num_rollouts_i=si["num_rollouts"]
         # parameters in strategy j
         weight_j=sj["weight"]
         policy_rollout_j=sj["policy_rollout"]
         depth_j=sj["depth"]
         num_rollouts_j=sj["num_rollouts"]
         # reset the game
         state=env.reset()
         # play a full game
         while True:
             # move recommended by strategy si
             action=alphago(env,weight_i,depth_i,
                            PG_net,value_net,fast_net,
                            policy_rollout_i,
                            num_rollouts_i)
             state,reward,done,_=env.step(action)
             if done:
                 result=abs(reward)
                 break
             # move recommended by strategy sj
             action=alphago(env,weight_j,depth_j,
                            PG_net,value_net,fast_net,
                            policy_rollout_j,
                            num_rollouts_j)
             state,reward,done,_=env.step(action)
             if done:
                 result=-abs(reward)
                 break
         return result
```

The function *one_game()* takes two game strategies s_i and s_j from the list *new_grid* as input. Game strategy s_i moves first while game strategy s_j moves second. The output of the function is the game outcome, which can take values -1, 0, or 1. If the first player (i.e., s_i) wins, the output is 1; if the second player (i.e., s_j) wins, the output is -1. If it's a tie game, the output is 0.

Next, we consider every possible permutation of (s_i, s_j), where s_i and s_j are from the list *new_grid* and they differ from each other. We'll play ten games for each permutation and record game results, like so:

```
)]:  # create a list to record game outcome
     results=[]
     # play ten games for each permutation
     for _ in range(10):
         for i in new_grid:
             for j in new_grid:
                 if i!=j:
                     result=one_game(i,j)
                     # record players and outcome
                     results.append((i,j,result))
                     print(i,j,result)
     # save the record to the computer
     import pickle
     with open("files/outcome.p","wb") as fb:
         pickle.dump(results, fb)
```

We create a list *results* to record the grid search outcome. We iterate through all permutations from the list *new_grid*. We call the *one_game()* function ten games and use (i, j) as the two arguments. After each game, we record (i, j, result) in the list *results*.

The above code cell takes about ten hours to run.

18.3.2 Find Out the Best Game Strategy

Next, we'll determine which game strategy is the best based on the grid search outcome recorded in the list *results*.

```
]:  # load the grid search results from the file
     import pickle
     with open("files/outcome.p","rb") as fb:
         outcome=pickle.load(fb)

     # Create a dictionary to count results
     rewards={}
     for i, x in enumerate(new_grid):
         rewards[i]=[]
     # iterate through all grid search results
     for x in outcome:
```

```
si, sj, r = x
# count the game outcome for the red player
rewards[new_grid.index(si)].append(r)
# count the game outcome for the yellow player
rewards[new_grid.index(sj)].append(-r)
```

We create a dictionary *rewards* to count the game outcomes for each game strategy. The keys in the dictionary *rewards* are 0, 1, ..., and 17, denoting the 18 game strategies in the list *new_grid*. The values for each game strategy in the dictionary *rewards* is a list of game results, which can be 0, 1, or −1.

Next, we calculate the average game outcome for each game strategy, as follows:

[12]:
```
# Create a dictionary to count average score
scores={}
# iterate through keys and values in rewards
for k, v in rewards.items():
    # calculate average score for each game strategy
    score=sum(v)/len(v)
    # record in the dictionary scores
    scores[k]=score
# print out the saverage scores
from pprint import pprint
pprint(scores)
```

```
{0: -0.1864406779661017,
 1: -0.2994350282485876,
 2: -0.2542372881355932,
 3: -0.11864406779661017,
 4: 0.096045197740113,
 5: 0.1694915254237288,
 6: -0.2138728323699422,
 7: -0.19254658385093168,
 8: -0.22784810126582278,
 9: 0.07586206896551724,
 10: 0.2357142857142857,
 11: 0.3023255813953488,
 12: -0.11627906976744186,
 13: -0.078125,
 14: -0.015748031496062992,
 15: 0.3333333333333333,
 16: 0.42857142857142855,
 17: 0.4523809523809524}
```

The above dictionary *scores* shows the average score of the 18 game strategies from the grid search process. It looks like the last game strategy has the highest score, with an average score of 0.45. We now print out the best game strategy and the hyperparameters associated with it, like this:

```
# the index of the best game strategy
best_idx=max(scores, key=scores.get)
print(best_idx)
best_parameters=new_grid[best_idx]
print(best_parameters)
```

```
17
{'depth': 45, 'num_rollouts': 584, 'policy_rollout': False,
'weight': 0.75}
```

We have identified the combination of the best hyperparameters for the AlphaGo agent, as shown above. With these optimized hyperparameters, the AlphaGo agent will not use the policy network to roll out games (i.e., *policy_rollout=False*) because doing so leads to slow game rollouts in MCTS. Instead, it will roll out games randomly so that it can roll out a large number of games within the allotted time limit. It will not use the value network either (since *depth=45*). It will look ahead a maximum of 45 steps. Since Connect Four has a maximum of 42 steps, this means the value network is never used to evaluate the game state. The AlphaGo agent will always roll out a game until a terminal state is reached. The agent rolls out 584 games every time it makes a move in an actual game, the maximum number allowed within the one second allotted time limit. Finally, when selecting the child node to roll out games, it places 75% of the weight on recommendations from the policy gradient network and 25% of the weight on rollout value.

18.4   TEST THE OPTIMIZED ALPHAGO AGENT IN CONNECT FOUR

Now that we have an AlphaGo agent with fine-tuned hyperparameters, we'll test it against the look-three-steps-ahead ruled-based AI that we developed in Chapter 6.

To save time, we will test only 10 games as we did earlier in this chapter. The optimized AlphaGo agent will make the first move, followed by the rule-based AI agent, as follows:

```
from utils.conn_simple_env import conn
from utils.ch17util import alphago

weight_i=best_parameters["weight"]
policy_rollout_i=best_parameters["policy_rollout"]
depth_i=best_parameters["depth"]
num_rollouts_i=best_parameters["num_rollouts"]
# initiate game environment
env=conn()
# test ten games
```

```
for i in range(10):
    state=env.reset()
    while True:
        # AlphaGo moves first
        action=alphago(env,weight_i,depth_i,PG_net,value_net,
                fast_net, policy_rollout_i,num_rollouts_i)
        state,reward,done,_=env.step(action)
        if done:
            print("AlphaGo wins!")
            break
        # move recommended by rule-based AI
        action=rule_based_AI(env)
        state,reward,done,_=env.step(action)
        if done:
            if reward==0:
                print("The game is tied!")
            else:
                print("Rule-based AI wins!")
            break
```

```
AlphaGo wins!
The game is tied!
Rule-based AI wins!
AlphaGo wins!
AlphaGo wins!
AlphaGo wins!
Rule-based AI wins!
AlphaGo wins!
Rule-based AI wins!
AlphaGo wins!
```

The result above show that our optimized AlphaGo agent is better than the rule-based AI algorithm we developed in Chapter 6. It won six games, lost three, and the remaining one is tied.

To level the playing field and eliminate the first-mover advantage, we test if the optimized AlphaGo agent can beat the rule-based AI if it plays second. We test ten games as follows:

```
[15]:   # test ten games
        for i in range(10):
            state=env.reset()
            while True:
                # Rule-based AI moves first
                action=rule_based_AI(env)
                state,reward,done,_=env.step(action)
```

```
            if done:
                print("Rule-based AI wins!")
                break
            # AlphaGo moves second
            action=alphago(env,weight_i,depth_i,PG_net,value_net,
                    fast_net, policy_rollout_i,num_rollouts_i)
            state,reward,done,_=env.step(action)
            if done:
                if reward==0:
                    print("The game is tied!")
                else:
                    print("AlphaGo wins!")
                break
```

```
AlphaGo wins!
Rule-based AI wins!
AlphaGo wins!
AlphaGo wins!
Rule-based AI wins!
Rule-based AI wins!
AlphaGo wins!
Rule-based AI wins!
AlphaGo wins!
AlphaGo wins!
```

The above results show that the optimized AlphaGo agent has won six games while the rule-based AI has won four games. There is no tie game. This shows that our optimized AlphaGo algorithm can beat the rule-based AI algorithm even when playing second. Keep in mind that the game outcome is random and you are likely to get different results.

Overall, these tests show that our optimized AlphaGo is stronger than the MiniMax agent who looks three steps ahead. If you compare this with our earlier results, hyperparameter tuning does produce a stronger AlphaGo agent.

To speed up testing, we allotted one second for the AlphaGo agent to make a move. If we allow the AlphaGo agent to take longer to make a move, the game strategies will be much stronger, of course.

In the last subsection, the optimized AlphaGo agent rolls out 584 games every time it makes a move. What if we allow the agent to roll out, say, 5000 games, how strong is the AlphaGo agent? Can it beat, say, a MiniMax agent that looks four steps ahead? We'll test it below.

```
]: # test ten games
   for i in range(10):
       state=env.reset()
```

```
if i%2==0:
    # Ruled-based AI moves
    action=rule_based_AI(env, depth=4)
    state,reward,done,_=env.step(action)
while True:
    # AlphaGo moves, setting num_rollouts=5000
    action=alphago(env,weight_i,depth_i,PG_net,value_net,
        fast_net, policy_rollout_i,num_rollouts=5000)
    state,reward,done,_=env.step(action)
    if done:
        if reward==0:
            print("The game is tied!")
        else:
            print("AlphaGo wins!")
        break
    # Rule-based AI moves
    action=rule_based_AI(env, depth=4)
    state,reward,done,_=env.step(action)
    if done:
        if reward==0:
            print("The game is tied!")
        else:
            print("Rule-based AI wins!")
        break
```

```
AlphaGo wins!
AlphaGo wins!
Rule-based AI wins!
Rule-based AI wins!
Rule-based AI wins!
AlphaGo wins!
Rule-based AI wins!
AlphaGo wins!
AlphaGo wins!
AlphaGo wins!
```

We have tested ten games by setting the *num_rollouts* argument to 5000 while keeping the other three hyperparameters at the optimized values from the last section. We set the *depth* argument to 4 when calling the *rule_base_AI()* function as the opponent. In five games, the AlphaGo agent moves first; in the other five games, the look-four-steps-ahead agent moves first. The results above show the AlphaGo agent won six games and lost the rest four. This shows that with better computation resources, we can make our AlphaGo agent even stronger.

Through this, you have successfully mastered the implementation of the AlphaGo algorithm across three different games: the coin game, Tic Tac Toe, and Connect

Four. The upcoming chapters will introduce you to AlphaZero, an enhanced variant of AlphaGo. Remarkably, AlphaZero doesn't depend on human expert moves for training the model. It learns to master any game autonomously, guided solely by the rules of the game, devoid of pre-existing human knowledge. You will discover that AlphaZero, with its advanced approach, yields even more powerful game strategies compared to AlphaGo.

18.5 GLOSSARY

- **Grid Search:** A common method used in hyperparameter tuning. The process involves experimenting with different combinations of these parameters to find the set that yields the best results, typically measured by the model's accuracy or performance on a validation set.
- **Hyperparameter:** Hyperparameters are the parameters that control the learning process in machine learning models. Their values are set before the learning process starts and will not change due to training. In contrast, non-hyperparameters are derived from the training process.
- **Hyperparameter Tuning:** Hyperparameter tuning is a critical step in the machine learning pipeline, focused on optimizing the parameters of a model that are not learned from data but are set before the training process. These hyperparameters, which include settings like learning rate or the number of layers in a neural network, greatly influence the performance of the model.

18.6 EXERCISES

18.1 What are hyperparameters in a machine-learning model? How are they different from other parameters in the model?

18.2 Describe the process of tuning hyperparameters. Which method is most frequently employed for this task?

18.3 Modify the two code cells in Section 18.1.2 and set *weight* to 0.8 and *depth* to 25 in the *alphago()* function. Rerun the two code cells and see how often the AlphaGo agent wins.

18.4 Modify the second code cell in Section 18.2.2 to calculate the maximum number of rollouts in two seconds instead of one second. Rerun the second and third code cells in Section 18.2.2 and see if the values of *num_rollouts* roughly double in each combination.

18.5 Modify the last code cell in Section 18.4 to set the value of *num_rollouts* to 6000. Rerun the code cell and see how often the AlphaGo agent wins.

## CHAPTER 19

The Actor-Critic Method and AlphaZero

"As it plays, the neural network is tuned and updated to predict moves, as well as the eventual winner of the games."
– David Silver and Demis Hassabis, 2017

IN 2017, the DeepMind team introduced an advanced version of AlphaGo, named AlphaGo Zero (which we'll refer to as AlphaZero in this book because we apply the algorithm to various games beyond Go) [3]. This version marked a significant departure from its predecessor, the AlphaGo that triumphed over World Go Champion Lee Sedol in 2016. Unlike the earlier version, AlphaZero's training relied exclusively on deep reinforcement learning, without any human-derived strategies or domain-specific knowledge, except for the basic rules of the game. It learned through self-play from scratch. This development has profound implications for AI. When confronting complex global issues, human expertise and domain knowledge often have their limitations. The challenge lies in how AI can devise intelligent solutions under such constraints. The success of AlphaZero, however, offers a beacon of hope in this endeavor.

You may be curious about what sets AlphaZero apart from AlphaGo in terms of power. A key factor is AlphaZero's use of larger and more complex neural networks, which significantly boost its learning abilities. However, in the context of the simpler games covered in this book, the additional layers in the neural networks don't substantially increase benefits. Therefore, we'll not explore this aspect of AlphaZero in this book.

Another element that has elevated AlphaZero above its predecessor is its application of an advanced deep reinforcement learning technique. As discussed in the previous

DOI: 10.1201/9781032722207-19

chapters of this book, the AlphaGo algorithm initially trains two policy networks using data from human experts. Following this, it employs self-play deep reinforcement learning to enhance one of these policy networks, creating a policy gradient network. It also leverages game experience data from self-play to train a value network for predicting game outcomes. In contrast, AlphaZero utilizes a single neural network with two outputs: one *policy head* for predicting the next move and a *value head* for forecasting game outcome, as highlighted by David Silver and Demis Hassabis in this chapter's introductory quote.

In this chapter, we'll delve into the advanced deep reinforcement learning strategy known as the actor-critic method, applying it specifically to the coin game. The concept of the *actor* in this method is straightforward: it's the game player who must determine the most advantageous next move. This actor is essentially the policy network we've examined in the policy-gradient methods in Chapters 13 to 15.

The *critic* refers to a different role – akin to another player – who evaluates the moves made thus far. The insights provided by the critic are instrumental in refining future moves. To implement this, we'll add an additional component to the deep neural network, resulting in two distinct outputs: a policy network for predicting the next move and a value network for estimating the game's outcome. The policy network assumes the actor's role, selecting the subsequent move, while the value network, as the critic, monitors the agent's progress throughout the game. This feedback is essential for the training process, serving a similar function to how a game review might enhance your own learning.

We'll focus on applying the actor-critic method to the coin game in this chapter. You'll learn how to develop an Actor-Critic (AC) deep reinforcement learning model. This model will feature two concurrent outputs: the policy network, serving as the "actor", and the value network, functioning as the "critic". Following this, you'll learn how to train this AC deep reinforcement model. Unlike our approach with the AlphaGo algorithm, where we used rule-based AI players as experts for generating training moves, here we'll start from scratch. We'll rely solely on self-play for training, without using expert moves as a guide.

Once you've successfully trained the AC deep reinforcement model, you'll integrate both the policy and value networks with Monte Carlo Tree Search (MCTS) for making decisions in actual games, mirroring the approach we took with the AlphaGo algorithm in Chapter 16. You'll observe that the AlphaZero agent, armed with this model, performs flawlessly and solves the game. It can beat the AlphaGo agent we developed in Chapter 16 if playing as Player 2.

What You'll Learn in This Chapter

- Understanding the theory behind the actor-critic method
- Creating an actor-critic agent in the coin game
- Training the actor-critic agent in the coin game from scratch, without human expert moves
- Creating an AlphaZero agent in the coin game
- Testing AlphaZero against the AlphaGo agent in the coin game

---

19.1 THE ACTOR CRITIC METHOD

This section introduces you to the actor-critic method. We'll first briefly review the idea behind the policy gradient method, which we discussed in Chapter 13. After that, we'll discuss the actor-critic approach, which is related to the policy gradient method, but with an additional parallel output layer.

19.1.1 Review the Policy-Gradient Method

In Chapter 13, we have discussed the policy-gradient method. We have learned that a policy, $\pi(a|s)$, represents any algorithm that advises the agent on the action to choose in a specific state. Policies can be stochastic, meaning the agent selects actions randomly, guided by a probability distribution. Alternatively, a policy might be deterministic, wherein the agent is certain about the action to take in a given scenario, executing it with 100% certainty.

Policy-gradient is an approach to tweak model parameters to optimize outcomes for a reinforcement learning (RL) agent.

In policy-based RL, the agent's goal is to learn an optimal policy that maximizes expected rewards over time. A policy, or strategy, is a decision rule that connects a specific state to a corresponding action, guiding the agent on what action to take in a given situation.

Consider a policy denoted as $\pi_\theta(a_t|s_t, \theta)$, where θ represents the model parameters, like weights in a neural network. This means the agent selects an action a_t at time t based on the current state s_t, influenced by the parameters θ. The agent aims to choose a series of actions $(a_0, a_1, \ldots, a_{T-1})$ to maximize her expected total rewards. In period t, upon observing state s_t and taking action a_t, the agent receives a reward $r(a_t, s_t)$. Given a discount rate γ, the agent's expected cumulative reward is calculated as:

$$R(s_0, a_0, \ldots, a_{T-1}, s_T) = \sum_{t=0}^{T-1} \gamma^t r(s_t, a_t) + \gamma^T r(s_T)$$

where s_T is the terminal state.

The objective of the agent is to find the optimal parameter values for the model, θ, to maximize the expected accumulative payoff:

$$\max_{\theta} E[R(s_0, a_0, \ldots, a_{T-1}, s_T)|\pi_\theta]$$

The maximization problem outlined above can be tackled using a gradient ascent algorithm. In this approach, we iteratively update the model parameters θ using the formula below until convergence is reached:

$$\theta \leftarrow \theta + lr * \nabla_\theta E[R|\pi_\theta]$$

Here, lr stands for the learning rate, a hyperparameter that determines the pace at which model parameters are updated. Essentially, this process involves training the model to predict the probability of choosing the correct action based on the current state. The formula for the solution becomes:

$$\theta \leftarrow \theta + lr \times E[\sum_{t=0}^{T-1} \nabla_\theta log\pi_\theta(a_t|s_t)R|\pi_\theta]$$

Readers interested in a deeper understanding of this solution can refer to the proof provided by OpenAI at the following link:

https://spinningup.openai.com/en/latest/spinningup/extra_pg_proof1.html.

19.1.2   The Actor-Critic Method

In the policy gradient method, the agent adjusts the model parameters in a manner proportional to the product of gradients and rewards to maximize cumulative rewards. This combination is represented by the following expression:

$$E[\sum_{t=0}^{T-1} \nabla_\theta log\pi_\theta(a_t|s_t)r_t(s_0, a_0, \ldots, a_{T-1}, s_T)|\pi_\theta]$$

The discounted reward at time t, denoted as $r_t(s_0, a_0, \ldots, a_{T-1}, s_T)$, is determined retrospectively after the final payoff R and the sequence of states and actions $(s_0, a_0, \ldots, a_{T-1}, s_T)$ are observed. Therefore, the agent's parameter adjustments are proportional to the product of the gradients and the rewards. The policy-based approach is advantageous due to its directness and efficiency in various scenarios. However, a potential drawback is the high variance in gradients, which can lead to instability and sometimes, non-convergence of parameters during training.

In contrast, the value-based approach focuses on determining value functions for each state-action pair. The agent selects the optimal action in each state by choosing the one with the highest value. While this approach is more stable, it often requires more time to train.

The actor-critic approach merges the strengths of both the value-based and policy-based methods, offering a more robust and effective method in reinforcement learning.

Actor-critic reinforcement learning models consist of two distinct networks: the critic, which is a value-based network, and the actor, which is a policy-based network. The critic's role is to estimate the expected outcome of the game (i.e., the value of the action chosen by the actor), while the actor's function is to determine the actions the agent should take.

In the actor-critic method, parameter adjustment is based not on the product of gradients and rewards but on the product of gradients and the advantage. The advantage is calculated as the difference between the actual reward and the expected outcome:

$$A(s_t, a_t) = r_t(s_0, a_0, \ldots, a_{T-1}, s_T) - V(s_t)$$

The rationale is as follows: if the agent anticipates a win (meaning the value $V(s_t)$ is high) and indeed wins, the action a_t taken at time t might not be particularly significant. Hence, there is little need for substantial adjustment of the model parameters. Conversely, if the agent expects to lose (where the value $V(s_t)$ is low) but ends up winning, the action a_t at time t is likely an excellent move. In this scenario, the model parameters should be adjusted more significantly to favor such effective moves. This approach offers a more efficient way of tuning the model parameters to develop more intelligent agents.

19.2 AN OVERVIEW OF THE TRAINING PROCESS

In this section, we'll first outline the process for training the AlphaZero agent from the ground up for the coin game, starting without any pre-existing data or human guidance. Following this, we'll describe the deep reinforcement learning model employed for this task.

19.2.1 Steps to Train an AlphaZero Agent

To train the AlphaZero agent in the coin game, we'll first develop a deep reinforcement model using the actor-critic approach. This method bears a resemblance to the policy gradient technique we employed in Chapter 13, with a key distinction: the model features two simultaneous output networks. One is a policy network for predicting actions, and the other, a value network for forecasting the game's outcome.

In Chapter 13, when training the policy gradient model for the coin game, we pitted it against a rule-based AI opponent. In contrast, for the actor-critic model in this chapter, the adversary is the actor-critic agent itself, exemplifying self-play.

Our training process for the coin game involves alternating between training Player 1 and training Player 2. In the initial set of ten games, Player 1 will make decisions using guidance from the policy network of our newly developed actor-critic model. This player competes against an opponent that also relies on decisions from the same model, hence the term "self-play." During these games, we gather data such as the natural logarithms of the predicted probabilities, discounted rewards, and the predicted game outcome from the value network to refine the model parameters.

For the subsequent set of ten games, Player 2 will use recommendations from the same policy network to compete against the model. We'll again collect similar data to enhance the model parameters, continuing this alternating training process for each player after every ten games.

To determine the appropriate time to stop training, we'll evaluate the model every 1000 episodes. If it can flawlessly play as the second player against the rule-based AI that we developed in Chapter 1, we'll conclude the training. However, it's important to note that the rule-based AI is solely for testing purposes and is not involved in the actual training process. We'll explore this training aspect further in Chapter 21 with the AlphaZero agent in Connect Four, where we completely abstain from external inputs, even in testing phases.

19.2.2   An Actor-Critic Agent for the Coin Game

Our design involves constructing a model that incorporates a single input layer, consisting of 22 values. This model is structured with two hidden layers. It features two distinct output layers: the first is a policy network, also known as the actor, which is responsible for predicting the subsequent move, while the second is a value network tasked with forecasting the outcome of the game. This model bears resemblance to the policy gradient model discussed in Chapter 13, but it is enhanced by the addition of an extra value network in its output.

The specific architecture of the model we are employing is detailed as follows:

```
]: import tensorflow as tf
   from tensorflow import keras
   from tensorflow.keras import layers

   num_inputs = 22
   num_actions = 2
   # The input layer
   inputs = layers.Input(shape=(22,))
   # The common layer
   common = layers.Dense(32, activation="relu")(inputs)
   common = layers.Dense(32, activation="relu")(common)
   # The policy network
   action = layers.Dense(num_actions, activation="softmax")(common)
   # The value network
   critic = layers.Dense(1, activation="tanh")(common)
   model = keras.Model(inputs=inputs, outputs=[action, critic])
```

Below, we specify the optimizer and the loss function we use to train the model.

```
[2]: optimizer = keras.optimizers.Adam(learning_rate=0.001)
     loss_func = keras.losses.MeanAbsoluteError()
```

Our model employs the Adam optimizer, set at a learning rate of 0.001. For the loss function, we utilize the mean absolute error loss function. This particular choice is beneficial as it is less punitive toward outliers when compared to other loss functions like Huber or mean squared error.

19.3 TRAIN THE ACTOR-CRITIC AGENT IN THE COIN GAME

This section delves into the detailed process of training the actor-critic agent for the coin game. We will be developing an AC (Actor-Critic) agent, which is based on the deep reinforcement learning model we crafted in the previous section. This agent will serve as the adversary for both Player 1 and Player 2 during self-play sessions.

The training involves simulating sets of ten games each. Upon the completion of these ten games, we gather data including predicted probabilities, discounted rewards, and anticipated game outcomes. This collected information is then utilized to update the parameters of our model.

19.3.1 Train the Two Players in the Actor-Critic Model

To train the actor-critic model, we need to create an opponent for both Player 1 and Player 2. The actor-critic agent plays against itself during training. Therefore, we'll first create an opponent who always selects moves based on the current actor-critic model. We'll let Player 1 play against the opponent for ten games and update model parameters. After that, we'll let Player 2 play against the same AC agent for ten games and update model parameters again.

For that purpose, we define an *AC_agent()* function as follows:

```
[3]: import numpy as np

     def onehot_encoder(state):
         onehot=np.zeros((1,22))
         onehot[0,state]=1
         return onehot

     def ACplayer(env):
         # estimate action probabilities and future rewards
         onehot_state = onehot_encoder(env.state)
         action_probs, _ = model(onehot_state)
         # select action with the highest probability
         action=np.random.choice([1,2],p=np.squeeze(action_probs))
         return action
```

Moving forward, we will establish a function named *playing_1()*. This function is designed to simulate an entire game, during which Player 1 will make decisions based on the policy network derived from the actor-critic model. The process is as follows:

```
from utils.coin_simple_env import coin_game
env=coin_game()
def playing_1():
    # create lists to record game history
    action_probs_history = []
    critic_value_history = []
    rewards_history = []
    state = env.reset()
    while True:
        # estimate action probabilities and future rewards
        onehot_state = onehot_encoder(env.state)
        action_probs, critic_value = model(onehot_state)
        # select action based on policy network
        action=np.random.choice([1,2],p=np.squeeze(action_probs))
        # record value history
        critic_value_history.append(critic_value[0, 0])
        # record log probabilities
        action_probs_history.append(\
                      tf.math.log(action_probs[0, action-1]))
        # Apply the sampled action in our environment
        state, reward, done, _ = env.step(action)
        if done:
            rewards_history.append(reward)
            break
        else:
            state, reward, done, _ = env.step(ACplayer(env))
            rewards_history.append(reward)
            if done:
                break
    return action_probs_history,critic_value_history,\
        rewards_history
```

The *playing_1()* function simulates a full game, meticulously tracking all the intermediate actions taken by the AC (Actor-Critic) agent. Upon completion, this function yields three lists:

- a list *action_probs_history* with the natural logarithm of the recommended probability of the action taken by the agent from the policy network;
- a list *critic_value_history* with the estimated future rewards from the value network;
- a list *rewards_history* with the rewards for each action taken by the agent in the game.

In reinforcement learning, the actions taken have consequences that extend beyond immediate rewards, influencing future rewards as well. This scenario presents the credit assignment problem, central to all reinforcement learning algorithms. To address this, we attribute value to preceding actions through the use of discounted rewards. Thus, discounted rewards are utilized to appropriately allocate credit. For that purpose, we define a function below:

```
[5]: def discount_rs(r):
         discounted_rs = np.zeros(len(r))
         running_add = 0
         for i in reversed(range(0, len(r))):
             running_add = gamma*running_add + r[i]
             discounted_rs[i] = running_add
         return discounted_rs.tolist()
```

Once Player 1 has undergone training for ten episodes, we will then allow Player 2 to compete against the identical opponent for a series of ten games, followed by another update of the model parameters. To be more precise, we will enable the opponent, as specified in the *ACplayer()* function mentioned earlier, to initiate the first move in the coin game. Below, we will outline the function *playing_2()* to facilitate the training of Player 2 within the actor-critic model, as follows:

```
[6]: def playing_2():
         # create lists to record game history
         action_probs_history = []
         critic_value_history = []
         rewards_history = []
         state = env.reset()
         state, reward, done, _ = env.step(ACplayer(env))
         while True:
             # estimate action probabilities and future rewards
             onehot_state = onehot_encoder(env.state)
             action_probs, critic_value = model(onehot_state)
             # select action based on policy network
             action=np.random.choice([1,2],p=np.squeeze(action_probs))
             # record value history
             critic_value_history.append(critic_value[0, 0])
             # record log probabilities
             action_probs_history.append(\
                         tf.math.log(action_probs[0, action-1]))
             # Apply the sampled action in our environment
             state, reward, done, _ = env.step(action)
             if done:
                 rewards_history.append(-reward)
                 break
```

```
        else:
            state, reward, done, _ = env.step(ACplayer(env))
            rewards_history.append(-reward)
            if done:
                break
    return action_probs_history,critic_value_history, \
        rewards_history
```

The *playing_2()* function simulates a full game, with the opponent, defined in the function *ACplayer()*, as the first player, and the actor-critic (AC) agent as the second player. Similar to the *playing_1()* function, the *playing_2()* function also returns three lists: *action_probs_history*, *critic_value_history*, and *rewards_history*.

19.3.2 Update Parameters During Training

Rather than adjusting the model parameters following each individual episode, we opt for stability by updating them after a set number of episodes. In this approach, we perform parameter updates every ten games, as illustrated below:

```
batch_size=10
def create_batch(playing_func):
    action_probs_history = []
    critic_value_history = []
    rewards_history = []
    for i in range(batch_size):
        aps,cvs,rs = playing_func()
        # rewards are discounted
        returns = discount_rs(rs)
        action_probs_history += aps
        critic_value_history += cvs
        rewards_history += returns
    return action_probs_history,critic_value_history,\
        rewards_history
```

Note that we discount the rewards associated with wins and losses due to the credit assignment problem we discussed above.

We'll update the parameters by alternating between training Player 1 and training Player 2. We'll define one single function *train_player()* below so that we can use it to train either Player 1 or Player 2 and update model parameters:

```
gamma=0.95
def train_player(playing_func):
    # Train the model for one batch (ten games)
    with tf.GradientTape() as tape:
        action_probs_history,critic_value_history,\
```

```
        rewards_history=create_batch(playing_func)
    # Calculating loss values to update our network
    tfdif=tf.convert_to_tensor(rewards_history,\
                               dtype=tf.float32)-\
    tf.convert_to_tensor(critic_value_history,dtype=tf.float32)
    alosses=-tf.multiply(tf.convert_to_tensor(\
      action_probs_history,dtype=tf.float32),tfdif)
    closs=loss_func(tf.convert_to_tensor(rewards_history,\
                              dtype=tf.float32),\
    tf.convert_to_tensor(critic_value_history,dtype=tf.float32))
    # Backpropagation
    loss_value = tf.reduce_sum(alosses) + closs
grads = tape.gradient(loss_value, model.trainable_variables)
optimizer.apply_gradients(zip(grads,\
                          model.trainable_variables))
```

Here, it's important to note that the parameter adjustments are made by multiplying the gradients with the advantage, which is calculated as the difference between the discounted rewards and the anticipated outcome of the game. This approach is tied to the solution for maximizing rewards in the actor-critic model, a topic we previously explored in this chapter.

19.3.3 The Training Loop

AlphaZero algorithms demand substantial computational resources, making the training process quite lengthy. Moreover, the complexity increases as we need to finely adjust various hyperparameters, such as the learning rate and the loss function, to ensure the model works effectively. Therefore, it's crucial to monitor the model's progress to ascertain whether it is developing correctly.

To achieve this, we will periodically test the model against a rule-based AI. This serves as a benchmark to gauge progress. It's important to note that the rule-based AI does not directly participate in training the model. Its role is solely to periodically evaluate the model's performance, without directly influencing the model itself.

For that purpose, we define the following *test()* function to test the performance of the actor-critic model periodically during training:

```
[9]: import random

     def rule_based_AI(state):
         if state%3 != 0:
             move = state%3
         else:
             move = random.choice([1,2])
         return move
```

```
def test():
    results=[]
    for i in range(100):
        env = coin_game()
        state=env.reset()
        while True:
            action = rule_based_AI(state)
            state, reward, done, info = env.step(action)
            if done:
                # record -1 if rule-based AI player won
                results.append(-1)
                break
            # estimate action probabilities and future rewards
            onehot_state = onehot_encoder(state)
            action_probs, _ = model(onehot_state)
            # select action with the highest probability
            action=np.argmax(action_probs[0])+1
            state, reward, done, info = env.step(action)
            if done:
                # record 1 if AC agent won
                results.append(1)
                break
    return results.count(1)
```

To systematically switch between training Player 1 and Player 2, we will implement a variable named *batches*, initially set to 0. With the completion of each batch (comprising ten games), we increment the value of *batches* by 1. The training is structured so that Player 1 is trained when the value of *batches* is an even number, and Player 2 is trained when it's odd.

The goal is to refine the model until it achieves perfection. For this purpose, after every 100 episodes of training, we will conduct a test against the rule-based AI to evaluate the model's progress. The training process will be deemed complete and will stop if the model consistently defeats the AI, achieving a 100% success rate in the test.

```
]: n = 0
batches=0
# Train the model
while True:
    if batches%2==0:
        train_player(playing_1)
    else:
        train_player(playing_2)
```

```
# Log details
n += batch_size
batches += 1
# print out progress
if n % 1000 == 0:
    model.save("files/ac_coin.h5")
    wins=test()
    print(f"at episode {n}, number of wins is {wins}/100")
    if wins==100:
        break
```

The model is successfully trained after 7000 episodes. Alternatively, you can download the trained model from the book's GitHub repository.

19.4 AN ALPHAZERO AGENT IN THE COIN GAME

Now that we have successfully trained an actor-critic agent who can both recommend perfect next moves and predict the game outcome, we'll construct an AlphaZero agent in the coin game.

The AlphaZero agent is similar to the AlphaGo agent we created in Chapter 16, except we'll use different policy and value networks.

In the local module *ch19util*, we'll implement the AlphaZero algorithm in the coin game. Download the file *ch19util.py* from the book's GitHub repository and place it in the folder /utils/ on your computer. Take some time to go through the details of the module. Below, I'll explain the logic behind the algorithm in the sequence of selection, expansion, simulation, and backpropagation.

19.4.1 Select, Expand, Simulate, and Backpropagate

In the local module *ch19util*, we first load up the trained actor-critic model, as follows:

```
from copy import deepcopy
import numpy as np
from tensorflow import keras

# Load the trained actor critic model
model=keras.models.load_model("files/ac_coin.h5")
```

We define a *select()* function in the local module to reflect how the AlphaZero agent selects a child node L based on the priors and the average rollout value, as follows:

```
def select(priors,env,results,weight):
    # weighted average of priors and rollout_value
    scores={}
    for k,v in results.items():
```

```
    # rollout_value for each next move
    if len(v)==0:
        vi=0
    else:
        vi=sum(v)/len(v)
    # scale the prior by (1+N(L))
    prior=priors[0][k-1]/(1+len(v))
    # calculate weighted average
    scores[k]=weight*prior+(1-weight)*vi
# select child node based on the weighted average
return max(scores,key=scores.get)
```

The *select()* function is defined the same way as that in Chapter 16.

In order to roll out games to evaluate different child nodes, we'll expand the game tree. To implement this, we define an *expand()* function in the local module *ch19util*, which is identical to the one we defined in Chapter 16.

Next, we roll out a game, starting from the child node. We stop the hypothetical game when the terminal state or the maximum depth is reached. After that, we evaluate the child node. If the terminal state is reached, we evaluate the child node with the actual game outcome. If the maximum depth is reached but the game is not over, we evaluate the node with the value network in the trained actor-critic model.

In the local module *ch19util*, we define the *simulate()* function as follows:

```
# roll out a game till terminal state or depth reached
def simulate(env_copy,done,reward,depth):
    # if the game has already ended
    if done==True:
        return reward
    for _ in range(depth):
        move=env_copy.sample()
        state,reward,done,info=env_copy.step(move)
        # if terminal state is reached, returns outcome
        if done==True:
            return reward
    # depth reached but game not over, evaluate
    onehot_state=onehot_encoder(state)
    # use the trained actor critic model to evaluate
    action_probs, critic_value = model(onehot_state)
    # output is predicted game outcome
    return critic_value[0,0]
```

The final step in the tree search is to update the game tree after each rollout. Specifically, if the current player is Player 2, we'll multiply the reward by -1 so that everything is from the current player's point of view, but from Player 1's point of view.

We define the *backpropagate()* function in the local module *ch19util*, which is identical to the one we defined in Chapter 16.

19.4.2   Create an AlphaZero Agent in the Coin Game

Now we are ready to define our AlphaZero agent in the coin game, by using the four functions defined above: *select()*, *expand()*, *simulate()*, and *backpropagate()*.

Specifically, we define the *alphazero_coin()* function in the local module as follows:

```
def alphazero_coin(env,weight,depth,num_rollouts=100):
    # if there is only one valid move left, take it
    if len(env.validinputs)==1:
        return env.validinputs[0]
    # get the prior from the AC policy network
    onehot_state = onehot_encoder(env.state)
    priors, _ = model(onehot_state)
    # create a dictionary results
    results={}
    for move in env.validinputs:
        results[move]=[]
    # roll out games
    for _ in range(num_rollouts):
        # select
        move=select(priors,env,results,weight)
        # expand
        env_copy, done, reward=expand(env,move)
        # simulate
        reward=simulate(env_copy,done,reward,depth)
        # backpropagate
        results=backpropagate(env,move,reward,results)
    # select the most visited child node
    visits={k:len(v) for k,v in results.items()}
    return max(visits,key=visits.get)
```

The *alphazero_coin()* is similar to the *alphago_coin()* function we defined in Chapter 16, except here, we extract the prior probabilities from the actor-critic model, instead of the trained policy gradient model.

19.4.3   AlphaZero versus AlphaGo in the Coin Game

Next, we'll test the AlphaZero agent against the AlphaGo agent we created in Chapter 16. We set the number of rollouts to 1000. Since Player 2 always wins if it makes perfect moves, we'll let Player 2 use the moves recommended by the AlphaZero algorithm. Player 1 will use the AlphaGo algorithm that we developed in Chapter 16.

Since each game takes about half a minute to finish, we'll test only ten games. In each game, the AlphaGo agent moves first and the AlphaZero agent moves second.

To level the playing field, we'll choose the same arguments when calling the two functions, *alphazero_coin()* and *alphago_coin()*. We set the *weight* argument to 0.95, the *depth* argument to 25 (it turns out that bypassing the value network is the best choice in this particular case), and roll out 1000 games before the agents make a move.

After each game, we print out the winner of the game, as follows:

```
from utils.coin_simple_env import coin_game
from utils.ch16util import alphago_coin
from utils.ch19util import alphazero_coin
# initiate game environment
env=coin_game()
# test ten games
for i in range(10):
    state=env.reset()
    while True:
        # The AlphaGo agent moves first
        action=alphago_coin(env,0.95,25,num_rollouts=1000)
        state,reward,done,_=env.step(action)
        if done:
            # print out the winner
            print("AlphaGo wins!")
            break
        # The AlphaZero agent moves second
        action=alphazero_coin(env,0.95,25,num_rollouts=1000)
        state,reward,done,_=env.step(action)
        if done:
            # print out the winner
            print("AlphaZero wins!")
            break
```

```
AlphaZero wins!
AlphaZero wins!
AlphaZero wins!
AlphaZero wins!
AlphaZero wins!
AlphaZero wins!
AlphaZero wins!
AlphaZero wins!
AlphaZero wins!
AlphaZero wins!
```

The Alpha Zero agent has won all ten games. This shows that we have created an AlphaZero agent in the coin game that makes perfect moves. We have trained the agent from scratch, without any pre-existing data or human guidance. And that is the main spirit in the design of AlphaZero by the DeepMind team.

In the next two chapters, we'll implement the AlphaZero algorithm in Tic Tac Toe and Connect Four.

19.5 GLOSSARY

- **Actor:** The policy network in the actor-critic model. It maps states to actions, deciding the best action to take in a given state based on the current policy.
- **Advantage:** The advantage is a measure used to indicate how much better (or worse) an action is compared to the average action in a given state. It's calculated by the critic as the difference between the predicted value of the action taken and the expected value of the current policy for that state. This advantage helps in updating the actor's policy more efficiently, focusing on actions that are better than average.
- **Critic:** The critic evaluates the actions taken by the actor. It's often a value network that estimates the value (or potential reward) of being in a certain state, or the value of a state-action pair. The critic's feedback is used to update both the actor's policy and the critic's own value estimation.
- **The Actor-Critic Method:** A deep reinforcement learning method similar to the policy gradient method. However, in the actor-critic method, parameter adjustment is based not on the product of gradients and rewards but on the product of gradients and the advantage, where advantage is calculated as the difference between the actual reward and the expected outcome.

19.6 EXERCISES

19.1 What is the actor-critic method? How is it related to the policy gradient method we discussed in Chapter 16?

19.2 What is *advantage* in the actor-critic method?

19.3 Explain the roles of the actor and the critic in the actor-critic method.

19.4 Modify the first code cell in Section 19.4.3 and set *weight* to 0.96 and *num_rollouts* to 500 in both *alphazero_coin()* and *alphago_coin()*. Rerun the code cell and see how often the AlphaZero agent wins.

## CHAPTER 20

Iterative Self-Play and AlphaZero in Tic Tac Toe

"This neural network improves the strength of the tree search, resulting in higher quality move selection and stronger self-play in the next iteration."
– *Mastering the game of Go without human knowledge (Nature 2017)*

IN THE PREVIOUS chapter, you successfully developed a streamlined version of AlphaZero for the coin game. The essence of AlphaZero's approach lies in honing a gaming strategy through self-play and deep reinforcement learning exclusively, bypassing the need for guidance from human experts or any specific knowledge beyond the rules of the game. A distinguishing feature of AlphaZero, setting it apart from its predecessor, AlphaGo, is its utilization of the actor-critic technique. This method employs two distinct networks for output: the policy network, which predicts the best subsequent actions, and the value network, which estimates the likely winner of the game. You acquired skills in training an actor-critic agent for the coin game and integrating it with Monte Carlo tree search (MCTS) to forge an AlphaZero agent. This AlphaZero agent is able to solve the game and execute impeccable moves in the coin game.

In this chapter, we will guide you through the process of constructing an AlphaZero agent for both Tic Tac Toe and Connect Four. The fact that the agent is multifunctional, capable of managing multiple games, minimizes code duplication and streamlines the process of applying the AlphaZero algorithm across a wider array of games. As we proceed to the next chapter to create an AlphaZero agent for Connect Four, our attention can be dedicated to developing the most effective policy gradient network without the concern of integrating it with MCTS to formulate an AlphaZero algorithm.

At the same time, we recognize that in straightforward games like Tic Tac Toe or Connect Four, the contribution of the value network to enhancing game strategies is minimal. Although a value network eliminates the need to play out game simulations all the way to the terminal state, employing a neural network for game state evaluation can also be time-consuming. Therefore, the effectiveness of using a value network in improving game strategy remains an empirical question. In Chapter 18, we have demonstrated that forgoing the value network in favor of rolling out games all the way to their terminal states is the most effective strategy.

Given these insights, we will not develop actor-critic networks for Tic Tac Toe or Connect Four. Instead, we will use the policy-gradient method for these games, which is advantageous because it involves only a single output network, making the training process less time-consuming and more efficient.

In this chapter, you'll learn to implement the AlphaZero algorithm in Tic Tac Toe by first constructing a policy gradient network. you'll then integrate this policy-gradient network with Monte Carlo Tree Search (MCTS) to develop an AlphaZero agent. This agent will select child nodes based on recommendations from the policy-gradient network in addition to average rollout values.

To train the AlphaZero agent in Tic Tac Toe, we start a policy gradient network from scratch and initialize it with random weights. During the training phase, the policy gradient agent competes against a more advanced version of itself: the AlphaZero agent (who utilizes both the policy gradient network and MCTS). As training progresses, both agents gradually improve their performance.

This training approach differs from the one described in Chapter 14, where the policy gradient agent faced opponents with static strategies. In the current training regimen, the policy gradient agent competes against its evolving self. This dynamic scenario presents a unique challenge, as the agent effectively faces a *moving target*, complicating the training process. The opponent, in this case the AlphaZero agent, employs the policy gradient network to choose child nodes during the game. Given that this network is simultaneously being trained, improvements in the agent's capabilities directly enhance the opponent's strength, as it relies on the same policy network for making decisions in MCTS simulations.

To address the challenge of this moving target, an iterative self-play approach is used. Initially, we keep the weights of the policy gradient network, as utilized by the AlphaZero agent, constant, while updating the weights within the policy gradient network itself. Once the policy gradient agent achieves a specified performance level, we conclude the first iteration of training and proceed to update the weights in the policy gradient network used by the AlphaZero agent. This process is repeated in successive iterations until the AlphaZero agent perfects its gameplay.

Finally, you'll test the AlphaZero agent in Tic Tac Toe by integrating the trained policy gradient network with MCTS. The agent ties all games when competing against the MiniMax agent we developed in Chapter 6. This shows that the trained AlphaZero agent also solves the Tic Tac Toe game, tying an agent that never loses.

What You'll Learn in This Chapter

- Creating an AlphaZero algorithm that can be applied to Tic Tac Toe and Connect Four
- Implementing AlphaZero in Tic Tac Toe by combining MCTS with a policy gradient network
- Training the policy gradient network (hence AlphaZero) from scratch, without human input
- Testing the effectiveness of the AlphaZero agent in Tic Tac Toe

20.1 AN ALPHAZERO AGENT FOR MULTIPLE GAMES

In the local module *ch20util*, we'll implement the AlphaZero algorithm that can be applied to both Tic Tac Toe and Connect Four. Download the file *ch20util.py* from the book's GitHub repository and place it in the folder /utils/ on your computer. Take some time to go through the details of the module.

Since MCTS is the backbone of AlphaZero's decision-making process, we'll explain the logic behind the algorithm in the sequence of the four steps of MCTS we outlined in Chapter 8: selection, expansion, simulation (i.e., rolling out games), and backpropagation.

20.1.1 Select, Expand, Roll Out, and Backpropagate

In the local module *ch20util*, we first define a *select()* function to select a child node to expand the game tree, as follows:

```python
def select(priors,env,results,weight):
    # weighted average of priors and rollout_value
    scores={}
    for k,v in results.items():
        # rollout_value for each next move
        if len(v)==0:
            vi=0
        else:
            vi=sum(v)/len(v)
        # scale the prior by (1+N(L))
        prior=priors[0][k-1]/(1+len(v))
        # calculate weighted average
        scores[k]=weight*prior+(1-weight)*vi
    # select child node based on the weighted average
    return max(scores,key=scores.get)
```

The *select()* function in this context is the same as the one in Chapter 17 when we constructed the AlphaGo agent, except that the argument *priors* is completely uninformative at the beginning of the training process. Therefore, the AlphaZero agent is trained from scratch without any guidance from human inputs. The agent uses a combination of the average rollout value and the prior distribution from the policy gradient network. As training progresses, the priors become more and more informative.

To assess various child nodes through game simulations, we need to grow the game tree. This expansion is accomplished by the AlphaZero agent performing a hypothetical next move, thereby reaching the chosen child node. To facilitate this, we introduce an *expand()* function within the *ch20util* local module, outlined as follows:

```
# expand the game tree by taking a hypothetical move
def expand(env,move):
    env_copy=deepcopy(env)
    state,reward,done,info=env_copy.step(move)
    return env_copy, done, reward
```

Following the selection of a child node, we simulate a game beginning from that node. This simulated game continues until it reaches a terminal state. Subsequently, we evaluate the chosen child node based on the outcome of the game.

To roll out a game, we define a *simulate()* function in the local module *ch20util* as follows:

```
# roll out a game till terminal state or depth reached
def simulate(env_copy,done,reward):
    # if the game has already ended
    if done==True:
        return reward
    # select moves based on fast policy network
    while True:
        move=env_copy.sample()
        state,reward,done,info=env_copy.step(move)
        # if terminal state is reached, returns outcome
        if done==True:
            return reward
```

The function starts by determining if the selected child node is in a terminal state. If it does, it directly returns the outcome of the game. If not, the function proceeds to simulate hypothetical random moves to advance the game, all the way to the terminal state. The *simulate()* function returns the outcome of the game rollout, which is from the perspective of the first player. We'll adjust the game rollout outcome to account for the current player's perspective later in the *backpropagate()* function.

The concluding phase in the tree search involves updating simulation results after each rollout. Particularly, if the current player is Player O, we invert the reward by multiplying it by -1. This adjustment ensures that the evaluation and subsequent decisions are based on the current player's perspective, rather than defaulting to the perspective of the first player.

To implement this, we introduce the *backpropagate()* function within our local module, outlined as follows:

```
def backpropagate(env,move,reward,results):
    # update results
    if env.turn=="X" or env.turn=="red":
        results[move].append(reward)
    # if current player is player 2,
    # multiply outcome with -1
    if env.turn=="O" or env.turn=="yellow":
        results[move].append(-reward)
    return results
```

The function *backpropagate()* modifies the *results* dictionary, ensuring it encompasses a comprehensive record of all outcomes from the rollouts. It's important to remember that these outcomes are initially from the perspective of Player X. Within the *backpropagate()* function, we adjust for this: if the active player is Player O, we invert the outcome by multiplying it by -1. This alteration ensures that the recorded outcome reflects the viewpoint of the current player. The *backpropagate()* function then returns this updated *results* dictionary.

20.1.2   AlphaZero for Tic Tac Toe and Connect Four

We're now equipped to construct our AlphaZero algorithm for both Tic Tac Toe and Connect Four, utilizing the four functions we've defined: *select()*, *expand()*, *simulate()*, and *backpropagate()*.

To achieve this, we have defined the *alphazero()* function within the *ch20util* local module, structured as follows:

```
def alphazero(env,weight,PG_net,num_rollouts=100):
    # if there is only one valid move left, take it
    if len(env.validinputs)==1:
        return env.validinputs[0]
    # get the prior from the PG policy network
    if env.turn=="X" or env.turn=="O":
        state = env.state.reshape(-1,9)
        conv_state = state.reshape(-1,3,3,1)
        if env.turn=="X":
            priors = PG_net([state,conv_state])
        elif env.turn=="O":
            priors = PG_net([-state,-conv_state])
    if env.turn=="red" or env.turn=="yellow":
        state = env.state.reshape(-1,42)
        conv_state = state.reshape(-1,7,6,1)
```

```
if env.turn=="red":
    priors = PG_net([state,conv_state])
elif env.turn=="yellow":
    priors = PG_net([-state,-conv_state])
# create a dictionary results
results={}
for move in env.validinputs:
    results[move]=[]
# roll out games
for _ in range(num_rollouts):
    # select
    move=select(priors,env,results,weight)
    # expand
    env_copy, done, reward=expand(env,move)
    # simulate
    reward=simulate(env_copy,done,reward)
    # backpropagate
    results=backpropagate(env,move,reward,results)
# select the most visited child node
visits={k:len(v) for k,v in results.items()}
return max(visits,key=visits.get)
```

The AlphaZero agent begins by determining if only one valid move remains. If that's the case, it proceeds with that move directly, bypassing any tree search. If there are multiple options, the agent computes the prior probabilities for selecting each potential child node, drawing upon the policy gradient network. These priors are then used to guide the agent in choosing child nodes through the *select()* function we previously defined.

The agent also sets up a dictionary, *results*, to keep track of the outcomes from the rollouts. Initially, this dictionary lists all valid moves as keys, with corresponding empty lists as values. During game rollouts, the dictionary *results* is updated with the outcomes for each child node. The value linked to each child node is a list of rewards for the first player following the completion of a rollout.

The parameter *num_rollouts* dictates the number of rollouts the AlphaZero agent performs before executing a move in the actual game. While the default value for *num_rollouts* is set to 100, it can be adjusted when calling the *alphazero()* function. In each rollout, the agent systematically follows the four steps defined in the functions *select()*, *expand()*, *simulate()*, and *backpropagate()*, with results being updated after each rollout.

After completing the pre-specified number of rollouts, the AlphaZero agent finalizes its move in the real game. This decision is based on selecting the child node that was visited the most during rollouts.

20.2   A BLUEPRINT TO TRAIN ALPHAZERO IN TIC TAC TOE

In this section, we'll first outline the process for training the AlphaZero agent from the ground up for Tic Tac Toe, starting without any pre-existing data or human guidance. Following this, we'll describe the deep reinforcement learning model employed for this task.

20.2.1   Steps to Train AlphaZero in Tic Tac Toe

To train the AlphaZero agent in Tic Tac Toe, we'll first develop a deep reinforcement model using the policy gradient approach. This method bears resemblance to the policy gradient technique we employed in Chapter 14, with a key difference. In Chapter 14, when training the policy gradient model for Tic Tac Toe, we pitted it against a rule-based AI opponent. In contrast, when training the policy gradient agent in this chapter, the opponent is a strengthened version of the policy gradient agent itself (i.e., the AlphaZero agent), exemplifying self-play.

Our training process for the policy gradient agent in Tic Tac Toe involves alternating between training Player X and training Player O. In the first set of ten games, Player X will make decisions using guidance from the policy gradient network. This player competes against an opponent that relies on decisions from the AlphaZero algorithm, which in turn utilizes the policy gradient network. During these games, we gather data such as natural logarithms of the predicted probabilities and discounted rewards to refine the model parameters.

For the subsequent set of ten games, Player O will use recommendations from the same policy gradient network to compete against the AlphaZero algorithm. We'll again collect similar data to enhance the model parameters, continuing this alternating training process for each player after every ten games. However, to overcome the moving target problem we have outlined in the introduction, we'll only update the model parameters in the policy gradient network used by Players X and O. We'll not update the model parameters in the policy gradient network used in the AlphaZero algorithm. That way, Players X and O are playing against a stationary target rather than a moving target.

To determine the appropriate time to stop training, we'll evaluate the model periodically. If the AlphaZero agent based on the current policy gradient network loses less than 40% of games against the MiniMax agent that we developed in Chapter 6, we'll stop training the policy gradient agent in the first iteration. After that, we'll move on to the second iteration of training by updating the weights in the policy gradient network used by the AlphaZero algorithm. We'll repeat what we have done in the first iteration, but stop training only when the AlphaZero agent based on the current policy gradient network loses less than 30% of games against the MiniMax agent. We'll repeat this process for three more iterations, and make sure that the AlphaZero agent based on the current policy gradient network loses less than 20%, 10%, and 0% of games against the MiniMax agent, respectively.

However, it's important to note that the rule-based AI is solely for testing purposes and is not involved in the actual training process. We'll explore this training aspect further in Chapter 21 with the AlphaZero agent in Connect Four, where we completely abstain from external inputs, even in testing phases.

20.2.2 A Policy Gradient Network in Tic Tac Toe

As we did in Chapter 14, we'll create two separate input networks first: one is a dense layer with 9 neurons and the other network has a convolutional layer that can detect the spatial features on the Tic Tac Toe game board. We'll then combine the two networks together using the *concat()* method in TensorFlow. We'll use the combined network as the input to our policy gradient model. The model has one output network with 9 neurons in it. We apply softmax activation on the output so they can be interpreted as the probability of choosing the next move (i.e., a policy network).

The code in the cell below creates such a model:

```
[1]:  import tensorflow as tf
      from tensorflow import keras
      from tensorflow.keras import layers


      num_inputs = 9
      num_actions = 9
      # The convolutional input layer
      conv_inputs = layers.Input(shape=(3,3,1))
      conv=layers.Conv2D(filters=64, kernel_size=(3,3),padding="same",
          input_shape=(3,3,1), activation="relu")(conv_inputs)
      # Flatten the output from the conv layer
      flat = layers.Flatten()(conv)
      # The dense input layer
      inputs = layers.Input(shape=(9,))
      # Combine the two into a single input layer
      two_inputs = tf.concat([flat,inputs],axis=1)
      # two hidden layers
      common = layers.Dense(128, activation="relu")(two_inputs)
      action = layers.Dense(32, activation="relu")(common)
      # Policy output network
      action = layers.Dense(num_actions, activation="softmax")(action)
      # The final model
      model = keras.Model(inputs=[inputs, conv_inputs],\
                          outputs=action)
```

Below, we specify the optimizer we use to train the model.

```
2]: optimizer=keras.optimizers.Adam(learning_rate=0.00025,
                              clipnorm=1)
```

We use the Adam optimizer with a learning rate of 0.00025.

20.3 TRAIN ALPHAZERO IN TIC TAC TOE

In this section, we'll discuss in detail how to train the policy gradient agent (hence the AlphaZero algorithm, which is a combination of the policy gradient network and MCTS) in Tic Tac Toe. Specifically, we'll let the policy gradient agent play against the AlphaZero agent and collect information such as natural logarithms of the recommended probabilities of actions taken by the agent and the rewards to update model parameters. We'll alternate between training Player X and training Player O.

20.3.1 Train Players X and O

To train the policy gradient model, we need to create an opponent for both Player X and Player O. The opponent is the AlphaZero agent we created in the first section of this chapter. However, we'll make sure that the AlphaZero agent uses a policy gradient network that doesn't update its parameters. This way, Players X and O are playing against a stationary rather than a moving target.

For that purpose, we define the *opponent()* function as follows:

```
3]: # An old policy gradient network that doesn't update
    old_model = keras.Model(inputs=[inputs, conv_inputs],\
                       outputs=action)

    from utils.ch20util import alphazero

    # define an opponent for the policy gradient agent
    weight=0.5
    num_rollouts=100
    def opponent(env):
        move=alphazero(env,weight,old_model,
                    num_rollouts=num_rollouts)
        return move
```

Next, we'll define a *playing_X()* function. The *playing_X()* function simulates a full game, with Player X selecting moves from the policy gradient network while the opponent chooses moves based on the *opponent()* function we just defined, as follows:

```
]: from utils.ttt_simple_env import ttt
   import numpy as np
```

```
# allow a maximum of 50 steps per game
max_steps=50
env=ttt()

def playing_X():
    # create lists to record game history
    action_probs_history = []
    wrongmoves_history = []
    rewards_history = []
    state = env.reset()
    for step in range(max_steps):
        state = state.reshape(-1,9,)
        conv_state = state.reshape(-1,3,3,1)
        # Predict action probabilities and future rewards
        action_probs = model([state,conv_state])
        # select action based on the policy network
        action=np.random.choice(num_actions,\
                            p=np.squeeze(action_probs))
        # record log probabilities
        action_probs_history.append(\
                    tf.math.log(action_probs[0, action]))
        # punish the agent if there is an illegal move
        if action+1 not in env.validinputs:
            rewards_history.append(0)
            wrongmoves_history.append(-1)
        # otherwise, place the move on the game board
        else:
        # Apply the sampled action in our environment
            state, reward, done, _ = env.step(action+1)
            if done:
                wrongmoves_history.append(0)
                rewards_history.append(reward)
                break
            else:
                state,reward,done,_=env.step(opponent(env))
                rewards_history.append(reward)
                wrongmoves_history.append(0)
                if done:
                    break
    return action_probs_history,\
            wrongmoves_history,rewards_history
```

The *playing_X()* function simulates a full game, and it records all the intermediate steps made by the policy gradient agent. The function returns three lists:

- a list *action_probs_history* with the natural logarithm of the recommended probability of the action taken by the agent;
- a list *wrongmoves_history* with the rewards related to illegal moves;
- a list *rewards_history* with the rewards to each legal action taken by the agent (Player X in this case) in the game.

In reinforcement learning, actions taken have consequences that extend beyond immediate rewards, influencing future rewards as well. This scenario presents the credit assignment problem, central to all reinforcement learning algorithms. To address this, we attribute value to preceding actions through the use of discounted rewards. Thus, discounted rewards are utilized to appropriately allocate credit. At the same time, we don't discount rewards associated with illegal moves, as we discussed in Chapter 14. Specifically, we define a function below:

```
gamma=0.95
def discount_rs(r,wrong):
    discounted_rs = np.zeros(len(r))
    running_add = 0
    for i in reversed(range(0, len(r))):
        if wrong[i]==0:
            running_add = gamma*running_add + r[i]
            discounted_rs[i] = running_add
    return discounted_rs.tolist()
```

The function takes two lists, *r* and *wrong*, as inputs, where *r* are the rewards related to legal moves while *wrong* are rewards related to illegal moves. We discount *r* but not *wrong*. The output is the properly discounted reward in each step when a legal move is made. Note that if an illegal move is made in a step, the reward is 0 from the output. We'll add in the reward of −1 for illegal moves later separately.

Once Player X has undergone training for ten episodes, we will then allow Player O to compete against the opponent for a series of ten games, followed by another update of the model parameters. To be more precise, we will enable the opponent, as specified in the *opponent()* function mentioned earlier, to initiate the first move in a Tic Tac Toe game. Below, we will outline the function *playing_O()* to facilitate the training of Player O, as follows:

```
def playing_O():
    # create lists to record game history
    action_probs_history = []
    wrongmoves_history = []
    rewards_history = []
    state = env.reset()
    # the opponent moves first
    state, reward, done, _ = env.step(opponent(env))
    for step in range(max_steps):
```

```
    state = state.reshape(-1,9,)
    conv_state = state.reshape(-1,3,3,1)
    # predict action probabilities; multiply the board by -1
    action_probs = model([-state,-conv_state])
    # select action based on the policy network
    action=np.random.choice(num_actions,\
                        p=np.squeeze(action_probs))
    # record log probabilities
    action_probs_history.append(\
                    tf.math.log(action_probs[0, action]))
    # punish the agent if there is an illegal move
    if action+1 not in env.validinputs:
        rewards_history.append(0)
        wrongmoves_history.append(-1)
    # otherwise, place the move on the game board
    else:
    # apply the sampled action in our environment
        state, reward, done, _ = env.step(action+1)
        if done:
            wrongmoves_history.append(0)
            rewards_history.append(-reward)
            break
        else:
            state,reward,done,_=env.step(opponent(env))
            rewards_history.append(-reward)
            wrongmoves_history.append(0)
            if done:
                break
    return action_probs_history,\
        wrongmoves_history,rewards_history
```

The *playing_O()* function simulates a full game, with the opponent, defined in the function *opponent()*, as the first player, and the policy gradient agent as the second player. Similar to the *playing_X()* function, the *playing_O()* function also returns three lists: *action_probs_history*, *wrongmoves_history*, and *rewards_history*.

Most importantly, we use $[-state, -conv\_state]$ instead of $[state, conv\_state]$ when we feed the game board to the model. This is because the game board has value 1 in a cell if Player X has placed a game piece in it, -1 if Player O has placed a game piece in it. To use the same network for both players, we multiply the input by -1 so that the model treats 1 as occupied by the current player and -1 as occupied by the opponent. This is how we make the model player-independent.

The second most important thing is to change the rewards. Instead of using 1 and -1 to denote a win for Players X and O, respectively, we'll use a reward of 1 to denote the current player has won and a reward of -1 to denote that the current player has lost. We accomplish this by using $-reward$ instead of $reward$ in the above function. Therefore, after Player O makes a move, the reward is now 1 if Player O wins and -1 if Player O loses.

20.3.2 Update Parameters in the Policy Gradient Network

Rather than adjusting the model parameters after each individual episode, we opt for stability by updating them after a set number of episodes. In this approach, we perform parameter updates every ten games. Here we update parameters every ten games to train Player X, as follows:

```
batch_size=10
def create_batch_X(batch_size):
    action_probs_history = []
    wrongmoves_history = []
    rewards_history = []
    for i in range(batch_size):
        aps,wms,rs = playing_X()
        # rewards are discounted
        returns = discount_rs(rs,wms)
        action_probs_history += aps
        # punishments for wrong moves are not discounted
        wrongmoves_history += wms
        # combine discounted rewards with punishments
        combined=np.array(returns)+np.array(wms)
        # add combined rewards to rewards history
        rewards_history += combined.tolist()
    return action_probs_history,rewards_history
```

We discount the rewards associated with wins and losses, but not the rewards associated with wrong moves, due to the credit assignment problem we discussed earlier. We then combine the discounted rewards with punishments associated with wrong moves and put the combined values in the list *rewards_history*. We'll use the combined value when deciding how much to adjust the model parameters later.

Similarly, we simulate ten games to train Player O, as follows:

```
def create_batch_O(batch_size):
    action_probs_history = []
    wrongmoves_history = []
    rewards_history = []
    for i in range(batch_size):
        aps,wms,rs = playing_O()
        # reward related to legal moves are discounted
        returns = discount_rs(rs,wms)
        action_probs_history += aps
```

```
        # punishments for wrong moves are not discounted
        wrongmoves_history += wms
        # combine discounted rewards with punishments
        combined=np.array(returns)+np.array(wms)
        # add combined rewards to rewards history
        rewards_history += combined.tolist()
    return action_probs_history,rewards_history
```

The output from the *create_batch_X()* and *create_batch_O()* functions are natural logarithms of the probabilities of chosen actions and the rewards. We'll use them to update model parameters later.

20.3.3   The Training Loop for AlphaZero in Tic Tac Toe

AlphaZero algorithms demand substantial computational resources, making the training process quite lengthy. Moreover, the complexity increases as we need to finely adjust various hyperparameters to ensure the model functions effectively. Therefore, it's crucial to monitor the model's progress to ascertain whether it is developing correctly.

To achieve this, we will periodically test the model against a rule-based AI. This serves as a benchmark to gauge progress. It's important to note that the rule-based AI does not directly participate in training the model. Its role is solely to periodically evaluate the model's performance, without directly influencing the model itself.

For that purpose, we define the following *test()* function to evaluate the performance of the policy-gradient model periodically during training:

[9]:
```python
from utils.ch06util import MiniMax_ab

def rule_based_AI(env):
    move = MiniMax_ab(env)
    return move

def test():
    results=[]
    for i in range(10):
        state=env.reset()
        while True:
            action = rule_based_AI(env)
            state, reward, done, info = env.step(action)
            if done:
                results.append(-abs(reward))
                break
            # AlphaZero moves
            action=alphazero(env,weight,model,
                num_rollouts=num_rollouts)
```

```
            state, reward, done, info = env.step(action)
            if done:
                results.append(abs(reward))
                break
    return results
```

To systematically switch between training Player X and Player O, we will implement a variable named *batches*, initially set to 0. With the completion of each batch, we increase the value of *batches* by 1. The training is designed so that Player X is trained when the value of *batches* is an even number, and Player O is trained when it's odd.

The goal is to train the model until its performance achieves a certain threshold. For this purpose, after every 100 episodes of training, we will conduct a test against the MiniMax agent to evaluate the model's progress. The training process will be deemed complete and will stop if the AlphaZero loses to the MiniMax agent no more than 40% of the time.

```
)]: from collections import deque


    tests=deque(maxlen=100)
    n = 0
    batches=0
    # Train the model
    while True:
        with tf.GradientTape() as tape:
            if batches%2==0:
                action_probs_history,\
        rewards_history=create_batch_X(batch_size)
            else:
                action_probs_history,\
        rewards_history=create_batch_O(batch_size)
            rets=tf.convert_to_tensor(rewards_history,\
                                    dtype=tf.float32)
            alosses=-tf.multiply(tf.convert_to_tensor(\
                action_probs_history,dtype=tf.float32),rets)
            loss_value = tf.reduce_sum(alosses)
        grads = tape.gradient(loss_value, model.trainable_variables)
        optimizer.apply_gradients(zip(grads,\
                                    model.trainable_variables))
        n += batch_size
        batches += 1
        if n % 100 == 0:
            results=test()
            tests += results
```

```
      losses = tests.count(-1)
      print(f"at episode {n}, lost {losses} games")
      if (losses<=40 and n>=1000) or n>=10000:
          print(f"Finished at episode {n}!")
          break
model.save("files/zero_ttt0.h5")
```

The above training takes an hour or so to complete.

Next, we'll iteratively strengthen the policy gradient network by adjusting the winning threshold, until the AlphaZero agent becomes a perfect player and solves the game.

[11]:
```
from collections import deque

for i in range(4):
    weight=0.5+(i+1)*0.1
    num_rollouts=100+(i+1)*100
    reload=keras.models.load_model(f"files/zero_ttt{i}.h5")
    model.set_weights(reload.get_weights())
    # update weights in the opponent
    old_model.set_weights(reload.get_weights())
    tests=deque(maxlen=100)
    n = 0
    batches=0
    # Train the model
    while True:
        with tf.GradientTape() as tape:
            if batches%2==0:
                action_probs_history,\
        rewards_history=create_batch_X(batch_size)
            else:
                action_probs_history,\
        rewards_history=create_batch_O(batch_size)
            rets=tf.convert_to_tensor(rewards_history,\
                                 dtype=tf.float32)
            alosses=-tf.multiply(tf.convert_to_tensor(\
                action_probs_history,dtype=tf.float32),rets)
            loss_value = tf.reduce_sum(alosses)
        grads = tape.gradient(loss_value, model.trainable_variables)
        optimizer.apply_gradients(zip(grads,\
                                 model.trainable_variables))
        n += batch_size
        batches += 1
        if n % 100 == 0:
```

```
        results=test()
        tests += results
        losses = tests.count(-1)
        print(f"at episode {n}, lost {losses} games")
        if (losses<=40-(i+1)*10 and n>=1000) or n>=10000:
            print(f"Finished at episode {n}!")
            break
    model.save(f"files/zero_ttt{i+1}.h5")
```

The above training takes several hours. Once done, we'll use the model *zero_ttt4.h5* as the trained policy gradient model to use in the AlphaZero algorithm. Alternatively, you can download it from the book's GitHub repository https://github.com/markhliu/AlphaGoSimplified.

20.4   TEST ALPHAZERO IN TIC TAC TOE

Next, we'll test the AlphaZero algorithm in Tic Tac Toe, setting the number of rollouts to 1000. To account for the inherent advantage of the first player, we will first have Player X employ the strategies suggested by AlphaZero. Following this, Player O will then adopt the AlphaZero algorithm as well. The opponent in these games is a rule-based AI that employs the MiniMax algorithm specifically for Tic Tac Toe, enhanced with alpha-beta pruning to expedite the tree search process.

To save time, we will conduct only 10 games for testing. In five games, the AlphaZero agent will make the first move. In the other five games, the rule-based AI agent makes the first move, like so:

```
# Use the trained PG model
reload=keras.models.load_model("files/zero_ttt4.h5")
model.set_weights(reload.get_weights())
env=ttt()
for i in range(10):
    state=env.reset()
    if i%2==0:
        action=rule_based_AI(env)
        state,reward,done,_=env.step(action)
    while True:
        # AlphaZero moves
        action=alphazero(env,0.9,model,
                num_rollouts=1000)
        state,reward,done,_=env.step(action)
        if done:
            if reward==0:
                print("The game is tied!")
            else:
```

```
                    print("AlphaZero wins!")
            break
        # MiniMax agent moves
        action=rule_based_AI(env)
        state,reward,done,_=env.step(action)
        if done:
            if reward==0:
                print("The game is tied!")
            else:
                print("AlphaZero loses!")
            break
```

```
The game is tied!
The game is tied!
The game is tied!
The game is tied!
The game is tied!
The game is tied!
The game is tied!
The game is tied!
The game is tied!
The game is tied!
```

All ten games are tied. This indicates that the AlphaZero agent is indeed as strong as the rule-based AI that solves the game. Our AlphaZero algorithm has successfully solved the Tic Tac Toe game.

In the next chapter, you'll implement the AlphaZero algorithm in Connect Four. We'll focus on how to train the strongest player possible when there is no rule-based AI to rely upon even in the testing stage.

20.5 EXERCISES

20.1 Modify the first code cell in Section 20.4 and set *weight* to 0.8 and *num_rollouts* to 2500 in the *alphazero()* function. Rerun the code cell and see how often the AlphaZero agent wins.

## CHAPTER 21

AlphaZero in Unsolved Games

"Our new program AlphaGo Zero achieved superhuman performance, winning
100–0 against the previously published, champion-defeating AlphaGo."
– *Mastering the game of Go without human knowledge (Nature 2017)*

IN THE PREVIOUS two chapters, we implemented the AlphaZero algorithm
in the coin game and Tic Tac Toe. The AlphaZero algorithm was trained
purely based on deep reinforcement learning, without human expert data, guidance,
or domain knowledge beyond game rules. However, we did use rule-based AI to periodically evaluate the AlphaZero agent to gauge its performance and decide whether
or not to stop training. Even though rule-based AI was not used in the training process directly, it was used for testing purposes to monitor the performance of the agent
to avoid unnecessary training.

However, in unsolved games such as Chess or Go, assessing the performance of AlphaZero is more difficult since we don't have an algorithm that's more powerful than
AlphaZero to use as the benchmark. How should we test the performance of AlphaZero and decide when to stop training in such cases? That's the question we are
going to answer in this chapter.

Even though Connect Four is a solved game, implementing a game-solving rule-based
algorithm involves too many steps. Therefore, we treat Connect Four as an unsolved
game. In this chapter, you'll train an AlphaZero agent from scratch in Connect Four.
To test the performance of AlphaZero and decide when to stop training, we use an
earlier version of AlphaZero as the benchmark. When AlphaZero outperforms an
earlier version of itself by a certain margin, we'll stop a training iteration. We then
update the parameters in the older version of AlphaZero and restart the training
process. We'll train the AlphaZero model for several iterations to strengthen the
AlphaZero agent.

DOI: 10.1201/9781032722207-21

After a couple of days of training, we test the trained AlphaZero agent against the AlphaGo agent we developed in Chapter 18. Our newly trained AlphaZero consistently outperforms its predecessor, AlphaGo!

What You'll Learn in This Chapter

- Implementing AlphaZero in Connect Four
- Iteratively training AlphaZero in Connect Four through self-play
- Testing AlphaZero against earlier versions of itself
- Pitting AlphaZero against AlphaGo

21.1   STEPS TO TRAIN ALPHAZERO IN CONNECT FOUR

In this section, we'll describe how to train the AlphaZero agent for Connect Four from scratch, without relying on any pre-existing data or human guidance. Unlike in previous chapters, we won't use human expert moves, not even during the testing phase.

21.1.1   A Blueprint to Train AlphaZero in Connect Four

To train the AlphaZero agent in Connect Four, we'll develop a deep reinforcement learning model using the policy gradient approach. This method is similar to the one we used in Chapter 15, but with a twist: the opponent is a stronger version of the policy gradient agent itself, namely the AlphaZero agent.

The training process for the policy gradient agent involves alternating between training the red and yellow players, as we did in Chapter 15. In the first set of 20 games, the red player makes decisions based on the policy gradient network, while competing against an opponent that relies on the AlphaZero algorithm, which also uses the policy gradient network. This is known as self-play. During these games, we collect data such as the natural logarithms of the predicted probabilities and discounted rewards to refine the model parameters.

In the next set of 20 games, the roles switch, and the yellow player uses the policy gradient network to compete against the AlphaZero algorithm. We continue to collect data to improve the model parameters, alternating the training process for each player after every 20 games. To address the moving target problem, we only update the model parameters in the policy gradient network used by the red and yellow players, keeping the parameters in the AlphaZero network constant. This temporarily creates a stationary target for the red and yellow players.

To decide when to stop training in the first iteration, we set a benchmark: the policy gradient agent must win at least 60% of the games against its opponent. After reaching this goal, we proceed to the second iteration of training by updating the weights in the policy gradient network used by AlphaZero. We repeat this process for four more iterations.

21.1.2 A Policy Gradient Network in Tic Tac Toe

As we did in Chapter 15, we'll create a policy gradient network as follows:

```
import tensorflow as tf
from tensorflow import keras
from tensorflow.keras import layers


num_inputs=42
num_actions=7
# The convolutional input layer
conv_inputs=layers.Input(shape=(7,6,1))
conv=layers.Conv2D(filters=128, kernel_size=(4,4),padding="same",
        input_shape=(7,6,1), activation="relu")(conv_inputs)
flat=layers.Flatten()(conv)
# The dense input layer
inputs = layers.Input(shape=(42,))
# Combine the two into a single input layer
two_inputs = tf.concat([flat,inputs],axis=1)
# hidden layers
common = layers.Dense(256, activation="relu")(two_inputs)
common = layers.Dense(64, activation="relu")(common)
# Policy output network
action = layers.Dense(num_actions, activation="softmax")(common)
# The final model
model = keras.Model(inputs=[inputs, conv_inputs],\
                    outputs=action)
```

Below, we specify the optimizer we use to train the model.

```
optimizer=keras.optimizers.Adam(learning_rate=0.00025,
                                clipnorm=1)
```

We use the Adam optimizer with a learning rate of 0.00025.

21.2 PREPARE TO TRAIN ALPHAZERO IN CONNECT FOUR

In this section, we'll prepare for the training process of the policy gradient agent, and consequently, the AlphaZero algorithm (which combines the policy gradient network with Monte Carlo Tree Search) in Connect Four. Specifically, we'll have the policy gradient agent play against the AlphaZero agent and collect information such as the natural logarithm of the recommended probability of the action taken by the agent and the discounted reward to update the model parameters. We'll alternate between training the red and yellow players.

21.2.1 Train the Red and Yellow Players

To train the policy gradient model, we'll set up an opponent for both players. This opponent will be the AlphaZero agent we created in Chapter 20. However, to ensure that the red and yellow players face a stationary target, we'll use a version of the AlphaZero agent with a policy gradient network whose parameters remain unchanged during training.

To achieve this, we define an *opponent()* function as follows:

```
[3]:  # An old policy gradient network that doesn't update
      old_model = keras.Model(inputs=[inputs, conv_inputs],\
                      outputs=action)

      from utils.ch20util import alphazero

      # define an opponent for the policy gradient agent
      weight=0.05
      num_rollouts=50
      def opponent(env):
          move=alphazero(env,weight,old_model,
                      num_rollouts=num_rollouts)
          return move
```

Next, we'll define a *playing_red()* function to simulate a full game. In this game, the red player will choose moves based on the policy gradient network, while the opponent will select moves using the *opponent()* function we just defined. The function is defined as follows:

```
[4]:  from utils.conn_simple_env import conn
      import numpy as np
      # allow a maximum of 50 steps per game
      max_steps=50
      env=conn()

      def playing_red():
          # create lists to record game history
          action_probs_history = []
          wrongmoves_history = []
          rewards_history = []
          episode_reward = 0
          state = env.reset()
          for step in range(max_steps):
```

```
        state = state.reshape(-1,42,)
        conv_state = state.reshape(-1,7,6,1)
        # Predict action probabilities and future rewards
        action_probs = model([state,conv_state])
        # select action based on the policy network
        action=np.random.choice(num_actions,\
                                p=np.squeeze(action_probs))
        # record log probabilities
        action_probs_history.append(\
                        tf.math.log(action_probs[0, action]))
        # punish the agent if there is an illegal move
        if action+1 not in env.validinputs:
            rewards_history.append(0)
            wrongmoves_history.append(-1)
        # otherwise, place the move on the game board
        else:
        # Apply the sampled action in our environment
            state, reward, done, _ = env.step(action+1)
            if done:
                wrongmoves_history.append(0)
                rewards_history.append(reward)
                episode_reward += reward
                break
            else:
                state,reward,done,_=env.step(opponent(env))
                rewards_history.append(reward)
                wrongmoves_history.append(0)
                episode_reward += reward
                if done:
                    break
    return action_probs_history,\
        wrongmoves_history,rewards_history,episode_reward
```

The *playing_red()* function simulates a full game and records all the intermediate steps taken by the red player. The function is similar to the one we defined in Chapter 15.

To appropriately allocate credit, we use discounted rewards. We define a function for this purpose as follows:

```
gamma=0.95
def discount_rs(r,wrong):
    discounted_rs = np.zeros(len(r))
    running_add = 0
    for i in reversed(range(0, len(r))):
```

```
        if wrong[i]==0:
            running_add = gamma*running_add + r[i]
            discounted_rs[i] = running_add
    return discounted_rs.tolist()
```

After the red player has completed training for 20 episodes, we will switch roles and allow the yellow player to compete against the opponent for a series of 20 games. Following this, we will update the model parameters again, as follows:

```
[6]: def playing_yellow():
        # create lists to record game history
        action_probs_history = []
        wrongmoves_history = []
        rewards_history = []
        state = env.reset()
        episode_reward = 0
        state, reward, done, _ = env.step(opponent(env))
        for step in range(max_steps):
            state = state.reshape(-1,42,)
            conv_state = state.reshape(-1,7,6,1)
            # Predict action probabilities and future rewards
            action_probs = model([-state,-conv_state])
            # select action based on the policy network
            action=np.random.choice(num_actions,\
                            p=np.squeeze(action_probs))
            # record log probabilities
            action_probs_history.append(\
                        tf.math.log(action_probs[0, action]))
            # punish the agent if there is an illegal move
            if action+1 not in env.validinputs:
                rewards_history.append(0)
                wrongmoves_history.append(-1)
            # otherwise, place the move on the game board
            else:
            # Apply the sampled action in our environment
                state, reward, done, _ = env.step(action+1)
                if done:
                    wrongmoves_history.append(0)
                    rewards_history.append(-reward)
                    episode_reward += -reward
                    break
                else:
                    state,reward,done,_=env.step(opponent(env))
                    rewards_history.append(-reward)
                    wrongmoves_history.append(0)
```

```
            episode_reward += -reward
            if done:
                break
    return action_probs_history,\
        wrongmoves_history,rewards_history,episode_reward
```

The *playing_yellow()* function simulates a full game, with the opponent, defined in the function *opponent()*, as the first player, and the policy gradient agent as the second player. The function returns four values: *action_probs_history, wrongmoves_history, rewards_history*, and *episode_reward*.

When feeding the game board to the model, we use $[-state, -conv\_state]$ instead of $[state, conv\_state]$. This adjustment makes the model player-independent.

21.2.2 Update Parameters in Training

Instead of updating the model parameters after each individual episode, we choose to enhance stability by updating them after every 20 episodes. Here, we create a batch of 20 games to train the red player:

```
]:  batch_size=20
    def create_batch_red(batch_size):
        action_probs_history = []
        wrongmoves_history = []
        rewards_history = []
        episode_rewards = []
        for i in range(batch_size):
            aps,wms,rs,er= playing_red()
            # rewards are discounted
            returns = discount_rs(rs,wms)
            action_probs_history += aps
            # punishments for wrong moves are not discounted
            wrongmoves_history += wms
            # combined discounted rewards with punishments
            combined=np.array(returns)+np.array(wms)
            # add combined rewards to rewards history
            rewards_history += combined.tolist()
            episode_rewards.append(er)
        return action_probs_history,\
            rewards_history,episode_rewards
```

Similarly, we simulate 20 games to train the yellow player, as follows:

```
]:  def create_batch_yellow(batch_size):
        action_probs_history = []
        wrongmoves_history = []
```

```
rewards_history = []
episode_rewards = []
for i in range(batch_size):
    aps,wms,rs,er= playing_yellow()
    # reward related to legal moves are discounted
    returns = discount_rs(rs,wms)
    action_probs_history += aps
    # punishments for wrong moves are not discounted
    wrongmoves_history += wms
    # combined discounted rewards with punishments
    combinod=np.array(returns)+np.array(wms)
    # add combined rewards to rewards history
    rewards_history += combined.tolist()
    episode_rewards.append(er)
return action_probs_history,\
    rewards_history,episode_rewards
```

The output from the *create_batch_red()* and *create_batch_yellow()* functions are the natural logarithm of the probabilities of chosen actions and the rewards. We'll use them to update model parameters later.

21.3 THE ACTUAL TRAINING OF ALPHAZERO IN CONNECT FOUR

In the first iteration, we keep the weights in the policy gradient model used by AlphaZero constant. We'll train the red and yellow players until they can beat AlphaZero at least 60% of the time.

After achieving this benchmark, we'll update the weights in the policy gradient model used by AlphaZero with the weights from the policy gradient agent. We'll then repeat the training process as in the first iteration. This process will be repeated for four more iterations.

21.3.1 The Training Loop in the First Iteration

To systematically alternate between training the red and yellow players, we'll use a variable named *batches*, initially set to 0. With each completed batch, we increase the value of batches by 1. The training is structured so that the red player is trained when the value of *batches* is an even number, and the yellow player is trained when it's odd.

The aim is to refine the model until it reaches a specific threshold. For this purpose, after every 100 episodes of training, we'll evaluate the model's progress. The training process will be considered complete and will stop if the policy gradient agent wins in at least 60% of the games (the average score should be at least 0.2, since 0.6 - 0.4 = 0.2).

```
9]: from collections import deque
    import numpy as np

    running_rewards=deque(maxlen=1000)
    episode_count = 0
    batches=0
    # Train the model
    while True:
        with tf.GradientTape() as tape:
            if batches%2==0:
                action_probs_history,rewards_history,\
                    episode_rewards=create_batch_red(batch_size)
            else:
                action_probs_history,rewards_history,\
                    episode_rewards=create_batch_yellow(batch_size)
            # Calculating loss values to update our network
            rets=tf.convert_to_tensor(rewards_history,\
                                      dtype=tf.float32)
            alosses=-tf.multiply(tf.convert_to_tensor(\
                action_probs_history,dtype=tf.float32),rets)
            # Backpropagation
            loss_value = tf.reduce_sum(alosses)
        grads = tape.gradient(loss_value, model.trainable_variables)
        optimizer.apply_gradients(zip(grads,\
                                  model.trainable_variables))
        # Log details
        episode_count += batch_size
        batches += 1
        running_rewards+=episode_rewards
        running_reward=np.mean(np.array(running_rewards))
        # print out progress
        if episode_count % 100 == 0:
            template = "running reward: {:.6f} at episode {}"
            print(template.format(running_reward, episode_count))
        # Stop if the game is solved
        if running_reward>=0.1 and episode_count>1000:
            print("Solved at episode {}!".format(episode_count))
            break
        if episode_count>25000:
            break
    model.save("files/CONNzero0.h5")
```

The training process described above takes approximately ten hours to complete.

Next, we'll iteratively update the weights in the policy gradient network in AlphaZero and retrain the policy gradient agent. This process will continue, making the policy gradient agent, and consequently the AlphaZero agent, increasingly stronger.

21.3.2 Train for More Iterations

Next, we'll iteratively enhance the policy gradient network by adjusting the hyperparameters in the training loop. This will continue until the AlphaZero agent becomes stronger with each iteration, as follows:

```
[10]: from collections import deque

for i in range(4):
    weight=0.1+(i+1)*0.2
    num_rollouts=50+(i+1)*50
    reload=keras.models.load_model(f"files/CONNzero{i}.h5")
    model.set_weights(reload.get_weights())
    # update weights in the opponent
    old_model.set_weights(reload.get_weights())
    running_rewards=deque(maxlen=1000)
    episode_count = 0
    batches=0
    # Train the model
    while True:
        with tf.GradientTape() as tape:
            if batches%2==0:
                action_probs_history,rewards_history,\
                    episode_rewards=create_batch_red(batch_size)
            else:
                action_probs_history,rewards_history,\
                    episode_rewards=create_batch_yellow(batch_size)
            # Calculating loss values to update our network
            rets=tf.convert_to_tensor(rewards_history,\
                                      dtype=tf.float32)
            alosses=-tf.multiply(tf.convert_to_tensor(\
                action_probs_history,dtype=tf.float32),rets)
            # Backpropagation
            loss_value = tf.reduce_sum(alosses)
        grads = tape.gradient(loss_value, model.trainable_variables)
        optimizer.apply_gradients(zip(grads,\
                                  model.trainable_variables))
        # Log details
        episode_count += batch_size
        batches += 1
        running_rewards+=episode_rewards
```

```
        running_reward=np.mean(np.array(running_rewards))
        # print out progress
        if episode_count % 100 == 0:
            template = "running reward: {:.6f} at episode {}"
            print(template.format(running_reward, episode_count))
        # Stop if the game is solved
        if running_reward>=0.1 and episode_count>1000:
            print("Solved at episode {}!".format(episode_count))
            break
        if episode_count>25000:
            break
    model.save(f"files/CONNzero{i+1}.h5")
```

We will conduct four additional iterations of training. In these iterations, the hyper-parameter *weight* will increase to 0.3, 0.5, 0.7, and 0.9, respectively. Simultaneously, the number of rollouts will increase to 100, 150, 200, and 250, respectively. After each iteration, we update the weights in the policy gradient network used by AlphaZero (referred to as *old_model* in the code) with the weights from the policy gradient agent's network (referred to as *model* in the code).

In each iteration, we train the policy gradient agent until it can beat AlphaZero at least 60% of the time, ensuring that the running reward is at least 0.2 (since $0.6 - 0.4 = 0.2$), or until there are more than 25,000 episodes of gameplay in the iteration. The trained models are saved as *CONNzero1.h5*, ..., *CONNzero4.h5*, respectively.

The training process takes a couple of days to complete. Once finished, we'll use the file *CONNzero4.h5* as the trained model for the AlphaZero algorithm. Alternatively, you can download the file from the book's GitHub repository at https://github.com/markhliu/AlphaGoSimplified.

21.3.3 Tips for Further Training

We have stopped training after five iterations, and the model is reasonably strong. For readers interested in tweaking the model to further improve its performance, here are some potential approaches for additional training:

Reducing the learning rate: If the model stops improving during training, consider reducing the learning rate. Currently, we have set the learning rate to 0.00025. You might consider lowering it further to, for example, 0.0001. This slows down the learning process but can help in further improving the model.

Changing the batch size: Currently, we update the model parameters after every 20 games (i.e., with a batch size of 20). Consider increasing the batch size to 25 or even 50. A larger batch size reduces the volatility of the average gradients, which in turn stabilizes the model.

Updating the opponent model more frequently: Currently, we update the opponent model parameters (i.e., the weights in the policy gradient network used by AlphaZero, *old_model*) when the policy gradient agent beats AlphaZero at least 60% of the time. Consider changing this threshold to 55% or even 50% to update the opponent model more frequently.

Increasing the number of rollouts: Consider increasing the number of rollouts in AlphaZero to an even larger number, such as 300. Note that training is slower when the number of rollouts is larger, but the trained model is also much stronger. There is a tradeoff between training speed and model strength.

By experimenting with these adjustments, you can further refine the model and potentially achieve better performance.

21.4   TEST ALPHAZERO IN CONNECT FOUR

Next, we'll test the AlphaZero algorithm in Connect Four, specifically against the AlphaGo agent we trained in Chapter 18. To ensure a fair comparison, we'll use the same hyperparameters for both algorithms. The only difference will be the strength of the policy gradient network used by the two agents.

As a reminder, in Chapter 18, we identified the optimal hyperparameters for the AlphaGo agent in Connect Four: the agent relies solely on the trained policy gradient network to select child nodes, bypassing both the fast policy network and the value network. It allocates 75% of the weight to recommendations from the policy gradient network and 25% to the average rollout value (i.e., *weight=0.75*). The AlphaGo agent performs 584 rollouts for each move in the real game, ensuring that a move takes no more than a second to make.

To level the playing field, we'll set the same hyperparameters for the AlphaZero algorithm, with *weight=0.75* and *num_rollouts=584*.

Below, we'll first define the AlphaGo agent in Connect Four:

```
[11]:   import numpy as np
        from tensorflow import keras
        from utils.ch17util import alphago

        weight=0.75
        num_rollouts=584

        # Load the trained fast policy network from Chapter 11
        fast_net=keras.models.load_model("files/policy_conn.h5")
        # Load the policy gradient network from Chapter 15
        PG_net=keras.models.load_model("files/PG_conn.h5")
        # Load the trained value network from Chapter 15
        value_net=keras.models.load_model("files/value_conn.h5")

        # Define alphago_move
```

```
def alphago_move(env):
    move=alphago(env,weight,45,PG_net,value_net,
        fast_net, policy_rollout=False,
            num_rollouts=num_rollouts)
    return move
```

Although the AlphaGo agent won't be using the fast policy network or the value network, we still need to import these two networks to use as arguments in the *alphago()* function. By setting *depth* to 45 and the *policy_rollout* argument to *False*, we ensure that these two networks are bypassed.

Now that we know the moves by AlphaGo, we'll define the move by AlphaZero as follows:

```
2]: # Define alphago_move
from utils.ch20util import alphazero

old_model=keras.models.load_model("files/CONNzero4.h5")
def alphazero_move(env):
    move=alphazero(env,weight,old_model,
                    num_rollouts=num_rollouts)
    return move
```

We update the weights in the policy gradient network used by AlphaZero (*old_model* in the code) with the trained weights from the policy gradient network, which are saved in the file *CONNzero4.h5*. The AlphaZero agent makes a move in real games by simulating 584 rollouts, the same number of rollouts used by AlphaGo.

For testing, we'll conduct 100 games. In 50 of these games, the AlphaZero agent will move first. In the other 50 games, the AlphaGo agent will move first, ensuring that neither agent has a first-mover advantage.

```
]: from utils.conn_simple_env import conn
env=conn()
results=[]
for i in range(100):
    state=env.reset()
    if i%2==0:
        action=alphago_move(env)
        state,reward,done,_=env.step(action)
    while True:
        # AlphaZero moves
        action=alphazero_move(env)
        state,reward,done,_=env.step(action)
        if done:
            results.append(abs(reward))
```

```
        break
    # AlphaGo moves
    action=alphago_move(env)
    state,reward,done,_=env.step(action)
    if done:
        results.append(-abs(reward))
        break
```

The test described above takes about 30 minutes to run, which means it takes about half a minute to finish a game. In this test, if AlphaZero wins, we add a 1 to the list *results*. If AlphaGo wins, we add a −1 to the list *results*. If the game ends in a tie, we add a 0 to the list *results*.

We can then count how many times the AlphaZero agent has won and lost:

```
[14]:  # Print out the number of games that AlphaZero won
       wins=results.count(1)
       print(f"The AlphaZero agent has won {wins} games.")
       # Print out the number of games that AlphaZero lost
       losses=results.count(-1)
       print(f"The AlphaZero agent has lost {losses} games.")
       # Print out the number of tie games
       ties=results.count(0)
       print(f"The game was tied {ties} times.")
```

```
The AlphaZero agent has won 79 games.
The AlphaZero agent has lost 21 games.
The game was tied 0 times.
```

The AlphaZero agent has won 79 games, while the AlphaGo agent won the remaining 21 games, with no ties. These results demonstrate that our AlphaZero agent is even stronger than the AlphaGo agent we trained in Chapter 18.

Through this journey, you have learned how to create AlphaZero agents from scratch for three everyday games: the coin game, Tic Tac Toe, and Connect Four. Along the way, you have gained insights into how rule-based AI and deep reinforcement learning work. More importantly, AlphaGo and its improved version, AlphaZero, have shown that combining rule-based AI with machine learning can lead to an algorithm that is stronger than either AI paradigm alone. In this case, the whole is indeed greater than the sum of its parts!

Bibliography

[1] Victor Allis. A Knowledge-Based Approach of Connect-Four. *ICGA Journal*, vol.11, no.4, 1988.

[2] David Silver et al. Mastering the game of go with deep neural networks and tree search. *Nature*, 2016.

[3] David Silver et al. Mastering the game of go without human knowledge. *Nature*, 2017.

[4] Larry Greenemeier. 20 years after deep blue: How AI has advanced since conquering chess https://www.scientificamerican.com/article/20-years-after-deep-blue-how-ai-has-advanced-since-conquering-chess/. *Scientific America*, 2017.

[5] Leaders. https://www.economist.com/leaders/2017/05/06/the-worlds-most-valuable-resource-is-no-longer-oil-but-data. *The Economist*, 2017.

[6] Mark Liu. *Machine Learning, Animated*. CRC Press, 2023.

[7] Bernard Marr. https://www.forbes.com/sites/bernardmarr/2018/12/31/the-most-amazing-artificial-intelligence-milestones-so-far/?sh=6698f5c37753. *Forbes*, 2018.

[8] Science and Technology. Showdown https://www.economist.com/science-and-technology/2016/03/12/showdown. *The Economist*, 2016.

[9] Charles Severance. *Python for Everyone: Exploring Data in Python 3*. 2016.

[10] David Silver and Demis Hassabis. AlphaGo: Mastering the ancient game of go with machine learning https://blog.research.google/2016/01/alphago-mastering-ancient-game-of-go.html, 2016.

Index

Note: Page numbers in *italics* and **bold** refer to figures and tables, respectively.

Printed in the United States
by Baker & Taylor Publisher Services